April 22, 1995

To Ralph & Meri Lüders
Best wishes und alles
Gute.
Sincerely,
Bert Lawrence
Publisher

Chicago – Our Beautiful City

Chicago is the kind of City one can truly love,
its skyline reaches to towering heights above.
Lake Michigan adds sparkle to the Outer Drive,
and keeps the city's pulse and tempo alive.

The world's tallest buildings are our own,
amongst other architectural wonders, to be shown.
The museums, Lyric Opera, and Orchestra Hall,
spread knowledge, entertainment and joy to all.

The city, commerce and industry work and meet,
as many up-beat people are crossing our streets.
Chicago is a city with culture and many treasures,
a great place to live, work and visit with pleasure.

Adapted from a song by Inge Braun, copyrighted 1994

Chicago – Unsere Schöne Stadt

Chicago ist eine schöne Stadt, die man wirklich gerne hat.
Die Silhouette ragt hoch wie ein Kliff aus Stahl und Sand.
Der Michigan See glänzt und wogt am Außenrand,
so wie die Stadt sich bewegt, frisch und gewandt.

Der Welt größten Gebäude sind hier zuhaus,
zwischen bunter Architektur und grüner Natur.
Galerien, Museen, Oper, Theater und Orchester Halle
belehren, bereichern, erfreuen das Publikum, alle.

Stadt, Wirtschaft und Industrie verpflegen
aufgeschlossene Menschen auf allen Wegen.
Chicago ist Klasse, Kultur und hat vieles mehr zu buchen,
ein Platz in der Welt zu leben, zu streben und zu besuchen.

Kuhn's International Delicatessen

116 South Waukegan Road, Deerfield, IL 60015, Telephone 708/272-4198 • 749 West Golf Road, Des Plaines, IL 60016, Telephone 708/640-0223

Also Page 173

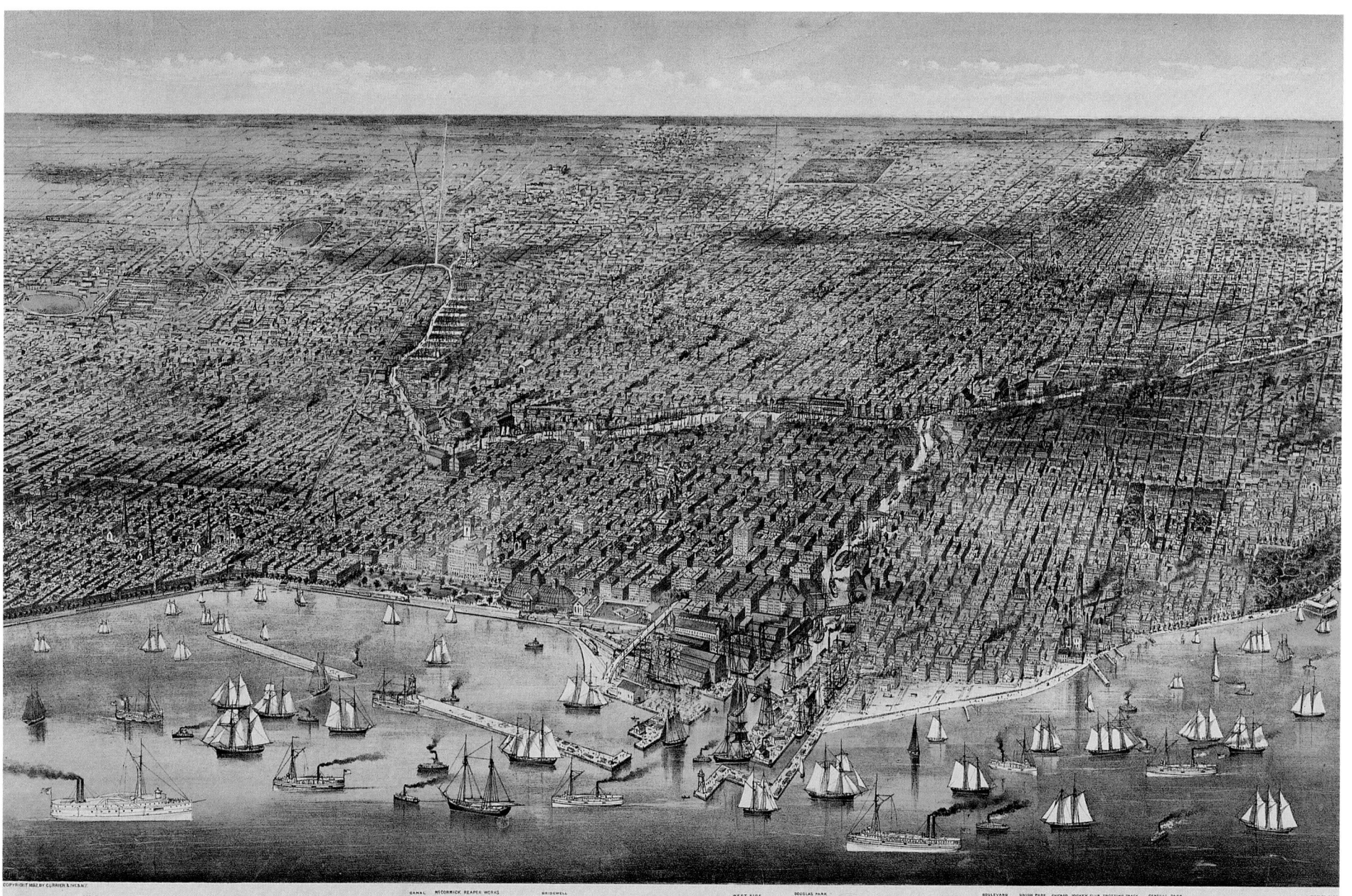

THE CITY OF CHICAGO.

Overleaf:
Chromolithograph, "The City of Chicago"
published by Currier & Ives, 1892

Rückseite:
Farbdruck "Die Stadt Chicago"
herausgegeben von Currier & Ives, 1892

Author and Publisher :	Bert Lachner	Autor und Herausgeber
Co-Author :	Niels Friedrichs	Co-Autor
Assistant :	Arlene Lachner	Assistent
Editors :	Mary Gekler	Redakteure
	Edward A. Michals	
Editorial Contributions :	Erich Himmel, CLUBS	Beiträge
	Ernst Ott, DANK	
	Marlis Schmidt, *Tune In*	
Official Information :	Ray Walters	Offizielles
Photography :	Bert Lachner & Associates	Fotografien
	Photo Credits on page 239	
Proofing :	L. C. Smith	Korrektur
Research :	Eva Schuchardt	Forschung
Translations :	Bruni Johnson, et al.	Übersetzungen
Art Direction :	David McFadden	Satz und Layout
	TypeTechs®	
Production :	The Irving Press, Inc.	Produktion
	Kurt Blumenthal, President	
	Misha Hendricks, Project Manager	
Marketing :	Klaus Rummer	Marketing

Chicagoland

a world-class Metropolis
eine Klasse-Stadt von Weltruf

A German-American Perspective
Eine deutsch-amerikanische Perspektive

Bert Lachner & Associates, Inc.

CHICAGOLAND
Published by Bert Lachner & Associates, Inc.
Copyright © 1994 by Bert Lachner & Associates, Inc.
389 Duane Street, Glen Ellyn, Illinois 60137-4389 U.S.A.

All rights reserved.

No part of this book may be reproduced, stored
in any form or by any means, without the prior
permission of Bert Lachner & Associates, Inc.

ISBN: 0-964-06590-8

Library of Congress Catalog Card Number: 94-096081

Manufactured in the United States of America.

4567890654321

Limited Edition,
May 1994

CHICAGOLAND
Herausgegeben von Bert Lachner & Associates, Inc.
Copyright © 1994 Bert Lachner & Associates, Inc.
389 Duane Street, Glen Ellyn, Illinois 60137-4389 USA

Alle Rechte vorbehalten.

Kein Teil dieses Buches darf reproduziert, kopiert
oder EDV verwahrt werden, ohne vorherige Elaubnis
von Bert Lachner & Associates, Inc.

ISBN # 0-964-06590-8

Kongreß-Bibliothek Katalog Nummer: 94-096081

Printed in U.S.A.

4567890654321

Begrenzte Ausgabe, Mai 1994

Contents / Inhalt

Contents		Page/Seite	Inhalt
Foreword			Vorwort
Governor Jim Edgar		9	Gouverneur Jim Edgar
Mayor Richard M. Daley		11	Bürgermeister R. M. Daley
Introduction		13	Einleitung
First Impressions		17	Ersten Eindrücke
Where in the World is Chicago		22	Wo auf der Welt liegt Chicago
CTA Mass Transit Map	M	25	CTA Verkehrsmittel Karte
A Stroll through the City		26	Ein Bummel durch die Stadt
Map of Central Chicago	M	30	Karte der Innenstadt
World Cup '94		47	Fussball WM '94
USA-Germany Comparison	M	55	USA-Deutschland Größen
Chamber of Commerce of Midwest		56	Deutsch-amerikanischer Handel
Welcome, Business Friends		58	Willkommen Geschäftsfreunde
Illinois Exports	S	62	Illinois Ausfuhren
German Counsulate General		63	Deutsches Generalkonsulat
Enjoying the Daily Drama		70	Spass am täglichen Drama
German/Ethnic Population	S	75	Deutsch/Völker Anteil
Zipcodes, numerical	S	76	USA Vorwahl, numerisch
Ten-Year City Development		77	Zehn Jahre Stadtentwicklung
Weights and Measures	S	82	Gewichte & Masse
Telephone Times/Dollar Value	S	83	Telefon Zeiten/Dollar Werte
Convention Capital		90	Ausstellungs Metropole
Map of Suburbia	M	108	Karte vom Chicagoland
The Suburbs of Chicago		109	Chicagos Vororte
Suburban Living		112	Leben in den Vororten
Places of Special Interest		119	Sehenswertes und Interessantes

Contents		Page/Seite	Inhalt
Seasons		124	Jahreszeiten
Chicago Temperatures	S	131	Durchschnittstemperaturen
Fly Away		135	Über den Wolken
O'Hare Airport Layout	M	137	O'Hare Flughafen Karte
Life and Leasure		143	Leben und Freizeit
Chicago Restaurant Guide		153	Chicago Restaurant Führer
Chicagoland Songs		163	Chicagoland Lieder
Chicago Sports		165	Chicago Profi Sport
Education		168	Schulwesen
A Woman's Point of View		170	Perspektive einer Frau
Shopping in Chicagoland		174	Einkaufen im Chicagoland
German Restaurants & Retailers		182	Deutsche Restaurants/Geschäfte
Club Life in Chicagoland		190	Vereinsleben im Chicagoland
Hamburg – Sistercity of Chicago		196	Hamburg – Chicagos Partnerstadt
Chicago's Beginnings	M	202	Die Anfänge Chicagos
German Carnival, a la Chicago		220	Deutscher Karneval, Chicago Art
German American Heritage		222	Das deutsch-amerikanische Erbe
German American Media		233	Deutsch-amerikanische Medien
Chicagoland's Future		236	Chicagolands Zukunft
Bibliography		238	Referenzen
Participants		238	Beteiligte Firmen
Photo Credits		239	Fotoquellen
Alphabetical Index		240	Alphabetisches Verzeichnis
Personal Photos and Notes		244	Eigene Bilder und Notizen

M = Maps / Karten   S = Statistics / Statistiken

The James R. Thompson Center was designed by German-born Helmut Jahn of Murphy/Jahn, Inc., a Chicago Architectural Firm. To his credit are such other landmark buildings as the Atrium of Northwestern Station, the Chicago Stock Exchange extension, and in the suburbs the 30 story Oakbrook Terrace Tower and the United Airlines Terminal at O'Hare.

Das James R. Thompson Zentrum, nach dem ehemaligen Gouverneur von Illinois benannt, wurde von dem berühmten, aus Deutschland stammenden Architekten Helmut Jahn der Chicagoer Architekten-Firma Murphy/Jahn, Inc. entworfen. Jahn war auch der Architekt anderer Wahrzeichen der Stadt, so zum Beispiel des Atriums des Northwestern-Bahnhofs, des Chicagoer Börsenanbaus - die Chicago Mercantile Exchange, und in den Vororten war er der Architekt des 30 Stockwerke hohen Oakbrook Terrace-Turms und des Terminals der United Airlines amO'Hare Flughafen.

From the Office of the Governor

Governor Jim Edgar (left) with Publisher Bert Lachner

Greetings:

As Governor of the State of Illinois, I am pleased to introduce you to the Chicagoland book.

This book is a lifestyle portrait of Illinois which focuses on the state's multi-national corporations and other international organizations and activities. Companies throughout the state who are involved in international trade and commerce play an important role in fostering travel, business and investment for the State of Illinois.

On behalf of the citizens of Illinois, I extend my personal welcome to you and invite you to experience the many historical landmarks, cultural points of interest and the natural beauty of our state.

Best regards,

Jim Edgar
GOVERNOR

Liebe Leser,

als Gouverneur des Bundesstaates Illinois ist es mir eine besonders große Freude, die einleitenden Worte zu diesem großartigen Chicago-Buch an Sie richten zu dürfen.

Dieses Buch ist mehr als nur eine Geschichte, es stellt ein Lebensporträt des Staates Illinois dar und ganz besonders der multi-nationalen Firmen und internationalen Organisationen mit ihren Aktivitäten. Firmen aus dem ganzen Staat sind aktiv im internationalen Handel tätig und spielen für Tourismus, Unternehmen und Investitionen im Staat Illinois eine große Rolle.

Im Namen der Bürger von Illinois möchte ich Sie persönlich willkommen heißen und lade Sie ein, die vielen historischen und kulturellen Stätten und die natürliche Schönheit unseres Bundesstaates selbst zu entdecken.

Mit freundlichem Gruß

Jim Edgar
Gouverneur

City Hall • Photo by Willy Schmidt © City of Chicago

Lachner "*CHICAGOLAND*"

From the Office of the Mayor

Mayor Richard M. Daley

Dear Friends,

Welcome to Chicago! We are delighted you are visiting our city.

Chicago is proud to host the opening ceremonies and five tournament games of the 1994 World Cup. We hope you will join us for the spectacular series of events we have planned to celebrate the World Cup in Chicago.

While you are here, you will experience Chicago's marvelous attractions, elegant accommodations, outstanding restaurants, renowned architecture, multicultural neighborhoods and beautiful lakefront parks and beaches. More importantly, you will discover Chicago's unsurpassed hospitality which keeps visitors coming back again and again.

Visitors to Chicago will find activities to suit every taste. From lakefront festivals and ethnic parades to outdoor concerts and neighborhood fairs, Chicago offers a variety of exciting events year-round.

Please visit our Information Booth in the landmark Chicago Cultural Center for free brochures and information about our world-class city. Friendly visitor information representatives will assist you in planning a wonderful Chicago tour.

Enjoy your stay in Chicago; we hope you will visit again soon.

Sincerely,

Richard M. Daley
Mayor

Liebe Gäste,

Willkommen in Chicago! Wir freuen uns sehr, Sie in unserer Stadt begrüßen zu dürfen.

Chicago ist stolz darauf, Gastgeberin für die Eröffnungsfeiern und fünf Wettspiele des World Cups 1994 zu sein. Wir hoffen, daß Sie mit uns an den spektakulären Veranstaltungen teilnehmen, die wir aus Anlaß des World Cups in Chicago geplant haben.

Während Ihres Aufenthaltes werden Sie die herausragenden Attraktionen von Chicago, elegante Unterkünfte, erlesene Restaurants, die berühmte Architektur, multikulturelle Stadtviertel und die wunderschönen Parks und Strände am See kennenlernen. Noch mehr beeindrucken wird Sie aber die beispiellose Gastfreundschaft unserer Stadt, die die Besucher veranlaßt, immer wieder zu uns zurückzukommen.

Besucher unserer Stadt finden Aktivitäten für jeden Geschmack. Von Festspielen am See und Paraden, die die Herkunft ethnischer Gruppen würdigen, bis zu Freiluftkonzerten und Volksfesten in den einzelnen Stadtvierteln bietet Chicago das ganze Jahr über eine Vielfalt unterhaltsamer Veranstaltungen.

Besuchen Sie bitte unseren Informationsstand im Chicago Cultural Center, einem der Wahrzeichen unserer Stadt, und lassen Sie sich kostenlose Broschüren und Unterlagen über unsere Weltstadt geben. Die freundlichen Mitarbeiter dieser Besucherzentrale werden Ihnen gern bei der Planung einer unterhaltsamen Besichtigungstour helfen.

Ich wünsche Ihnen einen unvergeßlichen Aufenthalt in Chicago und hoffe, daß Sie uns bald wieder besuchen.

Mit freundlichem Gruß

Richard M. Daley
Bürgermeister

Many families maintain a weekend home away from home. Whether it is a small cottage or an elaborate summer home by the lake, it is a place to relax, to shed the busy hours of the week and to enjoy family and friends.

Here, many good plans are made.

Viele Familien haben ein Wochenendplätzchen. Egal ob es ein kleines Häuschen ist oder eine feudale Sommervilla am See, es ist ein Ort zum Entspannen, wo man den Alltag ablegen und vergessen kann und Familie und Freunde unterhält.

Hier werden oft großartige Pläne geschmiedet.

Introduction

This is a dream come true:

To bring the City and suburbs, Chicagoland, to the visitors of my hometown, and show and tell of the many exciting discoveries I have made over 30 years.

Chicago, still wrapped in the mantle of its dramatic history, is really a bustling metropolis that works. The diversity of its people, the blend of modern and the conservative landscape, its solid business climate and infrastructure, and its dynamic lifestyle, all add up to a healthy, happy and prosperous environment.

This book is also your ready-made photo album to take home and reminisce; then use it to plan again. What you see are familiar sights, what you read will hopefully answer some questions and provide helpful information.

It is my personal observation, my point of view, as I see this world-class Metropolis.

Enjoy and explore...

Bert Lachner
Publisher

Einleitung

Es ist wie ein Traum, der in Erfüllung geht, meinen Landsleuten, Freunden und Touristen in Chicago das zeigen zu dürfen, was ich in über 30 Jahren in dieser Stadt und ihrem Umland, eben dem Chicagoland, entdeckt habe.

Obwohl Chicago ja eigentlich noch immer von seiner dramatischen Vergangenheit zehrt, ist es heute eine geschäftige Metropole, die funktioniert und lebt. Das bunte Gemisch an Menschen, die Verschmelzung von moderner und konservativer Architektur und Bauten, das solide Geschäftsklima, die Infrastruktur und der dynamische Lebensstil, sie alle tragen dazu bei, ein gesundes, blühendes und „happy" Umfeld zu schaffen.

Dieses Buch ist gleichzeitig ein Photoalbum, das wir für Sie zusammengestellt haben und das Sie mit nach Hause nehmen können, um Ihre Erinnerungen zu teilen. Vielleicht planen Sie hiermit Ihre nächste Reise nach Chicago. Wir stellen Ihnen hier die Sehenswürdigkeiten unserer Stadt vor und hoffen, daß wir einige Ihrer Fragen beantworten und informative Tips geben können.

Mit diesem Buch drücke ich meine persönliche Erfahrung aus, so wie ich Chicago sehe und erlebe. Eine Metropole von Weltklasse.
Viel Spaß beim Entdecken und genießen Sie Ihren Aufenthalt in Chicago.

Bert Lachner
Herausgeber

The skyline view from the Lake shows Grant Park and the Chicago and M.S.Columbia Yacht Clubs in the foreground. Other Grant Park features include the Buckingham Fountain, the Art Institute, the Petrillo Band Shell, tracks of the Illinois Southshore Railroad, extensive underground parking facilities and the Daley Sports Core. Grant Park was built from the debris of the Chicago Fire in 1871.

Of the major buildings we recognize from left to right: the Congress and Auditorium buildings with the new Washington Public Library (green roof) and the Main Post Office in the back of it. The red CNA Building is in front of the 311 South Wacker Building with the crown on top. The largest of all is the Sears Tower with the white antennae, then the AT&T Corporate Center covered partially by the 190 South LaSalle Building with the four gables. The square, grey building is the Mid Continental Plaza. Behind it the First National Bank Building with slanted sides, and the black Madison Plaza next to it.

The other black building is the Daley Center and then the Citi-Corp Building. The building with the diamond shaped roof is the Stone Container Building on the corner of Michigan and Randolph. Behind it, the dark building is the Leo Burnett Advertising and, with the green roof, the R.R. Donnelly Buildings. To the right are the Prudential Plaza and the Corporate Center. The white monolith is the Amoco Oil Building with the Fairmont Hotel next to it. To the front are a number of residential buildings with Harbor Point on the corner of Randolph and Lake Shore Drive.

On the North side of the Chicago River we see North Pier and the tall buildings, including the Ritz Carlton Hotel with Water Tower Place, the John Hancock Center with antennae, the Four Seasons Hotel with Bloomingdales Department Store and the Olympia Center to the left. Among the Michigan Avenue front buildings are the Fine Arts Building, Roosevelt University, the Chicago Title & Trust Building, Orchestra Hall, Borg-Warner and People's Gas Buildings. The early 1900 buildings to the North represent the Chicago School of Architecture, and finally the Chicago Cultural Center, housing among others the Broadcast Museum and the offices of the Department of Tourism and the Sister City Program.

Lachner "CHICAGOLAND"

Wenn wir vom See aus auf die Skyline von Chicago schauen, sehen wir im Vordergrund den Grant Park und die beiden Chicagoer Yacht-Clubs, Chicago und M.S. Columbia. Sehenswürdigkeiten im Grant Park sind: der Buckingham-Fountain, der eine Kopie des Latona-Springbrunnens in Versailles ist; Chicagos Gemäldegalerie, das „Art Institute,"; die Freilichtbühne „Petrillo Band Shell"; die Eisenbahnschienen der Illinois Southshore Railroad; die riesige Anlage der Untergrundparkplätze; und der Daley-Sportplatz. Grant Park wurde nach dem Chicagoer Großbrand 1871 aus den Trümmern aufgebaut.

An sehenswürdigen Gebäuden erkennen wir, wenn wir von links nach rechts schauen: das Congress-Gebäude und das Auditorium-Theater-Gebäude, dahinter das grüne Dach der neuen Stadtbibliothek, der Washington Public Library. Noch weiter im Westen sehen wir das riesige Gebäude des größten Postamtes der Welt, das Hauptpostamt Chicagos. Das rote Gebäude ist das CNA-Gebäude und liegt vor dem 311 South Wacker-Gebäude mit der Krone oben auf dem Dach. Das höchste Gebäude ist natürlich der „Sears Tower", der Turm mit den weißen Antennen. Wir sehen auch das Gebäude der Telefon-Gesellschaft, das AT&T Corporate Center, was aber zum Teil durch das Gebäude der 190 South LaSalle Street mit seinen vier Giebeln verdeckt wird. Das rechteckige, graue Gebäude ist der Mid Continental Plaza. Dahinter liegt das sich schräg in den Himmel streckende Gebäude der First National Bank, daneben das schwarze Madison Plaza-Gebäude.

Das andere schwarze Gebäude, das wir von hier aus sehen, ist das Daley-Zentrum und das CitiCorp-Gebäude. Das Gebäude mit dem rhombusförmigen Dach ist das Stone Container Building an der Ecke Michigan Avenue und Randolph-Street. Dahinter steht das dunkelgraue Gebäude der Leo Burnett Werbeagentur, und das Gebäude mit dem grünen Dach ist das R.R. Donnelly Building, Druckerei- und Herausgeberbetrieb. Schauen wir nun nach rechts, dann sehen wir die beiden, miteinander verbundenen Prudential-Versicherungsgebäude und das Corporate Center. Mit weißem Monolith verkleidet ist das Amoco-Oil-Gebäude, daneben gleich das Fairmont-Hotel. Vorne rechts sehen wir auch eine Reihe von Wohnhäusern mit Harbor Point an der Ecke Randolph Street und Lake Shore Drive.

Nördlich des Chicagoer Flußes sehen wir den Nord-Pier und unter den Hochhäusern befindet sich das Ritz-Carlton-Hotel mit dem Water Tower Place-Einkaufszentrum, das John-Hancock-Gebäude mit Antennen, das Hotel Four Seasons, das Kaufhaus Bloomingdales und zur Linken das Olympia-Zentrum. In der vorderen Reihe der Michigan Avenue sehen wir das Fine Arts Building, die Roosevelt Universität, das Gebäude der Chicago Title & Trust, die Orchestra Hall, das Borg-Warner und das People's Gas Gebäude. Die Hochhäuser zum Norden hin vertreten die Chicagoer Architekturschule mit Gebäuden der frühen zwanziger Jahre, und nicht zuletzt, das Chicago Cultural Center, wo u.a. das Broadcast oder Rundfunk-Museum zu finden ist, das Touristenbüro und das Büro für das Partnerstadt-Programm.

INTRODUCTION — EINFÜHRUNG

As the commercial aviation capital of the world, O'Hare International Airport has an average of 110 aircraft arrivals and departures each hour. Terminal 5, the new International Terminal opened in May of 1993 to efficiently accommodate 33 air carriers and handle 4000 passengers per hour for traveling to or from every major airporrt in the world.

110 Flugzeuge landen und starten hier stündlich. Denn O'Hare International Airport ist die Flugmetropole der Welt. Der neue Internationale Terminal 5 für Auslandsflüge wurde im Mai 1993 eröffnet und kann spielend leicht 33 Flugzeuge und 4000 Passagiere pro Stunde abfertigen.

First Impressions

Arriving by airplane, the visitor is welcomed to Chicagoland by towering skyscrapers and a vast expanse of surrounding neighborhoods. At night the city becomes a fairyland - a million lights dotting the way in three directions. The view is enhanced by the contrast between the dark expanse of Lake Michigan and this sprawling Metropolis on its Western Shore.

Streets are laid out in perfect symmetry. Square block after square block are interspersed by streets running diagonally away from the center of town. These are successors of the old wagon trails of 200 years ago.

2.7 million people live and work here. Another 3.8 million inhabit the surrounding area, often called Chicagoland, the suburbs and outskirts of the city.

Chicago's O'Hare International Airport features four major terminals, a six story parking facility, and the O'Hare Hilton Hotel. The new International Terminal lies East of the main terminals. All terminals, parking and the hotel are connected by a people-mover train for easy access and traffic flow.

VIsitors usually get their second wind after landing, as they emerge into the hustle and bustle of the concourse to claim their luggage and pass through customs. Conversations, smiles and helpful hints are trademarks of

Der Erste Eindruck

Wenn man sich per Flugzeug Chicagoland nähert, grüßen einen schon von weitem die Hochhäuser und die enorme Ausdehnung der Stadt und das sie umgebende Land. Nachts verwandelt sich diese City in ein Märchenland - Millionen von Lichtern verlieren sich weit hinaus in drei Richtungen. Dieses Lichtermeer wird durch den Kontrast zwischen der samtschwarzen Ausdehnung des Michigan Sees und der Metropole an der Westküste des Sees noch gesteigert.

Die Straßen sind in perfekter Symmetrie angeordnet. Die quadratischen, sich aneinanderreihenden Häuserblocks werden nur durch die Straßen unterbrochen, die diagonal vom Zentrum der Stadt aus in die Außenbezirke verlaufen. Die Straßenzüge sind eigentlich die alten Wagon Trails, auf denen die Pioniere mit ihren Wagen vor 200 Jahren entlang gezogen sind.

2,7 Millionen Menschen wohnen und arbeiten hier. Weitere 3,8 Millionen leben im Umland der City, die als Chicagoland bezeichneten Vororte und Außenbezirke.

Chicagos Internationaler Flughafen O'Hare verfügt über vier Terminals, einem sechsstöckigen Parkhaus und dem O'Hare Hilton-Hotel. Das neue Terminal für Auslandsflüge liegt an der Ostseite des Hauptterminals. Alle Terminals, Parkhaus/Parkplätze und das Hotel sind durch den People-Mover, einer computergesteuerten Transferbahn, miteinander verbunden, was den Transferverkehr auf dem Flughafengelände leichter fließen läßt.

Nach der Landung geht es dann zügig zur Gepäckabfertigung und durch die Zollkontrolle. Man wird auf typische Chicagoer Art empfangen. Die Menschen hier sind freundlich und einer Unterhaltung mit dem Nachbar nicht abgeneigt. Mit freundlichem Lächeln geben sie hilfsbereit Auskunft. Es erinnert an Frank Sinatras „It's my kind of town!" - „Eine Stadt nach meinem Herzen."

Die Innenstadt, also das „Downtown" Chicagos, ist ungefähr 30 Minuten vom Flughafen entfernt. Auf der Fahrt in die Stadt erhält man

Chicago's streets are laid out at 100 numbers per block. Eight blocks to a mile or 5 blocks to a kilometer. This helps estimating distances and locating addresses quickly.

Chicagos Straßenzüge sind so ausgelegt, daß jeder Straßenblock 100 Hausnummern enthält. Also sind acht Straßenblocks eine Meile oder fünf Straßenblocks ca. einen Kilometer lang. Dadurch kann man Entfernungen innerhalb der Stadt gut abschätzen und somit schnell eine Adresse ausfindig machen.

The Loop, named after the elevated train which makes a large square loop on the south side of the River on van Buren, Wabash, Lake and Wells Streets, has much to see and to offer. Walking the streets is the best may to discover the magic of the city.

Der Loop wurde nach der Hoch- oder Stadtbahn, „L" (von 'elevated' oder erhöht) benannt, die südlich vom Chicago-Fluß eine Schleife um die Innenstadt zieht, und Schleife heißt nun eben mal „Loop". Die Grenzen dieser Schleife bilden die Straßen Van Buren, Wabash, Lake und Wells. Am besten läuft man diese Straßen entlang, um die magische Zauberkraft der Stadt nachvollziehen zu können.

CHICAGO HOUSE NUMBER MAP

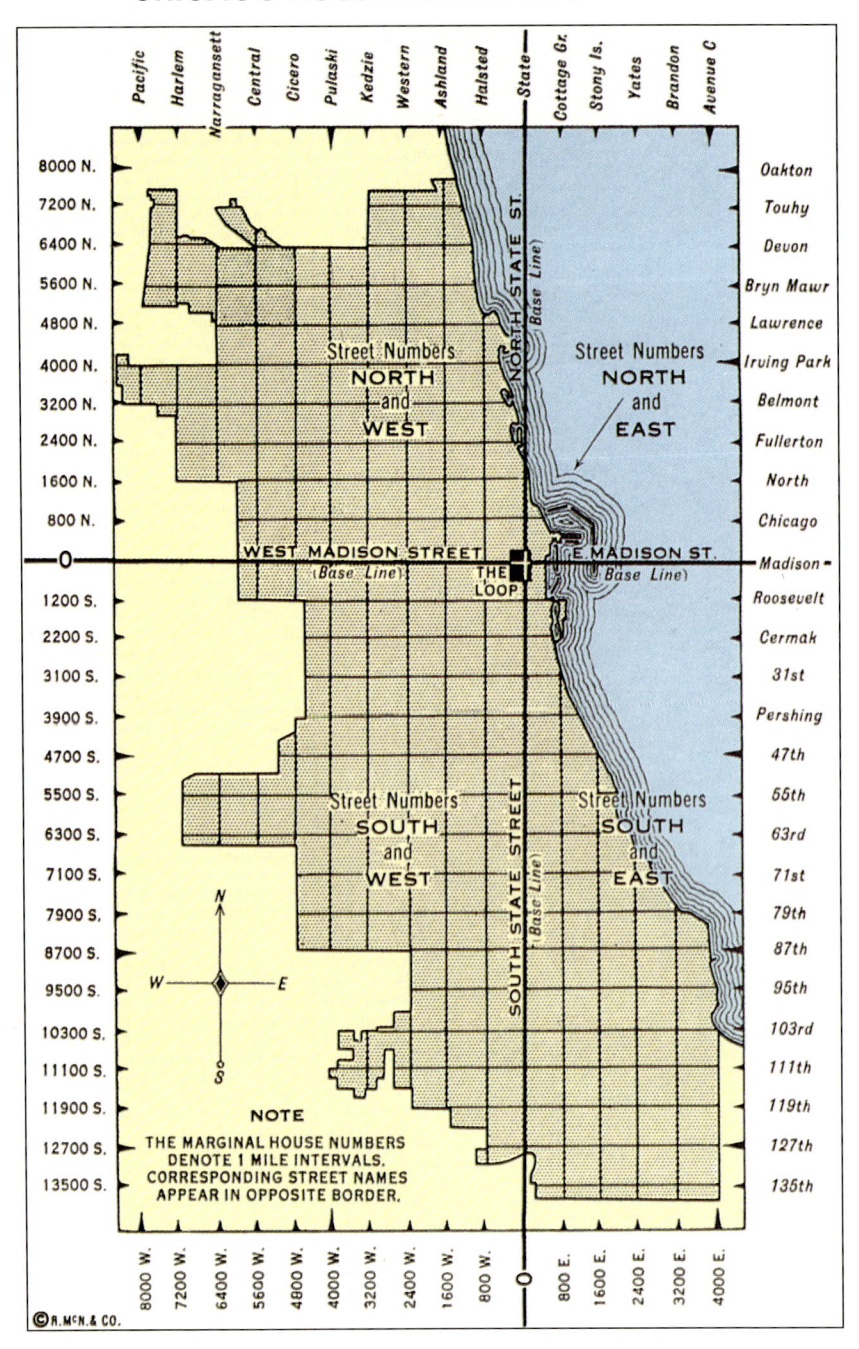

Chicago, reminders of Frank Sinatra singing "It's my kind of town!"

Downtown Chicago is about 30 minutes from O'Hare airport. Driving in, one gets a close-up look of the seemingly endless array of architecturally different buildings, old and new, high and low, bizarre towers of steel, concrete and glass. Chicago's architecture is legendary, its modern hue not more than 10 to 20 years old.

Arriving at our hotel, luggage is unloaded, welcoming hands are extended and introductions are made. One is impressed by the generous layout of the lobby. A comfortable meeting place with restaurants, coffee shop, lounge, gift and drug stores all in close proximity.

Before dinner, there is time to relax, talk with friends, make phone calls. The television news programs tell us what weather to expect the next day, our first full day in "The Windy City".

The next morning, after a good night's sleep, we are ready for breakfast. Fresh orange juice, bacon and eggs, toast and coffee, are an American tradition. Or you may prefer pancakes, hot or cold cereal, doughnuts or sweet roll with your coffee. Continental breakfast is available for those in a hurry.

Plans are made for the day—

schon einen ersten Eindruck von der anscheinend unendlichen Ansammlung an architektonisch verschiedenartigen Gebäuden, alten und neuen, hohen und niedrigen, bizarre Türme aus Stahl, Beton und Glas. Chicagos Architektur ist legendär, der moderne Ton ist keine 10 bis 20 Jahre alt.

Sobald man das Hotel erreicht hat, wird das Gepäck abgeladen, willkommenheißende Hände strecken sich einem entgegen und man stellt sich vor. Das erste was einem auffällt, sind die beeindruckenden, schönen Eingangshallen, die Lobbies, mit ihren einladenden Sitzecken, Restaurants, Kaffeestuben, Bars, Boutiquen und Zeitungsläden, alles in unmittelbarer Nähe.

Vor dem Abendessen hat man meistens noch etwas Zeit sich zu entspannen, mit Freunden zu plaudern, Telefongespräche zu führen. Und wie das Wetter am nächsten Tag werden wird, ihrem ersten Tag in der „Windigen Stadt", das erfahren Sie durch die Nachrichtenprogramme im Fernsehen oder dem Wetterkanal.

Ein typisch amerikanisches Frühstück erwartet Sie am nächsten Morgen. Orangensaft, gebratener Speck und Eier, Toast und Kaffee sind Tradition. Sie können aber auch Eierkuchen bestellen, oder Müslis und Cornflakes, Pfannkuchen oder Schnecken und Kaffee. Und wenn es schnell gehen soll, dann können Sie auch ein Continentales Frühstück bestellen, d.h. Kaffee mit Kleingebäck und Brötchen.

sightseeing, a visit to the mall or department store, a stroll through the park, maybe a little shopping. Note again how people interact, communicate and smile. Everyone is busy, but friendly.

Lunch is usually served from 11:00 to 2:00 p.m. The American midday meal is light. A softdrink with soup and sandwiches are popular, as are fruit or vegetable salads, hamburgers and fries, barbecue beef, and chicken or sausage. Full course entrees are served in finer restaurants and usually enjoyed with a glass of wine. Dessert, if desired, and a cup of coffee or tea, complete the meal. Tips are 15 to 20%.

Dinner is normally from 5:00 to 9:00 p.m., and is the main meal of the day. You have a wide choice of American, Italian, German, French, Oriental and other ethnic and exotic cuisines, and with the ambience to suit the occasion.

Domestic wines from California or New York State are excellent. American beers, many brewed in neighboring Wisconsin, are always served ice cold. Imported wines and beers are available everywhere.

Many restaurants are open 24 hours a day, so you can eat anytime you like. Americans don't have time for tea or sweets in the afternoon as a rule, but these, too, — a piece of pie perhaps - can be ordered at any hour. But do take time, now and then, to enjoy that American specialty, ice cream, cones or sundaes, in many different flavors.

In the evening you may want to go to the theater, a concert, night club, sporting event, movie or stay in and watch television. To get good seats, performance tickets should be purchased in advance. Restaurants always need reservations to seat you comfortably.

Jetzt wird das Tagesprogramm geplant. Stadtbesichtigung, ein Bummel durch ein Einkaufszentrum, das hier Mall heißt, ein Kaufhaus, ein Spaziergang im Park. Vielleicht fällt Ihnen auf, wie nett die Leute hier miteinander reden und stets freundlich lächeln, auch wenn Sie es eilig haben.

Mittagessen oder Lunch wird gewöhnlich von 11.00 Uhr bis 14.00 Uhr serviert. Die Amerikaner nehmen mittags meistens eine kleine Mahlzeit ein. Alkoholfreie Getränke, Suppe und Sandwiches werden bestellt, aber auch Obst- oder Gemüsesalat, Hamburger und Pommes, Barbecue Beef, Hühnchen oder Wurst. In den besseren Restaurants werden Vor- und Hauptspeisen mit allen Gängen und Dessert serviert und dazu vielleicht ein Glas Wein. Kaffee oder Tee schließen die Mahlzeit ab. Trinkgeld is 15 bis 20%.

Abendessen wird zwischen 17.00 und 21.00 Uhr serviert und stellt die Hauptmahlzeit des Tages dar. Ihnen steht eine große Auswahl an amerikanischen, italienischen, deutschen, französischen, orientalischen und anderen ethnischen und exotischen Küchen mit dazu gehörendem Ambiente zur Verfügung.

Es gibt gute Weine aus Kalifornien oder New York Staat. Bier wird immer eiskalt serviert. Ein großes Sortiment an Bieren wird im Nachbarstaat Wisconsin gebraut. Allerdings können Sie jederzeit und überall auch importierte Weine und Biere bestellen.

Da viele Restaurants 24 Stunden lang geöffnet haben, können Sie eigentlich essen gehen wann Sie wollen. Obwohl die Amerikaner normalerweise keine Zeit für einen Nachmittagstee oder Kaffee und Kuchen haben, so kann man sie dennoch überall und zu jeder Zeit bestellen. Sie sollten sich aber auf jeden Fall die Zeit nehmen, eine ganz besonders typische amerikanische Spezialität zu genießen, nämlich amerikanisches Eis in der Tüte oder im Eisbecher. Die Auswahl an Geschmacksrichtungen erscheint unendlich.

Abends können Sie ein Theater besuchen, ein Konzert, einen Night Club oder eine Sportveran-

Lunch hours are brief, a reason for fast food services and many small cafes everywhere. Often food is ordered in and consumed in the company lunchroom.

Die Zeit für Mittagspausen ist bemessen, also ein guter Grund für einen Schnellimbiß oder „fast food service" in einem der vielen kleinen Fast Food Restaurants der Stadt. Sehr häufig lassen sich die Angestellten ihr Essen auch in die Büros liefern, wo sie es in den eigens dazu eingerichteten Speisezimmern verzehren.

staltung. Sie können ins Kino gehen oder einfach Ihre Füsse ausstrecken und unter der Vielzahl der verschiedenen Kanäle und Programme des amerikanischen Fernsehens sich etwas für Ihren Geschmack auswählen. Karten für Theater, Konzerte oder Sportveranstaltungen sollten im Voraus gekauft werden, um, wenn überhaupt, einen guten Sitzplatz zu erhalten. Auch in den Restaurants ist es wünschenswert, einen Tisch zu reservieren.

FIRST IMPRESSIONS — ERSTEN EINDRÜCKE

Lachner "*CHICAGOLAND*"

FIRST IMPRESSIONS — ERSTEN EINDRÜCKE

Where in the World Is Chicago?

88° West and 42° North, 4,318 miles (6000 Km) west of Hamburg

Chicagoland's geographic location provides the region with a relatively flat landscape and a comfortable climate similar to that of central Europe.

Chicagoans enjoy more than 300 days of sunshine a year. It can be very windy, however, very cold in winter and very hot in summer. The extremes of temperature stem from the large land masses in the west and Lake Michigan's balancing effect to the east. Latitude is similar to that of Rome, Italy; Peking, China; Sapporo, Japan; and the state of Oregon on the West coast.

Chicago is located at the southern edge of the Canadian Shield which provides the city with the solid granite bedrock foundation for its many skyscrapers. Lake Michigan, like the other four Great Lakes, is filled to the brim with fresh water.

It has abundant marine life and

Lachner "CHICAGOLAND"

Photo by Alfred Blumenthal

Wo auf der Welt liegt Chicago?

88° West und 42° Nord

Chicagos geographische Lage zeichnet sich durch eine relativ flache Landschaft mit einem angenehmen Klima aus, das dem Zentral-Europas ähnlich ist.

Die Chicagoer genießen mehr als 300 Tage Sonnenschein im Jahr. Es kann sehr windig sein und es ist sehr kalt im Winter und sehr heiß im Sommer. Diese extremen Temperaturen rühren von der riesigen Landmasse im Westen her und werden vom Michigansee, der die Temperaturen etwas mäßigt, beeinflußt. Chicago liegt auf demselben Breitengrad wie Rom in Italien, Peking in China, Sapporo in Japan und der Staat von Oregon an der Westküste.

Chicago liegt am südlichsten Ende des „Canadian Shields," eine feste Granit Platte, die das Fundament für die zahlreichen Wolkenkratzer bildet.

WHERE IS CHICAGO — WO IST CHICAGO

A canal boat in the I&M Canal at Lockport around 1900
Ein Kanalboot im Illinois und Michigan Kanal bei Lockport – Anfang dieses Jahrhunderts

Lock #8 at Marseilles, beginning of the century
Die Schleuse Nr. 8 in Marseilles – Anfang dieses Jahrunderts

Today's canal at Morris
Der heutigen Kanal bei Morris

Photos courtesy of I&M Canal NHC Commission

provides the population around it with good drinking water. Lake Michigan, the second largest of the five Great Lakes, is approximately 330 miles long, 80 miles at its widest point and has an average depth of 300 feet. It provides ample space for commercial shipping and pleasure boating, such as the prestigious sailboat regatta to Mackinac Island, at the most northern tip of the Lake, each year in July.

The deepwater port of Lake Calumet Harbor, on the City's far southeast side, handles millions of tons of bulk cargo annually. Vast amounts of oil, gas, chemicals, coal and stone products are transported through the Great Lakes to and through Chicago. Giant barges are escorted by tugboats down the Chicago River, through the Sanitary Ship Canal, to the Illinois River, the Mississippi and Gulf of Mexico. The Great Lakes system is connected to the Atlantic by the St. Lawrence Seaway, able to handle ocean going vessels through its many locks. However, the long passage through the system is too slow for today's cargo transfer. Most goods coming over the Atlantic are transferred to rail service at the east coast ports and arrive in Chicago just two days later.

It is this large waterways network that makes Chicago, an inland City, an important port for commerce and industry.

Due to its strategic mid-continent location, Chicago is the transportation and distribution center of the United States, thereby creating its vast industrial and marketing base. Large amounts of cargo are shipped by rail and truck lines to cities and ports in all directions.

Chicago is the railroad capital of America, with passenger and freight traffic unmatched in the entire country. Interstate highways and local expressways make it the hub of the nation's trucking industry. Hundreds of giant truck terminals are located throughout the City and the suburbs.

Two major commercial airports service the Chi-cagoland area: Midway Airport, on the southwest side, which handles over seven million passengers a year. O'Hare International, the world's busiest airport, is on the northwest side, and accommodates 60 million passengers yearly, coming from and going to every major city in the U.S. and the world.

Tons of produce, products and machinery come into Chicago as air cargo. This enables Chicagoans to purchase oranges and strawberries out of season.

It also provides many jobs in manufacturing, assembly work, food processing, distribution and a variety of service companies.

Wie die anderen vier Großen Seen, ist auch der Michigansee ein Süßwassersee mit einer Fülle von Meerestieren und Meerespflanzen, und versorgt die Bevölkerung der umliegenden Ortschaften mit Trinkwasser. Der Michigan See, der zweitgrößte der fünf Großen Seen. Der See ist über 500 km lang, an seiner weitesten Stelle fast 130 km breit und hat eine Durchschnittstiefe von 100 m. Der Michigansee bietet ausreichend Platz für die Handelsschiffahrt wie auch für den Segel- und Motorbootsport. Jedes Jahr im Juli findet z.B. die bekannte Segelboot-Regatta nach Mackinac Island, der nördlichsten Spitze des Sees, statt.

Im Lake Calumet Harbor, einem Tiefwasserbinnenhafen an der Südostseite der Stadt, werden jährlich Millionen von Tonnen an Schüttgut verladen. Riesige Mengen an Öl, Gas, Chemikalien, Kohle und Steinprodukte werden von und über Chicago über die Großen Seen verschifft. Gigantische Frachtkähne werden von Schleppern den Chicago River hinuntergezogen, durch den Sanitary Ship-Kanal zum Illinois River, über den Mississippi zum Golf von Mexiko. Die fünf Großen Seen sind durch den St. Lorenz-Seeweg mit dem Atlantischen Ozean verbunden. Selbst Ozeandampfer sind somit in der Lage, mit Hilfe der vielen Schleusen über die fünf Großen Seen vom Atlantischen Ozean bis zum Golf von Mexiko zu fahren. Diese Route ist heute allerdings für den Transport von Gütern zu langsam. Die meisten Güter, die über den Atlantischen Ozean kommen, werden an der Ostküste durch Frachtzüge weiter transportiert und treffenen zwei Tage später in Chicago ein.

Dieses große Netzwerk an Wasserwegen macht die Binnenstadt Chicago zu einem der wichtigsten Häfen für Handel und Industrie.

Dank seiner günstigen Lage inmitten des Kontinents wurde Chicago zum Verkehrs- und Verteilerzentrum der Vereinigten Staaten und konnte somit eine solide Grundlage für Industrie und Marketing schaffen. Riesige Mengen an Fracht werden per Bahn und Lastwagen zu in allen Richtungen liegenden Städten und Häfen transportiert.

Chicago ist die „Eisenbahnhauptstadt" Amerikas. Die Anzahl der Passagiere und das Volumen an Frachtverkehr ist höher als in anderen Teilen des Landes. Durch Bundesstraßen und Schnellverkehrsstraßen wurde Chicago zum Mittelpunkt der Lastkraftwagenindustrie in Amerika. Hunderte von Lastwagen-Ladeplätzen sind in der Stadt und den Vororten zu finden.

Zwei große Handelsflughäfen stehen Chicagoland zur Verfügung: Midway Airport an der Südwestseite Chicagos fertigt jährlich 7 Millionen Passagiere ab. O'Hare International, der geschäftigste Flughafen der Welt, liegt an der Nordwest Seite und fertigt jährlich 60 Millionen Passagiere ab, die aus allen Teilen der Welt kommen.

Agrarerzeugnisse, Waren und Maschinen werden per Luftfracht nach Chicago gebracht und die Chicagoer können das ganze Jahr hindurch frische Orangen und Erdbeeren genießen. Dieser Umstand bringt außerdem viele Arbeitsstellen mit sich, so z.B. in der Herstellung, Montage, Verarbeitung von Nahrungsmitteln, im Verkauf und in einer Vielzahl von Dienstleistungsbetrieben.

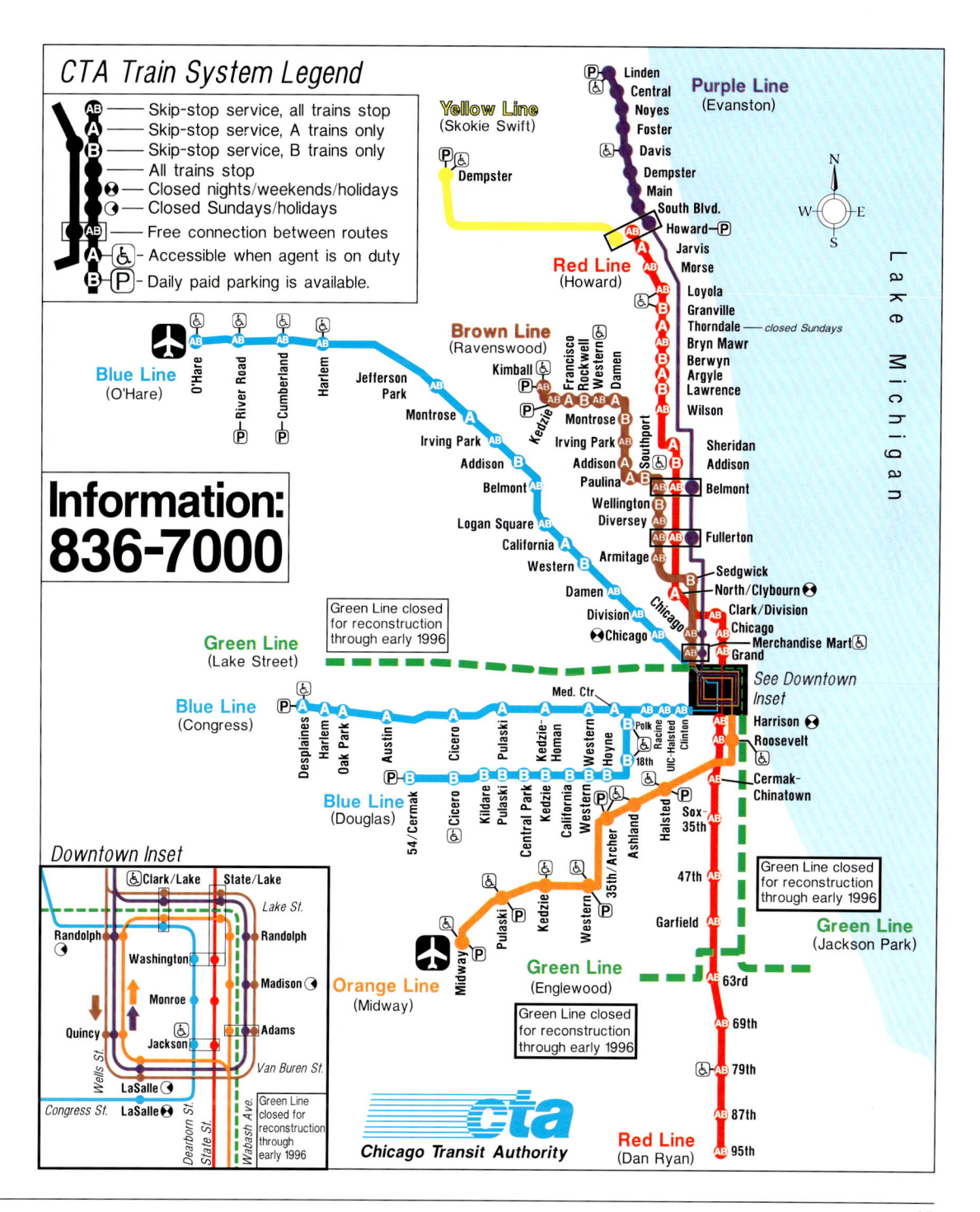

WHERE IS CHICAGO — WO IST CHICAGO

Behind this curtain of serenity, the bold, busy towers of activity
Hinter der ehrwürdigen Fassade verbirgt sich eine kühne und tatenreiche Stadt.

A Stroll through the City

Let us stroll through downtown Chicago, just like most visitors do when they have a few hours of leisure time.

After parking the car or leaving the train station, one is immediately overwhelmed by the conglomeration of tall buildings with their unusual designs, entrances and the elaborate architecture of their bold towers. At once, we are fascinated by the mix of old and new buildings, both have their creativity and charm. Most of the older buildings have been renovated and feature warm, welcoming lobbies in their grand splendor. The new buildings invite the visitor to large entrance halls, modern art and efficient traffic patterns.

Parking is available in one of the underground Grant Park garages on Monroe Street and Columbus Drive, or in any of hundreds of parking lots and garages in the City. For the stroll, you may want to wear comfortable sneakers with a cushioned sole. Walking on concrete can be very tiring.

When you get to Grant Park — Chicago's "Front Yard" —, it may be Jazzfest or Festa Italiana time, sponsored by Mayor Richard M. Daley, compliments of the City of

Ein Bummel durch die Stadt

Lassen Sie uns nun wie die vielen Besucher durch die Innenstadt bummeln gehen.

Sobald man das Parkhaus oder den Parkplatz bzw. den Zug verlassen hat, wird man von den hohen Gebäuden mit ihrer außergewöhnlichen Architektur, ihren kühn in den Himmel ragenden Türmen und den einladenden Portalen überwältigt. Eine breite Mischung an neuen und alten Gebäuden fasziniert einen mit immer neuer Kreativität und ihrem Charme. Der größte Teil der alten Gebäude wurde renoviert und mit warmen, einladenden und prachtvoll ausgestatteten Lobbies versehen. Die neuen Gebäude empfangen den Besucher in ihren großen, mit moderner Kunst eingerichteten Eingangshallen.

Parkmöglichkeiten bieten die Tiefgaragen an der Monroe Street und Columbus Drive und hunderte von Parkplätzen oder Parkhäusern in der Stadt. Bequeme Schuhe gegen das harte Pflaster sind schon angebracht.

Grant Park ist Chicagos „Vorgarten," und es kann gut möglich sein, daß, wenn Sie hier sind, eines der vielen Feste stattfindet, wie zum Beispiel das Jazzfest oder das Italienische Fest, die von unserem Bürgermeister, Richard M. Daley, gefördert und von der Stadt Chicago gesponsert werden. Das sind nur zwei der vielen Feste, die im Frühjahr und den

This Dixieland Band adds to the "Taste of Chicago"
Beim „Taste of Chicago" darf die Dixieland Band nicht fehlen

26   Lachner "CHICAGOLAND"

compliments of the City of Chicago. Those are only two of many fests held throughout the spring and summer at Grant Park at the Lakefront. Others include: Taste of Chicago, July 4th Concert and Fireworks, Gospel Music, Blues Bands, Symphony Concerts, Venetian Night and the Air and Water Show.

In connection with the main program, there are often side attractions, which keep people busy and in town for an extra few hours or even over night. On the morning of the Jazzfest, for example, thousands of youngsters were preparing to "Walk for Life," to raise money to fight the AIDS epidemic. Other people with families visit museums, go shopping or taste the great food of the City.

ganzen Sommer lang im Grant Park am Seeufer veranstaltet werden. Andere Festivals sind: der Taste of Chicago; 4. Juli (Unabhängigkeitstag) mit Konzert und Feuerwerk; das Gospel Music Festival, das Blues Festival, Symphoniekonzerte, die Venezianische Nacht und die Flug- und Wassershows.

Neben dem Hauptprogramm werden oftmals Nebenattraktionen zur weiteren Unterhaltung der Besucher organisiert, was sie oftmals längere Zeit in Chicago verweilen läßt. So bereiteten sich zum Beispiel am Morgen des Jazzfestes tausende von Jugendlichen auf den „Walk for Life" vor, um Spenden für die AIDS-Hilfe zu sammeln. Andere wiederum besuchen Museen, gehen in der Stadt einkaufen oder in einem der vielen verschiedenartigen Restaurants essen.

People in thousands of busy offices keep hundreds of sailboats waiting
Segelboote warten auf ihre Segler, die noch in den Büros arbeiten

Food and festivities by the Lake
Frohe Feste am Michigan See

A common cause motivates these youngsters
Ein gemeinsames Ziel motiviert diese jungen Menschen

A STROLL THROUGH THE CITY — STADT BUMMEL

Buckingham Fountain in Grant Park was donated by Kate Buckingham and dedicated in 1927. A computer regulates 1.5 million gallons of water feeding the fountain, and spewing as high as 140 feet at a rate of 14,000 gallons per minute. Illuminated at night by 650 multi-color lights, the fountain is a glorious sight on a summer evening.

Even more breathtaking is the skyline from the area of the Adler Planetarium. Some sightseers with their bikes are marvelling at the City's early light, the emerald green waters with many boats lazily going out into the Lake, the sail boats of the Chicago Yacht Club, tipping their masts and clanking their halyards in the morning breeze. Grant Park is often filled with joggers, roller-skaters, bikers and other exercise enthusiasts.

Der Buckingham Springbrunnen im Grant Park wurde von Kate Buckingham gestiftet und 1927 eingeweiht. Ein Computer steuert die rund 6 Millionen Liter Wasser, die den Springbrunnen speisen. Seine Fontäne speit mit 56.000 Litern pro Minute über 40 m in die Höhe. Nachts wird der Springbrunnen von 650 farbigen Lichtern beleuchtet – ein prächtiges Wasserspiel in einer lauen Sommernacht.

Noch atemberaubender ist Chicagos Skyline vom Adler Planetarium aus. Besucher auf ihren Fahrrädern bewundern die Morgenlichter der Stadt, das Smaragdgrün des Wassers mit den vielen Booten, die langsam in den See hinausgleiten und die Segelboote des Chicagoer Yacht-Clubs, die ihre Masten nicken und mit ihren Segeltauen im Morgenwind rasseln. Grant Park ist ein Paradies für Jogger, Rollschuhläufer, Fahrradfahrer und andere Sportenthusiasten.

Buckingham Fountain in the Center of Grant Park

Der Buckingham Fountain im Grant Park

Weddings and nature go together

Eine Hochzeit im Freien

In stark contrast you observe the Michigan Avenue Cliff, a row of buildings on South Michigan Avenue facing Grant Park and the Lake, many of which reflect the early Chicago School of Architecture. Like mountain tops behind them are the massive and bold buildings of Chicago's downtown area. These include, from left, the Hilton Hotel and Towers; the crowned building at 311 Wacker Drive; and the world's tallest occupied building, the Sears Tower with its 110 floors, standing 1,353 ft. above ground. The red colored building in the loop is the CNA Building. In the middle of the picture, is the white monolith of the Amoco Building, third tallest in Chicago, with the pointed Prudential Plaza standing guard next to it. Then the Ritz-Carlton Hotel and 97-story John Hancock Center, second tallest in Chicago, to the north. The tallest apartment building, Lake Point Tower, stands to the right by the Lake.

A private airplane comes in for landing at Meigs Field, the lakefront airport for many corporate planes and jets. In the same vicinity, at South 23rd Street and Lake Shore Drive is McCormick Place, America's largest exhibition and trade show complex.

Im starken Gegensatz dazu steht die Felswand der Michigan Avenue, eine Reihe von Hochhäusern auf der Süd-Michigan Avenue, die auf den Grant Park und den See schauen. Viele von diesen Gebäuden vertreten die frühe Chicagoer Schule der Architektur. Wie Bergspitzen ragen dahinter die massiven und kühnen Gebäude der Chicagoer Innenstadt hervor. Von links aus gesehen steht da das Hilton Hotel und Towers; das mit einer Krone versehene Gebäude am 311 Wacker Drive; das weltgrößte Bürogebäude, der Sears Tower, ragt mit seinen 110 Stockwerken 443 m in den Himmel. Das rotfarbige Stahlgerüstgebäude ist das CNA-Gebäude. In der Mitte des Bildes sehen wir die weißen Monolithen des Amoco-Gebäudes, dem dritthöchsten Gebäude in Chicago. Daneben steht das Prudential-Plaza-Gebäude mit dem spitzen Dach Wache. Das Ritz-Carlton Hotel und das 97 Stockwerk hohe John-Hancock-Center, das zweithöchste Gebäude der Stadt, sehen wir im Norden. Das größte Wohnhaus ist der Lake Point Tower, der rechts von uns aus am See steht.

Ein Privatflugzeug setzt zur Landung auf dem Meigs Field an, ein Flughafen am Seeufer für Firmen-Flugzeuge und Jets. Direkt daneben an der 23. Straße und Lake Shore Drive ist der McCormick Place, Amerikas größtes Ausstellungs- und Messegelände.

Peaceful Sunday morning by the lake   *Stiller Morgen*

Morning perspectives

Morgenansicht

A STROLL THROUGH THE CITY — STADT BUMMEL

Where Congress Parkway starts to run west from the Lake…

Am Congress Parkway…

At Congress Parkway and Michigan Avenue, stand the two beautiful, 17 ft. high bronze figures of American Indians on their horses. One is using his bow and arrow, the other is about to throw his lance, commemorating the "Dreams of Fulfillment".

Am Congress Parkway und Michigan Avenue stehen die wunderschönen Bronzefiguren von zwei Indianern zu Pferd. Diese Skulpturen sind über 5 m hoch. Der eine der beiden Indianer hält einen Pfeil und Bogen, der andere ist dabei, seinen Speer zu werfen. Sie erinnern an die „Dreams of Fulfillment" - Träume der Erfüllung.

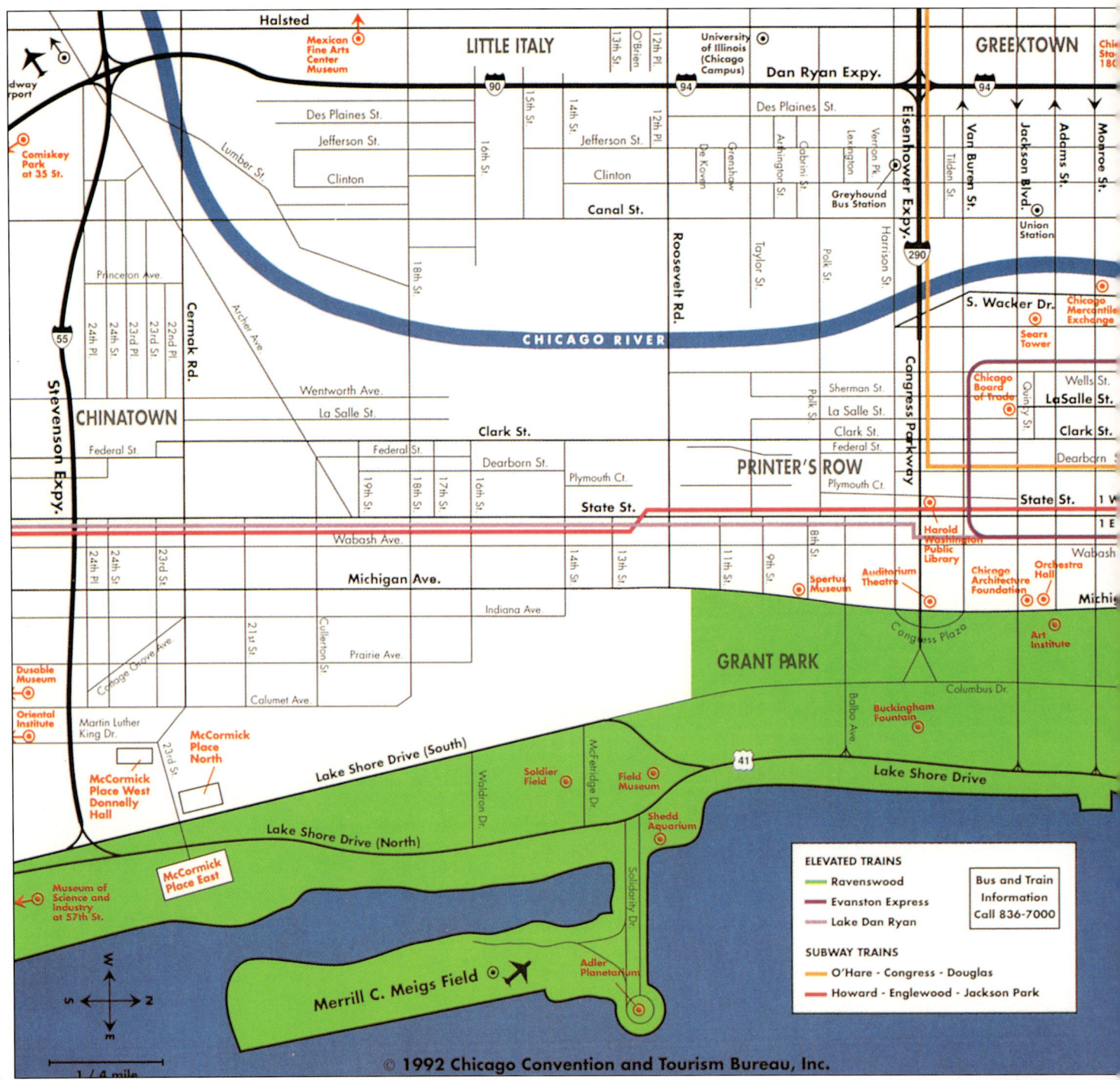

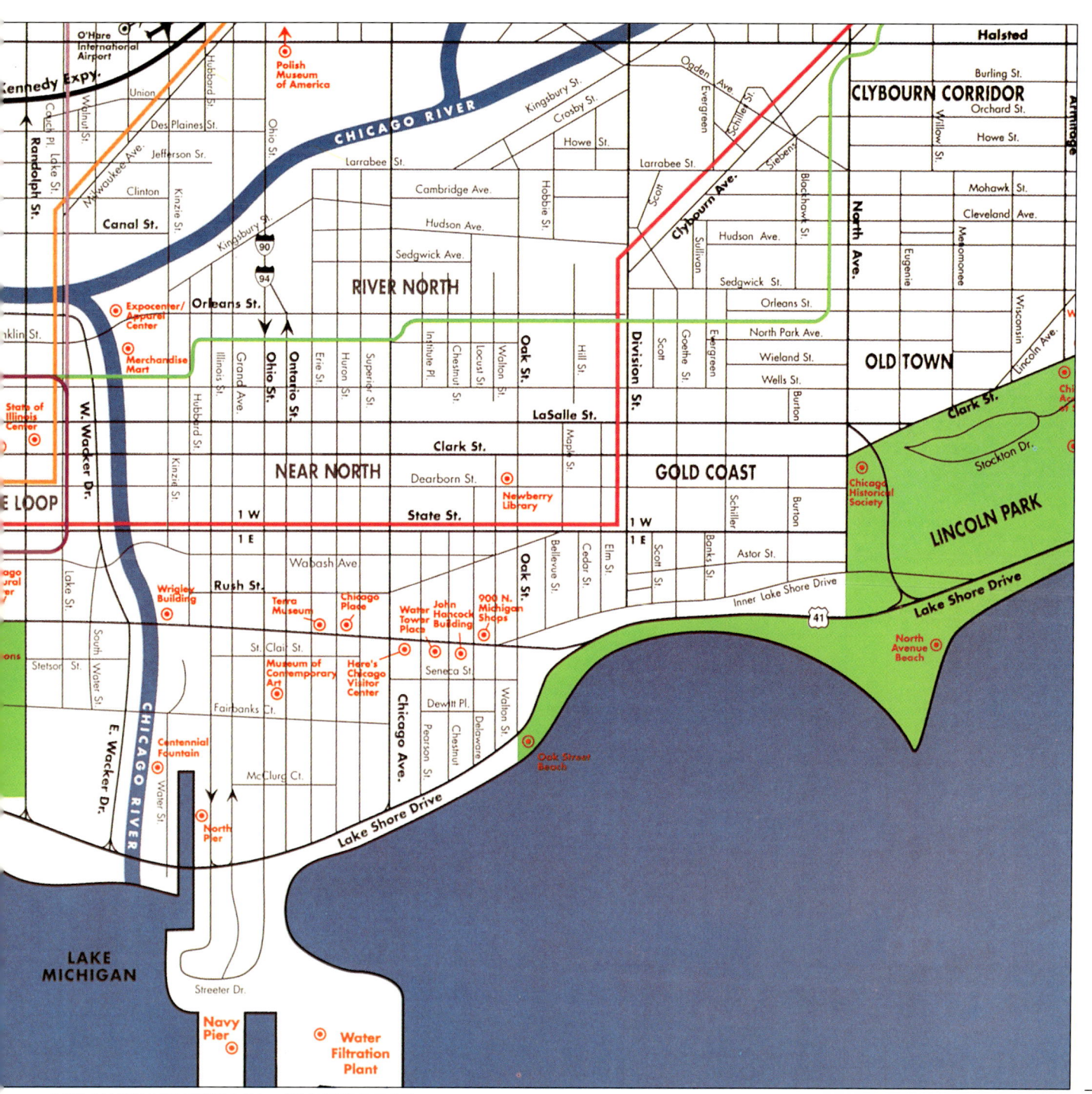

... two Native Americans display their hunting skills

...stehen die Statuen zweier jagenden Indianer

At the west side of Michigan Avenue, opposite the Art Institute, is the world-famous Orchestra Hall, built for the Chicago Symphony's first conductor, German-born Theodore Thomas.

Auf der Westseite der Michigan Avenue, gegenüber vom Art Institute, steht die weltberühmte Orchestra Hall, die für den ersten Dirigenten der Chicagoer Symphonie gebaut wurde, dem in Deutschland geborenen Theodore Thomas.

A STROLL THROUGH THE CITY — STADT BUMMEL

31

On Michigan Avenue, between Washington and Randolph Streets, you may visit the former public library building — today the Chicago Cultural Center.

This building houses sculptures, crafts, concerts, dance performances, lectures and films. It recently took over the Museum of Broadcasting, exhibiting early radio and television memorabilia. Here are also the offices of Chicago's Sister City program, including Hamburg as the German city. There is a profile of Hamburg on pages 196 to 201.

Auf der Michigan Avenue zwischen der Washington Street und der Randolph Street kann man die ehemalige Chicagoer Bibliothek besuchen. Sie ist heute Chicagos Kulturzentrum und beherbergt Skulpturen und kunstgewerbliche Gegenstände. Konzerte, Tanzvorstellungen, Vorträge und Filme werden hier geboten. Vor nicht allzu langer Zeit übernahm das Kulturzentrum das Broadcasting Museum für Funk und Fernsehen und stellt nun alte Radio-und Fernseherinnerungsstücke aus. Hier ist auch das Büro des Chicagoer Partnerstadt-Programms untergebracht, das Hamburg als deutsche Partnerstadt einschließt. Ein Profil Hamburgs finden Sie auf Seiten 196–201.

The Cultural Center (behind the bus) was built in 1897

Das Kulturzentrum (hinter dem Bus) wurde 1897 gebaut

"Chicago's First Lady" takes visitors up the River into the Lake

„Chicago's First Lady" fährt mit ihren Gästen auf dem River dem See zu

Halfway up on Michigan Avenue, you arrive at the Michigan Avenue bridge over the Chicago River. From here you might take a boat ride down the south branch of the Chicago River and back, and then go through the lock into Lake Michigan, traveling along the shoreline from the Gold Coast to the Planetarium.

Spanning the river are twenty-one unique, steel structured bridges, which rise one after another when tall-masted boats blow their horn for passage.

Weiter gen Norden, ungefähr auf der Hälfte der Michigan Avenue, kommt man zur Michigan Avenue-Brücke, die über den Chicago River führt. Von hier aus kann man eine Bootsrundfahrt hin und zurück zum südlichen Zweig des Chicago Rivers machen und fährt dann durch die Schleuse auf den Michigansee und an der Küstenlinie von der Goldküste bis zum Planetarium entlang.

21 einzigartige Stahlbrücken überspannen den Fluß, die, wenn Segelboote mit stehenden.

The double-deck Michigan Avenue Bridge offers a spectacular view in all directions, here the Wrigley Building and the Tribune Tower

Die Doppelstraßen der Michigan Avenue-Brücke bieten eine spektakuläre Sicht in alle Richtungen. Hier das Wrigley Gebäude und der Tribune Turm

Many bridges keep the Loop and Northside stitched together

Die vielen Brücken stellen die Verbindung zwischen Loop und der Nordseite her

A STROLL THROUGH THE CITY — STADT BUMMEL

United Insurance, Leo Burnett and R.R. Donnelley buildings

Die Gebäude der United Versicherungsgesellschaft, der Leo Burnett-Firma und dem R.R. Donnelley Unternehmen

Sightseers marvel at the array of famous real estate property

Touristen bewundern die vielen Hochhäuser

From the boat, the buildings look even taller. There are the twin Marina Towers, the IBM building, the Quaker Oats world headquarters, the Nikko Hotel and the red brick building of the Chicago traffic courts.

On the southside of the river, are the Jewelers Building, the black and gold topped Carbide and Carbon Building and the square tower of the United Insurance office. The new darkgreen Leo Burnett advertising agency building stands next to the light colored R.R. Donnelley & Sons tower, headquarters of the largest printing firm in the world.

Turning the corner going south, the former Merchandise Mart, now the World Trade Center, is reflected in the massive, convex glasswall of the 333 Wacker Drive building. The World Trade Center (WTC) is one of the largest office buildings in the United States. The WTC houses hundreds of wholesale display rooms

Mastendurch Chicago fahren will, nacheinander hochklappen, um die Boote passieren zu lassen. Vom Boot oder Schiff aus sehen die Gebäude noch imposanter aus. Man segelt am IBM-Gebäude vorbei, an den Zwillingstürmen - den Marina City Towers, am Nikko-Hotel, an der Hauptverwaltung der Quaker Oats Firma und am roten Backsteinbau des Chicagoer Verkehrsgerichts.

Auf der Südseite des Flußes stehen das Jewelers Building, das schwarze, mit Gold verzierte Carbide und Carbon-Gebäude und der eckige Turm des United Insurance-Gebäudes. Das neue, dunkelgraue Gebäude der Werbeagentur Leo Burnett steht neben dem hellfarbigen R.R. Donnelley & Sons-Turm, dem Firmensitz des größten Druckereiunternehmens der Welt.

Unsere Fahrt auf dem Fluß geht nun weiter zum südlichen Teil der Stadt. Dort wo der Chicago River sich in zwei Arme teilt, spiegelt sich der Merchandise Mart, jetzt das World Trade Center, in der massigen, grünen Glaswand des 333 Wacker Drive-Gebäudes wider. Das World Trade Center (WTC) ist eines der größten Bürohäuser in den Vereinigten Staaten. Im WTC haben hunderte von Großhändlern ihre Ausstellungsräume für Möbel, Haushaltsartikel und -geräte und Einrichtungsgegenstände aller Art

Lachner "*CHICAGOLAND*"

and suites for furniture, household appliances, furnishings of all kinds, as well as home and chemical products. In addition, there are design studios, consultant and service company offices. The building has its own zip code and telephone exchange. Next door, you will find the Chicago Apparel Center.

To the west are the Morton Salt headquarters with the tall clock tower, and the Northwestern Train Station, now enhanced by the modern terminal lobby and Atrium, designed by Helmut Jahn. The former Chicago Daily News Building, now the Riverside Plaza, was the first office complex built as a pedestrian plaza back in the 1930s. Another older, charming building is the Civic Opera House which from the river, looks like a huge armchair. Several large buildings in concrete, steel and glass follow in quick succession. Among them are the U.S. Gypsum Building, Hartford Plaza, the two identical highrise apartment buildings of the Riverfront Plaza, and finally Sears Tower. You can't miss it.

und chemische Produkte. Dort sind ebenfalls Design-Studios, und Beratungs- und Servicebüros untergebracht. Das Gebäude hat sogar seine eigene Postleitzahl und sein eigenes Fernsprechamt. Nebenan befindet sich das Modezentrum, das Chicago Apparel Center.

Jetzt geht es in westlicher Richtung weiter und wir kommen an der Morton Salt-Zentrale vorbei mit der großen Turmuhr. Dahinter sehen wir die Northwestern Train Station, ein Vorortsbahnhof, der durch den von Helmut Jahn entworfenen Glas- und Stahlanbau mit Lobby und Atrium modernisiert und verschönert wurde. Das ehemalige Gebäude der Chicago Daily News, jetzt der Riverside Plaza, war das erste Bürohaus, das in den dreißiger Jahren eine Fußgängerzone vor dem Gebäude angelegt hatte. Ein weiteres reizvolles altes Gebäude ist das Civic Opera House, das vom Fluß aus gesehen wie ein riesiger Sessel wirkt. Dann folgen hintereinander mehrere große Gebäude aus Zement, Stahl und Glas. Unter ihnen befindet sich das U.S. Gypsum-Gebäude, der Hartford Plaza, die zwei identischen Wohnhochhäuser des Riverfront Plazas und schließlich der Sears Tower. Er läßt sich nicht übersehen.

Morton Salt and Central & NW Railroad buildings dwarf the EL-Train gliding by

Neben den Gebäuden von Morton Salt und der Central & NW Railraod sieht die „L" Hochbahn wie ein Spielzeugzug aus.

Next to Helene Curtis HQ the mammoth WTC building and the Apparel Center

Neben der Hauptverwaltung von Helen Curtis steht das Mammut-Gebäude des WTC und das Modezentrum

A STROLL THROUGH THE CITY — STADT BUMMEL

After our ride back and out through the Lock into Lake Michigan, we get another breathtaking view of Chicago's skyline. The sound of fleeting powerboats and the sight of laboring sailboats going in and out of the harbor under power, make this harbor tour a special experience.

Sailboats are much more graceful under sail, when they cut the waves and lean before the wind, like those out beyond the breakwall which protects the harbor. The Lock permits the water of Lake Michigan to flow into the Chicago River. Earlier, the river flowed into the Lake. Later, as the Lake level rose, sandbanks prevented the water from running out of the Lake. This ridge or portage is still remembered by a historical marker in the Ridgeland area of Cicero. The original river delta was marshy lowland, smelling like onions. Local indians derived the name Chicago from this land.

Nach der Rückfahrt und dem Passieren der Schleuse haben wir vom Michigansee aus einen weiteren atemberaubenden Blick auf die Skyline von Chicago. Das Tuckern der vorbeifahrenden Boote und das Bild der Segelboote, die im Hafen hin- und hersegeln, lassen diese Hafentour zu einem besonderen schönen Erlebnis werden.

Unendlich elegant schneiden die graziösen Segelboote mit gespannten Segeln die Wellen und beugen sich im Winde. Die Schleuse läßt das Wasser des Michigansees in den Chicago River fließen. Früher floß der Fluß in den See. Später, als der Wasserspiegel des Sees stieg, verhinderten die Sandbänke, daß das Wasser aus dem See floß. Eine Gedenktafel in der Ridgeland-Gegend in Cicero erinnert an diese Wasserscheide oder Portage (Tragestelle). Das ursprüngliche Flußdelta war früher eine Sumpflandschaft gewesen, die nach Zwiebel gerochen hat. Bei den Indianern hier hieß Zwiebel Chicago, was der Stadt den Namen verlieh.

Boats are lifted 6-10 feet up to Lake Michigan
Die Schiffe werden 2 bis 3 m zum Wasserspiegel des Michigansees gehoben

Windy bay before the Windy City
Windige Bucht vor der Windigen Stadt

Lachner "CHICAGOLAND"

The City is rather concentrated and a pleasure to explore

Da in der Innenstadt alles zentral liegt, läßt sie sich leicht erforschen

When the Lake kicks up, look out!

Wenn die See stürmisch wird, ist Vorsicht geraten

The Chicago Police has its hands full, above and below the surface

Die Chicagoer Wasserpolizei hat alle Hände voll zu tun, über und unter dem Wasser

A STROLL THROUGH THE CITY — STADT BUMMEL

Monument of Robert Morris, General George Washington and Haym Salomon symbolizes law, government and business working together

Das Monument von Robert Morris, General George Washington und Haym Salomon symbolisiert Recht, Staat und Wirtschaft in harmonischer Zusammenarbeit

Back on dry land, you may want to explore the "Loop" which stretches from Wabash Avenue to Wells Street and from Lake Street to Van Buren Street. Starting out at Wacker Drive and Michigan Avenue, you may want to stroll south on State Street to Washington, then go west five blocks to Franklin, and south again to Sears Tower.

Wieder auf dem Trockenen, sollte man den „Loop" erforschen, der sich von der Wabash Avenue zur Wells Street und von der Lake Street zur Van Buren Street erstreckt. Fangen wir beim Wacker Drive und der Michigan Avenue an und bummeln südlich die State Street entlang zur Washington Street, dann fünf Blocks weiter westlich zur Franklin Street und wieder südlich bis zum Sears Tower.

Mural of Defense of Fort Dearborn 1812

Wandrelief von der Verteidigung des Fort Dearborns in 1812

Lachner "CHICAGOLAND"

State Street, that great street of Chicago and the Loop, is one of the main shopping areas of the Midwest. With only bus service operating now through its ten block long pedestrian plaza, it includes the renovated, elegant Chicago Theater, near Randolph Street and Marshall Field's flagship store, the fabulous department store for discriminating shoppers. One can spend hours here shopping, eating in one of several restaurants or viewing the windows. Visitors to Chicago usually take home a gift or box of candy from Fields.

State Street, the Great Street, ist Chicagos große Einkaufsstraße direkt im Loop und die Haupteinkaufsstraße des Mittelwestens. State Street ist eine sich über 10 Straßenblocks erstreckende Fußgängerzone, die nur von Bussen befahren werden darf. Dort finden wir das neu-renovierte Chicago Theater an der Ecke Randolph Street, und das Stammhaus des legendären Kaufhauses Marshall Field's, ein Kaufhaus für den anspruchsvolleren Geschmack. Man kann dort mit Leichtigkeit einen ganzen Tag mit Einkaufen verbringen, in einem der mehreren Restaurants essen gehen und sich die Schaufenster anschauen. Die meisten Chicago-Besucher nehmen ein kleines Geschenk oder eine Schachtel Pralinen von Field's mit nach Hause.

Hello, there! *Hallo ihr Süßen*

Marshall Field's traditional Christmas Tree in the Walnut Room
Der traditionelle Weihnachtsbaum im Walnut Room Cafe bei Marshall Field's

A STROLL THROUGH THE CITY — STADT BUMMEL

Near Dearborn and Washington you want to visit Civic Center (Daley) Plaza and City Hall. A large Picasso sculpture catches your eye, as well as the Eternal Flame, commemorating the men and women lost in all wars, and the Fountain Square, reminding us of our international heritage.

At Dearborn and Monroe, we take a rest at the Plaza of the First National Bank of Chicago, which features the colorful wall of Chagall's "Mosaic of the Seasons". This plaza, in the middle of the Loop, is a pleasant place, with trees, fountains and sidewalk cafes for a leisurely lunch.

Ecke Dearborn und Washington Street befindet sich der Civic Center Plaza mit dem Daley Plaza-Gerichtshof und auf der anderen Straßenseite die City Hall - das Chicagoer Rathaus. Auf dem Platz vor dem Gebäude stehen die große Picasso-Plastik und eine ewige Flamme in Erinnerung an die Kriegsgefallenen. Der Fountain Square steht zur Erinnerung an unser internationales Erbe.

Ecke Dearborn und Monroe machen wir auf dem Plaza der First National Bank of Chicago Pause und nehmen uns Zeit, Chagalls „Mosaik der Vier Jahreszeiten" zu bewundern. Dieser Plaza liegt mitten im Loop. Eine angenehme Oase in der Stadt, mit Bäumen, Springbrunnen und Straßencafés.

The Picasso statue: free spirit and reality of an unconventional city
Die Picasso-Skulptur: Verkörperung einer freigeistigen und unkonventionellen Stadt

International Fountain Square with City Hall, James Thompson Center and Civic Center Plaza
Der International Fountain Square auf dem Civic Center Plaza vor dem Rathaus. Im Hintergrund das James Thompson Center.

The Board of Trade Building

Continental Illinois Bank Building

American National Bank and Trust Building

On your way down LaSalle Street, Chicago's financial district with headquarters of most major Illinois banks, you will find the Chicago Mercantile Exchange, where commodities and currencies are traded. The Chicago Board of Trade, the world's largest grain trading center, is at the south end of LaSalle Street at Jackson Boulevard. The building is topped by a 30 foot statue of Ceres, the Roman goddess of grain. At 100 West Randolph, at LaSalle Street, towers the dramatic, glass encased State of Illinois Building, now renamed the James R. Thompson Center, also designed by German architect Helmut Jahn.

Die LaSalle Street führt direkt durch Chicagos Finanzviertel mit den Hauptzentralen der größeren Banken des Staates Illinois. Die Chicago Mercantile Exchange, wo Waren und Währungen gehandelt werden und die Chicago Board of Trade, der Welt größten Getreidebörse, liegen am südlichen Ende der LaSalle Street auf dem Jackson Boulevard. Das Gebäude wird mit einer 10 m hohen Statue der römischen Getreidegöttin Ceres gekrönt. Das aus Glas gebaute State of Illinois Building, das heute James R. Thompson Center heißt, steht auf der 100 West Randolph Ecke LaSalle Street. Architekt des Gebäudes war der deutsche Architekt Helmut Jahn.

The Northern Trust Company

Harris Bank Building

Guidance and security by Chicago's Finest
Chicagos Polizei, Dein Freund und Helfer

A STROLL THROUGH THE CITY — STADT BUMMEL

Hazy panorama seen from the Hancock Center

Chicago im Nebel - Panorama vom Hancock Center aus

A couple more blocks and you have arrived at the Sears Tower, the tallest commercial structure in the world. This building is occupied by hundreds of companies, minus one: Sears, Roebuck & Company, which moved to a large office complex in Hoffman Estates, northwest of Chicago.

The lineup for visitors to the Sears Tower Observation Deck is long, but it is a short wait. The elevators take you to the 103rd floor in about a minute. A sign advises you of the visibility on that day. The panoramic view of the Lake and City can be spectacular. On a clear day, you can see 50 miles in all directions. But you may also find it hazy, and you can see only the area below.

Noch ein paar Straßen weiter und wir befinden uns schon am Sears Tower, dem größten Bürohaus der Welt. Mehrere hundert Firmen sind dort untergebracht. Eine Firma fehlt allerdings, Sears, Roebuck & Company, die vor ein paar Jahren nach Hoffman Estates im Nordwesten von Chicago umgezogen ist.

Die Schlange der Besucher, die auf das Aussichts-Deck des Sears Towers wollen, ist lang, aber die Wartezeit ist kurz. Zwei Aufzüge bringen sie innerhalb von einer Minute zum 103. Stockwerk. Unten auf einer Tafel wird täglich die Sichtweite angegeben. Von oben ist das Panorama von See und Stadt ein großartiges Schauspiel. An einem klaren Tag kann man fast 80 km weit in alle Richtungen schauen. An trüben Tagen allerdings, ist wenig zu sehen.

Building canyons often create strong winds

In den steilen Häuserschluchten bilden sich oft heftige Winde

By now your feet will need a rest. At the Franklin Street entrance of Sears Tower, sightseeing buses are waiting to take you for a tour around the City. These double decker buses have an open top deck, some look like the trolley buses in London. The open deck provides a fine place from which to take photographs. These buses stop at various points throughout the City. You can usually take a break, explore and continue the tour on the next bus.

Sollten Sie vom Laufen müde geworden sein, warten vor dem Eingang des Sears Towers auf der Franklin Street Stadtrundfahrtbusse darauf, Sie durch die Stadt zu fahren. Diese Doppeldeckerbusse haben ein offenes Dach. Sie ähneln den Trolley Bussen in London. Von den offenen Decks aus läßt es sich besonders gut fotografieren. Die Busse halten an verschiedenen Sehenswürdigkeiten der Stadt an. Sie können jederzeit aussteigen, sich umschauen, und mit dem nächsten Bus weiterfahren.

Chicago's famous Christmas Tree and ice sculptures at the Daley Plaza. In the background toward the Southwest is the old Chicago Title & Trust building.

Chicagos berühmter Weihnachtsbaum und Eisskulpturen am Daley Plaza. Im Hintergrund das alte Gebäude der Chicago Title & Trust Company.

By the Children's Fountain near State and Wacker

Der Kinderspringbrunnen in der Nähe State und Wacker Streets

At Washington and LaSalle Streets the tour guide points out the financial district. Further east, he shows you the Civic Center Plaza.

Der Reiseführer zeigt Ihnen das Finanzviertel von der Washington und LaSalle Street aus. Weiter östlich zeigt er Ihnen den Civic Center Plaza.

Another look at Picasso's winged horse

Picassos beflügeltes Pferd

A STROLL THROUGH THE CITY — STADT BUMMEL

43

Chicago Theater, built in 1921, was the original flagship of the many elaborate movie houses throughout the city. Renovated to its early splendor in 1985, it now regularly presents spectacular musical productions, and also hosts big name movie stars such as Frank Sinatra.

Das 1921 erbaute und vor kurzem renovierte Chicago Theater bietet Sonderveranstaltungen.

Traveling south on Michigan Avenue to Grant Park, you pass the Chicago Art Institute with two majestic bronze lions at the front entrance. The Art Institute features a permanent display of internationally renowned collections of paintings including the finest French impressionists and post-impressionists. The works of Monet, Rembrandt, Matisse and Chagall and many other world-class painters and sculptures are on display.

The Luncheon Restaurant is open year around, as is the Courtyard Restaurant. Laredo Taft's fountain sculpture of the Five Great Lakes, outside, faces the south lawn and garden. The Art School offers studies in all the fine arts. The curator for the

On State Street, near the palatial Chicago Theater, you will notice many shoppers scurrying along the sidewalks and crossing the streets. Local buses are lined up at each corner for arrivals and departures in all directions. The subway, elevated trains and taxi cabs also provide public transportation in and around the City.

Wenn man auf der Michigan Avenue Richtung Süden zum Grant Park fährt, kommt man zum Chicago Art Institute mit seinen zwei majestätischen Löwen aus Bronze vor dem Eingang. Zum festen Bestand des Art Institutes gehören die Gemälde von internationalen Meistern und von den besten französischen Impressionisten und Post-Impressionisten. Darunter befinden sich Werke von Monet, Rembrandt, Matisse und Chagall sowie von vielen anderen Malern und Bildhauern von Weltklasse.

Das Restaurant im Art Institute ist mittags geöffnet. Ebenfalls das Courtyard Restaurant. Die Brunnenskulptur der „Fünf Großen Seen" von Lorado Taft steht auf der südlichen Seite in dem Garten des Art Institutes. Eine Kunstakademie ist dem Art Institute angeschlossen. John Zukowsky, Kurator der Abteilung für Architektur des Art Institute und Experte für Chicagoer und Hamburger Architektur, schrieb die einleitenden Worte für

Auf der State Street in der Nähe des palastartigen Chicago Theaters kann man die vielen Einkäufer beobachten. Linienbusse halten an jeder Ecke an und fahren von hier in alle Himmelsrichtungen. Weitere Verkehrsmittel in der Stadt sind die Untergrundbahn, die Hochbahn oder „L" und Taxis.

The beehive atmosphere in front of the Art Institute

Eine Bienenkorb-Atmosphäre herrscht vor dem Art Institute

Exhibits at the Art Institute   *Ausstellungen im Art Institute*

Art Institute's McKinlock Court
Das Courtyard Cafe im McKinlock Court des Art Institute

Department of Architecture of the Art Institute, John Zukowsky, is a scholar Chicago and Hamburg/Germany architecture. He introduced the Chicago book "The Sky's the Limit."

    The tour bus now turns onto Lake Shore Drive and stops at the Field Museum of Natural History. There are a huge, 3-story Brachiosaurus dinosaur skeleton and two large elephants in the Great Hall. This is one of the largest natural history museums known for its outstanding exhibits of animals in their natural habitat, American Indian life, Illinois landscapes, African and Egyptian history. It also features collections from the fields of anthropology, botany, geology and zoology. The special exhibit of the treasures from King Tut's tomb drew a million visitors. Come back and spend more time here, and at the nearby Adler Planetarium and Shedd Aquarium, with its new Oceanarium, featuring a marvelous display of the Northwest Wilderness with the now famous Beluga whales.

The Great Hall at the Field Museum   *Die Große Halle des Field Museums*

das Buch über Chicago: „The Sky's the Limit."
    Der Bus fährt jetzt zum Lake Shore Drive und hält am naturgeschichtlichen Museum, dem Field Museum of Natural History. Ein 3 Stockwerke hohes Brachiosaurus-Dinosaurierskelett und zwei riesige Elephanten begrüßen den Besucher in der Großen Halle. Wir befinden uns jetzt in einem der größten naturgeschichtlichen Museen, berühmt für seine hervorragenden Ausstellungen von Tieren in ihrem Lebensraum, vom Leben der Indianer, von Illinois Landschaften, von afrikanischer und ägyptischer Geschichte. Sammlungen in Anthropologie, Botanik, Geologie und Zoologie gehören zum festen Bestand des Museums. Die Sonderausstellung vom Schatz des König Tutanchamun hatte Millionen von Besucher angezogen. Kommen Sie wieder zurück nach Chicago und nehmen Sie sich etwas Zeit für das Museum und das danebenliegende Adler Planetarium und das Shedd-Aquarium mit seinem neuen Ozeanarium, das ganz im Stil der nordwestlichen Wildnis angelegt ist und die berühmten Beluga-Wale beherbergt.

McCormick Place by the Lake, as we know it

McCormick Ausstellungshallen am See, so wie es war

Driving north again, we pass McCormick Place, the largest exhibition hall in the United States, at South 23rd Street and Lake Michigan. It was created by German-born architect Ludwig Mies van der Rohe, who designed many public and residential buildings in Chicago. McCormick Place is being expanded for the third time and will open in 1997 with 2.2 million square feet of exibit space. To be connected to the North and East Halls will be a new South Hall and Mall of Nations. In the meantime, McCormick Place will operate as usual.

Der Bus fährt jetzt in südlicher Richtung weiter am McCormick Place vorbei, den größten Ausstellungshallen in den Vereinigten Staaten an der 23. Straße und Lake Michigan. McCormick Place wurde von dem Deutschen Ludwig Mies van der Rohe gebaut, Architekt vieler öffentlicher Gebäude und Wohnhäuser in Chicago. McCormick Place wird jetzt zum 3. Mal vergrößert und der neue Anbau wird 1997 mit über 0.2 Millionen Quadratmetern an Ausstellungsgelände eröffnet. An die Nord- und Osthallen werden eine neue Südhalle und die Halle der Nationen angebaut. In der Zwischenzeit geht der Betrieb aber weiter.

Soldier Field is a mile north, an open stadium of classic Greek/Roman architecture. This famed sports arena, seating 65,000 people, was built in 1926 as a memorial to those who lost their lives during World War I. It is home to the Chicago Bears football team and will be the site of the World Cup '94 Soccer Opening Ceremony and four Championship Games in June 1994.

Das Soldier Field-Sportsstadion liegt eine Meile nördlich davon. Das offene Stadion ist im klassischen griechisch-römischen Stil gebaut. Das Sportsstadion wurde 1926 mit 65.000 Sitzplätzen als Denkmal an alle, die im 1. Weltkrieg gefallen sind, gebaut. Es ist das Heim des Chicago Bears Football-Teams und im Juni 1994 werden dort die Eröffnungszeremonien und vier der Weltmeisterschaftsspiele des '94 World Soccer [Fußball] Cup" stattfinden.

This view shows Soldier Field and clockwise the Field Museum, Shedd Aquarium, the Adler Planetarium and Meig's Airfield across from Burnham Park Harbor.

Sicht auf das Soldier Field und, im Uhrzeigersinn, das Field Museum, das Shedd Aquarium, das Adler Planetarium und die Meig's Field-Landebahn auf der anderen Seite des Burnham Park-Hafens

Home of the Chicago Bears football team

Soldier Field, home of the Chicago Bears football team, will host the 1994 Opening Ceremony and four games of the World Cup '94 Soccer Championship

    June 17: Germany vs Bolivia
    June 21: Germany vs Spain
    June 26: Bulgaria vs Greece
    June 27: Bolivia vs Spain

Das Soldier Field ist das Heim des Chicago Bears Football Teams. 1994 werden dort die Eröffnungszeremonien und vier der 1994 Fußball-Weltmeisterschaftsspiele stattfinden.

A STROLL THROUGH THE CITY — STADT BUMMEL

Burnham Park Harbor, cradled between Lake Shore Drive and Meigs Field, is homeport to many commercial and private boats. It also harbors the Chicago charter fleets of fishing and excursion crafts.

On the point of the peninsula which connects Meigs Field to Lake Shore Drive is the Adler Planetarium. Daily programs depict the night skies, outer space explorations, solar and lunar eclipses. A moon rock, telescopes and early navigational instruments are on display.

Zwischen Lake Shore Drive und Meigs Field eingeschachtelt liegt der Burnham Park Hafen, wo viele kommerzielle und private Boote ihre Anlegestellen haben. Auch Charterflotten für Angelausflüge und Ausflugsboote ankern dort.

An der äußersten Spitze der Halbinsel, die die Verbindungsstraße zwischen Meigs Field und Lake Shore Drive ist, befindet sich das Adler Planetarium mit täglichen Vorstellungen vom Nachthimmel, vom Weltall und von Sonnen- und Mondeklipsen. Ein Mondstein, Ferngläser und alte Navigationsinstrumente sind ebenfalls dort zu sehen.

The Adler Planetarium entertains both stargazers and scientists alike
Das Adler Planetarium wird von Astronomen und Wissenschaftlern benutzt

Shedd Aquarium completed the addition of the Oceanarium in 1991

Das Oceanarium des Shedd Aquariums wurde 1991 fertiggestellt

A natural habitat for exotic fish and sea life

Naturgetreuer Lebensraum für exotische Fische und Seelebewesen

The Shedd Aquarium, at the base of the peninsula, is one of the world's largest indoor aquariums, housing over 6,000 species of fish in naturalistic habitats. The new Oceanarium holds three million gallons of saltwater and is home to Beluga whales, seals, dolphins, sea otters and penguins.

Das Shedd-Aquarium am unteren Ende der Halbinsel ist eines der größten Aquarien der Welt und zeigt über 6.000 Fischgattungen in ihrem Lebensraum. Das neue Ozeanarium mit Belugawalen, Robben, Delphinen, Seeottern und Pinguinen faßt 12 Millionen Liter Salzwasser.

Navy Pier, built to accommodate Great Lakes vessels, was later commissoned as a Naval Training Center and, until recently, used for special events. It is planned to re-open in 1995 as an entertainment and recreation center, bar none.

Der Navy Pier wurde ehemals für die großen Ozeandampfer gebaut, wurde dann als Marineakademie genutzt und später für Sonderveranstaltungen. Für 1995 plant man die Wiedereröffnung als Unterhaltungszentrum, das seines gleichen sucht.

From here, dinner and party cruises leave for an unprecedented view of the Chicago skyline, by day or night.

Von einer Dinner-Cruise auf dem Michigansee hat man einen unvergleichlichen Blick auf die Skyline von Chicago

A STROLL THROUGH THE CITY — STADT BUMMEL

Traveling three miles further north, past the Gold Coast luxury apartments, we arrive at Lincoln Park, the largest of Chicago's lakefront parks.

At the south end of the park is the Chicago Historical Society which preserves and displays artifacts from Fort Dearborn, the 1871 Chicago Fire, 1893 World's Columbian Exposition, and the 1933 Century of Progress World's Fair among many others.

Ungefähr 5 km nördlich fährt der Bus an den Luxusappartements der Gold-Küste vorbei zum Lincoln Park, dem größten der Chicagoer Parks, die am See liegen.

Am südlichen Ende des Parks hat die Chicagoer Historische Gesellschaft ihr Quartier, wo u.a. Artefakts von der Zeit des Fort Dearborn, dem Chicagoer Großbrand von 1871, der Kolumbus Weltausstellung von 1893 und der Weltausstellung von 1933, des „Century of Progress," aufbewahrt werden.

Lincoln Park Conservatory

The Lincoln Park Zoo is open every day of the year and is admission free. In addition to more than 2,000 mammals, birds and reptiles, it features a Children's Zoo, Farm, a Great Ape House, Conservatory and flower gardens. Over four million Chicagoans and tourists visit annually.

Der Lincoln Park-Zoo ist das ganze Jahr über täglich geöffnet. Der Eintritt ist frei. 2.000 verschiedene Säugetiere, Vögel und Reptilien, ein Kinderzoo, ein Bauernhof, eine menschenaffen-Haus, ein Gewächshaus und Blumengärten zählen zu den Attraktionen, die jährlich über 4 Millionen Besucher anziehen.

Lincoln Park Lagoon, a recreational paradise a cab ride from the city

Die Lincoln Park-Lagune ist ein Paradies für Wassersportler und nur eine kurze Taxifahrt vom Loop entfernt

Lachner "*CHICAGOLAND*"

Lake Michigan, inviting and forbidding, a freshwater ocean in the middle of the continent

Der Michigansee, ein Süßwasser-Ozean mitten im Kontinent. Er kann einladend und auch drohend sein

Formerly the Coast Guard station, it now houses the Chicago Harbor Police and visiting amphibious forces

In der ehemaligen Küstenwache ist heute die Chicagoer Hafenpolizei untergebracht und ist ein Übungsplatz für Wasserschutzkräfte.

A STROLL THROUGH THE CITY — STADT BUMMEL

Returning to the heart of the City via Michigan Avenue, we pass the landmark buildings of the Water Tower and Pumping Station, which survived the Great Fire, and the North Michigan Avenue shopping area known as the "Magnificent Mile". Elegant boutiques, cafes, and hotels line both sides of the street.

On the near Northside are restaurants owned by local celebrities Michael Jordan, Oprah Winfrey and Mike Ditka as well as the Hard Rock Cafe, Planet Hollywood and Rock 'n Roll McDonald's.

Auf dem Rückweg zur Innenstadt über die Michigan Avenue kommen wir an dem Wahrzeichen der Stadt, dem Wasserturm und der Wasserpumpstation vorbei, die den Großbrand überlebten, zum Einkaufsteil der Michigan Avenue, der als „magnificent mile" berühmt ist. Elegante Boutiquen, Cafés und Hotels liegen auf beiden Seiten der Straße.

Wieder dowtown, finden wir auf der Nordseite des Flußes Restaurants, solcher Persönlichkeiten wie Michael Jordan, Oprah Winfrey und Harry Caray sowie das Hard Rock Cafe, Planet Hollywood und Rock 'n Roll McDonald's.

North Lake Shore Drive features the beautiful Gold Coast apartments
Der Northlake Shore Drive mit seinen schönen Appartements an der Goldküste

Rock 'n Roll McDonald's and Planet Hollywood on the near north side
Rockn 'n Roll McDonald's und Planet Hollywood auf der Nordseite

52　　Lachner "CHICAGOLAND"

An official visitor's guide to all attractions, shopping and dining is available from the Chicago Convention and Tourism Bureau by calling 312/567-8500 or fax 312/567-8533. Uptodate information is also contained in the KEY and WHERE Brochures, available at all hotels.

Einen Stadtführer mit Beschreibung aller Attraktionen, Einkaufszentren und Restaurants können Sie vom Chicago Convention and Tourism Bureau erhalten unter der Rufnummer 312/567-8500 oder der Faxnummer 312/567-8533. Die neuesten und letzten Informationen sind auch in den Stadtführern, KEY und WHERE, enthalten, die in allen Hotels erhältlich sind.

*Chicago's Hard Rock Cafe,
a famous meeting place for young people of all ages*

*Chicagos Hard Rock Cafe -
ein beliebtes Ziel für alt und jung*

Good night, Chicago, and pleasant dreams

Gute Nacht Chicago und angenehme Träume

A STROLL THROUGH THE CITY — STADT BUMMEL

Chicago, with its million lights, has a million stories to tell. It also dares us to do good and great things. This is a city where dreams come true, if your shoulders are broad enough and the spirit makes no small plans.

Chicago mit seinen Millionen Lichtern kann uns Millionen Geschichten erzählen. Diese Stadt fordert uns auch zu guten und großen Taten heraus. In Chicago lassen sich Träume verwirklichen, wenn man dazu die berühmten breiten Chicagoer Schultern und den richtigen Schwung hat.

Lachner "*CHICAGOLAND*"

Comparative Geographical Representation

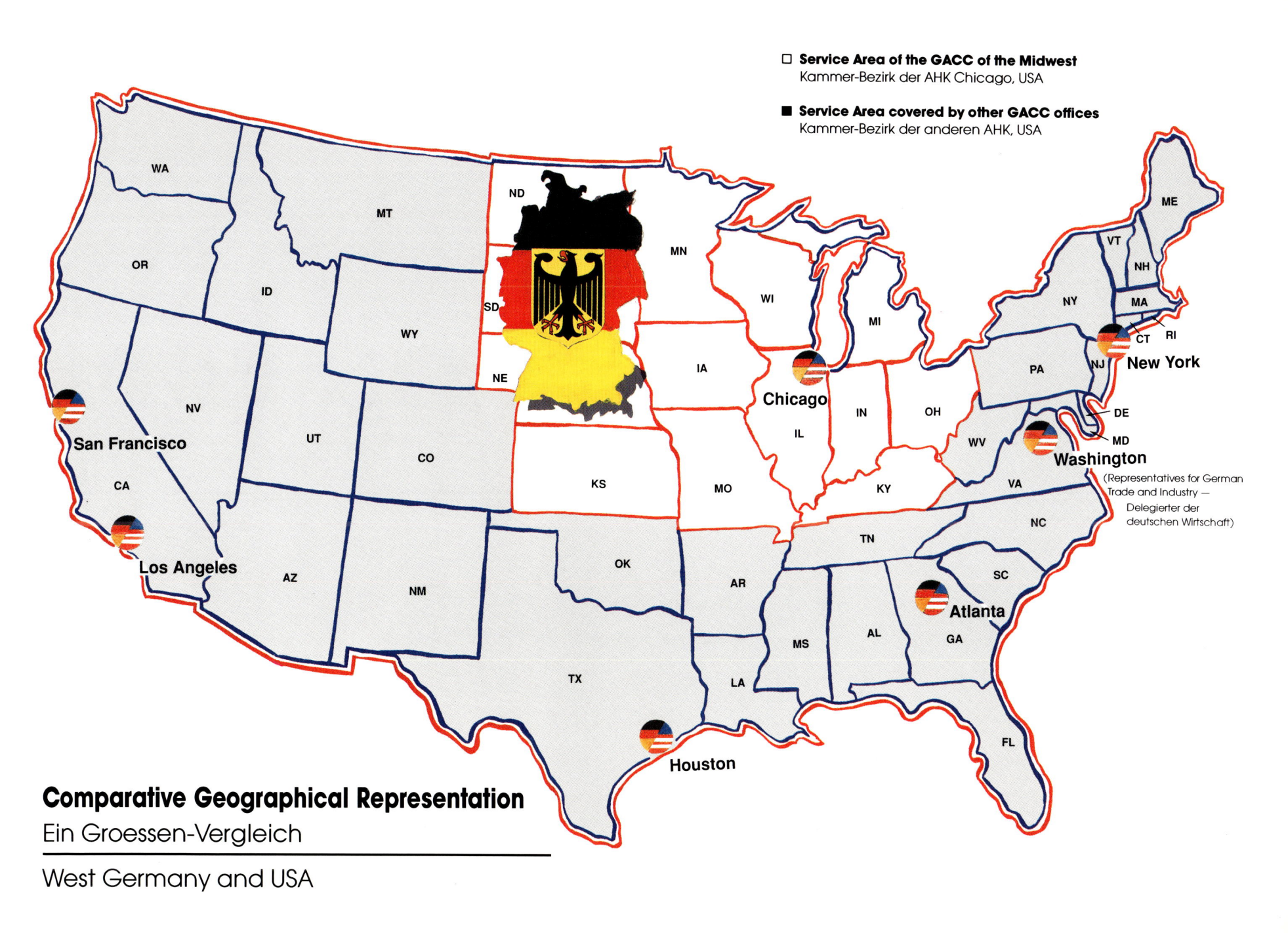

Ein Groessen-Vergleich

West Germany and USA

☐ **Service Area of the GACC of the Midwest**
Kammer-Bezirk der AHK Chicago, USA

■ **Service Area covered by other GACC offices**
Kammer-Bezirk der anderen AHK, USA

(Representatives for German Trade and Industry — Delegierter der deutschen Wirtschaft)

GERMAN AMERICAN CHAMBER OF COMMERCE

The German American Chamber of Commerce of the Midwest

by Niels Friedrichs, GACCoM, Managing Director

Background

The bilateral, non-government German American Chamber of Commerce of the Midwest (GACC) is incorporated under the laws of the State of Illinois as a private, non-profit membership organization. Similar offices are maintained in Atlanta, Chicago, Houston, Los Angeles, New York, and San Francisco, with some 2,500 firms and organizations in the United States and Germany making up the membership roster. The GACC is an integral part of the worldwide network of German Chambers of Commerce — 100 local and regional Chambers in the Federal Republic and 73 German Chambers abroad. Every enterprise in the Federal Republic, be it large or small, incorporated or unincorporated, with or without limited liability, is required by law to become a registered member of the local or regional Chamber of Commerce.

Since 1947 the GACC and its predecessors have actively promoted trade and business relations between the United States and the Federal Republic of Germany. The Chamber has assumed the day-to-day responsibilities for serving many non-official commercial interests of the business communities in both countries. This is based on an agreement between the Foreign Ministry in Bonn (BMWi), the German National Chamber of Commerce (DIHT) and the major German Institutions concerned with foreign trade and economic matters.

Thus, the GACC is able to maintain close contact with many thousands of German corporations to the benefit of American firms who wish to pursue business interests in the Federal Republic. Companies in the Federal Republic, in turn, take advantage of the Chamber's active link to the American business community.

Services

The promotion of free trade as a two-way street represents the common denominator of all of the Chamber's activities and services. One of the major objectives of the Chamber is to support the philosophy of free trade and to encourage its implementation through its consulting activities, publications, seminars, and speaking programs.

In its role as marketing consultant, the Chamber accommodates the increasingly specialized inquiries of both German and American companies by compiling an expanded reservoir of information and a comprehensive file of enterprises involved in every variety of commercial venture. It also assists firms in paving the way for overseas direct capital investments, providing much critical information and key contracts for both the corporate and individual investor.

Organisation

Die Deutsch-Amerikanische Handelskammer ist eine wirtschaftlichen Zielen verpflichtete bilaterale Mitgliederorganisation. Sie ist eine Körperschaft des amerikanischen Rechts und als "German American Chamber of Commerce of the Midwest" in das Handelsregister des Staates Illinois eingetragen.

Die Deutsch-Amerikanische Handelskammer ist Bestandteil der über die ganze Welt verteilten Organisationen der deutschen Handelskammern, davon 100 Kammern im Inland und 73 Kammern im Ausland. Kammern gibt es in Chicago, New York, San Francisco, Los Angeles, Atlanta, und Houston. Seit 1947 fördern die Deutsch-Amerikanischen Handelskammern und ihre Vorgängerorganisationen den Handel und die Geschäftsbeziehungen zwischen den Vereinigten Staaten und der Bundesrepublik Deutschland.

Mehr als 2.500 Firmen in den Vereinigten Staaten und der Bundesrepublik Deutschland sind Mitglieder der Kammer. Die Kammer bietet der Geschäftswelt in beiden Ländern ihre vielfältigen Dienstleistungen im Wirtschaftsbereich an. Diese Aufgabenstellung beruht auf einer Vereinbarung zwischen dem Auswärtigen Amt, dem Deutschen Industrie- und Handelstag und den zuständigen Stellen der deutschen Wirtschaft.

Dank ihrer Zugehörigkeit zum Deutschen Industrie- und Handelstag ist die Deutsch-Amerikanische Handelskammer in der Lage, einen engen Kontakt zu deutschen Unternehmen zu unterhalten, zum Vorteil einer großen Anzahl amerikanischer Firmen, die wirtschaftliche Interessen in der Bundesrepublik Deutschland wahrnehmen. Umgekehrt haben deutschen Firmen den Vorteil, in der Kammer eine aktive Kontaktstelle zur amerikanischen Geschäftswelt nutzen zu können.

Dienstleistungen

Die Förderung des gegenseitigen Handels ist wichtigster Bestandteil der Tätigkeit der Kammer.

Sie unterhält enge Beziehungen zu privaten Verbänden und Organisationen sowie öffentlichen Dienststellen der Wirtschaft in beiden Ländern.

Die Vielzahl der Dienstleistungen, die Mitgliedern entweder kostenlos oder zu Vorzugsgebühren zur Verfügung stehen, unterstreichen das breitgefächerte Leistungsangebot der Kammer sowie den Nutzen einer Mitgliedschaft. Das Leistungsangebot umfaßt vor allem:

- Kontaktherstellung zwischen Importeuren und Exporteuren
- Bezugsquellennachweis für Waren und Dienstleistungen
- Unterhaltung einer laufend ausgebauten Kartei von Firmen, die an der Gründung von Gemeinschaftsunternehmen interessiert sind
- Unterstützung und Beratung bei Direktinvestitionen und der Gründung von Gemeinschaftsunternehmen
- Vorbereitung und Mitarbeit beim Austausch von technischem Know-how, Erarbeitung von Markt- und Branchenstudien
- Einleitung von Lizenz-

The Chamber maintains a joint venture partner and licensee exchange that accommodates the requirements of another group of corporations on both sides of the Atlantic, arranges for the exchange of technological and business know-how, and facilitates licensing agreements and the utilization of patents.

Depending on the needs of individual firms, the Chamber can expedite the establishment of direct contacts between exporters and importers. These services range from customs procedures to the performance of market research and feasibility studies.

As participation in a German trade fair is very often the initial stage in gaining access to the German market, the GACC provides yet another special marketing service for American companies doing business in the Federal Republic.

The services of the Chamber are available to members at favorable rates or free of charge; non-members are charged a fee. Any company wishing to make extensive use of the GACC's services should consider becoming a member.

vereinbarungen und Hilfeleistung bei Patentverwertung
- Unterstützung bei Teilnahme an Messen und Ausstellungen
- Hilfeleistung beim Einzug von Außenständen
- Sammlung von Auswertung ökonomischer Daten und Statistiken
- Laufende Beobachtung und Beurteilung der Vorgänge auf dem amerikanischen Markt
- Studium und Bewertung neuer wirtschaftlicher und wirtschaftspolitischer Entwicklungen in den USA sowie gegebenenfalls Einleitung notwendiger Initiativen
- Publikationen

Niels G. Friedrichs and Deputy Managing Director Peter Flatzek

Seit 30 Jahren ist das „Monroe Building" auf der 104 S. Michigan Avenue in Chicago das Heim der Deutsch-Amerikanischen Handelskammer. Das Haus mit dem Giebeldach liegt auf der linken Seite der Monroe Street. Das Bemerkenswerte an diesem Bild sind die hohen, hellfarbigen Gebäude zur lchten Seite, die sich an das gotische Gebäude des „University Clubs" mit spitzem Gibeldach anreihen. Der University Club war das erste Stahlgerüst-Hochhaus in den USA überhaupt und steht jetzt unter Denkmalschutz. Mit diesen beiden Gebäuden wurde die „Chicago School der Architektur" um die Jahrhundertwende ins Leben gerufen.

Home of the GACCoM for now 30 years, the "Monroe Building" at 104 S. Michigan Avenue in Chicago is the gabled highrise on the left side of Monroe Street on whose bridge this photo (looking towards the West) was taken, on an icy cold January 1993 day. Remarkable on this picture are the narrow and high white colored highrise to the left and the red lower building to the right of Monroe Street, next to the gabled and Gothic styled "University Club" — being the very first highrise steel construction buildings in the USA — and now under historic monument protection. These two buildings established the "Chicago School of Architecture" around the turn of the century.

GERMAN AMERICAN CHAMBER OF COMMERCE OF THE MIDWEST

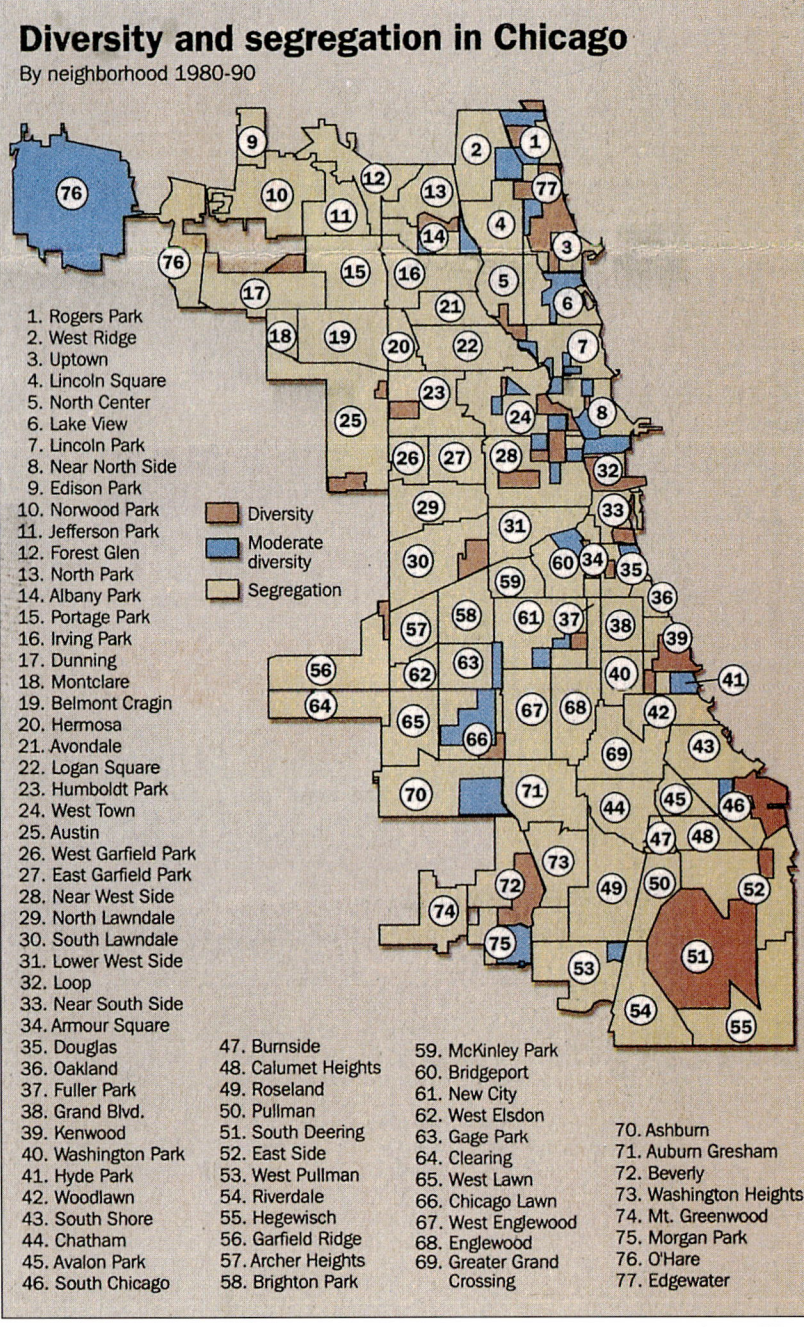

Diversity and segregation in Chicago
By neighborhood 1980-90

- Diversity
- Moderate diversity
- Segregation

1. Rogers Park
2. West Ridge
3. Uptown
4. Lincoln Square
5. North Center
6. Lake View
7. Lincoln Park
8. Near North Side
9. Edison Park
10. Norwood Park
11. Jefferson Park
12. Forest Glen
13. North Park
14. Albany Park
15. Portage Park
16. Irving Park
17. Dunning
18. Montclare
19. Belmont Cragin
20. Hermosa
21. Avondale
22. Logan Square
23. Humboldt Park
24. West Town
25. Austin
26. West Garfield Park
27. East Garfield Park
28. Near West Side
29. North Lawndale
30. South Lawndale
31. Lower West Side
32. Loop
33. Near South Side
34. Armour Square
35. Douglas
36. Oakland
37. Fuller Park
38. Grand Blvd.
39. Kenwood
40. Washington Park
41. Hyde Park
42. Woodlawn
43. South Shore
44. Chatham
45. Avalon Park
46. South Chicago
47. Burnside
48. Calumet Heights
49. Roseland
50. Pullman
51. South Deering
52. East Side
53. West Pullman
54. Riverdale
55. Hegewisch
56. Garfield Ridge
57. Archer Heights
58. Brighton Park
59. McKinley Park
60. Bridgeport
61. New City
62. West Elsdon
63. Gage Park
64. Clearing
65. West Lawn
66. Chicago Lawn
67. West Englewood
68. Englewood
69. Greater Grand Crossing
70. Ashburn
71. Auburn Gresham
72. Beverly
73. Washington Heights
74. Mt. Greenwood
75. Morgan Park
76. O'Hare
77. Edgewater

Source: Loyola University   Chicago Tribune

Welcome to Chicago!
by Niels G. Friedrichs

The German-American Chamber of Commerce of the Midwest and the Department of Planning and Development for the City of Chicago welcome you to Chicago, the "Windy City" on the shores of Lake Michigan. We hope that this "Chicago Story" will be of some help to you during your visit here, and also help to remind you of this friendly town when you are back home.

The German American Chamber of Commerce of the Midwest is one of more than fifty foreign chambers recognized by the German National Association of Chambers of Commerce in Bonn. In order to appropriately represent this enormous territory in the United States with its large markets, the first Chamber was set up in New York and then in 1963 the Chamber in Chicago followed. Consequently, in 1993 the Chicago Chamber celebrated its 30th anniversary. The Chambers in San Francisco and in Los Angeles, as well as in Houston, Texas, and in Atlanta, Georgia, were opened after Chicago.

The Chamber in Chicago is responsible for all 13 states in the Midwest, an area five times the size of the Federal Republic of Germany with a population of close to 88 million people!

Herzlich Willkommen!
von Niels G. Friedrichs

Die Deutsch-Amerikanische Handelskammer des Mittelwestens und das Chicagoer Amt für Wirtschaftsförderung und Planung heißen Sie herzlich willkommen in Chicago, der "windy city" am Rande des Lake Michigan. Wir hoffen, daß diese "Chicago Story" Ihnen eine kleine Hilfe bei Ihrem Besuch ist, und nach Ihrer Rückkehr eine Erinnerung an Ihren Aufenthalt in dieser gastfreundlichen Stadt.

Die Deutsch-Amerikanische Handelskammer des Mittelwestens ist eine der mehr als fünfzig vom Deutschen Industrie- und Handelstag in Bonn anerkannten Auslands-Handelskammern. Um das riesige Gebiet der USA und ihre großen Wirtschaftsräume zweckmäßig betreuen zu können, wurden zuerst die Kammer New York und dann im Jahre 1963 die Kammer Chicago gegründet - im Jahre 1993 kann sie nun also auf dreißig erfüllte Jahre Kammertätigkeit zurückblicken! Es folgten Kammern in San Francisco und Los Angeles sowie in Houston/Texas und in Atlanta/Georgia.

Die Kammer in Chicago ist für die 13 Staaten des Mittelwestens zuständig, einem Gebiet mit der fünffachen Fläche der Bundesrepublik und einer Bevölkerung von ca. 88 Millionen Menschen!

Vielseitigkeit ist Chicagos Stärke auf dem Weg in die neunziger Jahre

Es war im Jahre 1871 — da stolperte eine Kuh über eine brennende Laterne in der Scheune einer Frau O'Leary und löste einen Großbrand aus, der in

BMW of North America, Inc.

BMW of North America Central Region is one of four BMW regional offices located in the United States operating under BMW of North America headquarters in Woodcliff Lake, N.J. It is the largest subsidiary of BMW AG World Headquarters in Munich, Germany. Located in Schaumburg, Illinois, approximately 30 miles northwest of downtown Chicago, BMW of North America Central Region office is responsible for all activities pertaining to regional sales, marketing, distribution and Training encompassing 75 BMW dealers in 14 states.

Not surprisingly, Chicago boasts being the largest market for BMW of North America Central Region and fourth largest BMW market in the country with 11 BMW dealers located throughout the Chicagoland area. In 1993, BMW's retail sales in the Central Region reached 10,160 units an increase of over 23% over 1992, with Chicago generating 2,760 or 27% of those sales. Throughout 1994, BMW of North America and the Central Region, look forward to continuing thier success story by introducing new products to the current car line, while maintaining all the quality, luxury, performance and value that consumers have learned to expect from BMW of North America.

BMW of North America Central Region is also a strong contributor to many philanthropic causes, community clubs and high schools, and is a member of the German American Chamber of Commerce in the Chicagoland area. BMW's dedication and support for such activities is a philosophical mainstay instilled throughout all of BMW's subsidiaries and employees as a commitment to give back to those who have attributed to BMW's success in the past, present and future.

BMW of North America Central Region ist eine der vier regionalen Geschäftsstellen von BMW of North America in den Vereinigten Staaten. BMW of North America mit Sitz in Woodcliff Lake, New Jersey, ist die größte Tochtergesellschaft der BMW AG, deren internationale Zentralverwaltung in München zu Hause ist. Die regionale Geschäftsstelle für den zentralen Bereich von BMW of North America befindet sich in Schaumburg, Illinois, ca. 48 km nordwestlich vom Stadtzentrum Chicago. Sie ist für alle Aktivitäten hinsichtlich Verkauf, Marketing, Vertrieb und Schulung für 75 BMW-Händler in 14 Staaten zuständig.

Chicago und Umgebung stellen mit 11 BMW-Händlern den größten Markt für den Zentralbereich von BMW of North America und den viertgrößten BMW-Markt in den USA dar. 1993 konnte BMW im Zentralbereich 10.160 Einheiten absetzen, ein Anstieg von 23% gegenüber 1992, wobei 2.760 Einheiten oder 27% dieses Umsatzes auf Chicago entfielen. Auch für 1994 rechnen BMW of North America und der Zentralbereich mit weiteren Erfolgen. Das Unternehmen plant die Einführung neuer Modelle unter Beibehaltung des hohen Niveaus an Qualität, Luxus, Leistung und Wert, das die Kunden von BMW of North America erwarten.

Die Geschäftsstelle BMW of North America Central Region ist Mitglied der Deutsch-Amerikanischen Handelskammer in Chicago und unterstützt darüber hinaus viele philantropische Aktivitäten, Gemeindeclubs und Schulen. Dieses Engagement für gemeinnützige Zwecke ist ein integraler Bestandteil der Unternehmensphilosophie, mit der BMW und seine Mitarbeiter allen denen danken, die zum Erfolg des Unternehmens beitragen.

GERMAN-AMERICAN COMMERCE AND INDUSTRY

190 South LaSalle, Entrance also to the Dresdner Bank

Eingang auch zur Dresdner Bank

Hotels (from left) include the Fairmont Hotels, Hyatt Regency Hotel, Swissôtel and the new Sheraton International

Hotels von links sind das Fairmont, Hyatt Regency, Swissôtel und das neue Sheraton International

On its Way to the Nineties
Chicago's Strength lies in its Versatility

It was the year 1871 - when a cow in Mrs. O'Leary's barn tripped over a lantern and thus started the big fire that would rage through Chicago and totally destroy four square miles of this young town. Despite the enormous damages, its citizens immediately started to rebuild their town - and continued to build. Until by the end of the seventies Chicago had become the center of the manufacturing industry and a leading business community.

Luck played only a secondary role in this boom. Because in its history, Chicago repeatedly experienced far-reaching changes and each time it emerged as a different and a stronger town. During the time when U.S.-American industry was being restructured in the seventies and early eighties, hundreds of Chicago companies closed their doors and relocated, thus uprooting entire communities and neighborhoods. Today Chicago is proud to announce that $10 billion were invested in the city during the last few years alone. 500,000 new work places were created just in the inner city alone. The manufacturing industry has been modernized and automated. According to a recent Harris Poll of 404 CEOs, Chicago is the best location in the Midwest and it ranks fourth in the Nation.

Chicagos Zentrum wütete und vier Quadratmeilen der jungen Stadt völlig zerstörte. Die Bürger begannen trotz der großen Schäden sofort mit dem Wiederaufbau der Stadt - und bauten immer weiter. Ende der siebziger Jahre war Chicago zu einer Hochburg der herstellenden Industrien und zu einem führenden Wirtschaftszentrum geworden.

Glück spielte bei diesem Aufschwung eher eine untergeordnete Rolle. In seiner Geschichte hat Chicago wiederholte Male tiefgreifende Veränderungen durchgemacht und ist jedesmal als eine andere, stärkere Stadt daraus hervorgegangen. Im Zuge der großen Umstrukturierungen in der US-amerikanischen Industrie in den siebziger und frühen achtziger Jahren schlossen hunderte von Chicagoer Firmen ihre Tore und siedelten um. Ganze Stadtteile wurden dadurch aus dem Gleichgewicht geworfen. Heute kann Chicago auf stolze $10 Milliarden an in jüngerer Zeit in der Innenstadt getätigten Investitionen verweisen. 500.000 neue Arbeitsplätze wurden alleine im Stadtbereich geschaffen, die herstellende Industrie hat modernisiert und automatisiert. Nach einer kürzlichen Umfrage des Harris-Meinungsforschungsinstituts bei 404 Vorstandsvorsitzenden wurde Chicago am häufigsten als bester Wirtschaftsstandort im mittleren Westen und als viertbester im ganzen Land genannt.

Chicago ist ein ausgereiftes Wirtschaftszentrum auf Weltniveau. Siebzig internationale Banken und zwanzig ausländische Fluggesellschaften sind in der Stadt vertreten. Hotelgesellschaften haben seit 1980 in der Stadt Hotelkapazitäten in der Größenordnung von 10.000,

Lufthansa

Lufthansa Developments

Lufthansa, in keeping with its deserved reputation as one of the most innovative airlines of the world, continues to present new services and state-of-the-art technology.

Among newly introduced offerings are the brand-new A340, the four-engine Airbus, which employs the most up-to-date technical knowledge and experience from both sides of the Atlantic. There are personal video screens in every First and Business Class seat, CD-sound systems, satellite telephones, and Telefax. In addition, traditional high standards of cabin services and comfort are maintained.

Lufthansa Miles & More™ program, designed to be one of the most rewarding frequent flyer programs in the sky and on the ground, offers you the opportunity to accrue and redeem bonus miles on Lufthansa worldwide and on the global partner United Airlines operated flights, as well.

Lufthansa Entwicklungen

Um ihrem Ruf als eine der innovativsten Fluglinien der Welt gerecht zu werden, stellt Lufthansa permanent neue Dienstleistungen und modernste Technologie vor.

Zu den Neueinführungen gehören der brandneue vierstrahlige A340 Airbus, in den neueste technische Erkenntnisse und ein breites Erfahrungsspektrum von beiden Seiten des Atlantiks eingingen. Jeder Sitzplatz der First und Business Class ist mit eigenem Bildschirm, CD-Soundsystem, Satellitentelefon und Telefaxgerät ausgestattet..

Das Lufthansa Miles & More™ Programm ist eines der großzügigsten Vielfliegerprogramme in der Luft und auf dem Boden. Im Rahmen dieses Programms können Sie Bonusmeilen von Flügen der Lufthansa weltweit sammeln und eintauschen, wie ebenfalls auf den Flügen des globalen Partners United Airlines.

Lufthansa in Chicago

In April 1956, Lufthansa German Airlines established its operation in Chicago and today, after 38 years of continuous service, can truly call itself one of the pioneers of international aviation in Chicago.

Its daily nonstop service to Frankfurt provides direct links with over 180 cities in 87 countries which comprise Lufthansa's worldwide commercial and touristic network.

Now, with its new $40 million building at O'Hare International Airport, built in 1992 by architect William E. Brazley, Jr., Lufthansa once again sets the pace of progress in Chicago and demonstrates its faith in the future of the Midwest market. The Building, which houses Lufthansa's extensive Passenger and Cargo Services Administration is considered one of the prime architectural attractions of Chicago.

Lufthansa in Chicago

Im April 1956 nahm die Deutsche Lufthansa in Chicago den Flugbetrieb auf. Heute, nach 38 Jahren ununterbrochener Tätigkeit kann sie sich mit Recht als eine Pionierin der internationalen Luftfahrt in Chicago bezeichnen.

Der tägliche Nonstop-Service nach Frankfurt bietet direkte Verbindungen zu mehr als 180 Städten in 87 Ländern, die das weltweite kommerzielle und touristische Netz der Lufthansa umfassen.

Mit dem neuen $40 Millionen Gebäude am O'Hare International Airport, das 1992 vom Architekten William E. Brazley, Jr. erbaut wurde, setzt Lufthansa erneut ein Zeichen in der Entwicklung Chicagos und demonstriert Zuversicht und Vertrauen in die Zukunft des Mittleren Westens der Vereinigten Staaten. Das Gebäude, in dem die umfassende Passagier- und Frachtverwaltung der Lufthansa untergebracht ist, gilt als eine der herausragenden architektonischen Attraktionen in Chicago.

Photo: Mark Ballogg

Chicago has matured as an economic center and has attained world ranking. 70 international banks and 20 foreign airlines are represented in Chicago. Since 1980 Chicago has a capacity of 10,000 hotel rooms, and in Greater Chicago over 60,000 rooms were constructed or renovated. Chicago's stock exchanges have international standing and trade on markets in Germany, Thailand, Tokyo, Frankfurt and Sidney.

The Midwest is Celebrating a Comeback

Chicago is situated right in the heart of a reviving and flourishing industrial region in the Midwest of the U.S. The revival was accelerated through technological changes and foreign competition, something that was once considered to be early symptoms of decline. For example, Diamond-Star Motors in Bloomington, Illinois, a joint venture between Chrysler and Mitsubishi, is one of the most modern car manufacturers in the world. Caterpillar, the largest exporter in the region, invested $1 billion in modernizing and automating its manufacturing facilities near Peoria. And with newly built plants, Inland Steel and other steel companies, including German companies, all located on Lake Michigan, have made Chicago and Northwest Indiana the most important location for the steel industry in the nation.

im Großraum Chicago sogar über 60.000 Hotelzimmer neu gebaut bzw. von Grund auf renoviert. Chicagos Börsen haben internationale Reichweiten - sie handeln und verhandeln mit Deutschland ebenso wie mit Thailand, mit Tokio ebenso wie mit Frankfurt und Sidney.

Der mittlere Westen feiert sein Comeback

Chicago liegt im Herzen der wieder aufblühenden Industrieregion des Mittleren Westens der USA, wo technologischer Wandel und ausländischer Wettbewerb - einst als Vorboten des Niedergangs gefürchtet - die Wiederbelebung forciert haben. Die Diamond-Star Motors in Bloomington/Illinois zum Beispiel, ein Joint Venture von Chrysler und Mitsubishi, ist eine der modernsten Autofabriken der Welt. Caterpillar, der größte Exporteur der Region, investierte $1 Milliarde in die Modernisierung und Automatisierung seiner Fertigungsanlagen in der Gegend von Peoria. Und mit den jetzt neu aufgebauten Werken der Inland Steel und anderer, auch deutscher Stahlkonzerne am Lake Michigan haben sich Chicago und Nordwest-Indiana zum wichtigsten Standort der Stahlindustrie des Landes entwickelt. Auf sie entfallen 30% der gesamten Inlandsproduktion.

Chicago ist auch landesweit führender Standort für Technologieanwender. Hier gibt es die meisten Computer, wie man bei der International Data Corp. weiß. Die Konzentration von Anwendern modernster Telekommunikations-Technologien und Unternehmen in den Bereichen Information und Finanz

ILLINOIS EXPORTS BY DESTINATION
total dollar value of shipments by country and percent change 1991-92 for Illinois and U.S.

	Illinois 1992	Illinois 1991	% change Illinois	% change U.S.
Total all countries	$17,622,000,020	$16,518,500,756	+6.7%	+6.1%
Canada	5,234,134,326	5,318,899,532	-1.6	+5.9
Mexico	1,349,283,453	1,087,100,187	+24.1	+22.0
Japan	1,236,374,657	1,329,045,614	-7.0	-0.8
United Kingdom	950,563,135	857,599,396	+10.8	+3.4
Federal Republic of Germany	920,962,748	938,895,112	-1.9	-0.4
Australia	582,875,472	542,299,277	+7.5	+5.9
Republic of Korea	551,029,924	656,864,018	-16.1	-5.7
France	508,317,482	467,364,182	+8.8	-5.1
Singapore	497,407,335	457,939,112	+8.6	+9.3
Belgium	481,800,972	405,682,933	+18.8	-7.5
Netherlands	450,808,239	374,766,727	+20.3	+1.6
China (Taiwan)	431,210,412	317,616,265	+35.8	+15.3
Italy	360,624,497	419,999,482	-14.1	+1.4
Hong Kong	331,367,346	254,802,519	+30.0	+11.4
Spain	242,341,784	215,511,929	+12.4	+0.1

Source: Massachussetts Institute for Social and Economic Research, University of Massachusetts at Amherst

HARTING CONNECTORS

HARTING products are used throughout electrical and electronic industries wherever connectors, interconnection systems and solenoids are required specifically, where data processing, control and measurement applications are involved, e.g. from microprocessors to automatic car assembly lines.

HARTING interconnection products meet the most exacting requirements, including ISO 9001 certification, and are in daily use throughout the world in all fields of application. HARTING's close links with leading OEM companies has resulted in innovations which have set current trends and have found world-wide recognition. You will find that HARTING has a unique ability to produce high-quality connectors at a reasonable price plus the engineering and R&D potential to solve any problems you might have when it comes to connectors.

HARTING Produkte werden in allen Bereichen der industriellen Elektronik und Elektrotechnik eingesetzt. Steckverbinder, Interconnection Systeme und Elektromagnete werden in Datenverarbeitungsanlagen, Kontroll- und Meßeinrichtungen angewendet, wie z. B. in Mikroprozessoren und automatischen Kraftfahrzeug-Montagebändern.

HARTING Steckersysteme sind nach höchsten Anforderungen gefertigt, einschließlich ISO 9001 Zertifizierung, und werden täglich in allen Anwendungsbereichen weltweit eingesetzt. HARTING's enge Zusammenarbeit mit führenden Herstellern resultierte in Neuerungen, die aktuelle Trends gesetzt und weltweite Anerkennung gefunden haben. Sie werden feststellen, daß HARTING die außergewöhnliche Fähigkeit hat, hochwertige Steckverbinder zu einem günstigen Preis anzubieten und Ihre Entwicklungprobleme individuell zu lösen.

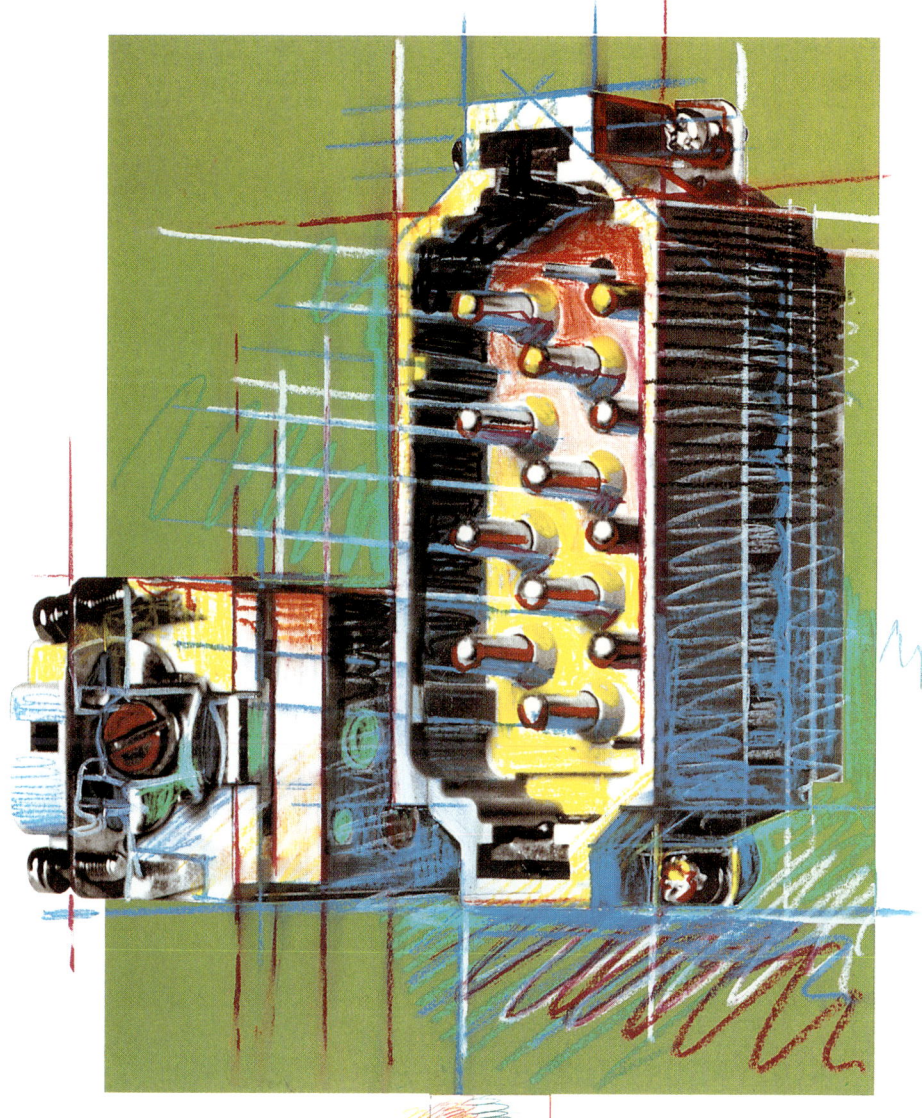

HARTING ELEKTRONIK, INC., 2155 Stonington Avenue, Hoffman Estates, Illinois 60195 USA

They produce 30% of the total domestic product.

Nationwide, Chicago is leading in user technology. International Data Corp. ascertained that we have more computers here than anywhere else. The high concentration of users of high-tech telecommunications and of the consulting and financial service industry serves as a motor for growth in glass fiber optics, software development and peripheral equipment. In turn, this attracted about 200,000 highly qualified skilled workers to northeast Illinois.

Mauro Walker, Vice President and Production Manager at Motorola, who recruits many of its engineers and scientists from the Illinois Institute of Technology, Northwestern University, University of Chicago and University of Illinois, believes that "Chicago has laid an excellent foundation for higher education." Motorola, which develops and produces switching systems and mobile telephones in Greater Chicago, is planning a new factory with 3,000 employees to keep up with high demands for mini mobile telephones on Japanese, European and U.S. markets.

The trend towards developing into a "Rust Belt" that was going nowhere has reversed itself a long time ago. Almost two thirds of the gross national product in the U.S. is manufactured in the vicinity of Chicago, within a radius of 500 miles.

dienstleistungen erweist sich als Wachstumsmotor für Glasfaseroptik, Software-Entwicklung und periphere Ausrüstungen. Das wiederum hat ein Potential von etwa 200.000 hochqualifizierten Fachkräften im Nordosten von Illinois nach sich gezogen.

"Chicago hat hervorragende Grundlagen im Hochschulwesen geschaffen", meint Mauro Walker, Vice President und Produktionsleiter bei Motorola, die viele ihrer Ingenieure und Wissenschaftler vom Illinois Institute of Technology, von der Northwestern University, der University of Chicago und der University of Illinois rekrutiert. Motorola entwickelt und produziert im Großraum Chicago Schaltsysteme und Mobiltelephone und plant eine neue Fabrikanlage mit 3.000 Mitarbeitern, um der kräftigen Nachfrage nach ihren Mini-Mobiltelephon am japanischen, europäischen und US-Markt gerecht zu werden.

Die Entwicklung zum "Rust Belt", die ins Abseits führt, hat sich längst umgekehrt. Fast zwei Drittel des Bruttosozialproduktes der USA werden im Umkreis von 500 Meilen von Chicago erwirtschaftet.

Chicagos Image zurechtrücken

Die Stärken von Chicago sind noch heute nicht selten durch völlig überholte Vorstellungen überschattet. Viele bringen die Stadt nach wie vor mit den Schlachthöfen vom Anfang des Jahrhunderts in Verbindung. Wenn Chicagoer Bürger auf Auslandsreisen den Namen ihrer Heimatstadt nennen, reagieren ihre Gesprächspartner oft mit Gesten, die einen revolverschwingenden Gangster nachahmen und sagen "Bäng Bäng! Al Capone!"

Illinois Institute of Technology

Transmission inspection at ZF North America, Inc.

Getriebe Inspektion bei ZF North America, Inc.

Mercedes-Benz of North America, Inc.

Headquartered in Montvale, New Jersey, Mercedes-Benz of North America, Inc. is responsible for the marketing, distribution and servicing of Mercedes-Benz passenger cars. Mercedes-Benz provides the broadest product selection of any premium automobile maker offering 19 U.S. models in four distinct classes: E-Class, S and SL-Class and the new award-winning C-Class. With some 400 dealers — including 13 in the Chicagoland area — MBNA expects to sell over 70,000 cars. Approximately 2,500 cars will be sold in Chicago, making it the company's third largest market in the country.

Besides introducing the popular E-Class and the new C-Class, Mercedes-Benz has recently made two important announcements:

• The first was the formulation of *MB Project, Inc.*, a new company which will be responsible for the production of a new multi-purpose vehicle. The MPV will be produced at a new $300 million U.S. manufacturing facility in Tuscaloosa, Alabama. The plant which will build an estimated 60,000 vehicles annually beginning in 1997, will employ some 1,500 workers locally and is expected to create an additional 10,000 jobs through suppliers and related industry by the end of the century.

• Secondly, shortly after the new plant announcement, Daimler-Benz, the parent company of Mercedes-Benz, became the first German company to be listed on the *New York Stock Exchange,* allowing the company access to the world's largest capital market.

The North Central Regional office of MBNA, as well as a vehicle preparation center and a parts distribution facility, are located in Chicagoland. The NCR office attends to over 100 Mercedes-Benz dealers in 19 states throughout the midwestern United States from Colorado to Pennsylvania.

Further news focuses on motorsport: After 100 years of racing, the oldest automaker will make its sceond debut at Indy 500, where partner Roger Penske will be using engines developed by Mercedes-Benz in cooperation with Ilmor Engineering.

Mercedes-Benz also has a longtime commitment to the Chicago Symphony Orchestra and has been named their exclusive automobile sponsor.

Each year Mercedes-Benz sponsors a vintage car show called the Chicago International Concours d'Elegance. This popular event, which is free to the public, is held in Grant Park near Buckingham Fountain and showcases over 100 cars of yester-year worth nearly $75 million. Pictured is a one-of-a-kind Mercedes race car which competed in the first-ever Indy 500 in 1910. This car, framed in the foreground of the magnificent Chicago skyline, was on loan from the Indianapolis Speedway museum.

In jedem Jahr sponsert Mercedes-Benz eine Oldtimer-Show, den Chicago International Concours d'Elegance. Diese allgemein beliebte Veranstaltung, die allen kostenlos offensteht, findet im Grant Park in der Nähe des Buckingham Fountain statt. Ausgestellt werden über 100 Automobilveteranen im Wert von nahezu $75 Millionen. Das Photo zeigt einen spezialgefertigten Mercedes-Rennwagen, der 1910 am ersten Indy 500 Rennen teilnahm. Dieses Auto, hier mit der imposanten Skyline von Chicago im Hintergrund, war eine Leihgabe des Indianapolis Speedway Museums.

The Mercedes-Benz C-Class has been a success throughout the world. It was recently named North American Car of the Year *by U.S. and Canadian journalists.*

Die Mercedes-Benz Klasse C, eine Erfolgsstory rund um die Welt, wurde vor kurzem von amerikanischen und kanadischen Journalisten zum North America Car of the Year *ernannt.*

Mercedes-Benz of North America, Inc. (MBNA) mit Sitz in Montvale, New Jersey, ist für Marketing, Vertrieb und Service der PKW-Flotte von Mercedes-Benz verantwortlich. Mit 19 US-Modellen in 4 Klassen, der E-Klasse, S und SL-Klasse und der neuen preisgekrönten C-Klasse, bietet Mercedes-Benz die breiteste Produktpalette unter den Herstellern hochwertiger Automobile. Über ein Netz von ca. 400 Händlern, darunter 13 im Raum Chicago, will MBNA mehr als 70.000 Wagen absetzen. Ca. 2.500 davon entfallen auf Chicago, das damit den drittgrößten US-Markt des Unternehmens darstellt.

Neben der Einführung der populären E-Klasse und der neuen C-Klasse gab Mercedes-Benz vor kurzem zwei weitere wichtige Neuentwicklungen bekannt:

• Einmal die Gründung eines neuen Unternehmens, *MB Project, Inc.,* für die Produktion eines neuen geländetauglichen Freizeitautos. Dieses Fahrzeug soll in einer neuen $300 Millionen teuren Fertigungsanlage in Tuscaloosa im US-Staat Alabama hergestellt werden. Ab 1997 wird das Werk schätzungsweise 60.000 Fahrzeuge pro Jahr produzieren, ca. 1.500 Mitarbeiter vor Ort beschäftigen und bis Ende des Jahrzehnts voraussichtlich 10.000 weitere Arbeitsplätze über Zulieferer und Begleitindustrien schaffen.

• Zum zweiten wurde Daimler-Benz, die Muttergesellschaft von Mercedes-Benz, kurz nach Bekanntgabe der Pläne für das neue Werk als erstes deutsches Unternehmen an der New Yorker Börse zugelassen, was dem Unternehmen Zugang zum größten Kapitalmarkt der Welt verschafft.

• Chicago ist Sitz der North Central Region (NCR) Niederlassung von MBNA. Eine Abteilung zur Fahrzeugauslieferung und ein Ersatzteil – Vertriebslager befinden sich ebenfalls im Raum Chicago. Die NCR-Niederlassung bedient mehr als 100 Mercedes-Benz-Händler in 19 Staaten des Mittleren Westens von Colorado bis Pennsylvanien.

Eine weitere Neuigkeit betrifft den Motorsport: Nach 100 Jahren Teilnahme an Autorennen wird der älteste Autohersteller der Welt zum zweiten Mal beim Indy 500 erscheinen. Partner Roger Penske wird Motoren verwenden, die von Mercedes-Benz in Zusammenarbeit mit Ilmor Engineering entwickelt wurden.

Mercedes-Benz unterhält seit langem enge Beziehungen zum Chicago Symphonieorchester und wurde zum alleinigen Automobilsponsor des Orchesters ernannt.

Intermodal Cargo Hub of North America

Speditions-Knotenpunkt von Nord-Amerika

Changing Chicago's Image

Totally obsolete misconceptions still cast a shadow on Chicago's strengths and good points. Chicago is still often associated with its stockyards that existed at the beginning of the century. And the first thing most foreigners still bring up when they meet a Chicagoan is the name of Al Capone along with the motion of a gun-slinging gangster.

Gangsters and the stockyards have long since vanished from Chicago and made room for art and culture. Today Chicago has 125 theaters, 150 art galleries, and its night clubs are world-famous for their blues and jazz. Concerts and art and theater festivals attract visitors from around the world. Chicago's new face is just about to be discovered. M.W. Newman, journalist for the 'Sun-Times' writes: "The steel-producing Chicago of yonder years, the 'strong-arm man of America' developed a surprisingly high cultural image during the nineties."

Jack Frazee from Virginia is amazed about the totally outmoded image people sometimes have of Chicago. The rust-belt era has long gone. Jack Frazee is chairman of Centel Corp., provider of telecommunications services with annual sales of $1.1 billion.

Die Gangster und die Schlachthöfe sind längst Vergangenheit in Chicago. Sie sind Kunst und Kultur gewichen. Heute zählt Chicago mehr als 125 Theater, 150 Kunstgalerien und die Nachtclubs mit ihrem weltberühmten Blues und Jazz.

Die Konzerte, Kunst- und Theaterfestivals der Stadt ziehen Besucher aus aller Welt an. Das neue Gesicht Chicagos werde eben erst entdeckt, schreibt Journalist M.W. Newman in der 'Sun-Times': "Das stahlproduzierende Chicago, ehemals 'Mr. Kraftprotz von Amerika', ist an der Schwelle zu den neunziger Jahren als Kulturstadt überraschend hoch angesiedelt."

"Ich wundere mich über die völlig veralteten Vorstellungen, die man vielerorts von Chicago hat. Die 'Rustbelt'-Zeiten sind doch längst vorbei", meint Jack Frazee, der aus Virginia stammt. Er ist Chairman der Centel Corp., einem Unternehmen für Telekommunikation mit einem Jahresumsatz von $1.1 Milliarden.

Innovation im Börsengeschehen

Die Stadt, die das Waren- und Finanztermingeschäft erfunden hat, bleibt darin weiter Vorreiter.

Die beiden Terminbörsen Chicago Board of Trade und Chicago Mercantile Exchange, deren fast 10.000 Händler und Hilfskräfte tagtäglich für Leben auf dem Börsenparkett sorgen, stehen für 60 Prozent des weltweiten Terminhandels. Doch während andere Länder Börsen etablieren, um Marktanteile zu erobern, marschieren die Chicagoer Börsen schon in Richtung auf vollcomputerisierte Handelssysteme für den internationalen Handel rund um die Uhr.

Lachner "CHICAGOLAND"

Schenker International

Schenker, Chicago is one of the strongest freight forwarders in the area. From the early 60's on, after Joerg "George" Launer, a native of Stuttgart, took over the helm of the Chicago office, the name *Schenker* has stood for the very best in international air and sea freight forwarding.

Exporters and importers appreciate the exactness, expertise and flexibility of this German company. Indeed, *Schenker International* has global presence and is backed up by strong resources. A subsidiary of the Schenker-Rhenus AG, which is part of Stinnes AG, it belongs to the VEBA Group. Its most important strategic guidelines are value creation, improved customer benefits and increased customer satisfaction. *Schenker* Chicago sees its greatest asset in its well trained, loyal and truly international work force in all its core service centers, including air and ocean import/export freight forwarding, customs house brokerage, warehousing, special projects and fairs/exhibitions. Also important is a good balance of human resources, financial strength and the most technologically advanced facilities, resulting in top efficiency and customer value.

Movement of goods urgent, cost sensitive, heavy, delicate, high value, oversize to and from all parts of the world is accomplished consistently and reliably. *Schenker* has the best freight forwarding system for land, air and sea; a sure documentation trail, fully computerized and global in scope. *Schenker International* communicates effectively, door to door, 24 hours a day, seven days a week.

Schenker International, Chicago, with its own state of the art cargo terminal located in view of O'Hare Airport, and easily accessible from all major expressways is the cornerstone of *Schenker*'s presence in the Midwest. The Chicago gateway works closely with other *Schenker* full service centers located in Minneapolis, Milwaukee, Kansas City, St. Louis, Indianapolis, Cincinnati, Columbus, Cleveland and Detroit.

Schenker International, the quality solution to Chicagoland's transportation needs.

Schenker, Chicago ist eines der leistungsstärksten Speditionsunternehmen im Mittleren Westen. Seit Anfang der 60er Jahre, als Jörg "George" Launer aus Stuttgart die Leitung der Niederlassung in Chicago übernahm, ist der Name *Schenker* gleichbedeutend mit optimaler Leistung im internationalen Luft- und Seefrachtverkehr.

Exporteure und Importeure wissen die Präzision, Fachkenntnisse, und Flexibilität dieses deutschen Unternehmens zu schätzen. *Schenker International* verfügt über eine globale Präsenz und Schenker International verfügt über eine globale präsenz und umfangreiche Resourcen. Als Tochtergesellschaft der Schenker-Rhenus AG, einem einem Unternehmen der Stinnes AG, gehört *Schenker International* zum VEBA Konzern. Seine wichtigsten strategischen Leitlinien sind die Schaffung von Wert, bessere Leistungen für den Kunden und erhöhte Kundenzufriedenheit. *Schenker* betrachtet seine gut ausgebildete, loyale und internationale Belegschaft als sein größtes Kapital. Diese Mitarbeiter sind in allen Kernabteilungen tätig, einschließlich Import-/Export-Frachtverkehr auf dem Luft- und Seeweg, Zollabfertigung, Lagerhaltung, Sonderprojekte sowie Messen und Ausstellungen. Ebenso wichtig ist ein ausgewogenes Verhältnis von Mitarbeitern, finanzieller Stärke und technologisch hochentwickelten Anlagen, das optimale Effizienz und Wertschaffung für den Kunden ermöglicht.

Die Bewegung von Gütern - dringenden, kostensensitiven, schweren, zerbrechlichen, großvolumigen und überdimensionierten Gütern von und nach allen Teilen der Welt - wird jederzeit zuverlässig abgewickelt. *Schenker* besitzt das beste Güterspeditionssystem auf dem Land-, Luft- und Seeweg sowie einen zuverlässigen, rechnergestützten Dokumentationsnachweis auf globaler Basis. *Schenker International* verfügt über ein wirksames Kommunikationssystem, von Tür zu Tür, rund um die Uhr, sieben Tage die Woche.

Mit einem eigenen, modernen Fracht-Terminal im Sichtbereich des O'Hare Airport und von allen großen Schnellstraßen leicht erreichbar, ist *Schenker International*, Chicago das Kernstück der *Schenker* Präsenz im Mittleren Westen. Die Niederlassung in Chicago arbeitet eng mit anderen *Schenker*-Geschäftsstellen in Minneapolis, Milwaukee, Kansas City, St. Louis, Indianapolis, Cincinnati, Columbus, Cleveland und Detroit zusammen, die ebenfalls über ein komplettes Leistungsangebot verfügen.

Schenker International, die Qualitätslösung für den Transportbedarf im Raum Chicago.

SCHENKER INTERNATIONAL

**Forwarding Air • Land • Sea
Storage • Consolidation
Exhibition Services**

*Luft-, Land- und Seefracht
Lagerhaltung • Sammelladungen
Messe Dienst*

Chicago Office: 123 Sivert Court, Bensenville, Illinois (USA) 60106 • Telephone: 708/595-0095   Telex No.: 206334   Telefax: 708/860-9166

Die Chicago Board of Trade an der Kreuzung von Jackson und LaSalle Street, ist die weltweit älteste und größte Warentermin- und Optionsbörse für Landwirtschaftsprodukte. Auf dem Börsenparkett werden Weizen, Mais, Sojabohnen, Rindfleisch usw. abgewickelt. Im Böesenstand-bereich für Finanztermingeschäfte handelt man in US-Schatzobligationen und Schatzanweisungen sowie Aktienindexen, Kommunalanleihen-Indexen usw.

Die Chicago Mercantile Exchange, 30 S. Wacker, der größte Handelsplatz für Termin- und Optionsgeschäfte auf der Welt, schlägt nahezu $100 Billionen pro Jahr um. Die vielfältigen Produkte der CME von landwirtschaftlichen Grundstoffen bis zu Devisen, Zinssatz- und Aktienindexen werden von Banken, Unternehmen und Investitionsspezialisten weltweit gehandelt. Die Besuchergalerie ist Montag bis Freitag von 8.00 bis 15.15 Uhr geöffnet. Für weitere Informationen rufen Sie die CME unter 312/930-1000 an.

The Chicago Board of Trade, located at Jackson and LaSalle, is the world's oldest and largest trader in agricultural and financial futures and options. The agricultural and commodities floor deals in orders for wheat, corn, soybeans, beef, etc. The financial futures pit does business in U.S. Treasury bonds and notes, stock indexes, municipal bond indexes, etc.

The Chicago Mercantile Exchange, al 30 S. Wacker, the world's largest marketplace for futures and options, trades nearly $100 trillion annually. The CME's divergent product lines of agricultural commodities, foreign currencies, interest rate and stock index instruments are used by banks, corporations, and investment specialists worldwide. The Visitors Gallery is open Monday thru Friday, 8:00 a.m. to 3:15 p,m, Call the CME at 312/930-1000 for more information.

Innovations in the World of the Exchanges

The City that invented trading in commodities and financial futures has remained the forerunner in this business.

60% of all futures trading in the world is transacted at Chicago's two futures exchanges, the Chicago Board of Trade and the Mercantile Exchange, with their 10,000 traders and runners who populate the floor every day. While other countries are attempting to launch exchanges in their countries to acquire a market share, Chicago's exchanges are already full steam on their way to a fully computerized 24-hour international trading system.

In some sort of competition with their archrivals, the "Merc" and Reuters were experimenting with GLOBEX, a worldwide trading system with automatic matching introduced in 1990. Meanwhile CBOT made the commitment for an even more elaborate electronic trading system called 'Aurora' which will provide the traders with a 24-hour marketplace that is in every respect competitive with the regular-hour market.

"The competitiveness between the 'Board' and the 'Merc' gives us an edge of three years over market places like New York, Tokyo and London," says Waite Rawls, Vice Chairman of Continental Bank. Rawls is particularly interested in this development, because he is responsible for the risk management of his bank, and he uses the

In einer Art Wettstreit zwischen den Erzrivalen bastelte die "Merc" mit Reuters an GLOBEX, einem weltweiten Handelssystem mit automatischem Matching, das 1990 eingeführt wurde. Derweil versprach die CBOT ein noch ausgefeilteres elektronisches Handelssystem namens 'Aurora', das den Händlern einen wettbewerbsintensiven 24-Stunden-Markt zur Verfügung stellen soll, der dem der normalen Handelszeiten in nichts nachsteht.

"Der Wettstreit zwischen "Board" und "Merc" verschafft uns einen Vorsprung von drei Jahren vor Plätzen wie New York, Tokio, und London", schätzt Waite Rawls, Vice Chairman der Continental Bank. Rawls ist an der Entwicklung besonders stark interessiert, weil er sich für das Risikomanagement seiner Bank verantwortlich zeichnet und die Handelssysteme der Börsen wie auch die neuen Finanzinstrumente tagtäglich nutzt.

"Die Kapitalbeschaffung ist heute nicht mehr das Problem für die Unternehmen — es gibt doch praktisch an jeder Ecke Investment-Banker mit Koffern voller Geld", meint Rawls. "Entscheidend ist vielmehr, die Volatilität bei Zinskosten und Währungen im Griff zu haben. Man muß wissen, wo und womit man sich absichern kann- und was das kostet."

Die Continental entwickelt auf der Basis von eingeführten Finanzprodukten kundenorientierte Over-the-counter-Instrumente wie Swaps, Caps, Collars oder Corridors. So konnte sie z.B. für ihren Firmenkunden L.L. Bean einen bestimmten Zinssatz über 30 Monate halten. Für einen anderen Kunden, die Firma Ocean Spray, kreierte die Bank einen Zweijahres-Swap, der Thanks-

Audi

From our birth in 1910, we at Audi have committed ourselves to creative engineering. Soaring above the traditional, with new ideas that change automotive history.

Our engineering experience is well-proven: it was Audi, after all, that pioneered front-wheel drive, turbocharging, and aerodynamics. Paths other carmakers have now chosen to follow.

Our social sensibilities inspired us to begin crash testing our cars in the Thirties. To initiate environmental planning as early as the Sixties.

And recently, to develop cars using aerospace light-alloy construction that is light, strong, and conserves natural resources.

And our discontent with conventional wisdom inspired quattro® —a full-time all-wheel drive system that offers up to twice the traction of conventional drive systems.

A moment behind the wheel will confirm our belief that driving is more than the functional process of traveling point to point. In an Audi, driving becomes an act of inspiration.

We believe that the only way to build cars is with our soul. For us, there simply is no other way.

Seit unserem Ursprung im Jahr 1910 sind wir bei Audi kreativer Technologie verpflichtet. Herkömmliches Denken lassen wir weit hinter uns - wir entwickeln neue Ideen, die die Geschichte des Automobils ändern.

Unsere technische Erfahrung steht außer Zweifel: Vorderradantrieb, Turbolader und Aerodynamik sind Konzepte aus dem Hause Audi. Wir schlugen Wege ein, auf denen andere Automobilhersteller heute folgen.

Unser Sozialbewußtsein bewog uns, in den dreißiger Jahren mit Crash-Tests zu beginnen, Umweltplanung bereits in den sechziger Jahren einzuführen. Und in jüngerer Zeit Autos im Leichtmetallbau der Luft- und Raumfahrt zu konstruieren, die gleichzeitig leicht und stark sind und unsere natürlichen Ressourcen schonen.

Aus unserer innovativen Denkweise entstand quattro® - ein permanentes Allradantriebssystem, das bis zum Zweifachen der Traktion herkömmlicher Antriebssysteme bietet.

Bereits eine kurze Probefahrt wird unsere Überzeugung bestätigen, daß Autofahren mehr ist als die funktionelle Fortbewegung von einem Ort zum anderen. In einem Audi wird Fahren zur Inspiration.

Wenn wir Autos bauen, sind wir mit jeder Faser unseres Herzens dabei. Etwas anderes kennen wir nicht.

Audi of America has a Central Zone Office in Lincolnshire, IL., 25 miles north of Chicago. This office is responsible for sales, service and parts activities in the central region which accounts for 16 states in the U.S. market.

The Chicago Stock Exchange (formerly the Midwest Stock Exchange) is the second largest stock exchange in the U.S. in terms of the dollar value of shares traded. The CHX and its wholly-owned subsidiaries provide trade and clearing, and data processing to the domestic and international securities and financial services industry.

Die Chicago Stock Exchange, also die Effektenbörse (früher Midwest Stock Exchange), ist die zweitgrößte Börse in den Vereinigten Staaten. DIE CHX und ihre 100%ige Tochtergesellschaft bieten der amerikanischen und ausländischen Finanzdienstleistungsbranche Börsenhandel, Clearing und Datenverarbeitung an.

trading systems of the exchanges as well as the new financial instruments on a daily basis.

"The problem today is no longer how to procure capital — because on practically every street corner we find investment bankers with deep pockets," says Rawls. "What is important, however, is the volatility of interest rates and understanding currencies. Important is to know where and how to protect yourself financially and the cost of it."

Using financial instruments as a basis, Continental developed over-the-counter instruments such as Swaps, Caps, Collars or Corridors for its clients. Thus, Continental was able to maintain a specific interest rate over a period of 30 months for one of its clients, L.L. Bean. For another client, Ocean Spray, the Bank created a two-year Swap, which was named 'Thanksgiving hedge.'

Leo Melamed, former consultant to the Merc, believes that "innovation is of critical importance to many industries, but especially for financial futures." Melamed was instrumental in helping along the success of financial futures. "This is the spirit for which Chicago is famous and which motivates the economy."

Enjoying the Daily Drama

One cultural event that happens virtually every day is giving hedge' ('Erntedank-Hedge') getauft wurde.

"Innovation ist ausschlaggebend in vielen Branchen, insbesondere aber bei Financial Futures", erklärte Leo Melamed, der ehemalige Sonderberater der Merc. Er hat Financial Futures mit zum Durchbruch verholfen. "Hier herrscht der Geist, der Chicago auszeichnet und die Wirtschaft antreibt."

Spaß am täglichen Drama

Ein Kulturereignis, das in Chicago praktisch konstant auf dem Programm steht, ist die Stadt selbst. Sie ändert sich ständig und langweilt nie. Vor siebzig Jahren beschrieb der Dichter Carl Sandburg Chicago als einen "tall, bold slugger", der unaufhörlich zerstört, neu plant, aufbaut, zertrümmert und wieder aufbaut. Heute kommt die Stadt ihren Bürgern nicht viel anders vor - und alle genießen das tägliche Drama.

Alles dreht sich jahrein jahraus um die drei großen Themen-Sport, Politik und Geschäft. Die achtziger Jahre waren besonders bewegt: die "Bears", (Chicagos erfolgreiches Footballteam) kämpften um die "Super Bowl", die "White Sox" (Baseballteam) brachten es zu einem neuen Stadion. Im Amt des Bürgermeisters gab es drei Wechsel, und manch bekannter Unternehmenschef kämpfte und überlebte in einer schier endlosen Serie von Firmenzusammenschlüßen und Übernahmen.

Scharfer Wettbewerb auch im Verlagswesen, etwa zwischen der "Tribune" (einer Tageszeitung mit gutem Wirtschaftsteil, internationaler Berichterstattung und den Kolumnen der Pulitzer-Preisträger Mike Royko und Clarence

the City itself. The City is constantly changing and never gets boring. Seventy years ago, poet Carl Sandburg described Chicago as a "tall, bold slugger," always tearing down, planning again, rebuilding, tearing down and building again. This has not changed today and everyone enjoys the daily drama.

Day in, day out, year in, year out everything centers around the three main events of this City - sports, politics and business. The eighties were particularly eventful. That was the decade when the Bears valiantly fought for the Super Bowl, and the White Sox got their new stadium. We had three different mayors during that time, and numerous companies fought for survival during an almost endless series of mergers and take-overs.

The world of publishing is also a world of fierce competition. There is the Tribune with its great business and international sections and the columns by Pulitzer-Prize winners Mike Royko and Clarence Page on the one side, and on the other side the Sun Times specializing in local news. We have six more regional papers all having their own special forte and readership. There are the weekly German papers "Eintracht" and "Amerika Woche," the "Korea Times," the "Polish Daily Zgoda" and "El Manana."

The development of Chicago's inner city after World War II was probably the most impressive

Page) auf der einen und der "Sun Times" (die in der lokalen Berichterstattung führt) auf der anderen Seite. Hinzu kommen sechs weitere regionale Tageszeitungen mit redaktionellen Schwerpunkten bzw. speziellen Leserkreisen, z.B. die deutschsprachige "Eintracht" und "Amerika Woche" wöchentlich, die "Korea Times", "Polish Daily Zgoda" und "El Manana".

Am meisten beeindruckt wohl die Entwicklung der Innenstadt von Chicago nach dem zweiten Weltkrieg. Komplette neue Wohngegenden entstanden auf alten Bahnhöfen und Gleisanlagen. Die Stadt ist auch jetzt voller Bauarbeiter. "Manchmal sieht es so aus, als hätte hier eine Bombe eingeschlagen", beklagt sich Lois Weisberg, im Stadtrat zuständig für kulturelle Angelegenheiten. Aber auch sie findet die neue Architektur beeindruckend, ihr gefallen die neu angelegten Grünanlagen und Gehwege entlang des Flusses, und sie freut sich, daß immer mehr Menschen in die Innenstadt ziehen und sie beleben. Denn das bedeutet ein besseres Umfeld für ihre Arbeit: mehr Platz für Festivals, mehr Chicagoer Bürger in der Lyric Opera oder in den Konzerten des Chicago Symphony Orchestra, mehr Künstler und Musiker, die den Straßen der Stadt Atmosphäre verleihen - und mehr Chicago-Fans.

"Viele kommen als Umsiedler aus anderen Städten, mit ihrer Firma oder wie auch immer. Sie haben meist keine Ahnung von dem, was Chicago wirklich ist", sagt Frau Weisberg. Sie betreut auch die Partnerschaften der Stadt. Es sind neue Partnerschaften geschlossen, zum Beispiel mit Hamburg und sechs weiteren Städten in aller Welt. Sie spricht aus

Wrigley, Chicago Tribune and Intercontinental Hotel Buildings

Chicago Sun-Times on the Chicago River

GERMAN-AMERICAN COMMERCE AND INDUSTRY

Automatic Liquid Packaging, Inc.

2200 W. Lake Shore Drive, Woodstock, Illinois (USA) 60098, Phone: 815/338-9500 Fax: 815/338-5504

Automatic Liquid Packaging, Inc. (ALP) is located in Woodstock, Illinois, an easy one-hour drive northwest of Chicago O'Hare Airport. For over 25 years they have built and marketed the ALP Blow/Fill/Seal Machine for the production of sterile, liquid pharmaceutical products.

This state-of-the-art, integrated system takes granular pellets of virtually any thermoplastic resin, extrudes, blow molds, fills and seals in one continuous operation.

In addition to marketing this machine, ALP employs almost 400 people in the operation of its modern, 350,000 square foot, FDA registered contract manufacturing facility. A wide variety of sterile liquid products are produced for an impressive list of clients.

Automatic Liquid Packaging, Inc. (ALP) mit Sitz in Woodstock, Illinois, ist etwa eine Autostunde nordwestlich vom Chicago O'Hare Airport gelegen. Seit mehr als 25 Jahren bekannt für die Produktion und den Verkauf dieser ALP Blow/Fill/Seal Maschine geeignet zur Verpackung von sterilen Flüssigkeiten.

In diesem hochmodernen, integrierten System wird Kunststoffgranulat aus praktisch jedem Thermoplastik in einem ununterbrochenen Prozeß hergestellt. Verkaufsfertige, gefüllte und verschlossene Behälter verlassen das Fliessband der Maschine.

Neben dem Verkauf dieser Maschine betreibt ALP ein modernes, FDA registriertes Unternehmen in Fläche von ca 35.000 m^2, mit nahezu 400 Mitarbeitern, die grösstenteils mit der Vertragsproduktion beschäftigt sind. Hier wird ein

Two (2) models of the ALP Blow/Fill/Seal machine are available, the Model 603 and 624. The hourly outputs range from 900 – 9,000 bottles per hour, depending upon size and container design.

Die ALP Blow/Fill/Seal Maschine ist in zwei (2) Ausführungen erhältlich, den Modellen 603 und 624. Im Durchschnitt liegt der Ausstoss bei 900 - 9.000 Flaschen pro Stunde je nach Größe und Behälterdesign.

ALP has always been committed to the creative application of high technology in the automatic packaging of liquid products for the pharmaceutical and healthcare industries. The ALP Blow/Fill/Seal System reflects this commitment resulting in the most advanced liquid packaging system available in the world today.

breites Spektrum steriler Flüssigprodukte für einen renommierten Kundenkreis produziert.

Die kreative Anwendung von High Technology auf die automatische Verpackung von Flüssigprodukten für die pharmazeutische Industrie und den Gesundheitssektor ist seit jeher eine Stärke von ALP. Ein Beweis hierfür ist das ALP Blow/Fill/Seal System, das modernste Flüssigverpackungssystem auf dem Weltmarkt.

Practically any package size or design from 0.2mL to 1000mL can be molded with the ALP process.

Mit dem ALP Prozeß lassen sich Packungen in praktisch allen Größen und Designs formen, von 0,2 ml bis 1000 ml.

GERMAN-AMERICAN COMMERCE AND INDUSTRY

Civic Opera House

Photo: Mary Gekler, 1953

*Orchestra Hall,
Home of the
Chicago Symphony
Orchestra*

Photo: Jim Steere

event. Entire new residential areas developed in old train stations and on train tracks. Today the city is once more one big construction site. "Sometimes it looks as if we were hit by a bomb," laments Lois Weisberg of the City Council responsible for cultural affairs. However, she also finds the new architecture very exciting. She likes the new landscaping and walkways along the river and she is particularly happy that more and more people move into the Loop, because this creates the right environment for her work, which is: to create more opportunities for festivals, to interest more people to visit the Lyric Opera or to attend a concert at the Chicago Symphony, to attract more artists and more musicians who add to the city's atmosphere, and to increase the number of Chicago fans.

"Many newcomers were relocated to Chicago from other cities through their companies. No matter what the reasons for their coming, most of them have no idea what Chicago is all about," says Ms. Weisberg. Ms. Weisberg is also responsible for the sister-city program of Chicago. New partnerships were entered into, as for instance with Hamburg and with six other cities all over the world. She speaks from experience when she says: "Most people who come to Chicago learn very quickly to love this city."

Erfahrung, wenn sie sagt: "Die meisten, die hierher kommen, lernen sehr schnell und werden dann zu wahren Liebhabern dieser Stadt."

Richtungsweisende Projekte hielten den Verfall auf

Viele der Umsiedler sind zu zentralen Figuren für das Wachstum der Stadt geworden und haben geholfen, Chicago vor dem Schicksal vieler anderer Städte im Norden der USA zu bewahren. Man denke beispielsweise an St. Louis oder an Detroit, wo die industrielle Neuorientierung und veränderte Bevölkerungsstrukturen zu überstürzten Abwanderungen führten. Auch Chicago hat in den siebziger Jahren mehr als 300.000 Einwohner verloren, meist wanderten sie in die Vorstädte ab. Aber die Stadt konnte das Ausbluten stoppen. Mit ihren Vororten hat die Stadt jetzt 8,85 Millionen Einwohner; im Innenbereich leben 2,8 Millionen Menschen. Davon sind 1,3 Millionen weißer und 1,1 Millionen schwarzer Hautfarbe. Unter den Minderheiten prägen besonders die Chinesen und Mittelamerikaner das Stadtbild; die "Hispanics" sind die am stärksten wachsende Bevölkerungsgruppe.

Die Wende setzte ein, als Unternehmen und finanzkräftige Pensionskassen in den frühen siebziger Jahren einen Bauboom in Gang setzten. Zuerst kamen die riesigen Wolkenkratzer: das John Hancock Center, die weiße Säule des Amoco Building und der 110 Stockwerke hohe Sears Tower, drei der höchsten Gebäude der Welt.

Eine bedeutende Rolle als "Architekt der Stadtsanierung" spielte der damalige Bürgermeister Richard J. Daley, Vater

Trendsetting Projects prevented the Cultural and Economic Decline

Many of those who were relocated became central figures in the growth of the city, and they were instrumental in preventing that Chicago met the same fate as the one that befell other cities in the north. To name a few, you only need to think of St. Louis or Detroit. Departures from the old ways in business and population led to an exodus from the cities. Chicago too lost more than 300,000 residents in the seventies. Most of them moved to the suburbs. However, Chicago was able to stop this trend. Chicago and suburbs now have 8.85 million people. 2.8 million people live in the inner city, of which 1.3 million are white and 1.1 million are black. Among the minority groups, Chinese and Hispanic ("central") Americans dominate. The "Hispanic population," however, is the fastest growing group.

Things started to change when businesses and financially strong pension funds started a building boom in Chicago during the seventies. It started with such gigantic skyscrapers as the John Hancock Center, the white columns of the Amoco Building and the 110-story high Sears Tower, three of the tallest buildings in the world.

Former Mayor Richard J. Daley, father of our present des heutigen Bürgermeisters von Chicago. 21 Jahre lang, bis zu seinem Tod im Jahre 1976, baute Daley Wohnhäuser, dazu McCormick Place, den Flughafen O'Hare, die University of Illinois, neue Highways und Schnellverbindungsstraßen sowie Versorgungswege zu den Baustellen in der Innenstadt. Im Bereich dieser Verkehrsadern füllte sich die Stadt langsam mit anspruchsvollen, oft mutigen und wegweisenden Projekten wie dem Dearborn Park, einer Wohngegend im South Loop mit 10.000 Einwohnern oder dem Water Tower Place, einem Geschäftszentrum, das die Michigan Avenue in die beliebteste Einkaufstraße des mittleren Westens verwandelte.

Wirtschaft und Verwaltung vereinen Kräfte

Chicagos Wachstum in der jüngsten Zeit kommt nicht von ungefähr. Einen großen Verdienst daran haben die öffentlich-privaten Partnerschaften unter der Führung von Persönlichkeiten der Wirtschaft, der Entwicklungsgesellschaften und der Verantwortlichen in den Ressorts Planung und Wirtschaftsförderung im Rathaus der Stadt.

Mehr als 500 Unternehmer und führende Köpfe der Stadtverwaltung arbeiten in der Economic Development Commission (EDC), dem Komitee für Wirtschaftsförderung der Stadt Chicago, und in Fördergruppen der freien Wirtschaft zusammen, um der Stadt bei der Erarbeitung von Strategien zur Erhaltung bzw. Verbesserung ihrer Wirtschaft zu helfen. Die "German American Chamber of Commerce of the Midwest",

German Speaking Population and Americans of German Speaking Ancestry based on updated 1990 census

in 1,000s

Entity	USA Country	Illinois State	Cook <	Lake Counties	DuPage >	Chicago City
Austrians	870	50	28	4	5	10
Germans	57,986	3,328	875	165	267	270
Swiss	1,046	47	11	3	4	4
Total group	59,902	3,425	914	172	276	284
Total Populus	296,380	14,176	6,010	689	1,110	2,945
% of total	20.2%	24.2	15.2%	25%	24.9%	9.6%

Source: U.S. Department of Commerce
Bureau of Census, Chicago

Tracking a person's roots

The U.S. Census in 1990 asked people to identify their "ancestry or ethnic origin." Here are ancestry totals, as a percentage of the total population:

1.	German	23.1%	24.	Portuguese	.46%
2.	Irish	15.59%		West Indian	.46%
3.	English	13.13%	26.	Greek	.45%
4.	Italian	5.92%	27.	Swiss	.42%
5.	Mexican	5.43%		Cuban	.42%
6.	American	5.25%	29.	Spaniard/Spanish	.39%
7.	French	4.16%	30.	Arab	.35%
8.	Polish	3.77%		Austrian	.35%
9.	Dutch	2.50%	32.	Japanese	.34%
10.	Scotch-Irish	2.26%	33.	Lithuanian	.33%
11.	Scottish	2.17%		Asian Indian	.33%
12.	Swedish	1.88%	35.	Korean	.32%
13.	Norwegian	1.56%	36.	Ukrainian	.30%
14.	Russian	1.19%	37.	Finnish	.26%
15.	French-Canadian	1.14%	38.	Vietnamese	.25%
16.	Puerto Rican	1.10%	39.	Salvadoran	.23%
17.	Welsh	.82%		Canadian	.23%
18.	Slovak	.76%	41.	Dominican	.22%
19.	Danish	.66%	42.	Sub-Sahara African	.20%
	Chinese	.66%		Yugoslavian	.20%
21.	Czech	.65%	44.	Belgian	.16%
22.	Hungarian	.64%	45.	Colombian	.15%
23.	Filipino	.57%		Romanian	.15%

Among the findings:
- Germans are the USA's largest ancestral group. The 1990 Census shows that almost one-fourth of Americans say they have at least some German ancestry.
- The next largest groups were Irish, 16%; English, 13%; Italian, 6%; Mexican, 5%; U.S. or American, 5%; and French and Polish, each 4%.

USA TODAY, August 4, 1992

USA Telephone Area Codes in Numerical Sequence
Amerikanische Vorwahl Ziffern in numerischer Reihenfolge

200		300	
201	Newark (NJ)	301	Baltimore (MD)
202	Washington (DC)	302	Delaware
203	Connecticut	302	Denver (CO)
204	Manitoba	304	West Virginia
205	Alabama	305	Miami (FL)
206	Seattle (WA)	306	Saskatchewan
207	Maine	307	Wyoming
208	Idaho	308	North Platte (NE)
209	Fresno (CA)	309	Peoria (IL)
210	San Antonio (TX)	310	Long Beach (CA)
211		311	
212	Manhattan, Bronx (NY)	312	Chicago (IL)
213	Los Angeles (CA)	313	Detroit (MI)
214	Dallas (TX)	314	St. Louis (MO)
215	Philadelphia (PA)	315	Syracuse (NY)
216	Cleveland (OH)	316	Wichita (KS)
217	Springfield (IL)	317	Indianapolis (IN)
218	Minnesota	318	Shreveport (LA)
219	South Bend (IN)	319	Dubuque (IA)
220		320	

400		500	
401	Rhode Island	501	Arkansas
402	Omaha (NE)	502	Louisville (KY)
403	Alberta, Yukon	503	Oregon
404	Atlanta (GA)	504	New Orleans (LA)
405	Oklahoma City (OK)	505	New Mexico
406	Montana	506	New Brunswick
407	Orlando (FL)	507	Rochester (MN)
408	San Jose (CA)	508	Lowell (MA)
409	Galveston (TX)	509	Spokane (WA)
410	Baltimore (MD)	510	Oakland (CA)
411	INFORMATION	511	
412	Pittsburgh (PA)	512	San Antonio (TX)
413	Springfield (MA)	513	Cincinnati (OH)
414	Milwaukee (WI)	514	Montreal (QE)
415	San Francisco (CA)	515	Des Moines (IA)
416	Toronto (ON)	516	Long Island (NY)
417	Springfield (MO)	517	Lansing (MI)
418	Quebec (QE)	518	Albany (NY)
419	Toledo (OH)	519	London (ON)
420		520	

This list was derived from carefully screening the area code maps of the United States. Diese Liste wurde sorgfältig von Vorwahlkarten der U.S.A. erarbeitet, jedoch ohne Gewähr.

Mayor in Chicago, played an important role as the "architect of urban renewal." For 21 years until he died in 1976, Mayor Daley built not only apartment buildings but also McCormick Place, O'Hare Airport, the University of Illinois, new highways and expressways, as well as new supply routes to construction sites in the Loop. In the vicinity of major thoroughfares ambitious and often trendsetting projects were developed such as Dearborn Park, a residential neighborhood in the South Loop with 10,000 residents, or Water Tower Place, a shopping center that transformed Michigan Avenue into the most popular shopping street of the Midwest.

Industry and Administration join Forces

Chicago's growth in recent years did not just happen haphazardly. Public and private interest groups under the direction of leaders in industry, development corporations and in City Government — Department of Planning and Development, played an important part in this development.

More than 500 businessmen and people in leading positions in City Administration work together in a commission for city planning — the Economic Development Commission (EDC), and in private development groups, to help Chicago work out strategies to

mit Sitz in Chicago, arbeitet mit allen diesen Gruppen von 'deutscher Seite aus' zusammen.

In den neunziger Jahren wird wiederum schwerpunktmäßig in McCormick Place investiert. Weitere Schwerpunkte sind die Entwicklung von Industrieparks und Programme zur Förderung wichtiger Branchen wie Lebensmittelverarbeitung und Finanzdienstleistungen. Die EDC und das städtische Department of Planning and Development haben fertige Pläne für mehrere Industrieparks in der City.

"Die Zusammenarbeit mit den Unternehmen und den Wirtschaftsförderungsgesellschaften versetzt uns in die Lage, Bedürfnisse schneller zu erkennen und entsprechend zu reagieren", meint der Commissioner im Department of Planning and Development, dem städtischen Amt für Wirtschaftsförderung.

Zehn Jahre Stadtentwicklung

Der Boom gewann Mitte der achtziger Jahre an Intensität, als -überraschend selbst für Experten im Immobiliengeschäft — expandierende Rechtsanwaltskanzleien und Unternehmensverwaltungen Jahr für Jahr 280.000 Quadratmeter an neuer Bürofläche belegten. Jetzt gibt es über 10 Millionen Quadratmeter Bürofläche in der Innenstadt; viele Firmen haben ihre neue Hauptverwaltung ins Zentrum von Chicago gelegt.

"Wir haben uns lange überlegt, ob wir in die City oder in einen der Vororte gehen sollten. Schließlich haben wir uns für die City entschieden, weil da alles in Reichweite ist, sei es zu Fuß oder mit

maintain and improve commerce and industry. Germany is also represented and lends its support. The German American Chamber of Commerce of the Midwest with its principal offices in Chicago, works closely together with all these groups.

During the nineties the expansion of McCormick Place is planned requiring large investments. Other important projects are the development of industrial parks and programs for the development of major food processing plants and financial services. The EDC and the City Department of Planning and Development have already finished plans for several industrial parks in the city.

"Working together with industry, businesses and development associations puts us in a better position to recognize needs faster and to react accordingly," says the Commissioner for the Department of Planning and Development.

Ten-Year Period of Development of the City

The boom intensified in the mid-eighties when - even to the surprise of real estate experts - steadily growing law firms and business administrations occupied almost 3 million square feet of new office space. Today we have over 100 million square feet of office space in the Loop alone. Many companies relo-

einer kurzen Taxifahrt", sagt Luther C. McKinney, Senior Vice President der Quaker Oats Company.

Die Transportfrage spielte bei der Entscheidung ebenfalls eine Rolle. Chicagos Highway-Netz, seine Schienenverkehrsnetze für Pendler und die Schnellverbindungsstraßen befördern täglich rund 850.000 Personen in die Innenstadt, in der Regel ohne Engpässe.

Das ausgefeilte Verkehrssystem bietet den in Chicago Beschäftigten nahezu unbegrenzte Möglichkeiten bei der Wahl ihres Wohnsitzes, sei es das moderne Einfamilienhaus oder die elegante Villa in einer der 263 angrenzenden Gemeinden. Die Distanz von der Innenstadt zum Flughafen O'Hare zum Beispiel schafft man in 35 Minuten zu einem Fahrpreis von $1,50. Ähnlich günstige Verbindungen bietet der Midway Airport.

Überraschungen im Zuge der Stadtentwicklung

Die Stadtplaner und Immobilien-Fachleute prognostizierten zwar einige der zu erwartenden Entwicklungen, etwa die Zunahme der Bürofläche im West Loop in der Nähe der Bahnstationen für Pendler. Was sie aber nicht voraussehen konnten, ist, daß die Innenstadt um das Vierfache wachsen und ihre Qualität völlig verändern würde.

Das alte Industriegebiet hinter dem Merchandise Mart wurde plötzlich zum "River North" - ein Paradies für 75 Kunstgalerien mit attraktiven antiken Interieur. Dann zogen namhafte Restaurants und Nachtclubs zu. Jede Nacht

600		700	
601	Mississippi	701	North Dakota
602	Arizona	702	Las Vegas (NV)
603	Concord (NH)	703	Roanoke (VA)
604	British Columbia	704	Charlotte (NC)
605	South Dakota	705	North Bay (ON)
606	Covington (KY)	706	Athens (GA)
607	Binghamton (NY)	707	Santa Rosa (CA)
608	Madison (WI)	708	Chicago Suburbs
609	Atlantic City (NJ)	709	Newfoundland
610		710	
611		711	
612	Minneapolis (MN)	712	Sioux City (IA)
613	Ottawa (ON)	713	Houston (TX)
614	Columbus (OH)	714	Anaheim (CA)
615	Nashville (TN)	715	Eau Claire (WI)
616	Grand Rapids (MI)	716	Buffalo (NY)
617	Boston (MA)	717	Harrisburg (PA)
618	Centralia (IL)	718	Brooklyn, Queens (NY)
619	San Diego (CA)	719	Pueblo (CO)
620		720	
800		900	
801	Utah	901	Memphis (TN)
802	Vermont	902	Nova Scotia
803	South Carolina	903	Tyler (TX)
804	Richmond (VA)	904	Jacksonville (FL)
805	Bakersfield (CA)	905	
806	Amarillo (TX)	906	Escanaba (MI)
807	Thunderbay (ON)	907	Alaska
808	Hawaii	908	Trenton (NJ)
809	Bermuda, Caribbean	909	San Bernadino (CA)
810	Detroit Suburbs	910	
811		911	EMERGENCY
812	Evansville (IN)	912	Savannah (GA)
813	Ft. Myers (FL)	913	Topeka (KS)
814	Altoona (PA)	914	White Plains (NY)
815	Morris (IL)	915	Abilene (TX)
816	Kansas City (MO)	916	Sacramento (CA)
817	Ft. Worth (TX)	917	
818	Pasadena (CA)	918	Tulsa (OK)
819	Sherbrooke (QE), NW Terr.	919	Raleigh (NC)
820		920	

Local information usually available through **411**, long distance information by dialling the respective area code, then 555-1212. Örtliche Telefonnummern sind über **411** zu erfahren, Telefonnummern für Ferngespräche erfragt man durch die entsprechende Vorwahl und dann 555-1212.

911 is the EMERGENCY Number in most areas. **911** wird in groessten Teilen USA als NOTRUF gewaehlt.

cated their new headquarters into the center of Chicago, the Loop.

"We deliberated for a long time whether we should move into the city or relocate to the suburbs. We finally decided for the city because everything is conveniently located and can be reached either by foot or with a short cab ride," said Luther C. McKinney, Senior Vice President of Quaker Oats Company.

The question of transportation also played an important part. Chicago's highway system, its commuter railway system and the expressways transport daily close to 850,000 commuters into the Loop and, as a rule, the transportation system functions smoothly.

The elaborate transportation system offers those who work in Chicago an almost unlimited possibility in the choice of their residents, be it the modern one-family home or an elegant mansion in one of the 263 outlying communities. And, as a rule, it takes only 35 minutes by train to get from O'Hare Airport to the Loop for a mere $1.50. The access from Midway Airport is similarly convenient.

Pleasant Surprises during City Planning

Although city planners and real estate experts predicted some of the developments expected, as, for instance, an erobern Tausende von Kongreßteilnehmern, Vorstadtbewohnern und Touristen die Strassen von River North aufs Neue.

Da zählt kaum eine Stunde Warten auf einen Tisch im "Scoozi!", einem italienischen Restaurant, das von einem der erfolgreichsten Chicagoer Restaurateure, Rich Melman, in einer alten Werkstatt eingerichtet wurde.

State Street war eine weitere Überraschung. Nach dem Auszug von vier alten Kaufhäusern entwickelt sich die Straße nun sehr zu ihrem Vorteil. An einem Ende steht nun die neue Bibliothek "Harold Washington Library", nicht weit von den sich ständig ausbreitenden Universitäten DePaul und Roosevelt sowie dem Columbia College. Weiter nördlich investierte Marshall Field's $110 Millionen in eine neue Kaufhaus-Konstruktion. Gegenüber soll auf einer großen Freifläche nach den Plänen des gebürtigen Deutschen Helmut Jahn ein neues Büro- und Einzelhandelszentrum gebaut werden.

Dann ist da die Wabash-Avenue, eine belebte Einkaufsstraße, durch die Chicagos berühmte Hochbahn läuft. Die Anlage steht heute unter Denkmalschutz.

Qualität ist Trumpf

Als die Ford Motor Firma $250 Millionen in die Modernisierung ihrer Montagehallen in Chicago investierte, wurden höhere Aufwendungen in Kauf genommen, damit die Montagearbeiter die Wagentüren vor dem Lackieren anbringen, um sie danach wieder abzumontieren, so daß die Monteure zu den Armaturenbrettern und Sitzen leichteren Zugang haben.

GERMAN-AMERICAN COMMERCE AND INDUSTRY

increase in office space in the west Loop near the commuter train stations, but what they could not predict was that the Loop would grow four times as much and totally change its value.

The old industrial section behind the Merchandise Mart suddenly turned into a paradise for 75 art galleries with attractive and antique interiors, an area known as "River North." They were followed by renowned restaurants and night clubs. Every night thousands of convention visitors, suburbanites and tourists conquer the streets of the River North anew.

Here it does not really matter, if you have to wait one hour for a table at "Scoozis," an Italian restaurant which was opened in an old workshop by one of Chicago's most successful restaurant owners, Rich Melman. State Street was another surprise. After four old department stores closed their doors or moved away, the street experienced a most favorable transformation. At one end is our new library, the Harold Washington Library. The library is not far from the ever expanding DePaul and Roosevelt Universities as well as Columbia College. A little further north is Marshall Field's, which invested $110 million in reconstructing its new department store. Across the street from Marshall Field's on a large open space German-born

"Das ist nur vernünftig", erklärt Frank Stafford, Leiter der Qualitätskontrolle, "denn wenn die Monteure leichteres Arbeiten haben, wird das Produkt besser."

Während das Montageband die Wagen langsam vorwärtsbewegt, messen und notieren die Mitarbeiter Toleranzen, überwachen die Roboter und überlegen sich mögliche Verbesserungen in der Montage. Die schlagen sie dann bei den wöchentlichen Gesprächsrunden vor, die speziell als Forum für den Meinungsaustausch eingerichtet wurden. Wenn ein Mangel entdeckt wird, halten die Arbeiter das ganze Montageband an - den Fehler lassen sie nicht durch.

Solche Eigenverantwortlichkeit der Mitarbeiter hat inzwischen bei vielen Unternehmen in allen Teilen des Landes hohe Priorität. Immer mehr Unternehmen legen besonderes Augenmerk auf Qualität als den wichtigsten Faktor für den Markterfolg.

Ein Vorreiter der Qualitätssicherung war die Firma Motorola in Schaumburg. Das Unternehmen richtete schon in den frühen achtziger Jahren weltweit Qualitätsprüfungen ein und machte Null-Fehler-Vorgaben, die kaum erfüllbar schienen. Seitdem hat das Qualitätssicherungsprogramm zu Einsparungen von $500 Millionen geführt, es wurde 1988 mit dem Malcolm Baldridge National Quality Award ausgezeichnet. "Man muß die Ziele hoch stecken", meint Richard C. Buetow, Vice President und im Vorstand zuständig für Qualitätskontrolle. "Es reicht nicht, 10% oder 15% Qualitätsverbesserung vorzugeben und die dann groß zu feiern. Man muß 10mal und

Harold Washington Library
— *Stadtbibliothek*

State Street with Marshall Field's Clock
Treffpunkt auf der State Street – die Uhr von Marshall Field's

Multi-Color Printing - The Irving Press - *Electronic Publishing*

Co-owners Kurt Blumenthal and Gerald "Jerry" Gaul understand that when it comes to building a commercial printing business, providing a variety of services is essential.

With a complete production system in-house, The Irving Press offers type and art, film work, printing, bindery and even fulfillment all under one roof. Their impressive list of equipment includes Heidelberg and Man Roland presses, G & K folders, Schneider cutters and everything else they need to produce high-quality sheet fed printing, including the latest in state-of-the-art electronic publishing capability.

Kurt and Jerry have taken the company from a small, storefront print shop, which was started by Kurt's father in 1918, to a busy, multi-color printing and finishing facility, now located in Elk Grove Village. The original shop was on Irving Park Road, in a picturesque German-American neighborhood on Chicago's northwest side.

The two-shift operation employs thirty-five people, most having worked there between 10 to 15 years. Despite being in a volatile industry, they've never had to lay anyone off.

Tucked away in Kurt's office is an old ledger used by his father. In beautiful handwriting it lists some of the firm's earliest accounts, including a 40-cent job business cards and $1.25 for handbills. They've come a long way since those modest beginnings, but the same old-world craftsmanship and personal attention that have always been Irving's hallmark remain unchanged.

Kurt Blumenthal und Gerald "Jerry" Gaul, die beiden Eigentümer von Irving Press, wissen, daß anhaltender Erfolg im Druckereigeschäft ein breitgefächtertes Serviceangebot voraussetzt.

Mit einem kompletten firmeneigenen Produktionssystem bietet Irving Press Setzen und Grafik, Filmbearbeitung, Druck, Buchbinderei und sogar Anfragenerfüllung unter einem Dach. Die eindrucksvolle Liste der Produktionsmaschinen umfaßt Heidelberg und MAN Roland Pressen, G & K Faltmaschinen, Schneider Cutters und alles, was zur Produktion von hochwertigem Bogendruck erforderlich ist, einschließlich modernster elektronischer Verlags-Kapazitäten.

Von einer kleinen Druckerei, die Kurts Vater 1918 gründete, hat sich die Firma unter der Leitung von Kurt und Jerry zu einer vielbeschäftigten Mehrfarbendruck- und Zurichtanlage mit heutigem Sitz in Elk Grove Village entwickelt. Die ursprüngliche Druckerei befand sich in der Irving Park Road in einem malerischen deutsch-amerikanischen Viertel im nordwestlichen Teil von Chicago.

Die Firma arbeitet im Zweischichtbetrieb und beschäftigt 35 Fachkräfte, von denen die Mehrzahl bereits 10 bis 15 Jahre bei der Firma arbeiten. Obwohl die Druckereibranche starken Konjunkturschwankungen unterliegt, konnte Irving Press bisher jegliche Personalfreisetzungen vermeiden.

In Kurts Büro ist ein altes Hauptbuch seines Vaters aufbewahrt. In wunderschöner Handschrift sind einige der ersten Konten aufgelistet, einschließlich eines 40 Cent-Auftrags für Visitenkarten und $1,25 für Flugblätter. Seit diesen bescheidenen Anfängen hat es die Firma weit gebracht. Unverändert blieben jedoch die Handwerkskunst der alten Welt und die persönliche Bedienung, für die Irving von Anfang an bekannt war.

Checking another quality press sheet.

Serving Chicagoland

TIP

for over 75 Years

Set-up on a high speed folder.

2530 United Lane / Elk Grove Village, IL 60007 / Phone: 708-595-6650 / Fax: 595-6610

Weights & Measures

AVOIRDUPOIS WEIGHT

27 11/32 grains	1 dram
16 drams	1 ounce
16 ounces	1 pound
25 pounds	1 quarter
4 quarters	1cwt
2,000 pounds	1 short ton
2,240 pounds	1 long ton

CUBIC MEASURE

1,728 cubic inches	1 cubic foot
27 cubic feet	1 cubic yard
128 cubic feet	1 cord (wood)
40 cubic feet	1 ton (shipping)
2,150.42 cubic inches	1 standard bu
231 cubic inches	1 U.S. standard gal
1 cubic foot	about 4/5 of a bushel

DRY MEASURE

2 pints	1 quart
8 quarts	1 peck
4 pecks	1 bushel
36 bushels	1 chaldron

LIQUID MEASURE

4 gills	1 pint
2 pints	1 quart
4 quarts	1 gallon
31* gallons	1 barrel
2 barrels	1 hogshead

LONG MEASURE

12 inches	1 foot
3 feet	1 yard
5* yards	1 rod
40 rods	1 furlong
8 furlongs	1 sta mile
3 miles	1 league

MARINERS' MEASURE

6 feet	1 fathom
120 fathoms	1 cable length
7* cable lengths	1 mile
5,280 feet	1 statute mile
6,080.2 feet	1 nautical mile

SQUARE MEASURE

144 sq inches	1 sq fr
9 sq ft	1 sq yard
30* sq yards	1 sq rod
40 sq rods	1 rood
4 roods	1 acre
640 acres	1 sq mile
36 sq miles	1 township

Source: *Sprint Telephone Directory*

METRIC EQUIVALENTS

Linear Measure

1 centimeter	0.3937 inches
1 inch	2.54 centimeters
1 decimeter	3.937 in...0.328 foot
1 foot	3.048 decimeters
1 meter	39.37 in....1.0936 yds
1 yard	0.9144 meter
1 dekameter	1.9884 rods
1 rod	0.5029 dekameter
1 kilometer	0.621 mile
1 mile	1.609 kilometers

Square Measure

1 square centimeter	0.1150 sq inches
1 square inch	6.452 square centimeters
1 square decimeter	0.1076 square foot
1 square foot	9.2903 square dec
1 square meter	1.196 square yds
1 square yard	0.8351 square meter
1 acre	160 square rods
1 square rod	0.00625 acre
1 hectare	2.47 acres
1 acre	0.4047 hectare
1 square kilometer	0.386 sq mile
1 square mile	2.59 sq kilometers

Measure of Volume

1 cubic centimeter	0.061 cu inch
1 cubic inch	16.39 cubic cent
1 cubic docimotor	0.0353 cubic foot
1 cubic foot	28.317 cubic dec
1 cubic meter	1.308 cubic yards
1 cubic yard	0.7646 cubic meter
1 liter	0.908 qt dry...1.0567 qts liq
1 quart dry	1.101 liters
1 quart liquid	0.9463 liter
1 dekaliter	2.6417 gals
1 gallon	0.3785 dekaliter
1 hektoliter	2.8375 bushels
1 bushel	0.3524 hekoliter

Weights

1 gram	0.3527 ounce
1 ounce	28.35 grams
1 kilogram	2.2046 pounds
1 pound	0.4536 kilogram
1 metric ton	0.98421 English ton
1 English ton	1.016 metric ton

Approximate Metric Equivalents

1 decimeter	4 inches
1 liter	1.06 quarts liquid, 0.9 qts dry
1 meter	1.1 yards
1 kilometer	5/8 of a mile
1 hektoliter	2 5/8 bushels
1 hectare	2* acres
1 kilogram	2 1/5 pounds
1 stere, or cubic meter	˜ of a cord
1 metric ton	2,204.6 pounds

---

architect Helmut Jahn plans to construct a new office and retail center.

And then there is Wabash Avenue, a busy shopping street, above which runs Chicago's famous elevated train, the "L." This structure has been declared a landmark.

Quality is Top Priority

When Ford Motor Co. invested $250 million in modernizing its assembly plant in Chicago, they put up with higher costs, so that the car doors could be mounted by the workers before being painted, only to be taken off again afterwards, so that the engineers had easy access to dashboards and seats. "This was the only reasonable thing to do," said Frank Stafford, Manager of Quality Control, "because if we make things easier for the engineers, we will have a better product."

While the assembly line slowly moves the cars along, the workers measure and record tolerances, monitor the robots and try to come up with improvements for the assembly. Ideas for improvements are then submitted during weekly meetings that are scheduled as a special forum to exchange ideas and suggestions. If an error is detected, the workers stop the entire assembly operation, because they don't let any errors go through.

Many companies around the country are now placing high

---

dann noch einmal 10mal bessere Qualität anstreben - dann kommt's hin."

Hunderte von Herstellern gehen inzwischen diesen Weg. Fred Steingraber, Chairman und Chief Executive Officer des Beratungsunternehmens A.T. Kearney, Inc., hält 'Lorbeeren' dennoch für verfrüht: "Die Unternehmen müssen lernen, daß es nicht damit getan ist, festgelegte Ziele zu erreichen. Wer Wettbewerbsvorteile erzielen will, muß das japanische Konzept des 'kaizen' (kontinuierliche Verbesserung) verfolgen und zur Kenntnis nehmen, daß ständiger Wandel in Zukunft unser Leben weit mehr als bisher bestimmen wird."

Architektur: "Keine mickrigen Pläne!"

Das abwechslungsreiche Innenstadtbild ergibt sich zum einen aus dem Alter der Stadt und zum anderen aus den neuen Flächennutzungsplänen, die auf Straßenniveau größere Annehmlichkeiten wie Einkaufszeilen, Plätze, Skulpturen oder Grünanlagen am Flußufer vorsehen, und die Bautätigkeit dafür in den Untergrund ausweiten. Anstatt Bürogebäude von Geschäfts- und Vergnügungszonen oder Wohngegenden zu trennen, fördert das Stadtbauamt bewußt eine Mischung aus allem.

Chicagos Tradition in großzügiger Stadtplanung geht auf das Jahr 1909 zurück. Damals beauftragte der Commercial Club of Chicago den Architekten Daniel Burnham mit der Erstellung einer Gesamtkonzeption für die Stadtplanung. "Denkt großzügig!", notierte Burnham seinerzeit, "denn mickrige Pläne lassen die Leute kalt." Er folgte seinem eigenen Rat und entwarf

priority on responsible workers. More and more businesses are turning their attention to quality as the most important factor for market success.

A leader in quality assurance is Motorola in Schaumburg. The company introduced already in the early eighties worldwide quality inspections and set zero-mistake standards that were almost impossible to live up to. Since that time, the quality assurance program led to a saving of $500 million and was awarded the Malcolm Baldridge National Quality Award in 1988. "One has to set high goals," says Richard D. Buetow, Vice President and member of the Board, who is responsible for quality control. "It is not enough to strive for a 10% or 15% quality improvement and then celebrate big, when it has been reached. You must strive for 10 times that and again 10 times better quality and then you will succeed."

Hundreds of manufacturers are by now using this approach. Fred Steingraber, Chairman and Chief Executive Officer of the consulting firm A.T.Kearney, Inc., believes that it is not enough to rest on one's laurels: "Companies must learn to accept that to reach one's goals is simply not sufficient. If you want to be competitive then you must pursue the Japanese concept of 'kaizen' (continuous improvements) and realize that perpetual changes will determine our life in the future much more than ever.

ein großartiges Muster von Boulevards und Parkanlagen mit Museen, Strandpromenaden und Hafenanlagen entlang der 4,5 Kilometer langen Seefront. Chicago hat diesen Rat nicht vergessen und profitiert heute jeden Sommer davon, wenn Millionen von Menschen am Seeufer flanieren oder die Konzerte und Festivals im Grant Park besuchen.

'Große' Pläne haben Chicago von Anfang an gestaltet. In Chicago wurden die ersten Wolkenkratzer des Landes errichtet, hier steht das einst größte Gebäude der Welt (der Merchandise Mart, heute zweitgrößtes Gebäude nach dem Pentagon). Und auch einige der ausgefallensten und umstrittensten Werke zeitgenössischer Architektur befinden sich hier.

Technologie verändert die Stadt

Nur eines, Technologie nämlich, gestaltet die Stadt heute noch mehr als die Architekten. Ihre Spuren finden sich überall, auch an ungewöhnlichen Plätzen wie etwa die alten Frachttunnel unter der Innenstadt, die jetzt mit Glasfaserkabel zur Datenübertragung mit Lichtgeschwindigkeit ausgestattet sind. Unerwartet für alle, füllten sich diese Tunnel im Jahre 1992 durch einen Einbruch unter dem Chicago River, und man hatte die erste "Unterflutung" einer Stadt in der Geschichte. Tagelang war die ganze Innenstadt ohne Strom, manche Büros waren für zwei Wochen geschlossen. In einer technischen Meisterleistung gelang es jedoch, das Tunnelsystem wieder trocken zu legen.

Die meisten der 4.300 Fabriken der Stadt sind in älteren Backsteingebäuden untergebracht, aber hinter den altehr —

Best telephone and fax times between Illinois and Germany

Günstigste Telefon- und Faxzeiten zwischen Illinois und Deutschland

6 pm (18:00) - 7 am (7:00)	LOW/guenstig,	Minute	$ 1.15/0.69
7 am (7:00) - 1 pm (13:00)	HIGH/teuer,	"	$ 1.77/1.09
1 pm (13:00) - 6 pm (18:00)	MEDIUM/OK	"	$ 1.47/0.84

CHICAGO (CST or CDT) times/Zeiten

Source/Quelle: **AT&T**

Dollar value at the end of each year

Dollarwert am Ende jeden Jahres

	1983	1984	1985	1986	1987	1988	1989	1990	1991	1992	1993
DM	2,726	3,152	2,447	1,926	1,586	1,772	1,690	1,497	1,519	1,617	1,714
SF	2,180	2,609	2,058	1,613	1,294	1,501	1,540	1,276	1,350	1,465	1,473
AS	19,24	22,10	17,22	13,55	11,18	12,47	11,90	10,53	10,69	11,38	12,05

DM	(Deutsche Mark)	German Marks
SF	(Schweizer Franken)	Swiss Francs
AS	(Oesterreicher Schilling)	Austrian Shillings

Source/Quelle: **Ruesch International**

Architecture: "No little plans!"

The diversified image of downtown Chicago is the result of a combination of age of the city and its new landscaping projects, because all amenities of importance, such as shopping strips, public squares, sculptures and parks are located on street level at the river's edge. Rather than separating office buildings from stores and entertainment or residential areas, the Municipal Office for City Planning consciously promotes a mixture of all these elements.

Chicago's tradition of generous city planning goes back to 1909. At that time the Commercial Club of Chicago commissioned architect Daniel Burnham to come up with an overall concept for the planning of the city. Burnham said: "Make no little plans, they have no magic to stir men's blood ..." He followed his own advice and drafted a grandiose design of boulevards and parks, lakefront promenades, beaches and harbors along the 2.8-mile lakefront. Chicago never forgot his advice and still benefits from it today every summer when millions of people stroll along the beach or enjoy the concerts and festivals in Grant Park.

'Big' plans is what created Chicago from the beginning. The first skyscrapers of the country were erected in Chicago. Chicago has what was once the largest building in the world, the Merchandise Mart. Today it is the second largest, the largest being the Pentagon. Chicago also has some of the more outrageous and controversial creations of contemporary architecture.

Changes through Technology

Only one other factor changes the city today more than architecture, and that is technology. Its traces are found everywhere, even in the most unusual places, such as the freight tunnels under the Loop where we find fiber optic cables for the transfer of data at the speed of light. In 1992, these tunnels filled up with water after a section of the Chicago river foundation collapsed, and for the first time in history a city was flooded underneath the ground level. For days the entire Loop was without electricity; some offices stayed closed for two weeks. However, in an amazing technological feat, the city managed to dry up the entire tunnel system.

The majority of the city's 4,300 factories are housed in older brick buildings; however, behind these old facades we oftentimes find the most modern manufacturing facilities — as, for example, the $25 million computerized assembly line system which the mail-order house Spiegel had installed in its 6-floor high distribution center. Spiegel, by the way, is a subsidiary of the German mail-order house Otto Versand AG.

würdigen Fassaden verbergen sich oft modernste Fertigungsanlagen - wie zum Beispiel die $25 Millionen teure computerisierte Fließbandanlage, die Versandhaus Spiegel in seinem sechs Stockwerke hohen Vetriebszentrum installiert hat. Spiegel ist übrigens eine Tochterfirma der deutschen Otto-Versand AG.

Oder in dem weitläufigen Gebäude aus dem Jahre 1924, in dem die Ford Motor Co. einst das legendäre Modell T baute und wo jetzt 3.000 Menschen und zahlreiche Roboter die Modelle "Ford Taurus" und "Mercury Sable" zusammenschweißen, lackieren, montieren und testen.

Technologie verändert auch das Gesicht des 100 Jahre alten Distrikts in der Nähe des Illinois Medical Center und der University of Illinois in Chicago. Westlich der Innenstadt, in Backsteinreihenhäusern und farbenfrohen viktorianischen Fachwerkhäusern hat sich der Chicago Technology Park etabliert, der kleinere Unternehmen aus den Bereichen Biotechnologie, Pharma-Forschung und Telekommunikation beherbergt. Weitere Anlagen sind ständig im Entstehen.

Ein zweiter Forschungspark in Evanston - ein Joint Venture dieser Vorstadt und der Northwestern University - wird von 30 Unternehmen der Region und dem staatlich geförderten Basic Industry Research Lab. entwickelt, um Grundlagenforschung für bessere Materialien und Herstellverfahren zu betreiben.

Beide Parks erwarten, daß aus ihrer Verbindung zu den großen Universitäten wissenschaftliche Zentren entstehen, ähnlich denen, die bereits im DuPage County existieren, wo es zwischen dem Argonne National Laboratory und dem Fermi National Accelerator Lab zahlreiche Forschungs- und Entwicklungseinrichtungen von Unternehmen gibt. Oder im Lake County, dem Standort der Großkonzerne Abbott Labs und Baxter International sowie rund 400 kleinerer Unternehmen aus dem medizinischen und dem High-Tech-Bereich.

Wie ein ertragskräftiger Investmentfonds

Das kräftige Wachstum der Technologie-Unternehmen bedeutet eine neue Dimension der Chicagoer Wirtschaft. Es verleiht der ohnehin bereits stark diversifizierten Wirtschaftsstruktur der Stadt noch mehr Tiefe. Seit den achtziger Jahren weiß man, daß die Wirtschaft auf lokaler oder regionaler Ebene ähnlich einem Investmentfonds funktioniert: viele verschiedene Vermögen fließen zusammen und produzieren stetiges, langfristiges Wachstum. Dabei können Regionen mit schmaler wirtschaftlicher Basis sehr rasch erstarken, aber genauso schnell auch wieder in den Hintergrund treten.

Das ist in Chicago kaum zu befürchten. Hier stehen 1,5 Millionen Arbeitsplätze im Dienstleistungsbereich und der herstellenden Industrie etwa 200.000 Arbeitsplätze im Groß- und Einzelhandel, im Transportwesen, im Finanzdienstleistungs- und im Immobilienbereich gegenüber. Jeder Sektor fördert die anderen und wächst zugleich mit ihnen. So kommen durch Innovation in der Hochtechnologie und bei Finanzdienstleistungen Einnahmen von jährlich $6 Milliarden aus dem Fremdenverkehr und Beschäftigung von

World Trade Centre in the Middle of downtown Chicago

GERMAN-AMERICAN COMMERCE AND INDUSTRY

German American Companies in Chicagoland

Thyssen Specialty Steels

Mercedes Benz Parts Distribution

Swiss-owned Buss America (Machine Sales)

Or in the spacious building from 1924, where Ford Motor Co. once built the legendary Model T and where today 3,000 workers and numerous robots assemble the Models "Ford Taurus" and "Mercury Sable," and where they paint them, mount them and test them.

Technology also changed the face of the 100-year old neighborhood near the Illinois Medical Center and the University of Illinois in Chicago. West of the Loop, in brick townhouses and colorful Victorian framework houses we find the Chicago Technology Park, home of small businesses in biotechnology, pharmaceutical research and telecommunications. Other new facilities are being added every day.

A second research park located in Evanston is a joint venture between the suburb and Northwestern University. 30 local businesses and the State-supported Basic Industry Research Lab are constructing the park to allow research and development of improved material and manufacturing processes.

Both parks hope that their association with large universities will eventually turn their facilities into scientific centers not unlike those that already exist in DuPage County, where Argonne National Laboratory and Fermi National Accelerator Laboratory in cooperation with the business community have developed

125.000 Arbeitern in der Bauindustrie zustande. Chicagos Museen und Künstler steuern weitere $600 Millionen jährlich zum Haushalt der Stadt bei.

"Die herstellende Industrie spielt nach wie vor eine Schlüsselrolle, aber wir haben auch Dienstleistungsunternehmen, die in ihren Geschäftsfeldern weltweit führend sind", erklärt Neil Springer, Chief Executive Officer des LKW-Herstellers "Navistar", ehemals International Harvester, "und das trägt ganz erheblich zur Wirtschaftskraft der Stadt bei."

Chicagos geografische Lage an einem der wichtigsten Verkehrsknotenpunkte des Landes spielt ebenfalls eine Rolle. Doch ebenso entscheidend sind zum einen die sehr aktive Unternehmerschaft der Stadt und zum anderen die Einwandererwellen, die in die Region schwappten und noch jede industrielle Entwicklung gemeistert haben. Sie brachten Unternehmerpersönlichkeiten mit, die immer wieder die nächsthöhere Stufe erklommen haben. Die Unternehmen sind heute in allen Bereichen involviert, von der Schulreform bis zur festen Verankerung der Software-Branche in der Region, die inzwischen 1.000 Unternehmen umfaßt. Und das Arbeitskräftepotential der Einwanderer könnte sich bei zunehmend engen Arbeitsmärkten als ein entscheidender Vorteil erweisen.

Flughafen und Messegelände

Chicago geht mit großen Schritten in die Zukunft und wird auf diesem Weg nicht haltmachen. Direkt am Ufer des Lake Michigan liegt das Messe-Zentrum McCormick Place, wo jährlich ca. 150

several Research and Development facilities. Lake County is the site of such large medical and high-tech corporate groups as Abbot Laboratories and Baxter International as well as close to 400 smaller businesses.

Similar to a Profitable Investment Fund

The high growth rate of technology businesses adds a new dimension to Chicago's economy. It adds more depth to an already existing diversified economic structure. Since the eighties we know that our local and regional economy functions like an investment fund: many different assets pool together and produce continuous, long-term growth. This allows a region with a low economic profile to grow rapidly, but it could also recede into the background just as rapidly.

We do not expect this to happen in Chicago. While 1.5 million jobs are available in the service industry and the manufacturing industry, there are about 200,000 work places in the wholesale and retail business, transportation, financial services and real estate. Each is growing through the support of the other. Income of $6 billion is generated annually through innovations in high technology and financial services, the tourism industry and the employment of 125.000 workers in the construction

große Wirtschaftsmessen stattfinden: die "National Houseware Show", die "Hardware Show" und die "Machine Tool Builders Show" und viele andere mehr. McCormick Place besteht aus drei riesigen Hallen. Außerdem gibt es noch die Hallen des O'Hare Expo Center und die des Merchandise Mart. Damit verfügt Chicago über die größte Ausstellungskapazität des ganzen Kontinents.

Es wurden Pläne für einen Erweiterungsbau von McCormick Place bekanntgegeben: die Arbeiten sollen 1994 beginnen und 1995 abgeschlossen sein. Damit wird die Kapazität des Zentrums verdoppelt.

Chicagos internationaler Flughafen O'Hare ist der geschäftigste der Welt, mit mehr als 59 Millionen Fluggästen und 1,07 Mio Tonnen Frachtgut jährlich; etwa 180.000 Arbeitsplätze sind von O'Hare abhängig.

Wesentlich kleiner ist der Midway Airport, der zweite und nur für Inlandsflüge genutzte Flughafen, mit mehr als 7,2 Millionen Fluggästen im Jahr. Insgesamt waren es im Jahr 1991 mehr als 1 Million Landungen. Daneben gibt es mit Meigs Field noch einen kleinen Flughafen für Privatfluzeuge direkt in der Stadt, am Ufer des Sees.

Chicago ist aber auch eine Hafenstadt. Über den St.Lorenz-Strom und die Großen Seen hat die Stadt Verbindung zum Atlantik, ausgelegt sogar für Hochseeschiffe, und über den Illinois River und den anschließenden Wasserweg Missisippi-Missouri-Ohio auch zum Golf von Mexiko.

Es ist daher nicht erstaunlich, daß so viele Transportunternehmen ihren Sitz in Chicago haben, darunter auch die Filialen vieler deutscher Speditionen.

Deutsch-Amerikanische Firmen in Chicagoland

TransTech America, Transfer Printing

Grohe Faucet Assembly & Distribution

Spiegel Catalog Sales

The new International Terminal at Chicago's O'Hare Airport

industry. Chicago museums and artists add another $600 million to the city's budget.

Neil Springer, Chief Executive Officer of heavy-duty truck manufacturer "Navistar," the former International Harvester, adds that "the manufacturing industry still plays a key role, but we also have service companies that are world leaders in their industry and are contributing to the strength of the city's business community.

Chicago's geographical location at one of the largest transportation centers in the country plays an equally important role. Another aspect that helped decide the fate of the city was its very active business community on the one hand and on the other hand the waves of immigrants that swept over the region and yet mastered any and all new industrial developments. The immigrants brought their enterprising spirits, escalating each time to the next higher level. Business today is involved in all areas, from school reforms to the solid establishment of the software industry in the region, comprising in the meantime 1,000 companies. With a changing job market, the work force potential of the immigrants may turn out to be a decisive advantage for the city.

Airports and Convention Center

With giant steps Chicago is on its way into the future and

Kongresshauptstadt der Welt

1993 war Chicago dank einer bemerkenswerten Unternehmerinitiative Veranstaltungsort des bislang größten Architekten- und Designerkongresses. Zwei Sommer zuvor -die Stadt stand in einem heftigen Wettbewerb mit Peking und Paris um den 1993er Kongreß des Internationalen Architektenverbandes- veranstalteten Vertreter des Chicagoer Convention & Tourism Bureau und der Merchandise Mart einen Charterflug für Architekten aus 90 Ländern. Sie nutzten die Gelegenheit und verteilten eine Sonderausgabe des italienischen Design-Magazins "Abitare", die auf 138 Seiten Architektur, Bauvorhaben und Stadtteil- ansichten von Chicago präsentierte.

Zurück am Boden entschieden sich die Architekten für Chicagos McCormick Place als Veranstaltungsort und terminierten die Tagung zeitgleich mit dem nationalen Kongreß des American Institutes of Architects und der NEOCON-Möbelmesse in The Merchandise Mart.

Als Tagungsort für große und kleine Veranstaltungen hat Chicago seit einem Jahrhundert Tradition. Mit zunehmendem Wettbewerb durch andere Tagungsorte hat die Stadt ihre Bemühungen um einen vorderen Platz als internationale Kongreßstadt verstärkt. Geplante bzw. im Bau befindliche Projekte sind:

• Erweiterung von McCormick Place: die für Jahre weitgehend ausgebuchte Ausstellungsfläche von mehr als 1,3 Mio m² wird um fast 1,7 Mio m² am südlichen Lake Shore Drive erweitert.

• International Terminal O'Hare: der neue Terminal letzter Teil der Erweiterung und Modernisierung des Flugha-

nothing can stop it. Chicago's Convention Center, McCormick Place, located directly at the shores of Lake Michigan, is the site of almost 150 trade shows and conventions annually. Its three gigantic halls accommodate such shows as the National Houseware Show, the Hardware Show and the Machine Tool Builders Show and many more. In addition to McCormick Place we also have the O'Hare Expo Center near O'Hare and the Merchandise Mart directly in the Loop. This gives Chicago the largest exhibition space on the entire continent.

Plans to expand McCormick Place have been announced, and the work is scheduled to start in 1994 and scheduled to be completed in 1995. This will double the center's capacity.

Chicago's International Airport O'Hare is indeed the busiest airport in the world with more than 60 million passengers and 1.07 million tons of freight annually and a work force of approximately 180,000 people. Midway Airport is considerably smaller than O'Hare and predominantly used for domestic flights with more than 7.2 million passengers annually. In 1991 it had 1 million arrivals. Additionally, we have Meigs Field, a small airport for private planes in the city at the shores of Lake Michigan and directly next to McCormick Place.

But Chicago also has a harbor. Via the St. Lawrence Seaway

fens, in die insgesamt $2 Mrd fließen- wird 1994 eröffnet. Er soll den rasch zunehmenden Flugverkehr von und nach Europa, Südamerika und Fernost bedienen.

Mit dem neuen Flughafen wurde eine Entwicklungsphase abgeschlossen, die nach dem 2. Weltkrieg begann, als der Trend in die Vorstädte einsetzte. Bis dahin waren die Vorstädte meist reine Wohngebiete gewesen. Doch nach der Eröffnung von O'Hare im Jahre 1962 entstanden Hauptverwaltungen und Forschungseinrichtungen von Unternehmen entlang den fünf Schnellstraßen von Chicago. Jetzt, da der Vorstadtring praktisch ausgereizt ist und die Innenstadt aus allen Nähten platzt, konzentriert sich die Entwicklung auf die angrenzenden Gemeinden.

Kampfgeist

Die Wende vollzieht sich just in dem Moment, da viele Chicagoer Unternehmen sich von ihren wirtschaftlichen Problemen wieder erholen. Viele Unternehmensleitungen -so bei den Großkonzernen Continental Bank, Inland Steel Industries und Sears, Roebuck & Co.- haben in der jüngeren Zeit Umstrukturierungen vorgenommen und ihre Unternehmen wieder flexibler und schlagkräftiger, kurz: wettbewerbsfähiger, gemacht.

"Navistar" zum Beispiel verbuchte in den frühen achtziger Jahren Verluste von $1 Mio täglich. Nach der Sanierung -Neil Springer nennt es "Erkennen der Realitäten"- macht das Unternehmen dank kürzerer Produktentwicklungszyklen und Automatisierung wieder

The McCormick Place expansion is now under construction

GERMAN-AMERICAN COMMERCE AND INDUSTRY

and the Great Lakes the city has access to the Atlantic Ocean and via the Illinois River and the Mississippi-Missouri Ohio seaways also to the Gulf of Mexico.

Therefore it comes as no surprise that so many freight companies have their offices in Chicago, many of them subsidiaries of German freight companies.

Convention Capital of the World

In 1993, thanks to a remarkable enterprising spirit, Chicago became the Convention City for the largest Architectural and Designer Convention. Two summers ago, Chicago was in fierce competition with Peking and Paris for the 1993 Congress of the International Architects Association. The Chicago Convention & Tourism Bureau and the Merchandise Mart organized a charter flight for architects from 90 countries and used the opportunity to distribute a special edition of the Italian Design magazine "Abitare" which presented Chicago's architecture, buildings, and areas on 138 pages.

The architects decided for Chicago's McCormick Place as Convention location and scheduled their Convention at the same time as the National Congress of the American Institutes of Architects and the NEOCON Furniture Fair in the Merchandise Mart.

Gewinne. "Unsere Erfahrungen", erinnert sich Springer,"schafften besseres Verständnis der wirtschaftlichen Logik und entfachten sozusagen unseren Kampfgeist."

Die Erfahrungen der Navistar werden in vielen Bereichen der Wirtschaft gemacht. Und viel von dem Kampfgeist findet sich in Städten wie Chicago, wo die hohe Konzentration von Unternehmen, Kongressen, Ausbildungsstätten und Universitäten die Probleme schneller an die Oberfläche bringt als anderswo. Jeden Tag fliegt die in Chicago ansässige Arthur Andersen Consulting einen ihrer 18.000 Professionals in ihre drei im Großraum Chicago angesiedelten Ausbildungszentren, um sie bei Systemintegration und "Management im Wandel" auf dem Laufenden zu halten. A. George 'Skip' Battle, Managing Partner im Bereich Marktentwicklung, prognostiziert, daß die Nachfrage nach Aus- und Fortbildung von Führungskräften noch zunehmen wird und daß Städte wie Chicago "Treffpunkte für diejenigen sein werden, die dem Wandel die Richtung geben."

Eine postindustrielle Stadt

Wandel ist eine Art Chicagoer Spezialität, seit eine Vorgängerin von Navistar, die Cyrus McCormick, 1847 ihre Nähmaschinenfabrik gründete. Damals war Chicago noch in erster Linie Handelsstadt. Andere Branchen etablierten sich rasch und zogen viele Einwanderer an, wobei die größte Bevölkerungsgruppe unter den Auswanderern die Deutschen waren. Sie fanden Arbeit in den Union Stock Yards, den berühm-

Chicago has a 100-year tradition for big and small conventions. Because of growing competition from other Cities, Chicago intensified its efforts to remain in the forefront as International Convention City. The following projects are planned or are already under construction:

• Expansion of McCormick Place: enlarging the present exhibition space of about 10.3 million square feet by more than 10.7 million square feet

• International Terminal O'Hare: the new terminal, which is the last leg in the expansion and modernization efforts of the airport at a cost of $2 billion. It will serve the rapidly increasing air traffic to and from Europe, South America and the Far East.

The new airport signifies the end of a phase of development that started after World War II, when the trend to expand to the suburbs started. Until then, the suburbs were purely residential areas. After the opening of O'Hare Airport in 1962, corporate headquarters and research facilities opened up along the five Chicago expressways. Now that the Loop is bursting at its seams and the suburbs are fully explored, development concentrates on the adjoining urban communities.

ten Chicagoer Schlachthöfen, in den Stahlwerken, bei der Telefongesellschaft Western Electric, die heute 40.000 Mitarbeiter beschäftigt, und in Tausenden anderer Fabriken, die von der ersten Welle der industriellen Reform in Amerika getragen wurden.

Viele dieser Fabriken gibt es inzwischen nicht mehr, und die Chicagoer fragten sich auf dem Höhepunkt des Exodus, was ihnen in der postindustriellen Ära wohl bleiben werde. Doch dann gestaltete sich diese Ära für Chicago besonders positiv. In der Region haben nach wie vor 43 "Fortune 500"-Unternehmen ihren Firmensitz. Die Zeitschrift "Crain's Chicago Business" machte bei einer Auflistung der größten Unternehmen der Region die Entdeckung, daß zahlreiche Unternehmen der herstellenden Industrie mit Einnahmen über $1 Mrd und 250 aus anderen Bereichen mit Umsätzen von über $50 Mio hier angesiedelt sind.

Seit Jahren befinden sich US-Filialen der Commerzbank, der Dresdner Bank, der Deutschen Bank und der Bayerischen Vereinsbank in der Stadt.

Aufschwung in den angrenzenden Gemeinden

Die zunehmende Beschäftigung in der Innenstadt und den Vororten hat bewirkt, daß sich in den letzten zehn Jahren auch die angrenzenden Gemeinden erholten. Das begann in Near North und Lincoln Park. Als hier dann die Preise für Zweifamilienhäuser und Reihenhäuser stiegen, breitete sich die Erholungswelle in Richtung Norden entlang dem Seeufer, in Richtung Nordwest entlang der Ravenswood-

AIR FRANCE
ASK THE WORLD OF US

The Concorde covers 3,621 miles (5,828 km) to Paris in 3:45 hours.

Air France in Chicago

Air France was the first airline to offer direct flights between Chicago and Paris, inaugurating service in 1953. Today the airline handles more than 100,000 passengers and over 35,000 metric tons of cargo annually at O'Hare International Airport. Chicago outranks all other Air France gateways except New York in cargo carried by the airline in and out of the U.S. Other points served by Air France in the U.S. are Boston, Houston, Los Angeles, Miami, Newark, New York/JFK, San Francisco and Washington.

In peak season, Air France offers daily passenger flights to the Air France hub at Charles de Gaulle Airport in Paris, where Air France connections are available to more than 100 points elsewhere in France and the rest of Europe. The airline also operates frequent all-cargo flights to Charles de Gaulle and Orly airports as well as to Toulouse, Mulhouse and Shannon (Ireland). Aircraft serving the Chicago route include the Boeing 767-300 and 747 all-cargo aircrafts.

Air France employs about 70 staff out of a U.S. total of over 800, with annual payroll and benefits worth over $4 million. In a typical year, the airline spends about $17 million out of a U.S. total budget of almost $250 million, including payroll and benefits, taxes, aviation fuel, supplies and services, sales commissions, flight catering, crew hotels and ground transportation. The airline's Chicago investments include a mammoth cargo warehouse at O'Hare opened in 1992.

AIR FRANCE war die erste Fluggesellschaft, die Direktflüge zwischen Chicago und Paris anbot. Dieser Service wurde 1953 eingeführt. Heutzutage befördert die Fluggesellschaft jährlich mehr als 100,000 Passagiere und über 35,000 Tonnen Frachtgut über den O'Hare Internationalen Flughafen. An Frachtbeförderung in und aus den Vereinigten Staaten übertrifft Chicago alle anderen AIR FRANCE Flughäfen mit Ausnahme von New York. Andere Städte, die von AIR FRANCE in den USA angeflogen werden, sind Boston, Houston, Los Angeles, Miami, Newark, New York/JFK, San Franzisko und Washington.

Während der Hochsaison fliegt AIR FRANCE täglich zum Charles de Gaulle Flughafen, dem Heimatflughafen der Fluglinie in Paris. Dort gibt es AIR FRANCE Verbindungsmöglichkeiten zu mehr als 100 Orten anderswo in Frankreich und dem Rest von Europa. Die Fluggesellschaft bietet auch zahlreiche reine Frachtflüge zu den Flughäfen Charles de Gaulle und Orly, wie auch nach Toulouse, Mulhouse und Shannon (Irland) an. Unter anderen fliegt man Boeing 767-300 und 747 Flugzeuge auf der Strecke von und nach Chicago.

AIR FRANCE hier beschäftigt etwa 70 Personen von einer US Gesamtzahl von über 800, mit einer jährlichen Lohnliste und Versicherungsleistungen (Kosten für Urlaub, Feier- und Krankheitstage) in der Höhe von mehr als 4 Millionen Dollar. In einem Durchschnittsjahr gibt die Fluggesellschaft hier ungefähr 17 Millionen Dollar, von einem US Budget von fast 250 Millionen Dollar, aus. Darin eingeschlossen sind der Gesamtbetrag der Löhne, Versicherungsleistungen, Steuern, Flugzeugtreibstoff, Vorräte und Service, Verkaufsprovisionen, Flugproviant, Hotelzimmer für die Besatzung und Bodenbeförderung. Die Investitionen der Fluggesellschaft in Chicago schließen ein riesiges Lagerhaus in O'Hare ein, welches in 1992 eröffnet wurde.

Air France Cargo warehouse at O'Hare

Express Cargo delivery and pick-up terminal

Fighting Spirit

This change set in just at a time when many Chicago businesses started to recover from their economic slumps. Management in several larger companies, like Continental Bank, Inland Steel Industries and Sears, Roebuck & Co. recently initiated major restructuring programs to become more competitive.

For example, "Navistar" used to post daily losses of $1 million in the early eighties. After they implemented their reorganization — Neil Springer calls it "Recognizing Reality" - the company started to make profit again. Springer recalls: "Our experience helped us to a better understanding of business logic and triggered the fighting spirit in us."

Navistar is not the only one that discovered its fighting spirit. We find it in cities like Chicago where a high concentration of businesses, conventions, educational institutions and universities spot a problem faster than elsewhere. Arthur Andersen Consulting Co., which has its headquarters in Chicago, every day flies at least one of their 18,000 professionals to one of their three training centers in Chicagoland, to keep them up to date as to the latest developments. A. George 'Skip' Battle, Managing Partner for Market Development, forecasts that the demand for higher education and continued education of management and

Hochbahnstrecke, in Richtung West nach University Village hin und nach Süden in die besseren schwarzen Wohngegenden wie South Shore und Gap in Nachbarschaft des Illinois Institute of Technology aus.

Harold Washington, der erste schwarze Bürgermeister der Stadt, spielte eine zentrale Rolle bei der Wiederbelebung der angrenzenden Gemeinden. 1983 als Reformkandidat gewählt, stand Washington zunächst einmal zwei Jahre einen "Verwaltungskrieg" durch, bevor er seine Politik der stärkeren Gemeinden, der Förderung kleinerer Unternehmen, der Bildung von Arbeitsgruppen aus führenden Köpfen der lokalen Wirtschaft, der Verwaltung und der Gemeinden durchsetzen und so die Stadt auf den Weg nach vorne bringen konnte.

Chicagos Sommerfestivals

Chicago hat einen Terminkalender voller Freilicht-Veranstaltungen, die inzwischen aus Chicagos Sommern nicht mehr wegzudenken sind.

Jedes Jahr ist noch mehr los als im Vorjahr. Nach dem Gospelfest und dem Blues-Festival an den ersten beiden Juni-Wochenenden kommt neun Tage lang das Stadtfest "Taste of Chicago". 3 Millionen Menschen werden sich dann an der "Lakefront" bei gutem Essen und Trinken vergnügen. Eine Woche später folgt das "All Star" Baseballspiel im Wrigley Field, dem efeubewachsenen Stadion der Cubs.

Der Sommer klingt aus mit der "Air and Water Show", mit dem Jazz Festival, das Musiker und Fans aus aller Welt

SIEMENS

A Strong Midwest Presence with Worldwide Impact on Healthcare

Developing advanced technology has always been a commitment of Siemens, a corporation with long-established roots in Germany and Europe. This Siemens commitment is carried out in the United States and in the Midwest, at places like Siemens Medical Systems, Inc., Nuclear Medicine Group located in Hoffman Estates, Illinois.

One of over 50 Siemens U.S. factories, this Chicago suburban facility employs over 800 people—people who design and manufacture nuclear medicine and digital angiography systems. The systems built in this midwestern plant are exported throughout the world.

Like other Siemens employees worldwide, we are dedicated to providing advanced technology that improves the quality of life for all.

Siemens Medical Systems, Inc.
2501 North Barrington Road • Hoffman Estates, IL 60195-7372 USA • Tel.: (708) 304-7700

Eine starke Präsenz im Mittleren Westen der USA mit weltweiten Auswirkungen auf das Gesundheitswesen

Die Entwicklung moderner Technologien ist seit jeher eine Verpflichtung von Siemens, einem Unternehmen mit tiefen Wurzeln in Deutschland und Europa. Diese Verpflichtung von Siemens wird auch in den Vereinigten Staaten und im Mittleren Westen realisiert, zum Beispiel bei Siemens Medical Systems, Inc., Nuclear Medicine Group, mit Sitz in Hoffman Estates, Illinois.

Als eines von mehr als 50 Siemens Werken in den USA beschäftigt die in einem Vorort von Chicago gelegene Anlage mehr als 800 Mitarbeiter - Mitarbeiter, die Systeme für die Nuklearmedizin und digitale Angiographie entwickeln und produzieren. Die hier hergestellten Systeme werden in die ganze Welt exportiert.

Zusammen mit den anderen Siemens Mitarbeitern weltweit widmen wir uns der Aufgabe, zukunftsweisende Technologie zur Verbesserung der Lebensqualität aller Menschen zu liefern.

Deutsches Generalkonsulat

Das Generalkonsulat Chicago ist die deutsche Auslandsvertretung im Mittleren Westen der USA. Zu seinem Amtsbezirk gehören neben der Stadt Chicago und dem Bundesstaat Illinois noch die amerikanischen Bundesstaaten Wisconsin, Iowa, Minnesota, Missouri, North und South Dakota, Nebraska und Kansas. Im Amtsbezirk leben rund 35 Millionen Einwohner, von denen etwa 40 % in der letzten Volkszählung angegeben haben, von deutschen Vorfahren abzustammen.

Die 24 Mitarbeiter des Generalkonsulats Chicago, das seit Juli 1993 von Generalkonsulin Dr. Gabriele von Malsen-Tilborch geleitet wird, nehmen alle Aufgaben einer deutschen Auslandsvertretung wahr mit Ausnahme der bilateralen deutsch-amerikanischen politischen Beziehungen, die Aufgabe der in der Hauptstadt Washington gelegenen Deutschen Botschaft sind. Es bleibt aber genug zu tun:

— Die *politische Öffentlichkeitsarbeit* ist eine zentrale Aufgabe des Generalkonsulats. Die Generalkonsulin und ihre Mitarbeiterinnen und Mitarbeiter halten laufend Vorträge vor allen relevanten Gruppen des öffentlichen Lebens im Amtsbezirk.

— Die *kulturpolitische* Zusammenarbeit Deutschlands mit dem amerikanischen Mittleren Westen steht sicherlich im Vordergrund. In enger Zusammenarbeit mit den Goethe-Instituten in Chicago und St. Louis gibt es vielfältige Verbindungen zu Schulen und Universitäten, Museen und Kunstgalerien, deutschen Vereinen und vielen Bürgern, die sich mit Anliegen an das Generalkonsulat wenden.

— Die *Wirtschaft* spielt für die Außenhandelsnation Deutschland auch hier eine besondere Rolle. In Zusammenarbeit mit und ergänzend zu der deutsch-amerikanischen Außenhandelskammer im Mittleren Westen (amerikanisches Kürzel: GACCoM) beobachtet und analysiert das Generalkonsulat wirtschaftliche Trends am Börsenplatz Chicago und in der Region und hält Kontakt zur hiesigen Geschäftswelt.

— Das *Pressereferat* hält ständigen und engen Kontakt zur hiesigen Presse, stellt Deutschland den Medien im Amtsbezirk vor und vermittelt Interessenten aus allen Bereichen Informationen über die aktuelle Lage in Deutschland.

— Das *Konsularreferat* ist für die hier lebenden Deutschen eine Art Einwohnermeldeamt, das Paßanträge bearbeitet. Hinzu kommen Rentenanträge und angesichts unserer historischen Verantwortung die Bearbeitung von Wiedergutmachungsanträgen von Opfern des Nationalsozialismus. Daneben hilft das Konsularreferat in Not geratenen Deutschen. Im Amtsbezirk lebende Ausländer aus Drittländern, die für Deutschland ein Visum benötigen, können dies im Generalkonsulat beantragen.

Mit seiner vielfältigen Tätigkeit dient das Generalkonsulat der Pflege und dem Ausbau der deutsch-amerikanischen Beziehungen.

Das Generalkonsulat befindet sich: 676 North Michigan Avenue, Suite 3200, Chicago, IL 60611 und ist wie folgt zu erreichen: Tel: 312/580-1199, Fax: 312/580-0099.

Chicago Marriott on North Michigan Avenue

Inter-Continental Hotel on the Magnificent Mile

executive personnel will increase, and that cities like Chicago will become the "meeting place for all those who are trendsetters."

A Post-Industrial City

Changing has become a Chicago specialty of sorts ever since Navistar's predecessor, Cyrus McCormick, opened an agricultural (reaper) factory in 1847. At that time, Chicago was mainly a commercial town. Other industries quickly became established here and attracted many immi-grants. The largest group among the immigrants were the Germans. They found work at the famous Union Stockyards, in steel factories, at the tele-phone company, Western Electric, which has 40,000 employees today, and a thousand other factories that arrived on the scene with the first wave of industrial reform in America.

Many of these factories no longer exist and at the peak of this exodus, Chicago asked itself what would remain in the post-industrial era. As it turned out, it would become a very positive era for Chicago. There are still 43 "Fortune 500" companies located in Chicago. Crain's Chicago Business just uncovered numerous manufacturing companies with incomes of over $1 billion and 250 companies from other industries with sales of $50 million.

Four large German banks,

anzieht, und dem "Viva Festival" für hispanische Musik.

Die Stadt sponsort außerdem 100 Stadtteilfeste. Chicago hat etwa 100 Tage im Jahr schönes Wetter, blauen Himmel und warme Temperaturen

High-Tech-Showrooms für der "Mart"

Mit Investitionen von $150 Mio will Chicagos Renommierbetrieb, der "Merchandise Mart" ständige Showrooms für Informationstechnologie und neue Verkaufsräume in dem schon jetzt weltweit größten Design-Center errichten. Damit wird die Mart zu einem der wichtigsten Geschäftszentren der Stadt in den neunziger Jahren.

Der Mart-Komplex - dazu gehören das Expocenter und 1.800 Austell-ungsräume für Möbel, Interieurs, Bekleidung und Geschenkartikel - zählt heute bereits 2.7 Mio Besucher jährlich. Jeden Sommer kommen mehr als 50.000 Architekten, Designer und Vertreter von Unternehmen aus 45 Ländern zur weltweit größten Möbelmesse NEOCON. Der Kalksteinbau ist mit einer Fläche von mehr als 3.5 Mio m2 das größte Geschäftsgebäude der Welt. Im Technology Center werden Compu-ter, Workstations und alles, was zur Telekommunikation gehört, zu sehen und zu kaufen sein. Dazu werden Kurse angeboten, die über die sinnvolle Anwendung der Ausrüstungen für ergonomisch gestaltete Arbeitsplätze informieren.

In dem Mart und dem angegliederten Apparell Center finden heute bereits 300 Veranstaltungen jährlich statt. Hier kommen Verkäufer und Kunden zusam-men.

Lufthansa / UNITED AIRLINES

Expect a new, unrivaled standard of excellence in passenger service:

Lufthansa and *United Airlines*,

A world of experience. Times two.

- Frequent flyer members combine ***United's Mileage Plus*®** and **Lufthansa's *Miles & More*™** programs, a world of choice.
- Coordination of flight schedules, together, **Lufthansa** and ***United*** offer nearly 3,000 flights to six continents every day.
- Advanced seat assignments reciprocal on **Lufthansa** and ***United Airlines***.
- Use of **Lufthansa's Senator, Frequent Flyers Lounges®** and ***United's* Red Carpet Club*®*** for qualified passengers.
- Advance boarding passes to the most modern aircrafts.
- One-stop check-in with baggage and boarding pass to final destination of ***United*** and **Lufthansa**.
- On worldwide **Lufthansa** and ***United*** flights, multilingual, helpful personnel who anticipate every passenger need at every stage of your journey.
- ***United*** and **Lufthansa**. A world of experience. Times two.

Ein neuer, bisher unerreichter Servicestandard für unsere Fluggäste:

Lufthansa und *United Airlines*

Eine Welt der Erfahrung. Mal zwei.

- Weltweites Angebot für Vielflieger durch Kombination der Programme *Mileage Plus*® (*United*) und **Miles & More**™ (**Lufthansa**).
- Nahezu 3,000 Flüge nach sechs Kontinenten täglich durch die Koordination der Flugpläne von **Lufthansa** und *United*.
- Gegenseitige Sitzplatzvorbestellung bei **Lufthansa** und *United Airlines*.
- Zugang zu den **Senator** und **Vielflieger Salons**® der **Lufthansa** und dem *Red Carpet Club*® von *United* für zutrittsberechtigte Passagiere.
- Bordkarten im voraus für die modernsten Flugzeuge.
- Check-in nur einmal erforderlich; Gepäck wird bis zum endgültigen Bestimmungsort abgefertigt.
- Weltweit auf **Lufthansa** und/oder *United* Flügen, mehrsprachiges, hilfsbereites Flugpersonal, das die Wünsche der Fluggäste auf allen Reiseabschnitten vorwegnimmt.
- *United* und **Lufthansa**. Eine Welt der Erfahrung. Mal zwei.

LaSalle National Bank

Federal Reserve Bank next to the Board of Trade Building

Commerzbank, Dresdner Bank, Deutsche Bank and Bayerische Vereinsbank have had a subsidiary in Chicago for a number of years.

Upswing in the Adjoining Urban Communities

Increasing employment in the inner city and suburbs fostered recovery in the adjoining urban communities during the last ten years. This trend started in the Near North and Lincoln Park area. After the price tag for two-family homes and townhouses started to go up, recovery spread north along the lake, northwest along the Ravenswood "L", west towards University Village and south into the better black neighborhoods like South Shore and Gap near the Illinois Institute of Technology.

Harold Washington, the first black Mayor of Chicago played a central role in the renewal of urban communities. Washington, who was elected in 1983 as a reformist, had to battle an "administrative war" for 2 years before he could launch his policy for stronger communities, promotion of the small businesses, formation of working groups within local businesses, government and communities and thus open the road into the future for Chicago.

Chicago's Summer Festivals

Chicago's appointment book is filled with outdoor events that

Chancen für eine Wiederbelebung

Das gemeinsame Interesse wird sich in Chicago in den neunziger Jahren gleichermaßen auf die Sanierung der angrenzenden Gemeinden konzentrieren. Die Stadt hofft den Erfolg des Industrieparks auf dem Gelände der früheren Schlachthöfe wiederholen zu können. Der Park ist eines der sechs staatlich geförderten Industriegebiete, wo jungen und expandierenden Unternehmen eine Vielfalt von Vorteilen geboten wird. Die Stadt hat verschiedene Standorte für zusätzliche Industrieparks bestimmt und plant Investitionen zur Sanierung der benachbarten Wohngebiete.

Gewerbliche Immobilien: Katalysator der Entwicklung

Für die Gemeinden sind die Entwicklungschancen jetzt deutlich besser. Im Norden bleibt zwar wenig Raum für neue Bauvorhaben, und die Vorstädte sehen sich zunehmend der Problematik von Verkehrsstaus und Arbeitskräftemangel gegenüber. Der Markt für gewerbliche Immobilien blieb jedoch weiter lebhaft.

Die Stadt hat Dutzende von angrenzenden Gemeinden, in denen in den kommenden Jahren mit Sicherheit Weiterentwicklung stattfindet:

• Im Südwesten, entlang der neuen Schnellverbindungsstraße zum Midway Airport, blühen kleinere Industriegebiete auf — und solide Bungalows im Ziegelbau kosten immer noch $60.000.

• In der Gemeinde Austin, in der

METAL POLISH
and Fiberglass Cleaner

Altus
Metal & Marble Maintenance, a restoration company in Stony Brook, New York, writes about FLITZ polish after the World Trade Center disaster:

"...The stainless steel was damaged excessively due to a combination of sticky soot and some heat damage. Flitz (polish) was able to remove the staining and help bring back the high polish shine to sheets and sheets of stainless steel..."

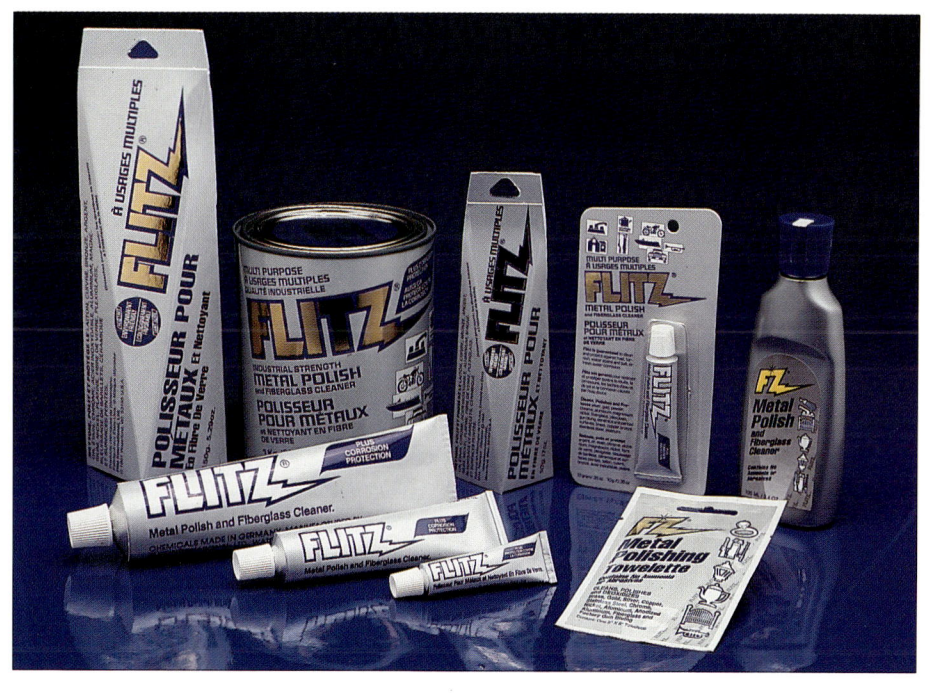

It started with a dedicated family in 1978.
Flitz was the first and foremost in introducing a Metal Polish effective for use on tarnished or oxidized metal as well as fiberglass. It works without abrasives and brings a brilliant shine to all metals and materials. It leaves a protective film for long lasting effect.
Today, **Flitz International** markets globally, obtains its raw materials from the best sources, spends a considerable amount of resources and effort on R&D, and provides the very best polish money can buy.
Flitz Polish is used in industrial/janitorial applications, by hunting and sporting goods and housewares trades, etc. Good for all your polishing needs: from sterling silver to gold, to copper, brass and stainless steel; fiberglass has never been maintained as easily with anything else.

Flitz is the one!

Altus
Metal & Marble Maintenance, ein Restaurationsunternehmen in Stony Brook, New York, schreibt nach dem Anschlag im World Trade Center über die FLITZ Politur:

„...Der Edelstahl war durch eine Kombination aus klebrigem Ruß und Hitze stark beschädigt. Flitz, die Polierpaste, konnte die Flecken entfernen und zahllose Platten aus rostfreiem Stahl wieder auf Hochglanz bringen..."

Es begann 1978 mit einer engagierten Familie.
Flitz stellte als erste Firma eine Metallpolitur vor, die sich für angelaufenes oder oxidiertes Metall wie auch für Glasfaser eignete. Die Politur arbeitet ohne Schleifmittel und verleiht allen Metallen und Materialien einen leuchtenden Glanz. Sie hinterläßt einen Schutzfilm und ist daher äußerst haltbar.
Heute vermarktet *Flitz International* seine Produkte weltweit, bezieht Rohstoffe aus den besten Quellen, stellt beträchtliche Arbeits- und Finanzmittel für F&E bereit und bietet die beste Politur auf dem Markt.
Flitz Polish wird in der Industrie und bei der professionellen Gebäudereinigung angewendet, für Jagd- und Sportausrüstungen, Haushaltsbranchen usw. *Flitz Polish* eignet sich für Ihren gesamten Polierbedarf: von Sterlingsilber bis Gold, Kupfer, Messing und Edelstahl; Glasfaser ließ sich nie leichter instandhalten.

Flitz und nichts anderes!

Flitz International, Ltd.   821 Mohr Avenue • Waterford, Wisconsin 53185 • Phone: 414/534-5898 • Fax: 414/534-2991

Tractor Pull at County Fair *Schlittenzug auf einem ländlichen Jahrmarkt*

Escape from the Windy City *Fern vom Alltag*

have become established routine on Chicago's summer calendar.

Every year there is yet more going on than the year before. The gospel festival during the first weekend in June is followed by the blues festival and the nine-day long "Taste of Chicago" event when 3 million people enjoy the "Lakefront" with good food and drinks. A week later we have the "All Star" baseball game in Wrigley Field.

Summers end with the Air and Water Show, the Jazz Festival which attracts musicians and fans from all over the world and the Viva Festival for hispanic music.

Chicago also enjoys hundreds of neighborhood festivals and fairs.

Chicago has 100 days of beautiful weather each year with blue skies and warm temperatures.

High-Tech Showrooms for the Mart

With an investment of $150 million, Chicago's showroom, the Merchandise Mart, plans to construct permanent showrooms for information technology and new sales rooms in its Design Center, which is already the largest in the world, thus making the Mart one of the most important business centers in the city.

Nähe von Oak Park, finden die Hypotheken der South Shore Bank gute Verwendung. Die Bank hat dem Ort South Shore über harte Zeiten hinweggeholfen, indem sie großzügige Darlehen für die Sanierung größerer Apartmenthäuser bewilligte. Mit der Hilfe der Stadt finanziert sie dort jetzt ein neues Einkaufszentrum. Die Bank hofft, diesen Entwicklungsprozeß in der Gemeinde Austin zu wiederholen.

• Im Südosten wurden in jüngerer Zeit beachtliche Investitionen von Zulieferern der Stahlindustrie und kleineren Unternehmen der herstellenden Industrie getätigt. Um den Illinois International Port herum hat sich ein blühendes Industriegebiet entwickelt. "Ein Standort erster Wahl", sagt Al McCaskill, ein Unternehmer aus New York, der hier seine Elektro-Vertriebsorganisation angesiedelt hat, "es ist die 'New Frontier' von Chicago".

Der Norden - ein Modell

Die nördliche Seefront der Stadt vermittelt einen Eindruck von dem, was die Entwicklung letztlich bewirken könnte. Der 22 km lange Gürtel vom South Loop bis Evanston zählt 500.000 Einwohner und ist sowohl in der Wirtschafts- als auch in der Bevölkerungsstruktur absolut ausgewogen. Eine Zeitlang bestanden Befürchtungen, daß die Immobilien im Zuge des Wandels ihren Wert verlieren würden. Statt dessen wurden hunderte von Millionen von Dollars in Gebäudesanierung und neue Bauvorhaben investiert. In Lincoln Park und am South Loop kostet eine Eigentumswohnung heute in der Regel

MAKING BUSINESS A PLEASURE.

The atmosphere in which you conduct business is as important as the business itself. At Chicago's Resorts we pride ourselves on creating the perfect atmosphere. We make business a pleasure.

Versatile meeting facilities allow us to accommodate 10 to 1,200 people. Providing everything you have come to expect-the best in service, accommodations, dining and entertainment. You'll find year-round recreation that includes championship golf, tennis, indoor & outdoor swimming and complete health club facilities.

For further information call **1-800-432-MEET** and discover the pleasure of doing business at Chicago's Resorts.

Ihre Geschäfte machen Freude…

Die Atmosphäre, in der Geschäfte getätigt werden, sollte so freundlich wie möglich sein. Das kennen wir, in den Chicago Resorts verbindet man gerne das geschäftliche und notwendige mit Freizeit und Gemütlichkeit. Sie werden sehen, wie gut das tut.

Es gibt bei uns Konferenzräume in allen Grössen und mit verschiedenster Ausstattung. Dazu den besten Dienst am Kunden, schöne Wohnzimmer, vorzügliches Essen und gute Unterhaltung. Das ganze Jahr lang ist etwas los: Golf, Tennis, Swimmen und ein feudaler Health Club.

Das alles ist unter der freien Nummer 1-800-432-MEET (6338) zu erreichen. Probieren Sie es einmal.

Nordic Hills Resort
Nordic Road   Itasca, IL 601243
708/773-2750

Oak Brook Hills Hotel & Resort
3500 Midwest Road   Oak Brook, IL 60522
708/850-5555

Indian Lakes Resort
250 W. Schick Road   Bloomingdale, IL 60108
708/529-0200

Chicago's Resorts

A scenic part of Chicagoland are its beautiful country estates.

Buffalo Rock, where the Chicago River changes to the Illinois River.

The Mart together with the Expo Center and 1,800 exhibition halls for furniture, interior decorating, clothing and gifts counts 2.7 million visitors annually. Every summer more than 50,000 architects, designers and representatives of businesses from 45 countries attend the world's largest furniture fair NEOCON. The limestone building covering an area of more than 30.5 million square feet is considered the largest commercial building in the world.

Computers, workstations and telecommunications equipment will be exhibited in the Technology Center. Courses will be offered in the use of the new gadgets in the ergonomic work place.

Presently 300 events take place annually in the Mart and the adjoining Apparel Center.

Opportunities for Revival

During the nineties, Chicago concentrates on the renewal of urban communities. Chicago hopes to repeat the success of the industrial parks on the site of the former stockyards. The park is one of six state-supported industrial sites for the benefit of young and expanding businesses. The city mapped out several sites for additional industrial parks and plans to invest in the rehabbing of adjoining residential areas.

um $500.000, in anderen Gemeinden sind die Preise unterschiedlich.

Jede Kultur brachte ihre Gotteshäuser, ihre Schulen und besonderen Fähigkeiten mit nach Chicago und die umliegenden Gemeinden, dazu ihre Restaurants, Buchläden und Festivals. Und jede bringt auch Arbeitskräfte für die Dienstleistungsbetriebe in der Stadt und die Fabriken in den Industriegebieten im Norden.

"Das Angebot der Stadt und ihres Umlandes ist enorm breit und tief", stellt Robert Wislow fest. Er wohnt in Lincoln Park und ist Inhaber der Immobilienfirma U.S. Equities, Bauherrin der neuen Bibliothek im Zentrum. Wislow sieht einen zunehmenden Trend zurück zur City voraus. "Städte", so Wislow, "eröffnen den Menschen eine ganze Welt voller neuer Erfahrungen."

Wislow ist einer von vielen Kennern der Stadt, die Chicago für die Herausforderungen der neunziger Jahre für gut gerüstet sehen. Als Gemeinwesen gereift, mit einer gesunden Mischung von Menschen unterschiedlicher Kulturen und einer stark diversifizierten Wirtschaft, mit nach neuesten Standards ausgelegten Flughäfen, Kongreßzentren und Verkehrsnetzen kann Chicago auf Wachstum zählen.

In einer Welt, die immer enger zusammenrückt, sind Zeitersparnis und leichter Zugang zu Waren und Dienstleistungen von entscheidender Bedeutung. In Chicago ist für beides gesorgt. Und auch das Timing stimmt. Führende Persönlichkeiten aus Chicagos schwarzen und hispanischen Gemeinden nehmen einen festen Platz in der Verwaltung der Stadt und der Hierarchie

German technology – U.S. manufacture and service

Take advantage of nearly a century of experience when you buy a press for the future.

As the first to offer welded presses to the world, Erfurt utilizes its 97-year global experience to provide a broad variety of advanced-technology presses to industry in North America. Whether you are looking for press consultation or innovative machinery, Erfurt experts can help you with straight-sided presses, transfer presses, multi-die presses, eccentric presses, and other presses or press lines—mechanical or hydraulic. Our U.S.-made presses have service available, too. Call today for details.

Worldwide forming experts

PRESSTECHNOLOGY
ERFURT

Erfurt, Inc.
5999 Wilke Road, Suite 101
Rolling Meadows, IL 60008
☎ 708/290-1483 Fax: 708/290-1783

Parks and Forest Preserves provide secure places to relax and reflect.

Swan on shore of a manmade pond of a commercial complex.

Commercial Real Estate: Catalyst

Communities today have a markedly better chance to develop. However, the North Side is faced with a shortage of available land for new construction and the suburbs are faced with increasing problems in traffic and a shortage in the work force. Commercial real estate, however, is still a lively market. There are a dozen adjoining communities with a chance for new development:

• South West, along the new expressway to Midway Airport we find a blossoming small industrial area where a solid brick bungalow still only costs $60,000.

• In the Austin area near Oak Park mortgages from the South Shore Bank are put to good use. The Bank has helped South Shore to get through hard times by granting major loans for the rehabbing of larger apartment buildings. A new shopping center is being built with financial support from the city. The Bank hopes to repeat the growth process in Austin.

• South East experienced considerable investment transactions by suppliers of the steel industry and smaller manufacturing businesses. A growing industrial area developed around the Illinois International Port. Al McGaskill, businessman from New York, who set up his electro distribution center here, calls it "a first-choice location — the 'New Frontier' of Chicago."

der Geschäftswelt ein. In ihrer Zielsetzung stimmen sie mit Major Daley und den anderen Gruppierungen der Wirtschaft der Stadt überein: die Qualifikation Arbeitskräfte mit den Anforderungen der Wachstumsindustrien auf einen Nenner zu bringen. "Die Motivation in den angrenzenden Gemeinden ist sehr hoch", stellt Doug Gill, Stadtentwickler in Kenwood-Oakland, fest, "das Potential ist vorhanden."

In Richtung Zukunft

Wenn Chicago und seine Unternehmen dieses Potential aktivieren und die Ressourcen der Innenstadt, der Vorstädte und der Umlandgemeinden weiter zusammenführen, wird Chicago zur Wende des Jahrhunderts -als eine der ersten Weltstädte- die Versprechen der neunziger Jahre einlösen.

Sollten Sie einen Spaziergang durch die Stadt machen wollen, so würden wir Ihnen vorschlagen, von Süden nach Norden zu gehen.

Fangen Sie auf dem Sears Tower, dem höchsten Gebäude der Welt an. Der Eintritt zum Aussichtsturm beträgt $3.00. Vom 103. Stockwerk haben Sie einen weiten Ausblick auf die Innenstadt von Chicago und Umgebung. Nach dem Besuch können Sie am Ausgang an der Ostseite des Gebäudes mit Doppeldecker Bussen gegen eine kleine Gebühr eine Stadtrundfahrt machen. Die Rundfahrt endet wieder am Einsteigeplatz.

Ca. 2 Blocks nördlich vom Searsgebäude befindet sich die zweite der größten Warentermin Märkte der Welt, der sog. Chicago Mercantile Exchange, an der Ecke Madison Street und Wacker Drive. Auch hier können Sie

In Chicagoland, we find large farms butting up to new subdivisions and expanding towns. These farms grow mainly corn, soybeans and cash crops for markets close by. The efficiency of American farmers is well known and is due, to a great extent, to modern implements. The picture shows a 24 double-station corn planter.

In Chicagoland grenzen ausgedehnte landwirtschaftliche Flächen direkt an die neuen Vororte und die ständig wachsenden Vorortsgemeinden. Auf den Feldern werden hauptsächlich Mais und Sojabohnen angebaut, sowie Obst und Gemüse für den sofortigen Verkauf auf den umliegenden Märkten. Die sprichwörtliche Wirtschaftlichkeit der amerikanischen Bauern mit ihren modernen Landwirtschaftsmaschinen ist ja weltbekannt. Auf dem Bild sehen wir eine Maispflanzmaschine, die 24 Körner gleichzeitig in die Erde setzt.

Water Tower, the only survivor of the Great Fire, in front of the Hancock Center.

Der Wassertum, das einzige Gebäude, das den Großbrand überlebte, vor dem Hancock Center.

As the sun sets in the West, the City is reflected in the 333 W. Wacker Building.

In der Abendsonne spiegelt sich die Stadt in der Glaswand des Gebäudes auf dem 333 W. Wacker Drive wider.

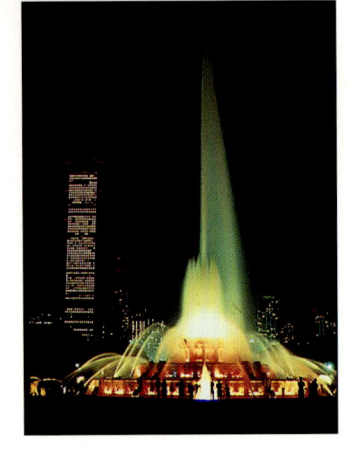

Buckingham Fountain rivaling the Amoco Building for attention.

Der Buckingham Fountain bei Nacht

The North - A Model

The North Shore of the city demonstrates the ultimate effects of this development. This 14-mile long stretch from the South Loop to Evanston counts 500,000 residents with a balanced mix of business and residential structures. For a long time it was feared that real estate would lose its value in the course of change. Instead, hundreds of millions of dollars were invested in the rehabbing of buildings and in new construction. A condominium in Lincoln Park and in the South Loop today as a rule sells for $500,000. However, prices differ in other communities.

Each culture brought its own church or house of worship, its own schools and its own skills to Chicago and the surrounding communities. They brought their own restaurants, bookstores and festivals. And they bring their own work force.

"The city and its suburbs have much to offer" opines Robert Wislow of Lincoln Park, owner of a real estate firm, U.S. Equities, who built the library there. Wislow predicts an increasing trend of people moving back into the city. He feels Cities open a whole new world full of experiences.

Wislow is one of many who knows the city well and believes that Chicago is good and ready for the challenges of the nineties. Chicago matured as a community and with a healthy

auf einen Besucher-Balkon gehen. (Eintritt frei.)

Von dort drei Blocks östlich gehen Sie zum "Board of Trade" auf der Jackson und LaSalle Street. Schauen Sie sich vom Besucherbalkon in der vierten Etage (Eintritt frei) das lebhafte Treiben dieser größten Produktbörse der Welt an. Direkt gegenüber der Börse sollten Sie in das Hochparterre von einer Chicago Bank, der Continental Illinois Bank, gehen. Eine große Halle mit bunten Fresken erwartet Sie dort.

Einige Häuser nördlich auf der LaSalle Street sind interessant. Schauen Sie sich das Jugendstil-Vestibül der "Rookery" an, ein Meisterwerk restaurierter Innenarchitektur. Gehen Sie auf der Monroe Street nach Osten, nach zwei Blocks stehen Sie auf der First National Bank Plaza. Der riesige Springbrunnen wird Sie erfreuen. Am Ostende der "Plaza" steht das große Chagall-Mosaik "Die vier Jahreszeiten", das der Stadt vom Künstler gegeben worden ist.

Wenn Sie von dort aus nach Süden schauen, dann steht eines der berühmtesten Gebäude des deutschgebürtigen Architekten Helmut Jahn vor Ihnen. Sie sehen das Xerox Gebäude, ein wuchtig-elegantes, weißgekleidetes Hochhaus. Dann gehen Sie vier Blocks nach Norden zur "Civic Plaza", auf dem Pablo Picasso seine berühmte Statue geschaffen hat. Einen Block nordwestlich von der Picasso Statue sehen Sie das große und im Jahre 1985 fertiggestellte Gebäude des Staates Illinois. Dieses Bauwerk des Architekten Jahn ist revolutionär im Baustil und erregte bereits viel Aufsehen. Schreiten Sie durch die Riesenlobby des Gebäudes und bestaunen Sie den "funktionellen" Baustil. Eine Fahrt mit dem Aufzug gibt Ihnen einen Blick "aus

Merz Apothecary

ESTABLISHED 1875

This old-time apothecary, with its timeless grace and beauty, has been serving the health care needs of Chicagoans since 1875. The stained-glass door chimes as you walk in, and the vast mirrors and glass cabinets framed in dark oak and giant apothecary jars sparkle beneath the brass chandeliers of the oldest pharmacy in the city. The pleasant odor of herbs, European bath soaps, oils and perfumes serves as the perfect environment for this escape into the past. The professional pharmacists will introduce you to natural, herbal, as well as homeopathic alternatives to convential medicine. Experience a touch of Europe and fill your prescription for the past and the present at the *Merz Apothecary*.

Merz Apotheke

Merz Apotheke, die älteste Apotheke in Chicago, sorgt seit 1875 für die Gesundheit der Einwohner von Chicago. Beim Betreten dieser alterwürdigen Apotheke von zeitloser Schönheit klingelt die Tür aus Buntglas, und die riesigen Spiegel, die von dunklem Eichenholz umrahmten Glasschränke und die enormen Arzneimittelgefäße funkeln unter den Leuchtern aus Messing. Der angenehme Duft von Kräutern, europäischen Badeseifen, Ölen und Parfüms liefert das perfekte Ambiente für diesen Ausflug in die Vergangenheit. Die erfahrenen Apotheker machen Sie gern mit Kräuterheilmitteln sowie natürlichen und homöopathischen Alternativen zur konventionellen Medizin bekannt. Hier empfinden Sie Glanz und Duft von einst und jetzt aus Europa. Wir laden Sie herzlich ein in die *Merz Apotheke*.

4716 North Lincoln Avenue
Chicago, Illinois 60625
Tel 312 989-0900 • Fax 312 989-8108

mix of people from different cultures and a diversified economy, with airports of the latest state of the art, convention centers and transportation systems, it is ready for the challenges of tomorrow.

In a shrinking world, saving time and easy access to goods and services is of paramount importance. Chicago can offer both. And the timing is right. Leading personalities from Chicago's black and hispanic communities have their established place in the administration of the city and hierarchy of the business community. Their objectives are the same as those of Mayor Daley and other business groups: to match a qualified work force with the challenges of a growing industry. "Motivation in the adjoining communities is very high," says Doug Gill, city developer of Kenwood-Oakland. "The potential is there."

Towards the Future

If Chicago and its suburbs activate their potentials and pool the resources of City, suburbs and collar counties, it will become one of the leading cosmopolitan cities in the world at the turn of the century.

der Höhe" eines riesigen Innenraumes.

Von dort aus sollten Sie nach Osten bis zur State Street gehen, an der das Groß- und Qualitätskaufhaus Marshall Fields liegt. Machen Sie einen kleinen Einkaufsbummel durch dieses riesige Kaufhaus, das dafür berühmt ist, nur Qualitätswaren und einmaligen Service zu verkaufen. Nach einem Luncheon in einem der unzähligen Restaurants schlendern Sie über die Michigan Avenue nach Norden. Nach dem Überqueren des Chicago Flusses am Wrigley "Kaugummi-Gebäude" gehen Sie über die goldene Meile, einer eleganten Ladenstraße in Richtung "Wasserturm". Dies ist das einzige Steingebäude, das nach dem großen Feuer im Jahre 1875 stehenblieb.

Nach einem Besuch im Atrium Shopping Center "Water Tower Place", das sich innerhalb des Water Tower Gebäudes befindet, sollten Sie sich einen weiteren Aussichtsturm gönnen: das John Hancock Building. Eingang zur "Observation Platform" ist von der Michigan Avenue Seite her. Vom 94. Stockwerk haben Sie einen herrlichen Blick, anders als vom Searsturm, weil näher zur eigentlichen Innenstadt und zum See-Ufer gelegen.

Viele andere Sehenswürdigkeiten, Museen und Ausstellungen warten auf Ihren Besuch. Chicago wird Sie nicht enttäuschen! Denn die Stadt Chicago ist durchaus besser und schöner als ihr Ruf.

Chicago, das Herz und die Seele der amerikanischen Wirtschaft und Industrie, die größte Stadt im Staate Illinois, in dem sich ca. 400 deutsche Firmen mit ihren USA-Niederlassungen angesiedelt haben.

CHICAGO'S NEW NAVY PIER - 1995
View from Lake Michigan with Ballroom and Festival Hall in foreground

CHICAGOS Neuer Navy Pier - 1995
Blick vom Michigansee auf den Navy Pier mit Ballsaal und Festhalle im Vordergrund

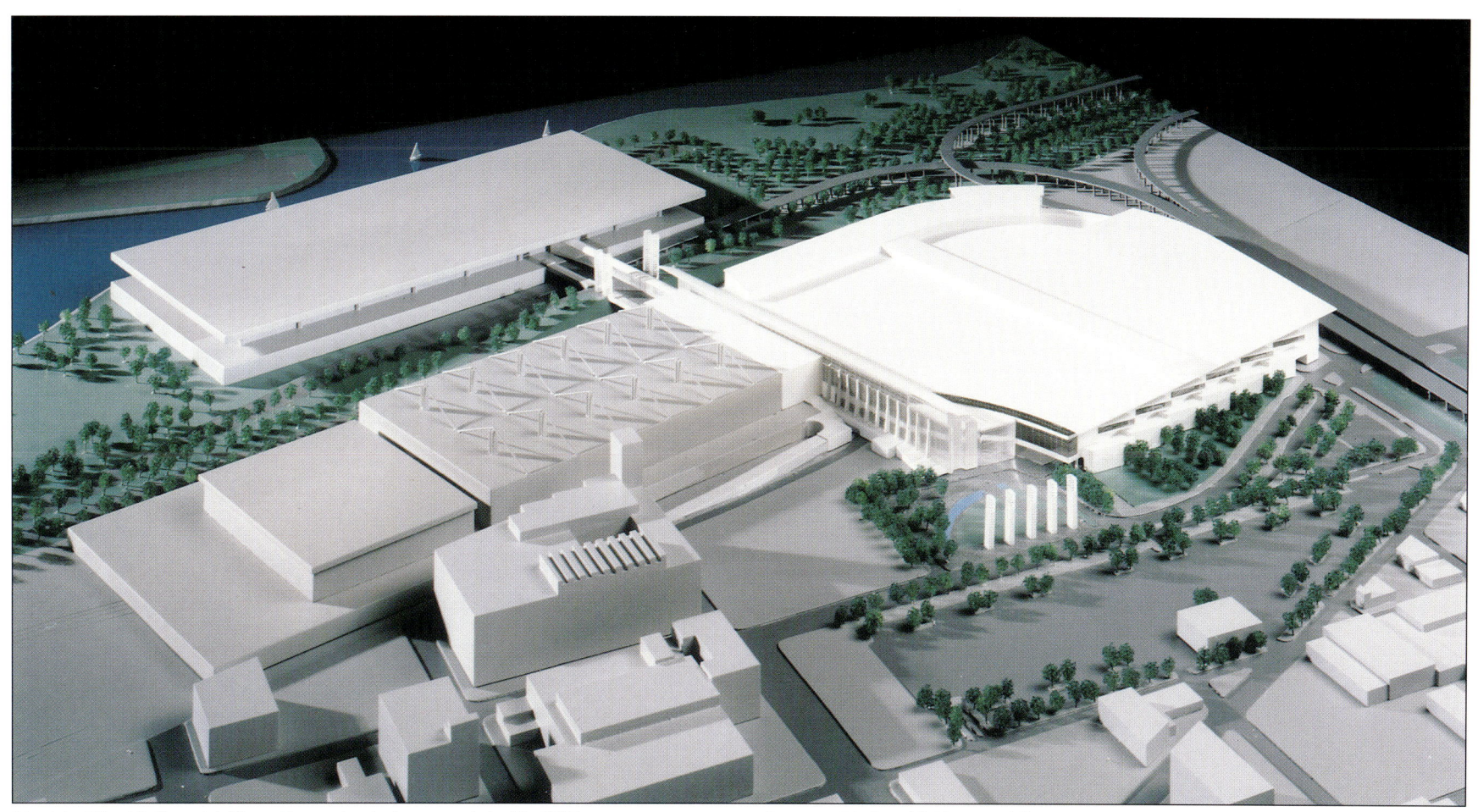

Model of the McCormick Place Expansion to be completed in 1997.　　　　　　　　Das neue McCormick Place-Modell

GERMAN-AMERICAN COMMERCE AND INDUSTRY

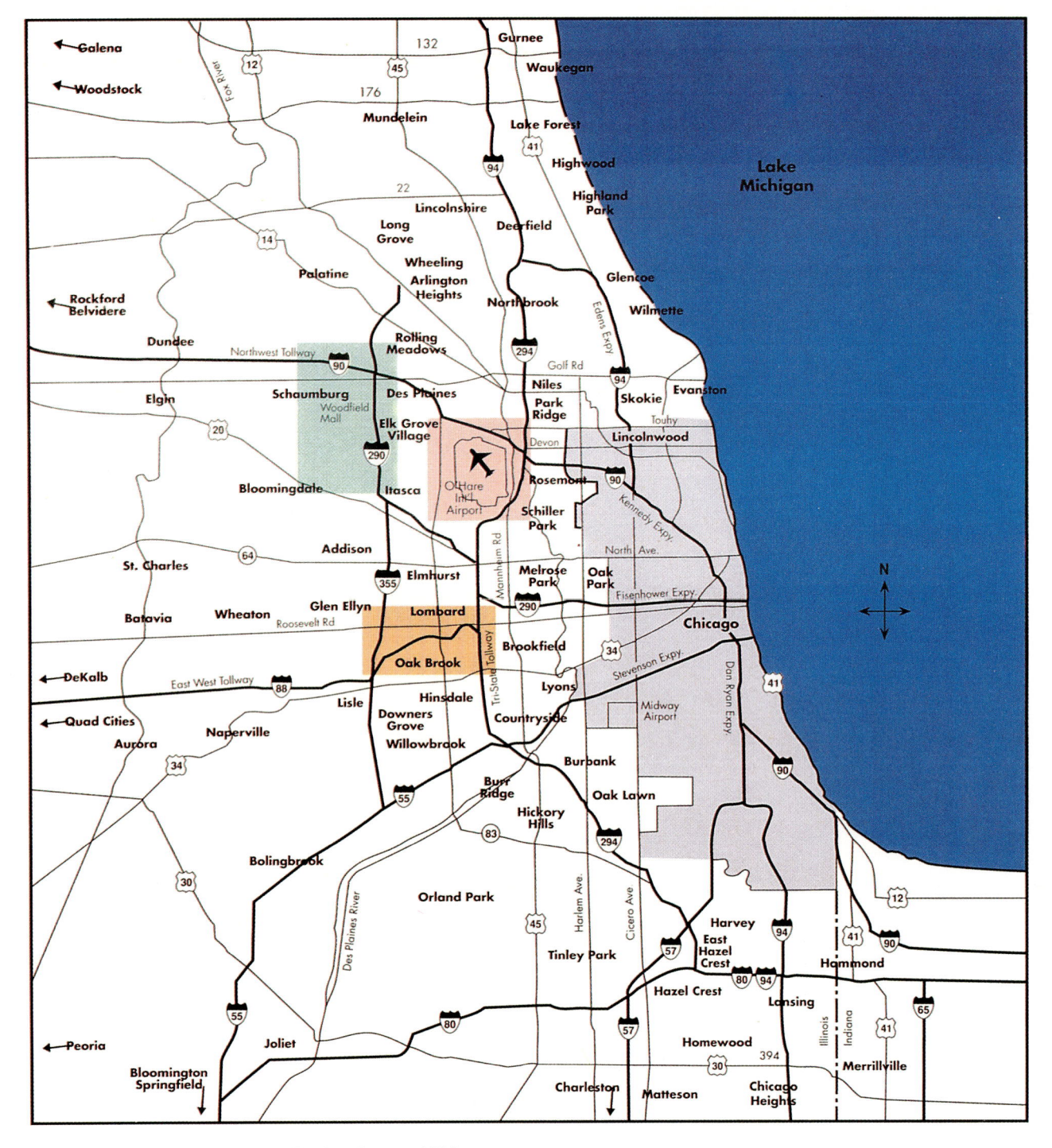

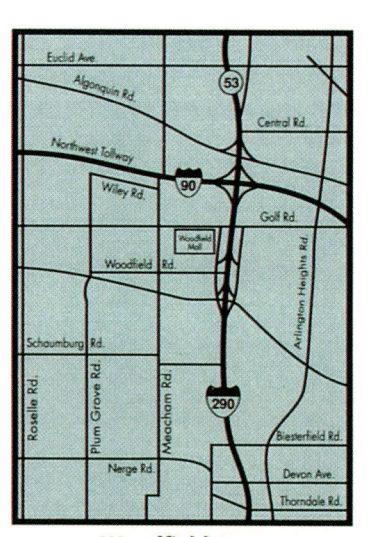

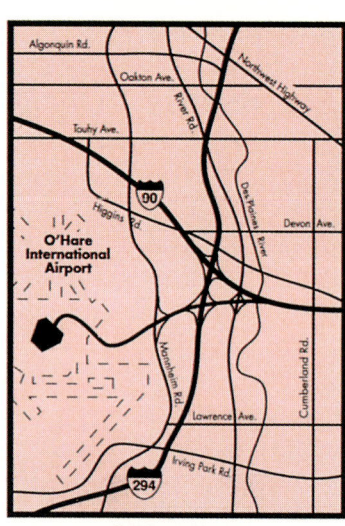

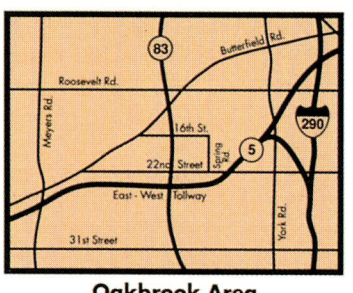

Courtesy of Chicago Convention and Tourism Bureau, 1994

Highways flow in all directions from Chicagoland, intermodal crossroads of the U.S.

Kombinierte US-Autostraßen führen von Chicago aus in alle Richtungen

The Suburbs of Chicago

The Greater Chicagoland metropolitan area embraces 2,400 square miles north, west, and south of the city, with a population of almost four million people. Each suburban community has its own municipal government, business district, schools, churches, light industry and shopping areas.

Several major expressways provide easy access to downtown Chicago: The **Edens** Expressway (Interstate I 94) goes to the northern suburbs and on to Milwaukee. The **Kennedy** Expressway (Interstate I 90) goes to O'Hare Airport and the northwest suburbs. **Congress Parkway** leading into the **Eisenhower** Expressway (Interstate I 290) extends to the western suburbs. The **Stevenson** Expressway (I 55) goes to the southwest suburbs and on to St. Louis. The **Dan Ryan** Expressway (Interstate I 94) and the **Chicago Skyway** (Interstate I 90)

Chicagos Vororte

Chicagoland dehnt sich zum Norden, Westen und Süden auf einer Fläche von 2.400 Quadratmeilen aus. Es hat eine Einwohnerzahl von fast vier Millionen Menschen. Jede Vorortsgemeinde hat ihre eigene Stadtverwaltung, Geschäftsviertel, Schulen, Kirchen, Industrie und Einkaufsviertel.

Mehrere größere Schnellstraßen führen direkt in die Innenstadt von Chicago: Der **Edens** Expressway (Interstate I 94) führt zu den nördlichen Vororten und nach Milwaukee. Der **Kennedy** Expressway (Interstate I 90) führt zum O'Hare Flughafen und in die nordwestlichen Vororte. **Congress Parkway** führt auf den **Eisenhower** Expressway (Interstate I 290), der sich bis zu den westlichen

Metra commuter train leaving Northwestern Station

Metra-Pendlerzug verläßt den Northwestern-Bahnhof

Vororten erstreckt. Der **Stevenson** Expressway (I 55) führt in die südwestlichen Vororte und nach St. Louis. Der **Dan Ryan** Expressway (Interstate I 94) und der **Chicago Skyway** (Interstate I 90) führen zum

Home-coming for those working in the City

Von der Arbeit in der Stadt auf dem Weg nach Hause

Chicago's "L" trains connect the outskirts with the Loop

Chicagos Hochbahn, "L", verbindet die Randbezirke mit dem Loop

lead south to northern Indiana. The **Tri-State Tollway** (Interstate I 294) makes a wide loop west around the city. The **Interstate I 57** goes to the far southern suburbs.

Chicago has excellent public transportation, bringing in nearly 1,000,000 people in and out of the City every day.

Metra (Metropolitan Rails) is a commuter train service for the six-county area around Chicago. *Metra/Chicago* and *Northwestern* Railroad trains serve the west, northwest and northern suburbs, leaving from the Northwestern Station at Canal and Madison Streets.

The *Metra/Burlington Northern* Railroad travels west as far as Aurora, leaving from Union Station at Canal Street and Jackson Boulevard.

The *Rock Island* Railroad goes to the far southwest suburbs and leaves from the LaSalle Street Station at Congress and LaSalle.

The *Illinois Central* and *South Shore* lines go south and southeast to Indiana and leave from the underground station at Michigan Avenue and Randolph Street.

The *Chicago Transit Authority* (CTA) operates a network of buses, elevated ("L") and subway trains throughout the city of Chicago and 38 nearby suburbs. Transfers are provided for making connections to any part of the City.

Pace operates 700 buses between Chicago and the suburbs, also connecting the various suburbs.

Amtrak, the government operated passenger train system, leaves from the Union Station on South Canal Street to all parts of the United States.

Greyhound/Trailways Bus Terminal, located at Harrison and Jefferson Streets, provides low cost, scenic highway coach transportation to anywhere in the country.

Süden und nach Nord-Indiana. Der Tri-State Tollway (Interstate I 295) macht einen Bogen westlich um die Stadt. Die Interstate I 57 geht weit raus in die südlichen Vororte.

Chicago hat ein hervorragendes öffentliches Verkehrssystem das täglich fast 1 Millionen Menschen in die Stadt und wieder zurück in die Vororte bringt.

Metra (Metropolitan Rails) ist eine Vorortszuglinie für die sechs um Chicago liegenden Counties (Verwaltungsbezirke).

Die Züge der Metra/ Chicago und Northwestern-Linie fahren von der Northwestern Station Ecke Canal und Madison Street in die westlichen, nordwestlichen und nördlichen Vororte.

Die Züge der Metra/ Burlington Northern-Linie fahren von der Union Station Ecke Canal Street und Jackson Boulevard in westliche Richtung und bis nach Aurora.

Die Rock Island-Linie fährt von der LaSalle Street Station Ecke Congress und LaSalle Street in die südwestlichen Vororte, die weit draußen liegen.

Die Illinois Central und South Shore Linien fahren von dem Untergrundbahnhof an der Michigan Avenue und Randolph Street in südlicher und südöstlicher Richtung nach Indiana.

Die Chicago Transit Authority (CTA) unterhält innerhalb der City von Chicago und den 38 direkt umliegenden Vororten ein Netzwerk an Bussen, Hochbahnen („L") und Untergrundbahnen. Mit Umsteigekarten kann man in alle Richtungen der Stadt Anschluß finden.

Pace, eine Busgesellschaft mit 700 Verkehrsbussen, verkehrt zwischen Chicago und den Vororten und verbindet auch die Vororte miteinander.

Amtrak ist eine staatliche Eisenbahngesellschaft, die von der Union Station an der South Canal Street aus in alle Teile des Landes fährt.

Der Busbahnhof der Greyhound/Trailways liegt Ecke Harrison Street und Jefferson Street, von wo die Busse zu erschwinglichen Preisen über das ganze Land fahren.

Amtrak yard on the City's southside

Amtrak-Rangierbahnhof auf der Südseite der Stadt

Metropolitan Chicago is headquarters for over 600 major companies who maintain executive and sales staff all over the world. World-wide communications are made possible by a network of telephones, telex, fax machines, mainframe and PC computers and other electronic systems.

Among the giants in the telecommunication industry, located in Chicagoland, are Ameritech (formerly Illinois Bell Telephone Company), AT&T (American Telephone & Telegraph), Motorola, Tellabs and Molex.

In der Metropole Chicago haben über 600 Großunternehmen ihre Hauptverwaltungen, die Management- und Verkaufspersonal auf der ganzen Welt verstreut beschäftigen. Diese weltweiten Verbindungen werden durch ein Netz von Telefonlinien, Telexanlagen, Faxmaschinen, Großrechnern und PC-Computern und anderen elektronischen Telekommunikationssystemen ermöglicht.

Unter den Giganten der Telekommunikationsindustrie in Chicagoland befinden sich Ameritech (ehemals die Illinois Telefongesellschaft), AT&T (American Telephone & Telegraph), Motorola, Tellabs und Molex.

One of the foremost tool makers in the suburbs

Namhafter Werkzeugmacher in den Vororten

McDonald's marketing facility also houses the famous thinktank and the Ray Kroc Museum

McDonald's Marketing-Zentrale mit dem berühmten "Thinktank" und dem Ray Kroc Museum

Hamburger University at McDonald's world headquarters campus in Oak Brook

Die "Hamburger Universität" und McDonald's Hauptverwaltung auf dem McDonald's Campus in Oak Brook

THE SUBURBS OF CHICAGO — CHICAGOS VORORTE

This 30-story building, the tallest between Chicago and Denver, is also headquarters for the German Media Group

In diesem 30 Stockwerk hohen Gebäude, dem höchsten zwischen Chicago und Denver, befindet sich auch die Hauptverwaltung der German Media Group

Suburban Living

People living in the Chicago suburbs enjoy more home and yard space, convenient shopping, good schools, plenty of recreational areas, and generally a pleasant and safe environment. Since many major companies have moved their offices and factories to the suburbs, to build larger or more modern facilities, employees can get to and from work more quickly.

Shopping Malls are found everywhere in and out of the city. Strip Malls, consisting of a row of stores, replaced the smaller, traditional neighborhood stores in many areas. Major Loop department stores have branches in larger shopping centers, which act as "magnets" for the lesser known stores.

Das Leben in den Vororten

Die Bewohner der Vororte genießen den Vorteil größerer Häuser und Gartenflächen, besser gelegener Einkaufsmöglichkeiten, guter Schulen, großzügig angelegter Sport- und Erholungsanlagen und im allgemeinen einer angenehmeren und sicheren Umgebung. Viele Großunternehmen haben aus Expansions- und Modernisierungsgründen ihre Verwaltungen und Fabriken in die Vororte verlegt. Für viele der Angestellten und Arbeiter ist somit der Weg zur Arbeit kürzer geworden.

Shopping Malls findet man überall. In der Stadt, in den Randbezirken, in den Vororten. Die Strip Malls, d.h. Geschäfte, die sich aneinanderreihen, haben in vielen Orten die kleineren, traditionellen Geschäfte und Tante Emma Läden ersetzt. Die großen

Spacious and gracious living in suburban condominiums

Geräumige und freundliche Eigentumswohnung im Vorort

Aerial view of Oak Brook, one of the most progressive communities in Chicagoland

Luftaufnahme von Oak Brook, einer der progressiveren Gemeinden in Chicagoland.

Some of the largest suburban shopping centers are Oak Brook, Fox Valley, Woodfield, Old Orchard, North Riverside, Hawthorne, Northbrook Court, Orland Square and Randhurst. Gurnee Mills, located near the Wisconsin border, is a wholesale outlet mall for people who want quantity and quality merchandise at bargain prices.

Kaufhäuser der Innenstadt sind in den größeren Shopping Centers durch Filialen vertreten, die wie ein Magnet auf die Käufer wirken. Davon profitieren auch weniger bekannte Geschäfte.

Große Shopping Malls finden wir in Oak Brook, Fox Valley, Woodfield, Old Orchard, North Riverside, Hawthorne, Northbrook Court, Orland Square und Randhurst. Das weltweit bekannte Gurnee Mills, das

Oak Brook Shopping Center, which opened in 1967, has approx. 150 stores in a beautiful, landscaped garden setting with trees and seasonal flower displays. To spend a few hours there, walking outside from store to store, stopping to rest, watching the fountains, or eating in one of the restaurants makes shopping a very pleasant experience.

kurz vor der Grenze zwischen Wisconsin und Illinois liegt, ist eine Mall für Großhändleroutlets, wo Quantität und Qualität zu niedrigen Preisen angeboten wird.

Zum Beispiel finden wir in dem 1967 eröffneten Oak Brook Shopping Center ungefähr 150 Geschäfte in schön angelegten Gartenanlagen mit Bäumen und das ganze Jahr hindurch blühenden Blumen. Man kann gut

THE SUBURBS OF CHICAGO — CHICAGOS VORORTE

Specialized boutiques are popular and plentiful

Boutiquen sind beliebt und im Überfluß vorhanden

Sport and recreational opportunities are abundant all year 'round in Chicagoland. Some of the finest golf courses in the Midwest are located throughout suburban Chicago. Private golf clubs require an annual membership fee, which includes clubhouse facilities, swimming, tennis, dining and other privileges. Public golf courses have a daily fee, and usually provide lunch and beverage service.

Private indoor or outdoor tennis clubs and public outdoor courts are available in many of the suburban parks. Most schools let the public play tennis on their courts in the afternoon and evening.

Polo is popular in Oak Brook and Naperville during the summer months. Matches are played against teams from Argentina, Mexico, England and Germany. Prince Charles of England has played at Oak Brook.

Horse races are held at Arlington International Race Course in Arlington Heights, at Hawthorne Park and Sportsman Park in Cicero. Night harness racing may be seen at Maywood Park.

Community parks and forest preserves offer numerous facilities for public outdoor use - picnic tables, swings, baseball diamonds, fishing in lakes and streams, tennis courts, hiking and bicycle trails.

Fishing is popular along the Fox and Des Plaines Rivers and on the many lakes north and west of Chicago. Smelt fishermen line the shores of Lake Michigan when these fish are running. A one year Illinois State fishing license is all that is required to fish anytime anywhere in Illinois.

Sailing, boating, canoeing and water skiing are fun on the many small rivers

und gerne mehrere Stunden dort verbringen und im Freien von Geschäft zu Geschäft bummeln oder in einem der Restaurants haltmachen, um sich auszuruhen.

Gelegenheiten für Sport und Erholung werden das ganze Jahr hindurch überall in Chicago in Hülle und Fülle angeboten. Einige der besten Golfplätze des Mittelwestens sind in den Vororten von Chicago zu finden. Private Golfclubs erheben einen Jahresmitgliedsbeitrag für die Nutzung von Klubhaus, Swimming Pools, Tennisplätzen, Restaurants und anderen Annehmlichkeiten. Öffentliche Golfplätze erheben eine Tagesgebühr. Dafür haben sie meistens nur eine Cafeteria.

In den meisten suburbanen Parkanlagen findet man private und öffentliche Tennisclubs und Tennisplätze. Auch die Tennisplätze vieler Oberschulen stehen der Öffentlichkeit nachmittags und abends zur Verfügung.

Oak Brook und Naperville sind in den Sommermonaten beliebte Polo-Ziele. Polo-Matches werden gegen Teams aus Argentinien, Mexiko, England und Deutschland ausgetragen. Sogar Prinz Charles von England hat schon in Oak Brook gespielt.

Zum Pferderennen geht man zur Pferderennbahn in Arlington Heights, zum Hawthorne Park oder zum Sportsman Park in Cicero. Im Maywood Park werden nachts Trabrennen veranstaltet.

Gemeindeparks und Naturschutzparks bieten den Besuchern Picknick-

Lakes and streams are stocked with game fish which are fun to catch. Most go back into the water

Seen und Bäche werden für die Angler mit Fischen besetzt. Aber die meisten Fische landen wieder im Wasser

This view of the Western Open Golf Tournament is typical of activities on weekends   *Ein typisches Wochenende: das Western Open Golf Turnier*

and lakes in the greater Chicago area.

In the Winter, ice skating and hockey can be enjoyed at both private and public rinks. Skiing and tobogganing are popular at Palos Hills, Villa Olivia and Four Lakes.

Indoor bowling is popular from Fall to Spring. Racquet ball courts are available in many communities.

From Spring to Fall, picnics are the most popular outdoor activity.

plätze, Kinderspielplätze, Baseball-Felder, Teiche und Bäche für Angler, Tennisplätze, Wander- und Fahrradwege.

Für den Angler bieten sich ebenfalls viele Gelegenheiten. Flüsse wie der Fox River und der Des Plaines River oder die vielen kleinen Seen nördlich und westlich von Chicago sind ein Paradies für Angler. Angler werfen ihre Angeln am Rande des Michigan Sees aus, um „Smelt," eine Art kleiner Lachsfisch, zu fangen. Mit einem Anglerschein, der gegen eine Gebühr erhältlich ist, kann der Angler überall in Illinois angeln gehen.

Unzählige kleine Flüsse und Seen um Chicago herum erlauben Segeln, Boot-, Kajak- und Wasserskifahren.

Dafür kann man dann im Winter auf privaten und öffentlichen Eisbahnen Schlittschuhlaufen gehen und Hockey spielen. Sogar für Skilaufen und Rodeln gibt es Gelegenheit auf den Hügeln der beliebten Palos Hills, Villa Olivia und Four Lakes.

Bowling und Racquetball sind das ganze Jahr über populär. Aber die populärste Beschäftigung von Frühling bis Herbst sind die Picknicks in den vielen Parks.

SUBURBAN LIVING — DAS LEBEN IN DEN VORORTEN

Resorts in the Suburbs

Oak Brook Hills Country Club, a place to relax or celebrate. It is also the temporary home of the German Soccer Champion Team

Der Oak Brook Hills Country Club, ein Ort zum Entspannen oder zum Feiern. Vorübergehendes Heim für die deutsche Fußball-Nationalmannschaft

Pheasant Run Resort, St. Charles, part of far western suburbs. 475 guest rooms. 18-hole golf course. Fitness center with spa and saunas. Indoor/outdoor swimming pools. Tennis courts. Pheasant Run Dinner Playhouse on premises.

Pheasant Run Resort in St. Charles, ein Vorort weit draußen im Westen Chicagos. Ferienhotel und -anlage mit 475 Gästezimmern, 18-Loch Golfplatz, Fitness-Center mit Bad und Saunas, Hallenbad und Freibad, Tennisplätzen und dem Pheasant Run Dinner-Theater.

Oak Brook Hills & Resort, Oak Brook, part of western suburbs. 400 luxury rooms on a 15-acre site. 18-hole golf course. Indoor/outdoor swimming pools. Health and fitness centers. Choice of six dining and lounge options. Near Drury Lane Oak Brook Dinner Playhouse.

Oak Brook Hills & Resort in Oak Brook, westlicher Vorort. Ferienhotel und -anlage mit 400 Luxusgästezimmern. 18-Loch Golfbahnen, Hallenbad, Freibad, Fitness-Center und sechs Restaurants und Bars. Nahebei das Drury Lane Oak Brook Dinner-Theater.

Resorts

Winter wonderland: Pheasant Run Theater and Resort

Pheasant Run Theater und Hotelkomplex im Winterkleid

Indian Lakes Resort, Bloomingdale, part of northwest suburbs. Six-story hexagonal modular building includes spectacular atrium. 18-hole golf course. Indoor/outdoor swimming pools. Tennis courts. Cross-country skiing during season. Health spa offers sauna, whirlpool, and massages. American or continental cuisine featured in 3 glamorous restaurants.

Indian Lakes Resort in Bloomingdale, Vorort im Nordwesten. Ein 6 Stockwerk hohes hexagonales Ferienhotel mit spektakulärem Atrium. 18-Loch Golfplatz, Hallenbad und Freibad, Tennisplätzen, Skilanglaufbahnen, Bäder und Saunas, Whirlpool und Massagen. In den 3 eleganten Restaurants wird amerikanische oder internationale Küche angeboten.

Nordic Hills Resort Secluded in a huge stand of majestic oak trees, Nordic Hills Resort offers the perfect hideway. The rustic Scandinavian building houses fine dining and banquet facilities, as well as a modern conference center.

Choose from a variety of recreational opportunities including golf, bowling, billiards, racquetball and swimming.

Lachner "CHICAGOLAND"

Indian Lakes Resort caters to corporate company functions, from sales and board meetings to Christmas parties and golf tournaments

Indian Lakes Resort wird für Konferenzen und Firmenaktivitäten wie Verkaufs- und Vorstandsitzungen bis hin zu Firmenweihnachtsfeiern und Golfturnieren gerne genutzt

Nordic Hills Resort
Verborgen, hinter einer Reihe majestätischer Eichen, finden wir Nordic Hills, ein ideales Wochenendhotel. Das rustikale Gebäude im skandinavischen Stil beherbergt elegante Restaurants, Bankett- und Konferenzzimmer.

Für den sportlichen Gast gibt es eine Anzahl von Freizeitsportanlagen, einschließlich Golf, Bowling, Billiards, Racquetball und Schwimmen.

Lincolnshire Marriott features a dinner-theater combination: it's reasonable, convenient and a great way to entertain guests

Lincolnshire Mariott, Restaurant und Theater in einem. Die Preise sind erschwinglich und die Lage angenehm. Ideal wenn man Gäste hat.

Marriott's Lincolnshire Resort, Lincolnshire, part of northern suburbs. 390 guest rooms. Indoor/outdoor swimming pools. Fully equipped health club. 18-hole golf course. Racquet club with 5 tennis courts. Cross-country skiing in season. Canoes, paddle boats, and Sunfish sailboats. Lincolnshire Theater Playhouse on premises.

Marriott's Lincolnshire Resort in Lincolnshire, Vorort im Norden. 390 Gästezimmer. Hallenbad und Freibad. Fitness-Center, 18-Loch Golfplatz, Racquet-Club mit 5 Tennisplätzen, Skilanglaufbahnen, Kajaks, Paddelbooten und Sunfish Segelbooten. Lincolnshire Theater.

Rustic Nordic Hills, a favorite resort for golf, weddings and other special parties.

Die ländlichen Nordic Hills sind als Golfplatz und für Hochzeitsfeiern und andere festliche Anlässe sehr beliebt.

Suburban towns take pride in their community and try to be unique. This made Naperville create its River Walk, a historical homestead community. Lombard has its Lilacia Park and Glen Ellyn loves its park around Lake Ellyn, an oasis in the middle of town for walks and play...

Jeder Vorort ist auf seine Gemeinde stolz und versucht etwas Besonderes anzubieten. Naperville richtete den „River Walk" ein, einen Wanderweg entlang der historischen Heimstätten- gemeinde. Lombard hat seinen Lilacia Park und Glen Ellyn liebt seinen Park um den Ellynsee, eine Oase inmitten der Stadt zum Spazierengehen und Spielen ...

...and skating in the wintertime
... und zum Schlittschuhlaufen im Winter

Lachner *CHICAGOLAND*

Highlights of Suburbia

Chicago's suburbs feature many outstanding tourist attractions that are well worth a visit when time permits.

Argonne National Laboratory. An experimental nuclear reactor facility in the southwest suburb of Lemont. When originally located on the University of Chicago campus, it was the site of the world's first nuclear chain reaction.

Sehenswertes und Interessantes in den Vororten

Die Vororte von Chicago bieten viel Sehenswertes für den Touristen an. Zu empfehlen wären:

Argonne National Laboratory. Eine experimentelle Kernreaktoranlage in Lemont im Südwesten von Chicago. In diesem Kernreaktor, der früher auf dem Gelände der University of Chicago stand, fand die erste nukleare Kettenreaktion statt.

Dolphins perform daily at Brookfield Zoo

Delphine zeigen täglich ihre Künste im Brookfield Zoo

N. Moore House, 1895-1923

Frank Thomas House, 1901

Wm. Winslow House, 1893

Mrs. Thomas Gale House, 1909

Frank Lloyd Wright Home and Studio in Oak Park. This was Wright's home for 19 years and where he raised his family. There are over 25 outstanding homes in Oak Park and River Forest designed by the world-famous and controversial architect, which may be viewed on a walking tour of these villages west of Chicago.

Frank Lloyd Wright Home and Studio in Oak Park. Hier arbeitete und lebte Frank Lloyd Wright mit seiner Familie 19 Jahre lang. Insgesamt gibt es 25 herausragende Häuser des weltberühmten und umstrittenen Architekten in Oak Park und River Forest, die man sich auf einer Tour zu Fuß durch diese beiden Orte anschauen kann.

Brookfield Zoo is an indoor and outdoor zoological park for 2,500 animals representing 400 different species of mammals, fish, reptiles and birds from every continent. Special exhibits are the Asian Rain Forest, the daily Dolphin Show, and the new African Savannah. Miniature trains and buses take visitors to all parts of this 204-acre park located 14 miles west of downtown Chicago.

Der Brookfield Zoo wurde als Zoologischer Park für über 2.500 Tiere angelegt und beherbergt 400 verschiedene Tierarten. Säugetiere, Reptilien, Fische und Vögel von jedem Kontinent sind hier vertreten. Zu den Attraktionen gehören der Asiatische Regenwald, eine Delphinen-Show und die neue Afrikanische Savanne. Miniaturzüge und -busse fahren die Besucher durch den 80-ha großen Park, rund 23 km von der Innenstadt Chicagos entfernt.

PLACES OF SPECIAL INTEREST IN THE SUBURBS — SEHENSWERTES UND INTERESSANTES IN DEN VORORTEN

Cantigny Memorial Park is in suburban Winfield, just west of Wheaton. This unique war museum is dedicated to the United States Army 1st Division and its battles, from the Revolutionary War through Desert Storm. This park is the elaborate former country estate of the late Colonel Robert R. McCormick, former publisher of the Chicago Tribune.

Sherman tanks, witnesses of an embattled past

Cantigny Memorial Park, liegt in Winfield, einem Vorort der westlich von Wheaton liegt. Das Museum ist als Ehrendenkmal der 1. Division der United States Armee und ihren Kämpfen im Revolutionskrieg bis zum Desert Storm gewidmet. Der Park steht auf dem früheren Landsitz des verstorbenen Colonel Robert R. McCormick, ehemals Herausgeber der Chicago Tribune.

Sherman Panzer, Zeugen einer kriegerischen Vergangenheit

A view of Robert Rathburn Wilson Hall at Fermilab. The 16-story building houses research laboratories and the administrative headquarters

Die Robert Rathburn Wilson Hall im Fermilab. In dem 16-stöckigen Gebäude sind das Forschungslabor und die Verwaltung untergebracht

The tunnel of the Main Accelerator at Fermilab. In the Tevatron, protons are accelerated to energies approaching 1 TeV.

Der Tunnel des Hauptteilchenbeschleuniger im Fermilab. Im Tevatron werden Protone zu Energien beschleunigt, die sich 1 TeV nähern.

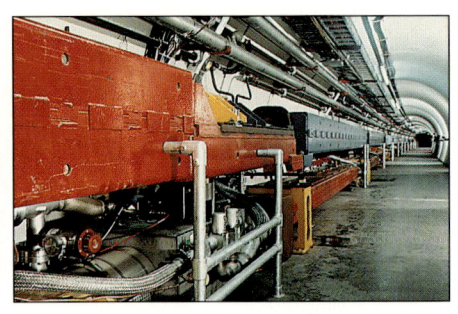

The collider detector was commissioned in October 1985 at Fermilab. Its calorimeters contain photomultipliers and electronics used to measure particle energies from the proton collision

Der Collider-Detektor wurde im Oktober 1985 im Fermilab in Auftrag gegeben. Seine Kalorimeter enthalten Photomultiplier und Elektronik, die zur Messung der aus Protonzusammenstössen entstehenden Teilchenenergie benutzt werden.

Despite the awesome technical advances it is still a beautiful environment

Trotz dieser überwältigenden fortgeschrittenen Technik, ist das Umland immer noch wunderschön

Fermilab, 40 miles west of Chicago near Batavia, is built on a 6800-acre site for energy research and development. The first particle accelarator atom smasher was built here in 1967. A fascinating place to view the super-conducting Super Collider which has the energy of nearly 1TeV, one trillion electron volts and travels at almost the speed of light. The Tevatron's main ring is four miles or 6.3 km in diameter.

Fermilab, über 60 km westlich von Chicago entfernt und in der Nähe von Batavia, wurde auf einer 2.720-ha großen Fläche errichtet und dient der Forschung und Entwicklung. Hier wurde 1967 der erste Teilchenbeschleuniger gebaut. Mit Faszination kann man sich hier den supraleitenden Super-Collider ansehen, mit einer Energie von fast 1 TeV, eine Billion Elektron Volt, also fast so schnell wie die Lichtgeschwindigkeit. Der große Ring des Tevatrons hat einen Durchmesser von 6,3 km.

Morton Arboretum in west suburban Lisle is an internationally known private 1,500-acre park, featuring ornamental trees and shrubs, and 4,500 plants from all parts of the world. One can drive through or walk the many woodland trails. It is especially beautiful in the Spring and Fall.

Morton Arboretum im westlichen Lisle ist ein international bekannter Privatpark. Auf einer 600-ha großen Fläche finden wir Zierpflanzen und -bäume, Sträucher und 4.500 Pflanzenarten aus der ganzen Welt. Man kann entweder durch den Park fahren oder auf den vielen Waldwegen wandern gehen. Der Park ist besonders schön im Frühjahr und Herbst.

Arlington International at its best
Arlington International zeigt sich von seiner besten Seite

The Knights of the Roundtable in full regalia
Die Ritter der Tafelrunde in voller Rüstung

Arlington International Race Course, in northwest Arlington Heights, conducts daily thoroughbred horse racing throughout the Summer. The new club house boasts several fine dining facilities, open from May to October. It frequently hosts the world's best jockeys, trainers and thoroughbreds.

Long Grove is a miniature early American shopping village with a bakery, apple cider plant, and numerous gift and antique shops, located 30 miles northwest of Chicago.

Baderbrau Brewery in west suburban Elmhurst is one of several German mini-breweries in the region.

Arlington International Race Course, Pferderennbahn im nordwestlichen Arlington Heights, die den ganzen Sommer lang Pferderennen mit reinrassigen Pferden veranstaltet. Das neue Klubhaus hat mehrere elegante Restaurants, die von Mai bis Oktober geöffnet sind. Die besten Jockeys, Trainer und Vollblutpferde sind hier anzutreffen.

Long Grove, Miniaturdorf im frühamerikanischen Stil, wo heute Boutiquen, Andenken- und Geschenkeläden, eine Bäckerei, eine große Apfelpresse und Antiquitätengeschäfte ihre Waren anmutig anbieten. Das Dorf liegt rund 48 km von Chicago entfernt.

Baderbrau Brewery im westlichen Vorort Elmhurst ist eine von vielen deutschen Mini-Brauerein in dieser Gegend.

Medieval Times, located in north-west Schaumburg, resembles an 11th century castle with its colorful pagentry and chivalry. It features exciting reenactments of knights on horseback, lance and sword fighting and jousting, while dinner is eaten without any silverware.

Mill Rose Restaurant & Brewery, in northwest Hoffman Estates, has a country store and restaurant serving a full menu, buffalo burgers and shark fin soup and venison in the Winter.

Medieval Times (Mittelalterliche Zeiten), ist ein Abenteuer, das man in Schaumburg, nordwestlich von Chicago, erleben kann. Hier läßt sich das bunte Treiben und Leben der Ritter und Bauern auf einer Burg aus dem 11. Jahrhundert nachvollziehen. Lebensnahe Ritterkämpfe und -turniere zu Pferd mit Speer und Schwert werden, während man seine Mahlzeit ohne Messer und Gabeln verzehrt, geboten.

Mill Rose Restaurant & Brewery im nordwestlichen Hoffman Estates, ein Restaurant mit rustikalem Charakter und einem Bauernladen. Das Restaurant serviert ein volles Menü. Spezialitäten sind Buffalo-Burger und Haifischsuppe und im Winter Wildfleisch.

PLACES OF SPECIAL INTEREST IN THE SUBURBS — SEHENSWERTES UND INTERESSANTES IN DEN VORORTEN

Northwestern University on the Northshore features the Kellogg School of Business and a very competitive football program

Die Northwestern University am Northshore mit ihrer wirtschaftlichen Fakultät und einem sehr starken Football-Programm

Ravinia Festival, an indoor-outdoor concert complex presenting great music, featuring the Chicago Symphony Orchestra plus a wide variety of musicians and world-renown soloists. "Music under the Stars" programs are held from June to September, in north suburban Highland Park.

Cuneo Museum and Gardens, near north suburban Lake Forest, features a 32-room Mediterranean style mansion containing opulent art treasures from around the world, plus a private chapel. The 75-acre estate includes lakes, a conservatory, formal gardens, fountains and a private golf course. There is also a herd of rare white deer that visitors can feed.

Ravinia Festival, Chicagos große Freilichtbühne im nördlichen Vorort Highland Park. Hier wird mit dem Chicago Symphony Orchestra große Musik gemacht. Berühmte Musiker und Solisten aus der ganzen Welt werden eingeladen, um hier von Juni bis September „Musik unter den Sternen" zu bieten.

Cuneo Museum und Gärten sind in der Nähe von Lake Forest im Norden Chicagos zu finden. Die Hauptattraktion ist eine Villa im Stil des Mittelmeers mit 32 Zimmern, die mit Kunstschätzen aus der ganzen Welt gefüllt ist und ihre eigene Kapelle besitzt. Das Grundstück mit Teichen, einem Konservatorium, angelegten Gärten, Springbrunnen und einem privaten Golfplatz ist 30 ha groß. Es gibt sogar eine Herde seltener weißer Hirsche, die sich von den Besuchern füttern lassen.

Baha'i Temple in Wilmette is a world-famous architectural landmark where religious services promote peace and coexistence of all people on earth. It is open to worshippers of every faith.

Der Baha'i Temple in Wilmette, ein architektonisches Meisterstück, dient der Baha'i Religionsgemeinschaft, die Frieden und Einheit aller Menschen auf Erden fördert. Der Tempel ist für alle Glaubensrichtungen offen.

The magnificent Bahai Temple provides solitude for all religions

Der überwältigend schöne Bahai Tempel ist für alle Religionen ein Ort der Besinnung

Six Flags Great America, a Theme Park, located on a 300-acre site in north suburban Gurnee, features the greatest collection of rides in the Midwest for people of all ages. There are over 100 thrilling rides, spectacular shows and attractions to experience throughout your fun-filled day.

Six Flags Great America, ein Vergnügungspark auf einer 120-ha großen Fläche im nördlichen Vorort Gurnee. Der größte Vergnügungspark des Mittelwestens bietet etwas für alle Altersstufen. Über 100 aufregende Fahrten, spektakuläre Shows und Attraktionen, genug, um sich einen ganzen Tag lang zu vergnügen.

This Shock Wave roller coaster is one of many exciting rides at Great America Theme Park
Diese Schockwellen Berg- und Talbahn ist nur eine von vielen aufregenden Fahrten im Great America Theme Park.

Waukegan Harbor, 50 miles north of Chicago on Lake Michigan, has the largest charter fishing fleet on the Lake. Coho salmon, weighing as much as 30 pounds, have been caught here.

Bristol Renaissance Faire, at I-94 North (Exit #1 at Russell Drive) near the Wisconsin border, is an Elizabethan countryfest, presented on nine weekends each Summer.

Waukegan Harbor ist ein Fischerei- oder Anglerhafen fast 90 km nördlich von Chicago mit der größten Charterflotte für Angler am Michigansee. Coho-Lachse bis zu 15 kg schwer wurden hier schon gefangen.

Bristol Renaissance Fair an der I-94 North (Abfahrt #1 am Russell Drive) nahe der Wisconsin Grenze, ist ein Jahrmarkt wie er zur Zeit Elizabeth I. von England üblich gewesen sein mochte. Der Jahrmarkt zieht sich über neun Sommerwochen hin.

Fox Lake is a great watersport area at the far northwest side of Chicagoland, a nearby weekend resort with many cottages, enjoyed by American and European families alike.

Fox Lake ist der größte See für Wassersport nordwestlich von Chicago. Ein beliebter Wochenenderholungsort, der von Amerikanern und Europäern aufgesucht wird.

PLACES OF SPECIAL INTEREST IN THE SUBURBS — SEHENSWERTES UND INTERESSANTES IN DEN VORORTEN

Flamingo. Located on Dearborn between Adams and Jackson, Alexander Calder's Flamingo has graced the Federal Plaza since 1974. The 53-foot tall structure is painted vermillion or "Calder red". Courtesy of the Chicago Convention Bureau/Gene Hickmott, photographer.

Der Flamengo von Alexander Calder steht seit 1974 zwischen Dearborn Street und Jackson Boulevard. Die über 17 m hohe Struktur ist Zinnoberrot oder „Calderrot." Mit Genehmigung des Chicago Convention Bureau/Gene Hickmott,

Weekends, Seasonal Activities and National Holidays

The biggest social nights of the week are Friday, Saturday and Sunday evenings. For many, Saturday is a time to do errands and work around the house.

After church on Sunday, it is pleasant to have brunch with family or friends. Brunch is a buffet lunch, offering a great variety of dishes, sometimes with a glass of champagne. Food is served "Smorgasbord" style — everyone serves himself from an assortment of breakfast items, omelettes and sweetrolls, to hot fried chicken, roast beef, ham and fish. A wide choice of salads and desserts are also available.

Sunday afternoon is a time for visiting friends, going to a ballgame, or entertaining at home.

The weather always changes in Chicago - day to day and season to season. Spring and Easter may be cool, but is lovely when the flowering trees and forsythia are in bloom.

Wochenende, Feiertage und Feste der Vier Jahreszeiten

Freitag, Sonnabend und Sonntag abends wird für Geselligkeit und Unterhaltung reserviert. Der Sonnabend wird natürlich auch zum Einkaufen und für die Hausarbeit genutzt.

Am Sonntag nach der Kirche geht man gerne mit der Familie oder Freunden zum „Brunch." Brunch ist ein büffetartiges Lunch mit einer großen Auswahl an Gerichten. Manchmal wird auch ein Glas Sekt serviert. Die Gerichte werden nach Art eines Smorgasbord angeboten, d.h. jeder bedient sich selbst von der großen Auswahl an Frühstücksvarianten - von Omelett über Gebäck oder Brötchen bis zum Brathühnchen, Rostbraten, gekochten Schinken und Fisch, findet man alles, was das Herz begehrt. Die Auswahl an Salaten und Desserts ist ebenfalls groß.

Sonntag nachmittags besucht man Freunde und Bekannte, geht zu einem Fußball- oder Baseballspiel, oder man lädt sich Gäste ein.

Das Wetter in Chicago wechselt ständig - von Tag zu Tag und von Jahreszeit zu Jahreszeit. Um die Osterzeit im Frühjahr kann es noch sehr kalt sein. Aber wenn die Bäume anfangen auszuschlagen und die Forsythien blühen ist es wunderschön.

Crocusses in front of a Kenilworth mansion

Krokusse vor einer Villa in Kenilworth

Spring

May 30th, Memorial Day, heralds the beginning of Summer, and is a United States holiday observed with memorial services honoring American servicemen killed in wars. Parades are held in almost every community.

In the Summer, outdoor barbecues are popular. Grilled spareribs, chicken, steak, hamburgers and hotdogs are often enjoyed by families in their backyards.

Families enjoy the many parks in and around Chicago

Familien genießen die vielen Parks in und um Chicago.

Lincoln Park Lagoon. Lincoln Park is an integral part of Chicago. Located on the lakefront, the 880-acre park provides a variety of jogging and biking paths, tennis courts and picnic areas. It has a golf course, conservatory, zoo and a number of museums. Paddle boats are available for rent. Courtesy of the Chicago Convention Bureau / Ron Schramm, photographer

Die Lincoln Park Lagune. Der am Seeufer gelegene Lincoln Park gehört zu Chicago und nimmt eine Fläche von 352 ha ein. Der Park ist ein Paradies für Jogger. Es gibt Fahrradwege, ein Konservatorium, einen Zoo und eine Reihe von Museen. Paddelboote stehen zur Ausleihe zur Verfügung.
Mit Genehmigung des Chicago Convention Bureau/Ron Schramm, Fotograf.

Der 30. Mai, der Gedenkfeiertag, kündet den Sommeranfang an. Es ist ein Tag, an dem die Vereinigten Staaten mit Gedenkfeiern und Paraden der gefallenen amerikanischen Soldaten gedenken.

Im Sommer ißt man gerne im Freien, und Grillen von Rippchen, Steaks, Hamburgern und Würstchen ist eine Lieblingsbeschäftigung amerikanischer Familien.

Frühling

GOOD TIMES — FREIZEIT

Summer in Chicago

Romantic dinner cruises on Lake Michigan are a special delight in the Summer time

Romantische Dinner-Cruises auf dem Michigansee sind eine besondere Attraktion im Sommer

The carnival is in town, fun for the young at heart

Ein Jahrmarkt ist in der Stadt und Alte werden wieder jung

A fresh breeze off the Lake clears the air

Vom See weht ein frischer Wind und reinigt die Luft

Envigorating bike rides along the Lake are good for body and soul

Eine Radtour am See entlang tut Körper und Seele gut

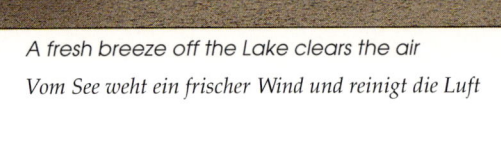

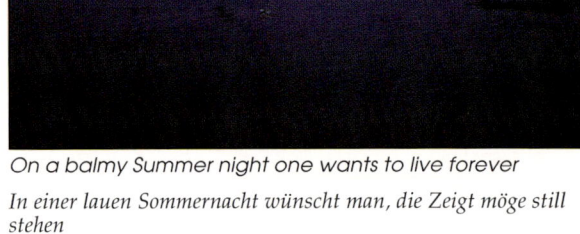

On a balmy Summer night one wants to live forever

In einer lauen Sommernacht wünscht man, die Zeigt möge still stehen

Lachner "CHICAGOLAND"

*Street musicians are a
part of Chicago's scene*

*Straßenmusikanten gehören
zum Straßenbild*

Sommer...

*Sailboats at Burnham Park Harbor
are waiting for their sailors*

*Segelboote liegen wartend im
Burnham Park Hafen*

July 4th celebration reflects our national values

In den Feierlichkeiten des 4. Juli spiegelt sich unser Nationalbewußtsein wider

*A little practice before the
Lake Shore crowd and the "Mac"*

*Ein paar Segelmanöver vor
der großen Regatta, die „Mac"*

*A little volleyball game
in the backyard*

Ein Volleyballspiel im Garten

GOOD TIMES — FREIZEIT

Homes are decorated with Christmas wreaths, trees and lights. The Christmas tree, a German custom, is observed all over the United States. Christmas cards and gifts are exchanged. Special cookies and cakes are prepared.

Christmas Eve services are attended by Protestants and Catholics alike. Then on Christmas Day, gifts are opened and family and friends come together for dinner at home.

The Adler Planetarium has a special presentation at Christmas telling how the stars were arranged at the time of Christ's birth. The Museum of Science and Industry has a marvelous program to celebrate Christmas around the world. The Nutcracker ballet is presented every year at the Arie Crown Theater in McCormick Place. The "Hallelujah" chorus from Handel's Messiah is sung in many churches.

New Year's Eve celebrations at hotels or at home welcome the new year with champagne. A "count down" of the last minutes of the old year brings hundreds of people into downtown Chicago at midnight.

New Year's Day is reserved for the Tournament of Roses Parade from Pasadena, California and the Collegiate Bowl Championship Football games.

Chicago may be very cold in January, but snow can be beautiful. Even in the City! But it is a good time to take a few days off, if possible, and go to Florida, the Caribbean islands, the Arizona desert, to Las Vegas, Nevada or the West Coast. A reprieve from shovelling snow is always pleasant. Most people stay in Chicagoland to enjoy the Winter - a hike in the park, ice skating and hockey, sledding and tobagganing, skiing and snowmobiling. Many hardy men have fun icefishing and ice-sailing. You might even see some hunters out braving the weather.

February means St. Valentine's Day and President's Day, honoring the birthdays of George Washington and Abraham Lincoln.

In March, everyone joins the Irish in celebrating St. Patrick's Day, on the 17th. The Chicago River is dyed green, restaurants serve green beer, and thousands of people watch the long and colorful St. Patrick's Day parade in the Loop as over 50 bands, floats and some 2,000 marchers pass by.

Easter usually comes in April and with it, warmer weather, green grass once again, snow drops, crocusses, daffodils and tulips.

May and June are busy months with graduations and weddings to attend. Kids are out of school for the Summer the middle of June. It's off to camp for a couple of weeks for the lucky youngsters, and vacation time until the end of August.

mit ihren Klingeln an das Fest der Liebe und des Gebens.

Die Häuser werden mit Adventskränzen, Weihnachtsbäumen und Lichtern geschmückt. Der Tannenbaum, eine aus Deutschland mitgebrachte Sitte, wird in ganz Amerika geschmückt. Weihnachtskarten und Geschenke werden ausgetauscht und es duftet nach Weihnachtsgebäck.

Protestanten und Katholiken gehen am Heilig Abend zum Gottesdienst. Am Ersten Feiertag werden die Geschenke ausgepackt und Familien und Freunde versammeln sich zum Festschmaus.

Das Adler Planetarium bietet um die Weihnachtszeit ein Sonderprogramm an und zeigt die Sternkonstellation zur Zeit der Geburt Christi. Das Museum of Science and Industry feiert Weihnachten mit einer wunderschönen Weihnachtsbaum-Ausstellung. Im Arie Crown Theater im McCormick Place kann man sich beim Nußknacker Ballet von Tschaikowsky weihnachtlichen Kinderträumen hingeben. Die Klänge des „Halleluja" aus dem Messias von Händel tönen uns aus vielen Kirchen entgegen.

Silvester feiert man in Hotels oder man heißt das Neue Jahr mit Freunden und Sekt zu Hause willkommen. Auch die Innenstadt wird kurz vor 24 Uhr lebendig, wenn sich Besucher und Gäste zusammentun, um das Neue Jahr einzuläuten.

Neujahrstag gehört der Parade des Tournament of Roses in Pasadena, Kalifornien, und dem Collegiate Bowl Championship Football-Spiel.

Im Januar kann es in Chicago sehr kalt werden, aber wenn hier Schnee liegt, verwandelt sich Chicagoland in eine Märchenwelt. Sogar in der Stadt!

Der Januar ist eigentlich ein guter Monat, sich ein paar Tage vom Schneeschaufeln und der Kälte zu erholen. Ein Urlaub in Florida, in der Karibik, in Arizona, in Las Vegas in Nevada oder an der Westküste steht bei vielen auf dem Kalender. Die meisten Menschen allerdings bleiben in Chicago und genießen den Winter, indem sie in den Parks spazierengehen, Schlittschuhlaufen oder Rodeln gehen, Hockey spielen, Skilaufen oder Snowmobiling gehen. Einige der abgehärteten Seelen gehen sogar Eisfischen oder Eissegeln. Hier und da sieht man auch einen Jäger, dem das kalte Wetter nichts ausmacht.

Valentinstag wird im Februar gefeiert. Im Februar feiert man auch die Geburtstage von George Washington und Abraham Lincoln.

Am 17. März wird jeder in Chicago Irisch und feiert den St. Patrickstag. Der Chicago River wird grün gefärbt, in den Kneipen wird grünes Bier serviert und zu tausenden stehen die Familien mit ihren Kindern und die Büroangestellten im Loop am Straßenrand und schauen der langen und farbenfreudigen St. Patrick's Day Parade zu, die mit 50 Bands, geschmückten Festwagen und 2000 Paradeteilnehmern vorbeimarschiert.

Ostern fällt meistens in den April, und bringt warmes Wetter, grünes Gras, Schneeglöckchen, Krokusse, Narzissen und Tulpen mit sich.

Mai und Juni sind angefüllt mit Schulabschlußfeiern und Hochzeiten. Die Sommerferien fangen Mitte Juni an und wer Glück hat, darf zwei Wochen lang zu einem Camp gehen. Die Großen Ferien gehen Ende August zu Ende.

*Street musicians are a
part of Chicago's scene*

Straßenmusikanten gehören
zum Straßenbild

Sommer...

*Sailboats at Burnham Park Harbor
are waiting for their sailors*

Segelboote liegen wartend im
Burnham Park Hafen

July 4th celebration reflects our national values

In den Feierlichkeiten des 4. Juli spiegelt sich unser Nationalbewußtsein wider

*A little practice before the
Lake Shore crowd and the "Mac"*

Ein paar Segelmanöver vor
der großen Regatta, die „Mac"

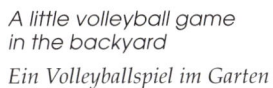

*A little volleyball game
in the backyard*

Ein Volleyballspiel im Garten

GOOD TIMES — FREIZEIT

This pony knows the company of children
Das Pony ist mit Kindern vertraut

Grant Park concerts are free, compliments of the Mayor of Chicago
Grant Park Konzerte sind frei und werden vom Bürgermeister der Stadt Chicago gesponsert

Fall or Autumn is the best time of the year in Chicagoland
Die schönste Zeit des Jahres in Chicago ist der Herbst

Summer

July 4th is Independence Day, another uniquely American holiday. All over the country, there are spirited parades by the citizenry down Main Street, band concerts in the park, family or neighborhood picnics, followed by colorful and noisy fireworks displays. Bipartisan patriotism reigns supreme all over the land, at least for this one day.

Labor Day Weekend ushers in the Fall season the first Monday of September. Students are back in school.

In the middle of September, through October, every German restaurant, club and community celebrates Oktoberfest. The Berghoff Restaurant in Chicago has downtown Adams Street blocked off for three days and serves bratwurst and beer outside. The Chicago Brauhaus on Lincoln Avenue celebrates for two weeks, starting with the Lincoln Mall Oktoberfest after the von Steuben Day Parade the end of September.

In early October, the German community celebrates German American Friendship Day and the Day of Unification. The German Consulate, the German American Chamber of Commerce, the DANK (German American National Congress) Group, and the United German Club Organizations, all participate. Homeland Clubs, like the Schwaben, Rhein-landers, Berliners, Bavarians, Niedersachsen and Hamburgians, have special programs.

Halloween is October 31st, the eve of All Saints Day, when

Sommer

Am 4. Juli feiert Amerika seine Unabhängigkeit mit dem Independence Day. Das ganze Land feiert. In farbenprächtigen Paraden marschiert das Volk die Straßen entlang, um sich danach in einem Park zu den Klängen einer Band zu amüsieren. Ein in allen Farben schillerndes und ohrenbetäubendes Feuerwerk bildet den Abschluß des Tages.

Der Tag der Arbeit, der Labor Day, fällt immer auf den ersten Montag im September. Er kündigt offiziell den Herbst an. Die Studenten und Schüler sind bereits in ihre Colleges, Universitäten und Schulen zurückgekehrt.

Von Mitte September bis Ende Oktober wird in jedem deutschen Restaurant, Club und jeder deutschen Gemeinde Oktoberfest gefeiert. In Downtown Chicago sperrt man sogar einen Teil der Adams Street vor dem Berghoff Restaurant ab, um drei Tage lang mit Bratwurst und Bier auf der Straße zu feiern. Das Chicago Brauhaus auf der Lincoln Avenue eröffnet das Oktoberfest auf der Lincoln Mall im Anschluß an die Steuben Parade Ende September und feiert dann zwei Wochen lang.

Anfang Oktober zelebriert die deutsche Gemeinde den Deutsch-Amerikanischen Freundschaftstag und den Tag der deutschen Einheit. Unterstützt vom Deutschen Konsulat, der Deutsch-Amerikanischen Handelskammer, dem DANK (Deutsch-Amerikanischer Nationalkongreß) und der Vereinigung Deutscher Clubs nehmen Heimatklubs wie der Schwabenverein, der Rheinische Verein, die Berliner Bären, der Bayerische Verein, die Niedersachsen und die Hamburger mit ihren Programmen daran teil.

Am Vorabend der Allerheiligen feiert man am 31. Oktober in Amerika

The sky before the thunderstorm, threatening yet beautiful
Der Himmel vor einem Gewitter - ein schauerlich schöner Anblick

Got the best pumpkin in the patch
Der größte Kürbis auf dem Feld

Trick or Treat?

Lachner "CHICAGOLAND"

Fall

children carve pumpkins, wear costumes to school and call on neighbors for "tricks or treats" often rewarded with candy, gum, cookies, apples or even a few pennies.

Opera, theater, ballet and concerts open for the Fall and Winter seasons of musical and dramatic programs.

Thanksgiving is a uniquely American national holiday at the end of November which commemorates the first harvest (1621) of the Pilgrims in New England, and their thanks to God for the year's blessings. It is a family holiday featuring the traditional roasted turkey dinner with dressing, cranberry sauce, mince and pumpkin pies, apple cider and cornbread.

Students, who enjoy Spring break and homecoming in the Fall, want to be with their friends and families on Thanksgiving. It is a time to reflect and share the experiences of the year just past, the tests and tasks achieved, to reminisce and talk about what was, could have been and what is to come.

After Thanksgiving, Christmas decorations appear in all the stores. The great Christmas tree in Chicago's Civic Center is lighted and dozens of trees on North Michigan Avenue are ablaze with lights. Santa Claus meets all the little ones and the Salvation Army collects donations for their good work with the poor and needy in the City. Their bells and kettles are on every street corner.

"Halloween." Kinder höhlen Kürbisse aus und mit gruseligen Kostümen und Masken verkleidet, ziehen sie mit ihren Kürbislaternen von Haus zu Haus, um sich mit Süßigkeiten, einem Apfel oder ein paar Pfennigen belohnen zu lassen, daß sie keinen Streich gespielt haben. Man nennt das Spiel hier „Trick or Treat."

Oper, Theater, Ballett und Konzerte eröffnen die Herbst- und Wintersaison.

„Thanksgiving" ist ein Feiertag, der nur in Amerika gefeiert wird. Ende November feiert Amerika das erste Erntedankfest (1621) der Pilgrims in New England, die ihrem Gott für den Segen des ersten Jahres dankten. Es ist ein typischer Familienfeiertag mit traditionell gefüllter Pute, Preiselbeeren, Pumpkin Pies, Apfelwein und Maisbrot.

Die Schüler und Studenten, die normalerweise ihre Osterferien oder Spring Break genießen und im Herbst das Homecoming, wollen den Thanksgiving-Feiertag mit Familie und Freunden verbringen. Es ist eine Zeit des Nachdenkens und eine Zeit, in der man mit der Familie die Erlebnisse des zurückliegenden Jahres, die Prüfungen und Erfolge teilen und über die Zukunft sprechen möchte.

Nach den Thanksgiving-Feiertagen fängt Amerika an, sich für Weihnachten zu schmücken. Die Lichter an dem großen Weihnachtsbaum auf dem Platz des Chicago Civic Centers werden angezündet und tausende von winzigen Lichtern erleuchten die Bäume auf der Nord-Michigan Avenue. Santa Claus nimmt die Wünsche der Kinder entgegen und die Heilsarmee sammelt Geschenke für die Armen und Bedürftigen der Stadt. Sie stehen mit ihren Sammelkesseln an jeder Straßenecke und ermahnen

Winter

Oktoberfest celebrations are held everywhere

Oktoberfeste wo man hinschaut

Indoor dining is back in vogue

Die richtige Jahreszeit für ein Diner im Restaurant

The Christmas tree is lighted the day after Thanksgiving

Die Lichter des Christbaums werden am Tag nach dem Thanksgiving-Fest angezündet

The Nutcracker Suite Ballet enchants children of all ages

Das Nußknacker-Ballett entzückt Kinder aller Altersstufen

Animated Christmas windows are worth the trip downtown

Der lange Weg in die Stadt hat sich gelohnt, wenn man zur Weihnachtszeit vor den geschmückten und animierten Schaufenstern der Kaufhäuser steht

On a fast, white trail with a snowmobile

Mit einem Motorschlitten auf schnellen, weißen Pfaden

GOOD TIMES — FREIZEIT

Homes are decorated with Christmas wreaths, trees and lights. The Christmas tree, a German custom, is observed all over the United States. Christmas cards and gifts are exchanged. Special cookies and cakes are prepared.

Christmas Eve services are attended by Protestants and Catholics alike. Then on Christmas Day, gifts are opened and family and friends come together for dinner at home.

The Adler Planetarium has a special presentation at Christmas telling how the stars were arranged at the time of Christ's birth. The Museum of Science and Industry has a marvelous program to celebrate Christmas around the world. The Nutcracker ballet is presented every year at the Arie Crown Theater in McCormick Place. The "Hallelujah" chorus from Handel's Messiah is sung in many churches.

New Year's Eve celebrations at hotels or at home welcome the new year with champagne. A "count down" of the last minutes of the old year brings hundreds of people into downtown Chicago at midnight.

New Year's Day is reserved for the Tournament of Roses Parade from Pasadena, California and the Collegiate Bowl Championship Football games.

Chicago may be very cold in January, but snow can be beautiful. Even in the City! But it is a good time to take a few days off, if possible, and go to Florida, the Caribbean islands, the Arizona desert, to Las Vegas, Nevada or the West Coast. A reprieve from shovelling snow is always pleasant. Most people stay in Chicagoland to enjoy the Winter - a hike in the park, ice skating and hockey, sledding and tobagganing, skiing and snowmobiling. Many hardy men have fun icefishing and ice-sailing. You might even see some hunters out braving the weather.

February means St. Valentine's Day and President's Day, honoring the birthdays of George Washington and Abraham Lincoln.

In March, everyone joins the Irish in celebrating St. Patrick's Day, on the 17th. The Chicago River is dyed green, restaurants serve green beer, and thousands of people watch the long and colorful St. Patrick's Day parade in the Loop as over 50 bands, floats and some 2,000 marchers pass by.

Easter usually comes in April and with it, warmer weather, green grass once again, snow drops, crocusses, daffodils and tulips.

May and June are busy months with graduations and weddings to attend. Kids are out of school for the Summer the middle of June. It's off to camp for a couple of weeks for the lucky youngsters, and vacation time until the end of August.

mit ihren Klingeln an das Fest der Liebe und des Gebens.

Die Häuser werden mit Adventskränzen, Weihnachtsbäumen und Lichtern geschmückt. Der Tannenbaum, eine aus Deutschland mitgebrachte Sitte, wird in ganz Amerika geschmückt. Weihnachtskarten und Geschenke werden ausgetauscht und es duftet nach Weihnachtsgebäck.

Protestanten und Katholiken gehen am Heilig Abend zum Gottesdienst. Am Ersten Feiertag werden die Geschenke ausgepackt und Familien und Freunde versammeln sich zum Festschmaus.

Das Adler Planetarium bietet um die Weihnachtszeit ein Sonderprogramm an und zeigt die Sternkonstellation zur Zeit der Geburt Christi. Das Museum of Science and Industry feiert Weihnachten mit einer wunderschönen Weihnachtsbaum-Ausstellung. Im Arie Crown Theater im McCormick Place kann man sich beim Nußknacker Ballet von Tschaikowsky weihnachtlichen Kinderträumen hingeben. Die Klänge des „Halleluja" aus dem Messias von Händel tönen uns aus vielen Kirchen entgegen.

Silvester feiert man in Hotels oder man heißt das Neue Jahr mit Freunden und Sekt zu Hause willkommen. Auch die Innenstadt wird kurz vor 24 Uhr lebendig, wenn sich Besucher und Gäste zusammentun, um das Neue Jahr einzuläuten.

Neujahrstag gehört der Parade des Tournament of Roses in Pasadena, Kalifornien, und dem Collegiate Bowl Championship Football-Spiel.

Im Januar kann es in Chicago sehr kalt werden, aber wenn hier Schnee liegt, verwandelt sich Chicagoland in eine Märchenwelt. Sogar in der Stadt!

Der Januar ist eigentlich ein guter Monat, sich ein paar Tage vom Schneeschaufeln und der Kälte zu erholen. Ein Urlaub in Florida, in der Karibik, in Arizona, in Las Vegas in Nevada oder an der Westküste steht bei vielen auf dem Kalender. Die meisten Menschen allerdings bleiben in Chicago und genießen den Winter, indem sie in den Parks spazierengehen, Schlittschuhlaufen oder Rodeln gehen, Hockey spielen, Skilaufen oder Snowmobiling gehen. Einige der abgehärteten Seelen gehen sogar Eisfischen oder Eissegeln. Hier und da sieht man auch einen Jäger, dem das kalte Wetter nichts ausmacht.

Valentinstag wird im Februar gefeiert. Im Februar feiert man auch die Geburtstage von George Washington und Abraham Lincoln.

Am 17. März wird jeder in Chicago Irisch und feiert den St. Patrickstag. Der Chicago River wird grün gefärbt, in den Kneipen wird grünes Bier serviert und zu tausenden stehen die Familien mit ihren Kindern und die Büroangestellten im Loop am Straßenrand und schauen der langen und farbenfreudigen St. Patrick's Day Parade zu, die mit 50 Bands, geschmückten Festwagen und 2000 Paradeteilnehmern vorbeimarschiert.

Ostern fällt meistens in den April, und bringt warmes Wetter, grünes Gras, Schneeglöckchen, Krokusse, Narzissen und Tulpen mit sich.

Mai und Juni sind angefüllt mit Schulabschlußfeiern und Hochzeiten. Die Sommerferien fangen Mitte Juni an und wer Glück hat, darf zwei Wochen lang zu einem Camp gehen. Die Großen Ferien gehen Ende August zu Ende.

Chicago Temperatures (Average)

Durchschnittstemperaturen in Chicago

Month/Monat	Fahrenheit degrees	Celsius Grade
January	21.0-	-6,10-
February	25.4-	-3,67-
March	37.2	+ 2,89
April	48.6	+ 9,20
May	58.9	+14,94
June	68.6	+20,30
July	73.2+	+22,89+
August	71.7+	+22,10+
September	64.4	+18,00
October	52.8	+11,56
November	40.0	+ 4,40
December	26.6	- 3,00

Source/Quelle: Farmers' Almanac

The "State of Copernicus", one of the pioneers in modern astronomy, highlights the entrance to Chicago's Adler Planetarium
Courtesy of the Chicago Convention Bureau
Ron Schramm, photographer

Kopernikus, Pionier moderner Astronomie, am Eingang zum Adler Planetarium in Chicago
Mit Genehmigung des Chicago Convention Bureau/
Ron Schramm, Fotograf

Chicago is noted for its exciting vibrant nightlife, including comedy, dance, blues and jazz clubs
Courtesy of Chicago Convention Bureau
Ron Schramm, photographer

Chicago ist für sein aufregendes und belebtes Nachtleben berühmt, einschließlich Komödien, Tanzclubs, und Blues- und Jazzclubs.
Mit Genehmigung des Chicago Convention Bureau/
Ron Schramm, Fotograf

GOOD TIMES — FREIZEIT

At the Art Institue of Chicago, noted for its Impressionist Collection, Renaissance oils, Thorne minature rooms, garden restaurant and a special museum for Children Ron Schramm, photographer

Das Art Institute of Chicago ist berühmt für seine Sammlung französischer Impressionisten und Ölgemälden aus der Renaissancezeit, dem Thorne-Saal für Miniaturen, einem Gartenrestaurant und einem Kindermuseum
Ron Schramm, Fotograf

Lincoln Park Conservatory has hosted visitors since 1892 and features a magnificent collection of orchids, palms and other hothouse plants
Courtesy Chicago Convention Bureau / Ron Schramm, photographer

Lincoln Park Conservatory entzückt seine Besucher seit 1892 mit einer herrlichen Sammlung an Orchideen, Palmen und anderen Gewächshauspflanzen
Mit Genehmigung des Chicago Convention Bureau/ Ron Schramm, Fotograf

The Shedd Aquarium, Field Museum of Natural History and Adler Planetarium are located on south Lake Shore Drive, minutes from the Loop
Courtesy Chicago Convention Bureau / Gene Hickmott, photographer

Das Shedd Aquarium, Field Museum of Natural History und das Adler Planetarium befinden sich auf dem Süd-Lake Shore Drive nur Minuten vom Loop entfernt.
Mit Genehmigung des Chicago Convention Bureau/Gene Kickmott, Fotograf

Chicago is known for its abundance of architectural styles, each adding to the magnificent skyline. Anchored by the John Hancock Center built in 1969, the Michigan Avenue area boasts a variety of landmark buildings as well as a world-class shopping district Ron Schramm, photographer

Die atemberaubende Skyline Chicagos ist das Ergebnis der Architektur verschiedener Stilrichtungen. Das in 1969 erbaute John Hancock Center gibt den Ton an auf der Michigan Avenue, auf der sich ein Wahrzeichen nach dem anderen reiht und ein exklusives Geschäft nach dem anderen.   Mit Genehmigung des Chicago Convention Bureau/Ron Schramm, Fotograf

Lachner "CHICAGOLAND"

333 Wacker Drive. This 36-floor granite and glass building is curved as its mirrored facade reflects the Chicago River. In 1984, the design was recognized by the American Institute of Architects
Courtesy Chicago Convention Bureau / Ron Schramm, photographer

333 Wacker Drive. Ein 36 Stockwerk hohes Gebäude aus Granit und Glas, in dessen Rundfassade sich der Chicago River widerspiegelt. Das Design wurde 1984 vom American Institute of Architects ausgezeichnet.
Mit Genehmigung des Chicago Convention Bureau / Ron Schramm, Fotograf

"The Discoverers" sculpture on the southeast tower of the Michigan Avenue bridge depicts French explorers Louis Jolliet and Jacques Marquette (center), along with other explorers Rene Robert Cavelier, Sieur De LaSalle, Henri De Tonti and a kneeling Native American in the foreground.
Photo by Ron Schramm

Die Skulptur der „Discoverers" am südöstlichen Turm der Michigan Avenue-Brücke stellt die französischen Entdecker Louis Jolliet und Jacques Marquette (Mitte) zusammen mit den anderen Entdeckern Rene Robert Cavelier, Sieur De LaSalle, Henri De Tonti und einem knieenden Indianer im Vordergrund dar.
Foto Ron Schramm

A pair of huge bronze Lions have guarded the Art Institute since 1883
Photo: Mary Gekler, August 1958

Zwei riesige Bronzelöwen stehen seit 1883 vor dem Art Institute Wache
Foto: Mary Gekler, August 1958

The evening sun is reflected in this river view of the skyline
Courtesy Chicago Convention Bureau / Ron Schramm, photographer

Die Abendsonne reflektiert sich in der Fluß-Ansicht der Skyline
Mit Genehmigung des Convention Bureau / Ron Schramm, Fotograf

GOOD TIMES — FREIZEIT

The new International Terminal at O'Hare Airport

Lachner *"CHICAGOLAND"*

United Airlines is headquartered at O'Hare International Airport

Fly Away on Vacation, for Business, or Plain Fun

Americans, like Europeans, enjoy traveling. This chapter describes the airports around Chicagoland. In addition there are many airstrips used by private pilots, flying farmers and executives, who park their plane in their backyards, as in southwest, suburban Brookhaven.

O'Hare International Airport is located northwest, 15 miles from the City. Almost a city in itself, it works very well and runs smoothly except during major weather disturbances. Everything moves in and out with great efficiency. It has to, as this is the busiest airport in the world, handling approx. 69 million passengers a year. At the present time only an eastern expressway leads vehicular traffic in and out of the airport. The Chicago Transit Authority (CTA) transports light-traveling passengers by subway to and from downtown to the Airport in 40 minutes. There is also helicopter service to downtown's Meigs Field and Midway Airport on the southwest side.

Five major terminals, and the Hilton Airport Hotel, are the main buildings in the passenger part of the airport facility.

Über den Wolken - auf dem Weg in die Ferien, auf Geschäftsreisen oder einfach nur zum Vergnügen oder Sport

Wie die Europäer gehen auch die Amerikaner gern auf Reisen. In diesem Kapitel werden die Flughäfen, die um Chicago herum liegen, beschrieben. Darüber hinaus gibt es hier viele private Landebahnen, die von Privatpersonen, Großbauern und leitenden Angestellten der Industrie für ihre Zivilflugzeuge genutzt werden, die sie meist auf ihren eigenen Grundstücken abstellen. Zum Beispiel in dem südwestlichen Vorort Brookhaven.

O'Hare International Airport liegt rund 24 km vom Zentrum der Stadt entfernt. Der Flughafen ist fast eine eigenständige Stadt. Auf diesem Flughafen läuft alles wie am Schnürchen und nur bei schlechtem Wetter können kleine Pannen auftreten. Mit äußerster Präzision wird der Verkehr abgewickelt und das muß so sein, denn der O'Hare International Airport ist der geschäftigste Flughafen der Welt, auf dem jährlich ca. 69 Millionen Passagiere abgefertigt werden. Gegenwärtig führt nur eine Schnellstraße zum Flughafen. Reisenden mit leichtem Gepäck steht die Chicago Transit Authority (CTA) zur Verfügung, die die Fluggäste innerhalb von 40 Minuten in die Stadt bzw. zum Flughafen bringt. Außerdem gibt es einen Hubschrauberservice zu dem in der Stadt liegenden Meigs Field und zum Midway Airport, der weiter südwestlich liegt.

United Airlines Terminal, bright and efficient

FLY AWAY — ÜBER DEN WOLKEN

Terminal 1 is Chicago headquarters of United Airline's futuristic facility, consisting of two glass-domed buildings, designed by German-born Architect Helmut Jahn.

Terminal 2 accommodates a great variety of domestic airlines. It is opposite from the Hilton Hotel, where one can reserve rooms for rest between flights, or rent meeting rooms by the hour.

Terminal 3 houses American and Delta Airlines, the first and third largest U. S. carriers.

Terminal 4 provides facilities for emergencies, special events and charters. It is located in the six story parking facility, and was used for years as the temporary International Terminal.

Terminal 5 is the new International Terminal which now elegantly and appropriately welcomes visitors from all continents. It is bright, efficient and convenient, located a mile east of the other terminals.

All terminals and the hotel are connected by a French MATRA people-mover train system, which also carries passengers to and from the remote parking facilities. Rental car customers are shuttled to their respective agency locations by buses which constantly roam the circular drive at the terminal's lower level.

Fünf große Terminals und das Hilton Hotel bilden das Hauptgebäude für den Passagierverkehr.

In dem futuristisch anmutenden **Terminal 1** ist die United Airline untergebracht. Das mit zwei Glaskuppeln überdachte Gebäude wurde von dem deutschen Architekten Helmut Jahn entworfen.

Im **Terminal 2** sind die Inlandfluggesellschaften untergebracht. Er liegt dem Hilton Hotel gegenüber, wo man zwischen Flügen übernachten oder auch stundenweise Konferenzräume mieten kann.

Im **Terminal 3** finden wir die American und Delta Fluggesellschaften, die erst- bzw. drittgrößten Fluggesellschaften Amerikas.

Terminal 4 steht jetzt Notstationen und Charterfluggesellschaften zur Verfügung. Es ist in dem 6-stöckigen Parkhaus untergebracht, das jahrelang als vorübergehender Internationaler Terminal diente.

Im **Terminal 5** endlich ist der neue Internationale Terminal untergebracht, der mit seiner eleganten und funktionalen Gestaltung Besuchern aus der ganzen Welt den richtigen Weg weist. Der Terminal ist ein helles, freundliches, effizientes und praktisches Gebäude, das etwa 1 1/2 km östlich von den anderen Terminals liegt.

Zubringerbusse und der „People Mover" (computergesteuerte Transferbahn) drehen ununterbrochen auf der Flughafenringstraße ihre Runden und bringen die Fluggäste zu den fünf großen Terminals, dem Hilton Hotel, den Parkhäusern bzw. -plätzen und den Autovermietungen.

The airport property also accommodates the large cargo terminals of all major carriers. Lufthansa, the largest cargo airline, shares facilities with Air France. There are freight terminals for KLM, British Airways, Air Canada, Japan Air Lines, etc. Federal Express and United Parcel Service (UPS). The United States Post Office maintains operations that can handle huge amounts of mail and parcels efficiently and timely. A letter or parcel dropped off by noon will be on a plane to Europe that afternoon, guaranteed.

Punctual Parcel Delivery

Pünktliche Paket Zustellung

Auf dem Flughafengelände sind auch die Frachtterminals der großen Fluggesellschaften untergebracht. Die Lufthansa, die größte Luftfrachtgesellschaft, teilt ihre Anlage mit der Air France. Aber auch die KLM, British Airways, Air Canada, Japan Air Lines, Federal Express und United Parcel Service (UPS) verfügen über Kargoterminals. Die amerikanische Bundespost hat dort ebenfalls einen eigenen Betrieb, der riesige Mengen an Post und Postsendungen schnell und pünktlich weiterleitet. Briefe oder Pakete, die gegen Mittag aufgegeben werden, sind unter Garantie am Nachmittag im Flugzeug unterwegs nach Europa.

Express Letter Carriers

Schneller Briefverkehr

FLY AWAY — ÜBER DEN WOLKEN

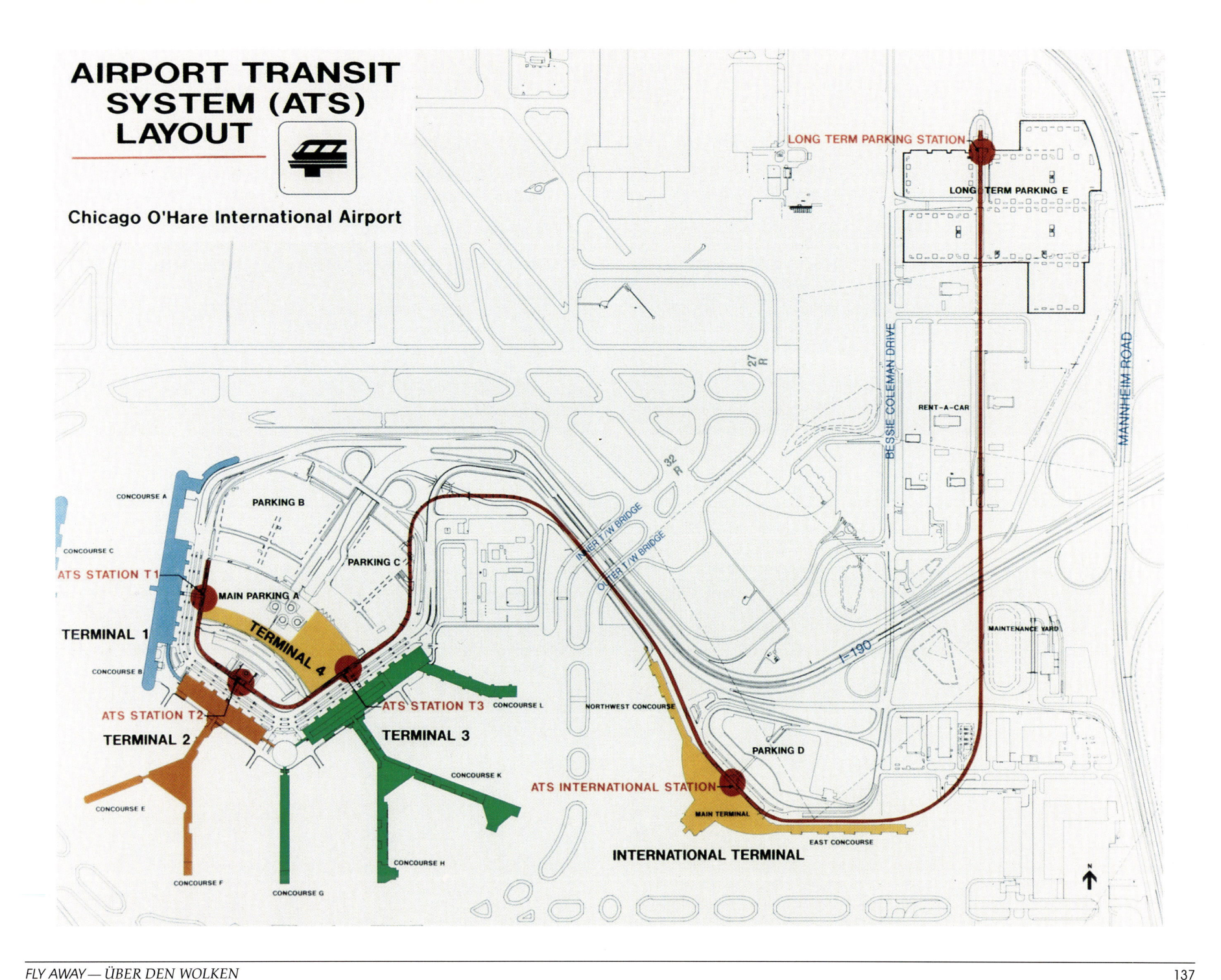

Midway Airport, on the city's Southwest side, was dedicated in 1927 and has undergone several major renovations. In 1992 as Chicago's second airport, 7,950,000 passengers arrived or departed through its gates.

Midway Airport, an der Südseite der Stadt, wurde 1927 eröffnet und wurde vor kurzem renoviert. 7,95 Millionen Passagiere passierten durch seine Sperren.

Lachner "CHICAGOLAND"

Midway Airport, Chicago's original airline terminal, is located nine miles southwest of the Loop. Seven million passengers arrive or depart from this airport annually. It is served by a number of regional air carriers for transfers or shorter flights. There is one terminal building divided into three concourses. The Terminal A & C extensions are for arrival and departures, and Terminal B, the central part of the terminal, is where information booths and limousine, taxi and vehicle pick-up services are available. From here, you can walk to everything in a few minutes. Parking is close by, or easily reached by frequent shuttles, if the car is parked in one of several remote lots. Various car rental agencies are located nearby. The new CTA, Subway/Elevated train serves Midway from downtown in approximately 30 minutes.

Midway Airport ist eigentlich Chicagos erster Flughafen. Er liegt rund 15 km südwestlich vom Loop. Jährlich kommen etwa sieben Millionen Passagiere auf diesem Flughafen an oder fliegen von dort ab. Der Flughafen dient hauptsächlich regionalen Fluggesellschaften für Transport- oder kurze Inlandsflüge. Das Flughafengebäude ist in drei Terminals eingeteilt. Terminals A und C sind für Ankunft und Abflug bestimmt. Terminal B liegt in der Mitte des Gebäudes, wo Informationsstände, Limousinen- und Taxiservice sowie Autovermietungen zu finden sind. Von hier aus kann man alles innerhalb von wenigen Minuten zu Fuß erreichen. Ein Parkplatz liegt direkt vor dem Gebäude. Ein Zubringerbusse zu den entfernter liegenden Parkplätzen hält vor der Tür und die Autovermietungen liegen nahebei. Die neue CTA-Verbindung - Untergrund-Stadtbahn - verbindet Midway mit der Innenstadt innerhalb von 30 Minuten.

DuPage County Airport in west suburban St. Charles is the third busiest in Illinois and provides excellent facilities for private and corporate air travel. This airport offers professional air and ground communications, long and wide runways, modern storage hangars and maintenance shops. You can train here, belong to a flying club and share a small fleet of airplanes. Or you can charter a plane, with pilot, to go anywhere. You can also make this home-base for your own prop or jet airplane.

DuPage County Airpot im westlichen St. Charles ist der drittgrößte Flughafen in Illinois und bietet für Privat- und Geschäftsflüge einen hervorragenden Service. Der Flughafen ist mit den modernsten Luft- und Bodenkontrollanlagen, langen und breiten Start- und Landebahnen und modernen Flugzeughallen und Reparaturwerkstätten ausgerüstet. Hobbyflieger können hier trainieren, einem Fliegerclub beitreten, das eigene Flugzeug hier abstellen oder sogar kleine Flugflotten mit anderen Fliegern teilen. Fliegt man selber nicht, kann ein Flugzeug mit Pilot gemietet werden.

DuPage County Airport

Meigs Field is located at 15th Street, just east of Lake Shore Drive, across from McCormick Place. It accommodates small business and private planes for convenient access to downtown and near north, south and west locations. 165,000 passengers arrive or depart from Meigs Field yearly.

Meigs Field liegt an der 15. Straße direkt an der Ostseite des Lake Shore Drives, gegenüber von McCormick Place. Es dient kleineren Geschäfts- und Privatflugzeugen, und bietet schnellen, bequemen Zugang zur Innenstadt sowie zu nördlichen, südlichen und westlich Destinationen nahebei. Meigs Field bewältigt jährlich 165.000 Passagiere.

Meigs Field

FLY AWAY — ÜBER DEN WOLKEN

Pal-Waukee Airport in north suburban Wheeling is 30 minutes from the Loop, providing fuel, maintenance, charter services and flight crew facilities for business and corporate aircraft.

Hinckley Airport is a small but very active sports facility, located in a western rural area near Aurora. Parachute training and skydiving exercises are performed on a regular basis. Gliderflying either by motor-plane or motorcar tow are very popular. The surrounding fields with different crops provide excellent thermal drafts for soaring.

Pal-Waukee Flughafen liegt im nördlichen Wheeling, etwa 30 Minuten vom Loop entfernt. Hier kann man sein Privatflugzeug auftanken und warten lassen. Desweiteren werden Charterservices, Flugbesatzungen und Ausrüstungen für Geschäftsflüge angeboten.

Hinckley Airport ist ein kleiner Flughafen für Sportflugzeuge in einer ländlichen Gegend in der Nähe des westlichen Auroras gelegen. Ausbildungen im Fallschirmspringen und Skydiving-Übungen werden dort regelmäßig durchgeführt. Segel- oder Gleitfliegen ist sehr populär. Die umliegenden Felder und Äcker sorgen für den dazu notwendigen Wärmeauftrieb.

Ballooning out of suburban Plainfield at the southwest region of Chicagoland, is an exclusive airborne activity. There is room for only four people: the pilot, and three passengers in the wicker basket, called a Gondola. The balloon is inflated with a large fan drawing in cold air, the pilot then uses propane burners warming up the air in the balloon, making it light, and soon the balloon stands upright. Hop in and away you go! Weather permitting, the large and colorful hot-air balloon will quickly lift you up to a safe height and then drift in total silence across the countryside, chasing deer, allowing marvelous photography of a dramatic sky at dawn or dusk. Always accompanied by a shadow, and with occasional radio contact with the chase truck, it eventually comes to rest at a field where the farmer's family may join the balloonists for a traditional toast of champagne.

Das einmalige Erlebnis einer Ballonfahrt kann man im vorortlichen Plainfield im südwestlichen Chicagoland erleben. Die Gondel, ein Ballonkorb, faßt nur vier Personen: den Piloten und drei Passagiere. Der Ballon wird mit Hilfe eines Kaltluftgebläses aufgeblasen. Nachdem der Pilot dann die Luft im Ballon mit einem Propangasbrenner erwärmt hat, steigt der leichter gewordene Ballon auf. Jetzt hineinspringen und davonfliegen. Je nach Wetterbedingungen steigen die großen und bunten luftgefüllten Ballons schnell in sichere Höhen, um dann in totaler Stille über die Landschaften zu gleiten und mit ihrem Schatten dem Wild hinterher zu jagen. Die Aufnahmen, die man früh am Morgen bei Sonnenaufgang oder am Abend bei Sonnenuntergang von dort oben machen kann, sind einfach einmalig. Der Ballon steht mit dem Begleitfahrzeug in Funkverbindung. Manchmal landet er auf dem Acker eines Bauern, der dann mit seiner Familie und den Ballonpassagieren beim traditionellen Champagnertoast mit anstößt.

Life in the suburbs can be uplifting!
Das Leben in den Vororten kann ein 'beflügelndes' Erlebnis sein!

Tollroad gate designed for heavy traffic
Mautschranke ideal für viel Verkehr

Lachner "CHICAGOLAND"

Chicago, looking north

Chicago's colorful skyline after Thanksgiving — Chicagos farbenprächtige Silhouette nach Thanksgiving

Photo by Bob Horsch

Life and Leisure...

The *Chicago Tribune*'s Friday "Entertainment Section" and the *Chicago Sun-Times*, the two city newspapers, keep their readers informed on entertainment events in and around the city. Other helpful publications are "Key" and "Where" booklets available at all major hotels, and the "Chicago Magazine", which is publisdhed monthly.

"Crain's Chicago Business" and "The Wall Street Journal" provide weekly business, financial, corporate and international news. The "German American Journal Midwest", published bi-monthly circulates to 4,500 German American executives in Chicago, and other cities in the United States and Germany.

Chicago, sister city of Hamburg, Germany, so designated in a 1994 Proclamation, maintains an active exchange of business, travel, cultural and entertainment programs. The Sister City Program includes bringing news from the German and other ethnic communities of Chicago to the cities of Gothenburg, Prague, Kiev, Warsaw, Osaka, Shenyang, Milan, Casablanca and Toronto.

Chicago has many hotels available for conventions, exhibitions, and business meetings. They are listed in the "Chicago Official Visitors Guide" and in the Yellow pages of the city telephone book. Your travel agent can help you find the hotel at the best location for your business, personal and family needs.

Leben und Freizeit...

Die „Entertainment Sections," Beilagen der Freitagsausgaben der Chicago Tribune und der Sun-Times, der zwei großen Chicagoer Tageszeitungen, informieren ihre Leser über die Veranstaltungen in der Stadt und der näheren Umgebung. Andere hilfreiche Publikationen sind „Key" und „WHERE", die in allen größeren Hotels ausliegen und das „Chicago Magazine", das monatlich herausgebracht wird.

"Crain's Chicago Business" und "The Wall Street Journal" sind die führenden Wirtschaftszeitungen und bringen die neuesten Nachrichten aus der nationalen und internationalen Geschäftswelt und von den Finanzmärkten. Das alle zwei Monate erscheinende „German American Journal Midwest" wird an 4,500 Deutsch-Amerikaner in Chicago und andere Städte in den Vereinigten Staaten und in Deutschland geschickt.

Chicago, dessen deutsche Partnerstadt laut einer Proklamation von 1994 Hamburg ist, unterhält einen aktiven Austausch von Geschäfts-, Reise-, Kultur-, und Veranstaltungsprogrammen. Das Partnerstadtprogramm bringt u.a. Nachrichten aus Deutschland und anderen Partnerstädten wie Göteborg, Prag, Kiew, Warschau, Osaka, Shenyang, Mailand, Casablanca und Toronto nach Chicago.

Chicago hat zahlreiche Hotels, die Räumlichkeiten für Tagungen, Konferenzen, Ausstellungen und Geschäftstreffen zur Verfügung stellen. Sie sind im „Chicago Official Visitors Guide" und in den Gelben Seiten der Telephonbücher aufgeführt. Bei der Suche nach einem gutgelegenen Hotel, das Ihren Ansprüchen entspricht, kann Ihnen ebenfalls Ihr Reisebüro behilflich sein.

St. Michaels Cathedral was built by the German community in 1869.

St. Michaels Cathedrale wurde von der deutschen Gemeinde im Jahre 1869 gebaut.

Churches in Chicagoland

Traditionally, the Church takes care of its own congregation, and many still do.

Today, with a shifting, pluralistic society, the modern Church has many opportunities to be a spiritual leader, a guide for those affected by the changes and transitions of modern life, and comfort for those in need.

Christ Church of Oak Brook, is a non-demoninational Church, which bases its services on the Bible, and has active teaching and counselling programs, supports a vast network of missionaries and preaches the gospel through weekly outreach programs via TV and radio. With a congregation of 5,000, it is sensitive to provide a meaningful message to each individual.

Kirchen

Früher kümmerte sich die Kirche eigenverantwortlich um ihre Gemeinde, so auch noch häufig in diesen Tagen.

Heute bieten sich der modernen Kirche, aufgrund einer sich fortwährend ändernden und pluralistischen Gesellschaft, zahlreiche Möglichkeiten, eine Führungsrolle einzunehmen, sei es in spiritueller Hinsicht oder als eine Stütze für die Menschen, die von den Veränderungen und Umwälzungen im modernen Leben in Mitleidenschaft gezogen werden und Hilfe brauchen.

Die „Christ Church of Oak Brook" ist eine konfessionslose Kirche, die ihren Glauben auf die Bibel zurückführt. Sie bietet eine Reihe lehrreicher und ratgebender Programme an und unterhält ein ausgedehntes Missionarsnetz. In wöchentlich ausgestrahlten Radio- und Fernsehsendungen predigt sie das Evangelium. Sie ist sehr darum bemüht, ihrer Gemeinde von 5,000 Mitgliedern eine bedeutungsvolle Botschaft mitzuteilen.

Christ Church of Oak Brook

The Music Scene   *Musik*

Gala opera throng during intermission in the Daniel F. and Ada L. Rice Grand Foyer of the Lyric Opera of Chicago, at Wacker Drive and Madison Street. 40 years of exemplary artistry and extraordinary entertainment has resulted in 102% capacity subscriptions for the last six years.

Während einer Pause im Daniel F. und Ada L. Rice Grand Foyer der Chicagoer Lyric Opera am Wacker Drive und Madison Street. Ein 102%er Verkauf von Abonnements in den letzten Jahren spiegelt den Erfolg vierzig Jahre außergewöhnlicher Kunst wider.

CHICAGO OPERA THEATRE
20 East Jackson Boulevard
(312) 663-0555

CHICAGO SINFONIETTA
105 West Adams Street
Suite 3330
(312) 857-1072

CHICAGO SYMPHONY ORCHESTRA
Orchestra Hall
220 South Michigan Avenue
PhoneCharge: (312) 435-6666

GRANT PARK MUSIC FESTIVAL
Petrillo Band Shell
235 S. Columbus Dr. (at Jackson)
(312) 819-0614

LYRIC OPERA
20 North Wacker Drive
(312) 332-2244

OLD TOWN SCHOOL OF FOLK MUSIC
909 West Armitage
(312) 525-7793

ORCHESTRA HALL
220 South Michigan Avenue
(312) 435-6666

RAVINIA FESTIVAL
1575 Oakwood Avenue
Lake-Cook & Green Bay Roads
Highland Park
(312) R-A-V-I-N-I-A

The Chicago Symphony Orchestra in its second century enjoys an enviable position in the music world. Performances are greeted with enthusiasm both at home and abroad. Best-selling recordings continue to win prestigious international awards. Syndicated radio broadcasts are heard by millions in every corner of the world.

Im zweiten Jahrhundert ihres Bestehens genießt das Chicago Symphony Orchestra einen ausgezeichneten Ruf in der Musikwelt. Die Konzerte ernten sowohl in Chicago als auch im Ausland enthusiastische Beifallsstürme. Die erfolgreich verkauften Aufnahmen gewinnen zudem angesehene, internationale Musikpreise. Lizenzsierte Radioübertragungen werden von Millionen in aller Welt gehört.

Orchestra Hall

LIFE AND LEISURE — LEBEN UND FREIZEIT

Chicagoland Theatres / Theater

APPLE TREE THEATRE
595 Elm Place, Highland Park
(708) 432-4335

ATHENAEUM THEATRE
2936 North Southport
(312) 525-0195

AUDITORIUM THEATRE
50 East Congress Parkway
(312) 922-4046
Ticketmaster: (312) 559-2900

BAILIWICK REPERTORY
Theatre Building, 1225 West Belmont
(312) 327-5252

CANDLELIGHT DINNER PLAYHOUSE
5620 South Harlem Avenue, Summit
(708) 496-3000

CANDLELIGHT'S FORUM THEATRE
5620 South Harlem Avenue, Summit
(708) 496-3000

CHICAGO THEATRE
175 North State Street
Ticketmaster: (312) 902-1500

CITY LIT
Chicago Cultural Center
77 E. Randolph Street, (312) 271-1100

COMEDYSPORTZ
520 South Michigan Avenue
(312) 549-8080

CLASSICS ON STAGE!
Pickwick Theatre, Park Ridge
(708) 989-0598

COURT THEATRE
University of Chicago
5535 South Ellis Avenue
(312) 753-4472

DEPAUL UNIVERSITY, THE THEATRE SCHOOL
Merle Reskin Theatre
60 East Balbo
(312) 362-8455

DES PLAINES THEATRE GUILD
515 East Thacker, Des Plaines
(708) 390-5720

DRURY LANE DINNER THEATRE
2500 West 95th Place, Evergreen Park
(708) 422-0404

DRURY LANE OAK BROOK
100 Drury Lane, Oak Brook
(708) 530-8300
Ticketmaster: (312) 902-1500

DRY GULCH DINNER THEATRE
9351 West Irving Park Rd., Schiller Park
(708) 671-6644

ETA CREATIVE ARTS FOUNDATION
7558 South Chicago Avenue
(312) 752-3955

FAMOUS DOOR THEATRE CO.
3212 North Broadway
(312) 404-8283

GOODMAN THEATRE
200 South Columbus Drive
(312) 443-3800

ILLINOIS THEATRE CENTER
400A Lakewood Boulevard, Park Forest
(708) 481-3510

INTERPLAY
Piper's Alley, 1608 North Wells
(312) 654-1055

LIFELINE THEATRE
6912 North Glenwood
(312) 761-4477, (708) 634-0200

LOOKINGGLASS THEATRE CO.
At Steppenwolf Theatre
1650 North Halsted, (312) 335-1650

MARRIOTT'S LINCOLNSHIRE THEATRE
10 Marriott Drive, Lincolnshire
(708) 634-0200

MAYFAIR THEATRE
636 South Michigan Avenue
(312) 786-9120

NATIONAL JEWISH THEATRE
5050 West Church, Skokie
(708) 675-2200

NEXT THEATRE CO.
927 Noyes Street, Evanston
(708) 475-1875

NORTHLIGHT THEATRE
817 Chicago Avenue, Evanston
(708) 869-7278

O'MALLEY THEATRE
430 South Michigan Avenue, 7th Floor
(312) 341-3719

PEGASUS PLAYERS
1145 West Wilson
(312) 271-2638

PHEASANT RUN DINNER THEATRE
Route 64, St. Charles
(708) 584-6300
Ticketmaster: (312) 902-1500

RAVEN THEATRE
6931 North Clark Street
(312) 338-2177

ROYAL GEORGE CABARET
1641 North Halsted Street
(312) 988-9000

ROYAL GEORGE THEATRE
1641 North Halsted Street
(312) 988-9000

THE SECOND CITY
1616 North Wells Street
(312) 337-3992

THE SECOND CITY E.T.C.
1608 North Wells Street
(312) 642-8189

THE SECOND CITY NORTHWEST
Continental Towers
1701 West Golf Road, Rolling Meadows
(708) 806-1555

SHAKESPEARE REPERTORY
817 Chicago Avenue, Evanston
(708) 869-7278

SHUBERT THEATRE
22 West Monroe Street
Ticketmaster: (312) 902-1500

STEPPENWOLF THEATRE
1650 North Halsted Street
(312) 335-1650

STRAWDOG THEATRE CO.
3829 North Broadway
(312) 528-9696

TOUCHSTONE THEATRE
2851 North Halsted
(312) 404-4700

VICTORY GARDENS THEATER
2257 North Lincoln Avenue
(312) 871-3000

WELLINGTON THEATRE
750 West Wellington
(312) 975-7171

Chicago Theatre Today   *Das Chicago Theater heute*

Museums and Other Good Places to Visit

Museen und andere sehenswerte Plätze

ADLER PLANETARIUM
1300 South Lake Shore Drive
24-hour info. hotline (312) 922-STAR
TDD/TT: (312) 322-0995

AMERICAN POLICE CENTER AND MUSEUM
1705-25 South State Street
(312) 431-0005

ART INSTITUTE OF CHICAGO
111 South Michigan Avenue
(South Michigan Ave. at Adams Street)
(312) 443-3600

BALZEKAS MUSEUM OF LITHUANIAN CULTURE
6500 South Pulaski Road
(312) 582-6500

BICYCLE MUSEUM OF AMERICA
435 East Illinois Street
(312) 222-0500

BLOCK GALLERY
Northwestern University
1967 South Campus Drive on the Arts Circle, Evanston, (708) 491-4000

CAPONE'S CHICAGO
605 North Clark Street
(312) 654-1919

CHARLES GATES DAWES HOUSE
225 Greenwood Avenue, Evanston
(708) 475-3410

CHICAGO ACADEMY OF SCIENCES
2001 North Clark Street at Armitage
(312) 871-2668

CHICAGO ARCHITECTURE FOUNDATION
224 South Michigan Avenue
(312) 922-TOUR

THE CHICAGO ATHENAEUM
Museum of Architecture and Design
1165 North Clark Street
(312) 280-0131

CHICAGO CULTURAL CENTER
78 East Washington Street
(312) 346-3278

CHICAGO HISTORICAL SOCIETY
1629 North Clark Street at North Avenue
(312) 642-4600

CHILDREN'S ARTIFACT CENTER
Spertus Museum
618 South Michigan Avenue
(312) 922-9012 x 248

CUNEO MUSEUM
1350 North Milwaukee Ave., Vernon Hills
(708) 362-3042

DUSABLE MUSEUM
740 East 56th Place
(312) 947-0600

Viewing one of the many exhibits at the Field Museum

Kinder im Field Museum

EVANSTON ART CENTER - CENTER FOR THE VISUAL ARTS
2603 Sheridan Road, Evanston
(708) 475-5300

EVANSTON HISTORICAL SOCIETY
225 Greenwood Avenue, Evanston
(708) 475-3410

FEET FIRST: THE SCHOOL STORY
1001 North Dearborn Street
(312) 280-2939

FIELD MUSEUM OF NATURAL HISTORY
Roosevelt Road at Lake Shore Drive
(312) 922-9410

FRANK LLOYD WRIGHT HOME AND STUDIO
951 Chicago Avenue, Oak Park
(708) 848-1978

HAROLD WASHINGTON LIBRARY
400 South State Street
(312) 747-4130

HELLENIC MUSEUM AND CULTURAL CENTER
400 North Franklin Street
(312) 467-4622

HISTORIC PULLMAN DISTRICT
614 East 113th Street
(312) 785-8181

JANE ADDAMS HULL HOUSE
800 South Halsted Street
(312) 413-5353

KOHL CHILDREN'S MUSEUM
165 Green Bay Road, Wilmette
(708) 256-6056

LIZZADRO MUSEUM OF LAPIDARY ART
220 Cottage Hill - Wilder Park,
Elmhurst, (708) 833-1616

MEXICAN FINE ARTS CENTER MUSEUM
1852 West 19th Street
(312) 785-8181

MUSEUM OF BROADCAST COMMUNICATIONS
Chicago Cultural Center
Michigan Avenue at Washington Street
(312) 629-6000

MUSEUM OF CONTEMPORARY ART
237 East Ontario Street
(312) 280-5161

MUSEUM OF CONTEMPORARY PHOTOGRAPHY
600 South Michigan Avenue
(312) 663-5554

MUSEUM OF HOLOGRAPHY
1134 West Washington Boulevard
(312) 226-1007

MUSEUM OF SCIENCE & INDUSTRY
57th Street at Lake Shore Drive
(312) 684-1414

NAPER SETTLEMENT MUSEUM VILLAGE
201 West Porter Avenue, Naperville
(708) 420-6010

ORIENTAL INSTITUTE MUSEUM
At the University of Chicago
1155 East 58th Street, (312) 702-9521

POLISH MUSEUM OF AMERICA
984 North Milwaukee Avenue
(312) 384-3352

THE POWER HOUSE
101 Shiloh Boulevard, Zion
(708) 291-3367

PRINTER'S ROW PRINTING MUSEUM
731 South Plymouth Court
(312) 987-1059

SCULPTURE CHICAGO
20 North Michigan Avenue, Suite 400
(312) 456-7140

SHEDD AQUARIUM
1200 South Lake Shore Drive
(312) 939-2438 - General Information
(312) 599-0200 - Ticketmaster

THE SMART MUSEUM OF ART
5550 South Greenwood Avenue
(312) 702-0200

SPERTUS MUSEUM/CHILDREN'S ARTIFACT CENTER
618 South Michigan Avenue
(312) 922-9012

SWEDISH AMERICAN MUSEUM CENTER
5211 North Clark Street
(312) 728-8111

TERRA MUSEUM OF AMERICAN ART
666 North Michigan Avenue
(312) 664-3939

UKRANIAN NATIONAL MUSEUM
2453 West Chicago Avenue
(312) 276-6565

LIFE AND LEISURE — LEBEN UND FREIZEIT

Parks and Recreation

Parks und Freizeitanlagen

CHICAGO BOTANIC GARDEN
Lake Cook Road/East of Edens Expressway, Glencoe
(708) 835-5440

A 300-acre living museum, offers visitors of all ages and interests the unparalleled beauty of more than 20 different gardens.

Ein 120ha großes „lebendes" Museum, das Besuchern aller Altersgruppen und Interessenslagen die unvergleichliche Schönheit von mehr als 20 Gärten näherbringt.

CHICAGO PARK DISTRICT
(312) 294-2493

GARFIELD PARK CONSERVATORY
300 North Central Park Boulevard
(312) 533-1281

LINCOLN PARK CONSERVATORY
2400 North Stockton Drive
(312) 294-4770

MORTON ARBORETUM
Route 53, Lisle
(708) 968-0074

A 1500 acre outdoor museum with trails and visitor center. Collections of cultivated trees, shrubs and woody vines from various parts of the world. Visitor center has restaurant, book and gift shop.

Ein 600ha großer Botanischer Garten mit Wanderwegen, einem Informationszentrum und der Ansammlung veredelter Bäume, Sträucher und Weinstöcke von verschiedenen Kontinenten. Das Informationszentrum hat ein Restaurant und einen Buch- und Andenkenladen.

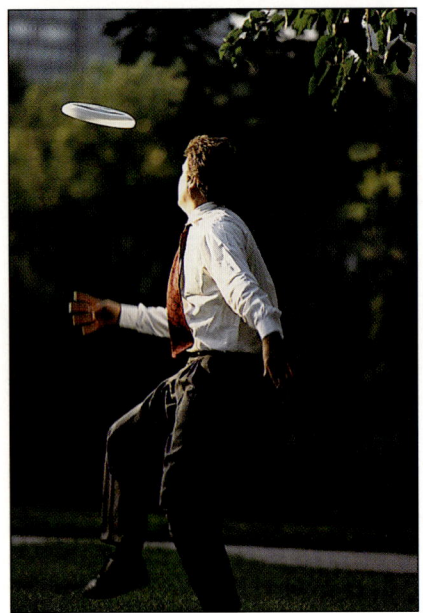

Spirit of the Great Lakes at the Art Institute
Der Geist der Großen Seen

Lincoln Park Conservatory

Lakefront - North from the Aquarium, 1953
Das Seeufer nördlich vom Aquarium, 1953

Frisbie in the Park
Frisbiespieler im Park

148 Lachner "CHICAGOLAND"

Zoos

BROOKFIELD ZOO
8400 West 31st Street, Brookfield
(708) 485-2200

Brookfield Zoo is open daily 10 a.m. to 4:30 p.m. Visitors can tour the zoo via motorized safari rides from late Spring through early Fall. Besides the many seasonal special exhibits there is a permanent exhibit - "Habitat Africa!" - a 5-acre savannah exhibit that highlights Africa's diverse wildlife, habitats, and conservation issues to encourage humans to act on behalf of the world's wild places.

Der Brookfield Zoo ist täglich von 10-16.30 Uhr geöffnet. Vom Frühling bis zum Herbst können Besucher den Zoo mit einer motorisierten Safari-Bahn erkunden. Neben vielen saisonbedingten Sonderausstellungen gibt es eine Dauerausstellung -„Habitat Africa!"- Auf einer 2ha großen Fläche wurde die afrikanische Savanne mit ihrem Wildleben dargestellt. Der Mensch wird hier aufgefordert, die Natur und die vom Aussterben bedrohten Tiere zu achten und zu schützen.

Welcome to Lincoln Park Zoo *Willkommen im Lincoln Park Zoo*

LINCOLN PARK ZOO
2200 North Stockton Drive
(312) 294-4660

Located just 5 minutes from downtown Chicago. Free, first-class city zoo open 365 days a year.

Ein reizender, kleiner Zoo gerade 5 Min. vom Zentrum Chicagos entfernt. Der Eintritt ist frei und der Zoo ist 365 Tage geöffnet

Brookfield Zoo (Photos by Mike Greer, courtesy Chicago Zoological Society/Brookfield)

"Habitat Africa!"    *Elephant Demonstrations — weather permitting*    *Walrus at the Seven Seas Panorama Seascape*

LIFE AND LEISURE — LEBEN UND FREIZEIT

Golf and Picnics

There are more golf courses in the six counties surrounding Chicago than any place in the country. In the 1990 census, more than 250 public and private courses accommodate golfers of varying skills who enjoy the game and friendships.

In den sechs Counties um Chicago gibt es mehr Golfplätze als an irgendeinem anderen Ort im Land. In der 1990er Saison standen mehr als 250 private und öffentliche Plätze Golfern verschiedener Handicaps zur Verfügung, um das Spiel und Freundschaften zu genießen.

Family picnics, friend reunions, and company social gatherings are held during the summer months in the vast Cook County Forest Preserves rimming Chicago. The district maintains 137 major woods, including 2,300 picnic groves, 36 lakes and ponds, and many more recreational facilities.

Familien, Freunde und Arbeitskollegen treffen sich in den Sommermonaten in den weitläufigen Cook County Forest Preserves am Rande von Chicago zu Picknicks. Zu dem Distrikt gehören 137 Wälder, einschließlich 2300 Picknickplätze, 36 Seen und Teiche und zahlreiche andere Freizeitanlagen.

Wanderwege und Bootfahrten

The Morton Arboretum, in west suburban Lisle, is world renowned for its 1500 acres of outdoor wooded plants. Open all year long, visitors enjoy all of nature's beauties throughout all of its seasons. There are trails throughout the park for a walking tour, or you can tour in your automobile.

Das Morton Arboretum im westlichen Vorort Lisle ist weltbekannt für seine mit hölzernen Gewächsen bepflanzte 600ha große Fläche. Da der Park das ganze Jahr über geöffnet ist, genießen Besucher die natürliche Schönheit zu allen Jahreszeiten. Wanderwege im Park laden zu herrlichen Spaziergängen ein oder man erkundet das Gelände mit dem Auto.

Ten boat sightseeing companies offer cruises either along the Chicago River or Lake Michigan. Historical or architectural cruises are scheduled frequently throughout the day, except during winter. An evening cruise along the lake's shoreline provides a spectacular view of the city's skyline at night.

Zehn Schiffahrtsgesellschaften bieten Fahrten auf dem Chicago River und dem Lake Michigan an. Historische und architektonische Bootsfahrten werden im Sommer mehrere Male am Tag angeboten. Eine Abendfahrt entlang des Seeufers gestattet einen atemberaubenden Blick auf die Skyline

LIFE AND LEISURE — LEBEN UND FREIZEIT

Happy Chicagoans

152 Lachner "*CHICAGOLAND*"

Restaurants in Chicagoland

LIFE AND LEISURE — LEBEN UND FREIZEIT

Dining in Chicagoland

Chez Paul

Lawry's

Szechwan House

American

ALEXANDER'S
2875 North Milwaukee Ave.,
Northbrook
(708) 298-2525

ALLIE'S BAKERY
(Chicago Marriott)
540 North Michigan Avenue
(312) 836-6334

ALL SEASONS CAFE
(Hyatt Regency Chicago)
151 East Wacker Drive
(312) 565-1234

A MURDER ON THE TRAIN
3525 West Peterson, Suite 200
(312) 604-4200

ARNIE'S RESTAURANT
1030 North State Street
(312) 266-4800

THE ART INSTITUTE OF CHICAGO
(Restaurant on the Park)
111 South Michigan Avenue
(312) 443-3543

ASCOTS
(Oak Brook Hills Hotel & Resort)
3500 Midwest Road, Oak Brook
(708) 850-5555

ATRIUM CAFE
(Indian Lakes Resort)
250 West Schick Road, Bloomingdale
(708) 529-0200

AVENUE CAFE & RESTAURANT, THE
(Allerton Hotel)
701 North Michigan Avenue
(312) 944-8200

BARLEY'S
(Clarion Intl./Quality Inn O'Hare)
6810 North Manheim Road, Rosemont
(708) 297-1234

BEAU NASH, THE
(Omni Ambassador East)
1300 North State Parkway
(312) 787-7900

BENJAMIN'S
(Inn At University Village)
625 South Ashland Avenue,
at Harrison Street, (312) 243-7191

BENNIGAN'S
150 South Michigan Avenue
(312) 427-0577

BERGHOFF RESTAURANT, THE
17 West Adams Street
(312) 427-3170

BLACKHAWK LODGE
41 East Superior Street,
at Wabash Avenue, (312) 280-4080

BOOGIE'S DINER
923 North Rush Street
(312) 915-0555

BREAKFAST CLUB, THE
1381 West Hubbard Street
(312) 666-3166

BROTHER JIMMY'S B.B.Q. & BOOZE
2909 North Sheffield
(312) 528-0888

BUB CITY CRABSHACK & BAR-B-QUE
901 West Weed Street
(312) 266-1200

BUTCH MCGUIRE'S
20 West Division Street
(312) 337-9080

CAFE 525
(Forum Hotel)
525 North Michigan Avenue,
Lobby Level, (312) 321-8766

CARSON'S, THE PLACE FOR RIBS
612 North Wells Street
(312) 280-9200

CELEBRITY CAFE
(Hotel Nikko)
320 North Dearborn Parkway
(312) 744-1900

CENTRE CAFE
(Holiday Inn Chicago City Centre)
300 East Ohio Street
(312) 787-6100

CHALET, THE
(Bismarck Hotel)
171 West Randolph Street
(312) 236-0123

CHICAGO BRAUHAUS
4732-34 North Lincoln Avenue
(312) 784-4444

**CHICAGO'S FRONT ROW/
CHARLESTONS DINING ROOM**
555 West Madison Street
(312) 902-2900

CHRISTIE'S AT COLUMBUS
233 East Wacker Drive
(312) 856-1810

CHRISTOPHER'S ON HALSTED
1633 North Halsted Street
(312) 642-8484

CITYSIDE BISTRO & BAR
(Guest Quarters Suite Hotel)
198 East Delaware Place
(312) 664-1100

COUNTRY HOUSE
55th Street & Clarendon Hills Road
Clarendon Hills
(708) 325-1444
6460 College Road, Lisle
(708) 983-0545

CORGI'S STEAKS & SEAFOOD RESTAURANT
(Holiday Inn O'Hare)
5440 North River Road, Rosemont
(708) 6712-6350

DENNY'S RESTAURANT O'HARE
8225 West Higgins Road
(312) 399-1190

DICK'S LAST RESORT
(North Pier)
435 East Illinois Street
(312) 836-7870

DON ROTH'S RESTAURANT
61 North Milwaukee Avenue, Wheeling
(708) 537-5800

ECCENTRIC
159 West Erie Street
(312) 787-8390

ED DEBEVIC'S
640 North Wells Street, (312) 664-1707
660 Lake Cook Road, Deerfield
(708) 945-3242

ELLINGTON'S
(Embassy Suites Hotel O'Hare)
6501 North Mannheim Road,
Rosemont, (708) 699-6300

EXCHANGE RESTAURANT, THE
(Midland Hotel)
172 West Adams Street
(312) 332-1200

FIREPLACE INN, THE
1448 North Wells Street
(312) 664-5264

FOOD COURT
111 North State Street, Lower Level
(312) 781-3647

FRONTIER BAR & GRILL
(Indian Lakes Resort)
250 West Schick Road, Bloomingdale
(708) 529-0200

GARDEN TERRACE RESTAURANT
(Hyatt Regency O'Hare)
9300 West Bryn Mawr Avenue,
Rosemont, (708) 696-1234

GAZEBO RESTAURANT, THE
(Congress Hotel)
520 South Michigan Avenue
(312) 427-3800

GOOSE ISLAND BREWING COMPANY
1800 North Clybourn Avenue
(312) 915-0071

GORDON
500 North Clark Street
(312) 467-9780

GREAT STREET RESTAURANT & BAR
(Stouffer Riviere Hotel)
One West Wacker Drive
(312) 372-7200

GRILLE 198
(Guest Quarters Suite Hotel)
198 East Delaware Place
(312) 664-1100

GYPSY
211 East Ohio Street
(312) 644-9779

HAMBURGER HAMLET
1024 N. Rush Street
(312) 649-6601

HARD ROCK CAFE
63 West Ontario Street
(312) 943-2252

HAWKEYE'S BAR & GRILL
1458 West Taylor Street
(312) 226-3951

HOGAN'S SPORTS BAR & GRILL
(Oak Brook Hills Hotel & Resort)
3500 Midwest Road, Oak Brook
(708) 850-5555

HOOTERS OF CHICAGO
660 North Wells Street
(312) 944-8800

HOUSTON'S RESTAURANT
616 North Rush Street
(312) 649-1121

JAXX
(Park Hyatt Chicago)
800 North Michigan Avenue
(312) 280-2230

J.W.'S
(Chicago Marriott)
540 North Michigan Avenue
(312) 836-6336

KINZIE STREET CHOP HOUSE
400 North Wells Street
(312) 822-0191

LAKE SHORE CAFE
(Ramada Inn Lake Shore)
4900 South Lake Shore Drive
(312) 288-5800

LAKE SHORE CAFE
(Days Inn Lake Shore)
644 North Lake Shore Drive
(312) 943-9200

LOU MITCHELL'S
565 West Jackson Boulevard
(312) 939-3111

THE MARC
318 West Superior Street
(312) 642-3810

MARKETPLACE RESTAURANT
(Holiday Inn O'Hare Intl.)
5440 North River Road, Rosemont
(708) 671-6350

MICHAEL JORDAN'S RESTAURANT
500 North LaSalle Street
(312) 644-3865

MILLER'S PUB
134 South Wabash Avenue (at Adams)
(312) 263-4988

MOONRAKER
733 South Dearborn Parkway
(312) 922-2019

MOOSEHEAD BAR & GRILL
240 East Ontario Street
(312) 649-9113

MRS. O'LEARY'S RESTAURANT
(Hyatt Regency Chicago)
151 East Wacker Drive
(312) 565-1234

NEWSMAKERS RESTAURANT
(Best Western Inn of Chicago)
162 East Ohio Street (at Michigan
Avenue), (312) 787-3100

O'BRIEN'S RESTAURANT
1528 North Wells Street
(312) 787-3131

ODYSSEY (Cruise Ship)
Navy Pier
(708) 990-0800

OLD COUNTRY BUFFET INC.
6560 West Fullerton Avenue
Bricktown Square Center
(312) 745-7024

ONDINE
(Wyndham Hamilton)
400 Park Boulevard, Itasca
(708) 773-4000

ORIGINAL A-1
401 East Illinois Street
(312) 644-0300

Miller's Pub

Planet Hollywood

Hard Rock Cafe

LIFE AND LEISURE — LEBEN UND FREIZEIT

Billy Goat Tavern

Marina City

Harry Caray's

PINNACLE
(Days Inn Lake Shore Drive)
644 North Lake Shore Drive
(312) 943-9200

PLANET HOLLYWOOD
633 North Wells Street
(312) 266-7827

PLAZA CAFE
(Quality Inn Downtown)
One South Halsted Street
(312) 829-5000

PRAIRIE
500 South Dearborn Parkway
(312) 663-1143

PUMP ROOM, THE
1301 North State Parkway
(312) 266-0360

RAGAMUFFIN
350 North Orleans Street
(312) 836-5000

RELISH
2044 North Halsted Street
(312) 868-9034

ROCK 'N ROLL McDONALD'S
600 North Clark Street
(312) 664-7940

ROSEWOOD RESTAURANT AND BANQUETS
9421 West Higgins Road, Rosemont
(708) 696-9494

SALOON, THE
200 East Chestnut Street
(312) 280-5454

SEASONS RESTAURANT
(Four Seasons Hotel)
120 East Delaware Place
(312) 280-8800

SIGNATURE ROOM AT THE 95TH
875 North Michigan Avenue
(312) 787-9596

SKYWAY RESTAURANT
(Hyatt Regency Chicago)
151 East Wacker Drive
(312) 565-1234

SPIRIT OF CHICAGO
455 East Illinois Street
(312) 321-1241

STREETERVILLE GRILLE & BAR
(Sheraton Chicago Hotel & Towers)
301 East North Water Street
(312) 464-1000

STREETSIDE CHICAGO
One First National Plaza
(Corner of Clark and Monroe)
(312) 346-4700

TESSY'S
(Radisson Hotel Lincolnwood)
4500 West Touhy Avenue, Lincolnwood
(708) 677-1234

T.G.I. FRIDAY'S
153 East Erie Street, (312) 664-9820
222 Merchandise Mart Plaza,
(312) 527-0900

30 EAST AMERICAN BISTRO
(Courtyard by Marriott)
30 East Hubbard Street
(312) 329-2500

TICKER TAPE BAR & BISTRO
(Midland Hotel)
172 West Adams Street
(312) 332-1200

VULCANS FORGE
(Nordic Hills Resort)
Nordic Road, Itasca
(708) 773-2750

WALTON PLACE CAFE, THE
(Knickerbocker Hotel)
163 East Walton Place
(312) 751-8100

WALNUT ROOM, THE
(Marshall Field & Co.)
111 North State Street, 7th Floor
(312) 781-3697

WHITNEY'S BAR AND GRILLE
(Oak Lawn Hilton)
9333 South Cicero Avenue, Oak Lawn
(708) 425-6000

Caribbean

TASTE OF JAMAICA
1372 East 53rd Street
(312) 955-4373

Chinese

HAYLEMON RESTAURANT
2201 South Wentworth Avenue
(312) 225-0891

HONG MIN RESTAURANT
221 West Cermak Road
(312) 842-5026

HOUSE OF HUNAN
535 North Michigan Avenue
(312) 329-9494

HUNAN CAFE
625 North Michigan Avenue
(312) 482-9898

JIAS
2 East Delaware Place
(312) 642-0626

KING WAH RESTAURANT
2225 South Wentworth Avenue
(312) 842-1404

MANDAR-INN RESTAURANT
2249 South Wentworth Avenue
(312) 842-4014

65 SEAFOOD RESTAURANT
2414 South Wentworth Avenue
(312) 372-0306

SZECHWAN HOUSE
600 North Michigan Avenue
(312) 642-3900

Continental

BIGGS RESTAURANT
1150 North Dearborn Parkway
(312) 787-0900

BISTRO 1800 EAST
(Arlington Park Hilton and Conference Center)
1800 East Golf Road, Schaumburg
(708) 605-1234

BLACK RAM RESTAURANT
1414 East Oakton Street, Des Plaines
(708) 824-1227

BRASSERIE BELLEVUE
(Le Meriden Chicago)
21 East Bellevue Place
(312) 266-2100

CAFE DE L BONNE VIE
(Holiday Inn O'Hare)
5440 North River Road, Rosemont
(708) 671-6350

CAFE LA CAVE
2777 North Mannheim Road,
Des Plaines, (708) 827-7818

CAFE SUISSE
(Swissôtel Chicago)
323 East Wacker Drive
(312) 565-0565

CAFE, THE
(Ritz-Carlton)
160 East Pearson Street
(312) 266-1000

CHELSEA, THE
(Westin Hotel Chicago)
909 North Michigan Avenue
(312) 943-7200

Cité AT THE TOP OF LAKE POINT
505 North Lake Shore Drive
(312) 644-4050

CRICKETS RESTAURANT & BAR
100 East Chestnut Street
(312) 280-2100

DINING ROOM, THE
(Ritz Carlton)
160 East Pearson Street
(312) 266-1000

ENTRE NOUS
(Fairmont Hotel)
200 North Columbus Drive
(312) 565-8000

KIKI'S BISTRO
900 North Franklin Street
(312) 335-5454

KLAY OVEN RESTAURANT
414 North Orleans Street
(312) 527-3999

LASALLE BAR & RESTAURANT
(Executive Plaza/A Clarion Hotel)
71 East Wacker Drive
(312) 346-7100

LUTZ CONTINENTAL CAFE
2458 West Montrose Avenue
(312) 478-7785

MARINA 300 RESTAURANT
300 North State Street
(312) 321-0786

MRS. CANDY'S RESTAURANT
(Hyatt Regency Oak Brook)
1909 Spring Road, Oak Brook
(708) 573-1234

"MY NEIGHBORHOOD"
(Claridge Hotel)
1244 North Dearborn Parkway
(312) 787-4980

RAPHAEL, THE
(Raphael Hotel)
201 East Delaware Place
(312) 943-5000

SCANDINAVIAN RESTAURANT
(Nordic Hills Resort)
Nordic Road, Itasca
(708) 773-2750

SUNDAY CHAMPAGNE BRUNCH
(Hyatt Regency O'Hare)
9300 West Bryn Mawr Avenue,
Rosemont
(708) 696-1234

TIFF'S TOO RESTAURANT
(Sheraton Plaza Hotel)
160 East Huron Street
(312) 787-2900

T.J. PEPPERCORN'S
(Radisson Hotel Lincolnwood)
4500 West Touhy Avenue, Lincolnwood
(708) 677-5400

WATERFORD
(Oak Brook Hills Hotel and Resort)
3500 Midwest Road, Oak Brook
(708) 850-5555

WEDGEWOOD HOUSE RESTAURANT
(Omni Orrington Hotel)
1710 Orrington Avenue, Evanston
(708) 866-8700

WILLIAM TELL RESTAURANT
(Holiday Inn Countryside/LaGrange)
6201 Joliet Road, Countryside
(708) 352-1101

WOLF POINT GRILL
(Holiday Inn Mart Plaza)
350 North Orleans Street
(312) 836-5000

ZAVEN'S
260 East Chestnut Street
(312) 787-8260

Delicatessen

BAGEL RESTAURANT & DELI
50 Old Orchard Court, Skokie
(708) 677-0100

BAGEL RESTAURANT, THE
3107 North Broadway
(312) 477-0300

D.B. KAPLAN'S RESTAURANT
845 North Michigan Avenue, 7th Floor
(312) 280-2700

8TH STREET DELI
800 South Michigan Avenue
(312) 939-2800

ENGLISH ROOM/FISH & CHIPS
(Marshall Field & Co.)
111 North State Street, 7th Floor
(312) 781-3695

MANNY'S COFFEE SHOP & DELI
1141 South Jefferson Street
(312) 939-2855

MOE'S DELI & PUB
611 North Rush Street
(312) 828-0110

Won Kow

Honda

North Pier

LIFE AND LEISURE — LEBEN UND FREIZEIT

MRS. LEVY'S DELICATESSEN
233 S. Wacker Drive (Restaurant Level)
(312) 993-0530

WINKLESTEIN'S
858 North Orleans Street
(312) 642-3354

European - Oriental

JACKIE'S RESTAURANT
2478 North Lincoln Avenue
(312) 880-0003

PAMPANGA RESTAURANT
6407 North Caldwell Street
(312) 763-1781

French

AMBRIA
2300 North Lincoln Park West
(312) 472-5959

BISTRO 110
110 East Pearson Street
(312) 266-3110

CAFE BERNARD
2100 North Halsted Street
(312) 871-2100

CAFE DE PARIS
(Hotel Sofitel)
5550 North River Road, Rosemont
(708) 678-4488

CHARLIE TROTTER'S
816 West Armitage
(312) 248-6228

CHEZ COLETTE
(Hotel Sofitel)
5550 North River Road, Rosemont
(708) 678-4488

CHEZ PAUL
660 North Rush Street
(312) 944-6680

EVEREST
(Chicago Stock Exchange)
440 South LaSalle Street, 40th Floor
(312) 663-8920

le MARGAUX
2442 North Clark Street
(312) 871-3033

L'ESCARGOT ON HALSTED
2925 North Halsted Street
(312) 525-5522

MARCHE
833 West Randolph Street
(312) 226-8399

PORTICO RESTAURANT
(Ramada Hotel O'Hare)
6600 North Mannheim Road,
Rosemont, (708) 827-5131

RUE SAINT CLAIR
162 East Ontario Street
(312) 787-3580

SAINT GERMAIN
1210 North State Parkway
(312) 266-9900

UN GRAND CAFE
2300 North Lincoln Park West
(312) 348-8887

YVETTE
1206 North State Street
(312) 280-1700

YVETTE WINTERGARDEN
311 South Wacker Drive
(312) 408-1242

German
(See complete list on page 184)

BERGHOFF RESTAURANT, THE
17 West Adams Street
(312) 427-3170

CHICAGO BRAUHAUS
4732-34 North Lincoln Avenue
(312) 784-4444

GOLDEN OX RESTAURANT
1578-82 Clybourn Avenue
(312) 664-0780

HEIDELBERGER FASS
4300 North Lincoln Avenue
(312) 478-2486

METRO CLUB
3032 North Lincoln Avenue
(312) 929-0622

MIRABELL RESTAURANT
3454 West Addison Street
(312) 463-1962

ZUM DEUTSCHEN ECK
2924 North Southport Avenue
(312) 525-8121

Greek

COURTYARDS OF PLAKA
340 South Halsted Street
(312) 263-0767

DENI'S DEN
2941 North Clark Street
(312) 348-8888

GREEK ISLANDS
200 South Halsted Street
(312) 782-9855

PAPAGUS
600 North State Street
(312) 642-8450

PARTHENON, THE
314 South Halsted Street
(312) 726-2407

SANTORINI'S RESTAURANT
800 West Adams Street
(312) 829-8820

Indian

BUKHARA RESTAURANT & BAR
(Ontario Place)
2 East Ontario Street
(312) 943-0188

CHOWPATTI VEGETARIAN RESTAURANT
1035 South Arlington Heights Road,
Arlington Heights
(708) 640-9554

DAAVAT RESTAURANT
211 West Walton Street
(312) 335-1001

GAYLORD INDIA
678 North Clark Street
(312) 664-1700

KLAY OVEN RESTAURANT
414 North Orleans Street
(312) 527-3999

Irish

KITTY O'SHEAS IRISH PUB
(Chicago Hilton)
720 South Michigan Avenue, Lobby
Level, (312) 922-4400

Italian

ALDO'S
(Hyatt Regency O'Hare)
9300 West Bryn Mawr Avenue,
Rosemont, (708) 696-1234

ALFO'S RISTORANTE
2512 South Oakley Avenue
(312) 523-6994

ANTHONY'S ITALIAN CHOP HOUSE & BAR
(Hyatt Regency Oak Brook)
1909 Spring Road, Oak Brook
(708) 573-1234

ARMANDO'S RESTAURANT
735 North Rush Street
(312) 337-7672

ARTIE "G"S SORRISO
321 North Clark Street
(312) 644-0283

AVANZARE RESTAURANT
161 E. Huron Street
(312) 337-8056

BACCHANALIA RISTORANTE
2413 South Oakley Avenue
(312) 254-6555

BAGUETTI'S
1800 E. Golf Road, Schaumburg
(708) 605-1234

BLEEA VISTA
1001 West Belmont Avenue
(312) 404-0111

BICE RISTORANTE
158 East Ontario Street
(312) 664-1474

BRUNA'S RISTORANTE
2424 South Oakley Avenue
(312) 254-5550

CAFE SPIAGGIA
980 North Michigan Avenue
(312) 280-2764

CANNELLA'S RESTAURANT
1820 North Wells Street
(312) 787-3511

CARLUCCI RESTAURANT
2215 North Halsted Street
(312) 281-1220

CENTRO
710 North Wells Street
(312) 988-7775

CLUB GENE & GEORGETTI, LTD.
500 North Franklin Street
(312) 527-3718

CLUB LUCKY
1824 West Wabansia Avenue
(312) 227-2300

COCO PAZZO
300 West Hubbard Street
(312) 836-0900

COMO INN RESTAURANT
546 North Milwaukee Avenue
(312) 421-5222

DA NICOLA RISTORANTE
3114 North Lincoln Avenue
(312) 935-8000

DOMINICK'S
(North Shore Hotel Moraine)
700 North Sheridan Road
(708) 433-5566

DRINK
541 West Fulton Avenue
(312) 441-0818

FEBO RESTAURANT
2501 South Western Avenue
(312) 523-0869

GENNARO'S RESTAURANT
1352 West Taylor Street
(312) 243-1035

HARRY CARAY'S RESTAURANT
33 West Kinzie Street
(312) 828-0966

IL VICINATO
2435 South Western Avenue
(312) 927-5444

ITALIAN VILLAGE
71 West Monroe Street
(312) 332-7005

LA LOCANDA
743 North LaSalle Street
(312) 335-9550

LA PLAZA ITALIAN RESTAURANT
(Chicago Marriott)
540 North Michigan Avenue
(312) 836-6335

La RISOTTERIA NORD
2324 North Clark Street
(312) 348-2106

La STRADA RISTORANTE
155 North Michigan Avenue
(312) 565-2200

LEO NELLO'S RISTORANTE
340 East Ohio Street
(312) 787-2222

LIMIT UP!, THE
30 South Wacker Drive
(312) 207-1400

LINO'S RESTAURANT
222 West Ontario Street
(312) 266-0616

LUIGI OF HONG KONG
923 West Weed Street
(312) 573-1900

MAGGIANO'S
516 North Clark Street
(312) 644-7700

MIA TORRE RESTAURANT
233 South Wacker Drive (Sears Tower)
(312) 474-1350

O'FAME RESTAURANT
750 West Webster Street
(312) 929-5111

ORCHID ROOM
(North Shore Hotel Moraine)
700 North Sheridan Road, Highwood
(708) 433-5566

ORSO'S RESTAURANT
1401 N. Wells Street
(312) 787-6604

PASTA VINO
4200 River Road, Schiller Park
(708) 678-2000

PRIMAVERA RISTORANTE
(Fairmont Hotel)
200 North Columbus Drive
(312) 565-8000

PRONTO RISTORANTE
200 East Chestnut Street
(312) 664-6181

RINALLI'S RESTAURANT
24 West Elm Street
(312) 440-7000

RICO'S RESTAURANT
626 South Racine Avenue
(312) 421-7262

ROSEBUD CAFE, THE NEW
1500 West Taylor Street
(312) 942-1117

ROSEBUD ON RUSH
55 East Superior Street
(312) 266-6444

SABATINO'S RESTAURANT
4441 West Irving Park Road
(312) 283-8331

SALVATORE'S RISTORANTE
525 West Arlington Place
(312) 528-1200

SOPHIA'S
250 West Schick Road
Bloomingdale
(708) 529-0200

SPIAGGIA RESTAURANT
980 North Michigan Avenue, 2nd Floor
(312) 280-2750

STEFANI'S
1418 West Fullerton Parkway
(312) 348-0111

STEFANI'S OF NORTHBROOK
601 Skokie Boulevard, Northbrook
(708) 498-9810

SYLVIANO'S RISTORANTE
2809 Butterfield Road, Oak Brook
(708) 571-3600

THAT STEAK JOYNT
1610 North Wells Street
(312) 943-5091

TOPO GIGIO RISTORANTE
1437 North Wells Street
(312) 266-9355

TRATTORIA CONVITO
11 East Chestnut Street
(312) 943-2984

TRATTORIA GIANNI
1711 North Halsted Street
(312) 266-1976

TRATTORIA NO. 10
10 North Dearborn
(312) 984-1718

"TUFANOS" VERNON PARK TAP
1073 West Vernon Park Place
(312) 733-3393

TUSCANY
1014 West Taylor Street
(312) 829-1990

TUTTAPOSTO
646 North Franklin Street
(312) 943-6262

VILLA MARCONI RESTAURANT
2358 South Oakley Avenue
(312) 847-3168

VINCI RESTAURANT
1732 North Halsted Street
(312) 266-1199

Chop House

Como Inn

Heidelberg Restaurant & Deli

VINNY'S
1014 West Taylor Street
(312) 829-1990

VIVO
838 West Randolph Street
(312) 733-3379

Japanese

BENIHANA OF TOKYO
166 East Superior Street
(312) 664-9643
747 Easst Butterfield Road, Lombard
(708) 571-4440

BENKAY
(Hotel Nikko)
320 North Dearborn Parkway
(312) 836-5490

HONDA JAPANESE RESTAURANT
540 North Wells Street
(312) 923-1010

KYORI RESTAURANT
316 North Michigan Avenue
(312) 346-2559

SUNTORY RESTAURANT
13 East Huron Street
(312) 664-3344

Korean

BANDO RESTAURANT
2200 West Lawrence Avenue
(312) 728-0100

Mediterranean

BOULEVARD RESTAURANT
505 North Michigan Avenue, 2nd Floor
(312) 321-8888

CAFE SARANDA
405 North Wabash Avenue
(312) 527-3100

CUISINES
(Souffer Riviere Hotel)
One W. Wacker Drive
(312) 372-7200

TUTTAPOSTO
646 North Franklin Street
(312) 943-6262

Mexican

DOS HERMANOS MEXICAN RESTAURANT & CANTINA
(Sears Tower, Restaurant Level)
233 South Wacker Drive
(312) 280-2780

EL JARDIN RESTAURANT
3335 North Clark Street
(312) 528-6775

ESTA LOCA
2 West Elm Street
(312) 337-2474

LA TERRAZA RESTAURANT
2603 North Halsted Street
(312) 871-8840

LINDAS MARGARITA'S
47 West Polk Street
(312) 939-6600

LINDO MEXICO
2642 North Lincoln Avenue
(312) 871-4832

Middle Eastern

A 1000 NITES
1612 North Sedgewick Street
(312) 944-4811

Persian

REZA RESTAURANT
432 West Ontario Street, (312) 664-4500
5255 North Clark Street, (312) 561-1898

Pizza

BACINO'S STUFFED PIZZA
75 East Wacker Drive, (312) 263-0070
2204 North Lincoln Avenue,
(312) 472-7400

BOOEY MONGERS O'HARE
1504 Minor Street, Des Plaines
(708) 299-7656

CALIFORNIA PIZZA KITCHEN
551 Oakbrook Center, (708) 571-7800
414 North Orleans Street,
(312) 222-9030
835 North Michigan Avenue
(Water Tower Place), 7th Level,
(312) 787-7300

CHICAGO STYLE PIZZA AND EATERY
120 South Michigan Avenue
(312) 427-0968

CONNIE'S PIZZA
2373 South Archer Avenue
(312) 326-3443

DOWN & UNDER ITALIAN DELI & PIZZERIA
308 West Erie Street, Lower Level
(312) 787-6691

EDWARDO'S NATURAL PIZZA
1212 North Dearborn Parkway
(312) 337-4490
521 South Dearborn Parkway
(312) 939-3366

EXCHEQUER PUB
226 South Wabash Avenue
(312) 939-5633

GINO'S EAST
160 East Superior Street
(312) 943-1124

GIORDANO'S
747 North Rush Street, (312) 951-0747
236 South Wabash Avenue,
(312) 939-4646
310 West Randolph Street,
(312) 401-1440
815 West Van Buren Street
(312) 421-1221
1840 North Clark Street, (312) 944-6100
1040 West Belmont Avenue,
(312) 327-1200
9415 West Higgins Road, Rosemont,
(708) 292-2600

LOU MALNATI'S PIZZERIA
439 North Wells Street
(312) 828-9800

Lachner "*CHICAGOLAND*"

O'FAME RESTAURANT
750 West Webster Street
(312) 929-5111

PIZZERIA DUE
619 North Wabash Avenue
(312) 943-2400

Polish

LUTNIA CONTINENTAL CAFE
5532 West Belmont Avenue
(312) 282-5335

SAWA'S OLD WARSAW RESTAURANT
9200 Cermak Road (at 17th Avenue),
Broadview, (708) 343-9040

Polynesian

TRADER VIC'S
(Palmer House Hilton)
17 East Monroe Street
(312) 726-7500

Ribs

HICKORY PIT RESTAURANT LOUNGE AND BANQUET
2801 South Halsted Street
(312) 842-7600

MILLER'S PUB
134 South Wabash (at Adams)
(312) 263-4988

TWIN ANCHORS
1655 North Sedgwick Street
(312) 266-1616

Romanian

LIL BUCHAREST RESTAURANT
3001 North Ashland Avenue
(312) 929-8640

Russian

MOSCOW NIGHTS
7800 North Caldwell, Niles
(708) 470-1090

Seafood

BOB CHINN'S CRAB HOUSE RESTAURANT
393 South Milwuakee Avenue,
Wheeling, (708) 520-3633

CAPE COD ROOM
(Drake Hotel)
140 East Walton Place
(312) 787-2200

CATCH THIRTY FIVE
35 West Wacker Drive, (312) 346-3500

CRABS & THINGS
1249 South Elmhurst Road, Des Plaines
(708) 437-1595

KINGS WHARF, THE
(Marriott Lincolnshire Resort)
10 Marriott Drive, Lincolnshire
(708) 634-0100

MOONRAKER
733 South Dearborn Parkway
(312) 922-2019

NICK'S FISHMARKET
One First National Plaza
(312) 621-0200

NICK'S FISHMARKET ROSEMONT
10275 West Higgins Road, Rosemont
(708) 298-8200

OLD CAROLINA CRAB HOUSE
455 East Illinois Street, at North Pier
(312) 321-8400

SHAW'S CRAB HOUSE
21 East Hubbard Street
(312) 527-2722

SHUCKER'S RESTAURANT
150 East Ontario Street
(312) 266-6057

65 SEAFOOD RESTAURANT
2414 South Wentworh Avenue
(312) 372-0306

VENTANA'S REVOLVING ROOFTOP
(Hyatt Regency O'Hare)
9300 West Bryn Mawr Avenue,
Rosemont
(708) 696-1234

WATERFRONT RESTAURANT
16 West Maple Street
(312) 943-7494

Steak & Beef

BARNEY'S MARKET CLUB STEAKHOUSE
741 West Randolph Street
(312) 372-6466

BUCKINGHAM'S STEAK HOUSE & BAR
720 South Michigan Avenue
(312) 922-4400

BUTCHER SHOP STEAKHOUSE, THE
358 West Ontario Street
(312) 440-4900

CHICAGO CHOP HOUSE
60 West Ontario Street
(312) 787-7100

CHICAGO PALM RESTAURANT
181 East Lake Shore Drive
(312) 944-0135

CHOPS
(Best Western River North)
125 West Ohio Street
(312) 467-1776

DELANEY AND MURPHY
(Arlington Park Hilton and Conference Center)
3400 West Euclid Avenue, Arlington
Heights, (708) 394-2000

ELI'S - A PLACE FOR STEAK
215 East Chicago Avenue
(312) 642-1393

GIBSONS BAR & STEAKHOUSE
1028 North Rush Street
(312) 266-8999

GRAND & WELLS TAP
531 North Wells Street
(312) 645-1255

LAWRY'S THE PRIME RIB
100 East Ontario Street
(312) 787-5000

MORTON'S OF CHICAGO
1050 North State Street
(312) 266-4820

Ruth's Steak House

Palmer's Steak & Seafood House

Pegasus Restaurant & Taverna

LIFE AND LEISURE — LEBEN UND FREIZEIT

MORTON'S OF CHICAGO
9525 W. Bryn Mawr Avenue, Rosemont
(708) 678-5155

MORTON'S OF CHICAGO
1 Westbrook Corporate Center,
Westchester
(708) 562-7000

OTHER PLACE RESTAURANT, THE
(Hyatt Regency O'Hare)
9300 West Bryn Mawr Avenue,
Rosemont
(708) 696-1234

PALMER'S STEAK & SEAFOOD HOUSE
(Palmer House Hilton)
17 East Monroe Street
(312) 726-7500

RUTH'S STEAK HOUSE
431 North Dearborn Parkway
(312) 321-2725

STETSON'S CHOP HOUSE
(Hyatt Regency Chicago)
151 East Wacker Drive
(312) 565-1234

THAT STEAK JOYNT
1610 North Wells Street
(312) 943-5091

Tapas

BOSSA NOVA
1960 North Clybourn Avenue
(312) 248-4800

CAFE BABA REEBA
2024 North Halsted Street
(312) 935-5000

Thai

DAO THAI RESTAURANT
105 East Ontario Street
(312) 664-9600

PATTAYA RESTAURANT
114 West Chicago Avenue
(312) 944-3753

STAR OF SIAM
11 East Illinois Street
(312) 670-0100

STAR OF THAILAND
3133 North Clark Street
(312) 935-6711

THAI STAR CAFE
660 North State Street
(312) 951-1196

Vegetarian

CAFE VOLTAIRE
3231 North Clark Street
(312) 528-3136

CHOWPATTI VEGETARIAN RESTAURANT
1035 South Arlington Heights Road,
Arlington Heights
(708) 640-9554

REZA RESTAURANT
432 West Ontario Street
(312) 664-4500
5255 North Clark Street
(312) 561-1898

After dining at a loop restaurant, a carriage ride is the perfect way to end the evening

Nach einem Abendessen im Loop, bildet eine Pferdekutschenfahrt einen schönen Abschluß

Photo: James A. Rasmussen

Lachner "*CHICAGOLAND*"

CHICAGOLAND

From far away shores we have come to u-nite at the
heart-land of the U. S. He-re
at the shores of Lake Mi-chi-gan, at the out-skirts of the prairie. We have found Chi-ca-go-land, a
glo-ri-ous land to be. Na-na-na-
na, na-na-na-na, na-na-na-na, na-na-na
na-hei-hei! We have found Chi-ca-go-
land a glo-ri-ous land to be.

We've ta-ken the boats, we have lan-ded by plane, and were
ta-ken by storm, we con-fess

2. Overlooking the Lake, the impressive array
Of the skyscrapers' towering height
And below spacious parks that invite us to play
And your theatres sparkle at night
You have laughter and life, joy and danger galore
You have plenty to show and to hide
You're the city that works, who could ask for more
"Windy City" - we call you with pride
Nananana . . . hei, hei!
You're the city that works, who could ask for more
"Windy City" - we call you with pride

3. Like a long string of pearls on the outskirts of town
Are your suburbs - your tranquil retreat
With their wide open space and a tree-studded crown
They fulfill the American dream
Elmhurst, Naperville, Highland Park, Lake Bluff
And Aurora, Mount Prospect, Gurnee
Indeed, Chicagoland
You're a glorious land to be
Nananana . . . hei, hei!
Indeed, Chicagoland
You're a glorious land to be

Traditional: German pirate song/19th century ("Der maechtigste Koenig im Luftrevier"); English Lyrics: Marlis Schmidt, 1994

LIFE AND LEISURE — LEBEN UND FREIZEIT

Professional Sports   *Der Profi-Sport*

CHICAGO BEARS

Chicago Bears playing professional football on a Sunday afternoon during November in Soldier Field, located at McFetridge and the Outer Drives. The rabid, loyal Chicago area fans form a "ticket-sellout-crowd" regardless of the team's standing in its league.

Die Chicago Bears bei einem ihrer Spiele an einem Sonntag nachmittag im Soldier-Field-Stadion, das am McFetridge und Outer Drives gelegen ist. Egal auf welchem Platz die Mannschaft steht, die Chicagoer sind treue Fans und die Spiele sind immer ausverkauft.

Bear Mark Bortz

Thousands of Chicagoans attend a variety of spectator sports all-year-round and are great fans of Chicago's professional teams.

Professional Sports Teams in Chicago:

National League's **Chicago Cubs** (baseball) at Wrigley Field, on the north side.

American League's **Chicago White Sox** (baseball) at Comiskey Park, on the south side.

Chicago Bulls (basketball) at Chicago Stadium; triple National Champions.

Chicago Blackhawks (ice hockey) at Chicago Stadium; competitive contenders.

Chicago Bears (football) at Soldier Field; Super Bowl Champions in 1986.

Chicago Soccer Team Power at Rosemont Horizon; attendance will pick up after World Cub Matches.

CHICAGO CUBS

Wrigley Field is the home of the Chicago Cubs of the National League. The Cubs were the last baseball team in the professional leagues to install giant lighting fixtures throughout the park for nighttime games.

Wrigley Field ist das Stadion der Chicago Cubs, die in der National League spielen. Aus Rücksicht auf die Anwohner, waren die Cubs die letzte Mannschaft in der Profi-Liga, deren Stadion eine Flutlichtanlage für Nachtspiele installiert bekam.

BLACKHAWKS

Chicago Blackhawks at the Chicago Stadium

Lachner "CHICAGOLAND"

Die Chicagoer besuchen das ganze Jahr über zu Tausenden die verschiedenen Sportveranstaltungen und sind treue Fans ihrer Chicagoer Mannschaften.

Die professionellen Chicagoer Teams sind:

Die **Chicago Cubs**, ein Baseballteam, das in der National League spielt. Ihr Stadion ist das Wrigley Field Stadium auf Chicagos Nordseite.

Das Baseballteam der **Chicago White Sox** spielt in der American League. Ihre Heimspiele finden im Comiskey Park Stadium auf Chicagos Südseite statt.

Die **Chicago Bulls** (Basketball) sind dreifache nationale Meister und spielen im Chicago Stadium.

Das starke Eishockeyteam, die **Chicago Blackhawks**, spielt ebenfalls im Chicago Stadium.

Die **Chicago Bears** (Football) waren 1986 die Champions des Super Bowls. Ihr Stadion ist das Soldier Field.

Die Fußballer des **Chicago Soccer Team Power** hoffen, daß nach der in Amerika ausgetragenen Fußballweltmeisterschaft mehr Zuschauer im Rosemont-Horizon-Stadion zu ihren Spielen kommen.

The Chicago Power, a member of the National Professional Soccer League, plays a 40-game indoor soccer schedule each winter, and plays its home games at the Rosemont Horizon near O'Hare Airport. Player/coach Pato Margetic, formerly of Germany's Bundesliga, led his team to the 1990-91 NPSL championship.

Die Chicago Power, Fußballmannschaft in der National Professional Soccer League, spielt jeden Winter 40 Spiele in der Halle. Die Spiele finden im Rosemont Horizon in der Nähe des O'Hare Flughafens statt. Spieler und Trainer Pato Margetic, früher ein Spieler in der deutschen Fußballbundesliga, führte sein Team 1990/91 zur NPSL Meisterschaft.

Photo by Dale Tait

BULLS

CHICAGO WHITE SOX

The Chicago White Sox's newly completed Comiskey Park on the city's near Southeast side of town. The White Sox were American League champions in the Central Division at the end of the 1993 baseball season.

Das neue Comiskey-Park-Stadion der Chicago White Sox liegt auf der südöstlichen Seite der Stadt. Die White Sox waren am Ende der 1993er Baseballsaison Meister der Central Division.

Chicago Bulls   Photo courtesy of Chicago Convention and Tourism Bureau

The new Comiskey Park on Opening Day 1991

LIFE AND LEISURE — LEBEN UND FREIZEIT

University Campuses and Hospitals
Universitäten und Krankenhäuser
Northwestern Memorial Hospital

Northwestern Memorial Hospital, on Chicago's near north side, is a primary teaching hospital for residents and fellows of Northwestern University Medical School. The hospital complex consists of 5 distinct buildings, housing a staff of 1000 physicians.

Northwestern Memorial Hospital auf Chicagos Nordseite ist ein Universitätskrankenhaus, das Bürgern und Studenten der medizinischen Fakultät der Northwestern University zur Verfügung steht. Der Krankenhauskomplex umfaßt fünf große Gebäude, in denen das Personal von 1.000 Ärzten untergebracht ist.

The University of Illinois at Chicago

The 28-story University Hall, which houses administrative and faculty offices at the University of Illinois at Chicago, is a landmark on Chicago's Near West Side."

Die 28 Stockwerk hohe University Hall, welche die Büros der Verwaltung und der Fakultäten der University of Illinois in Chicago beherbergt, ist ein Markstein auf Chicagos Westseite.

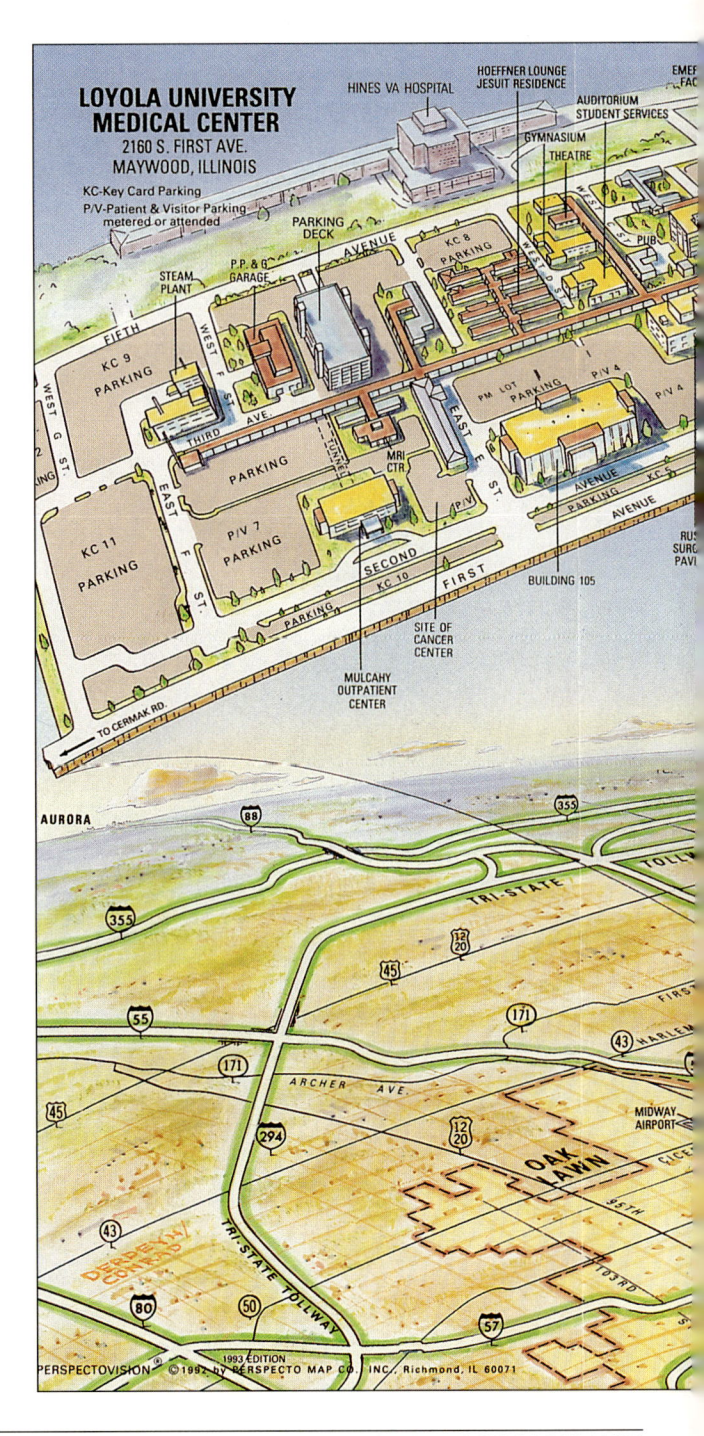

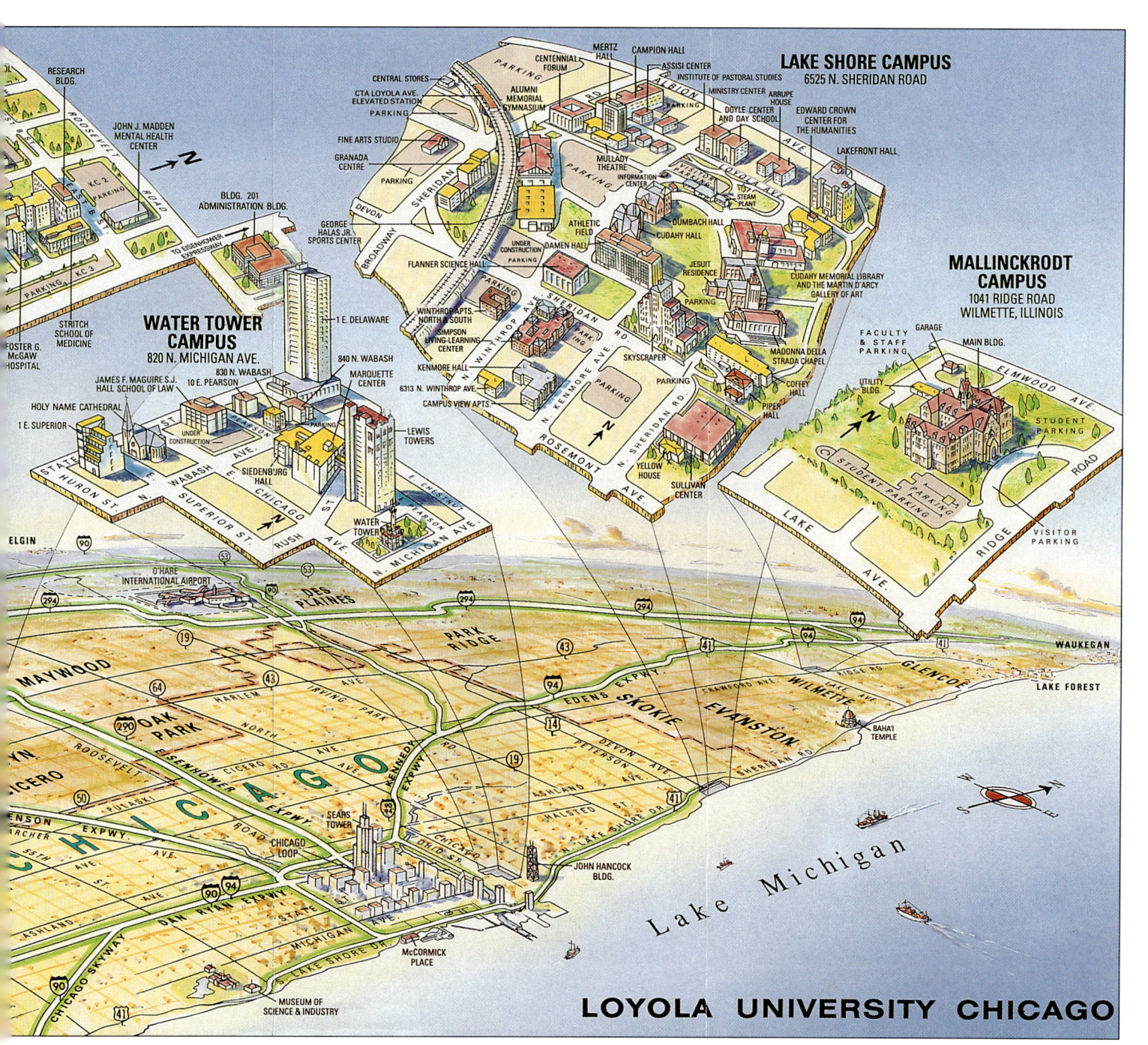

Typical of the major universities in and around Chicago is the multi-campus Loyola University. The main **Lake Shore Campus** is on North Sheridan Road, the downtown **Water Tower Campus** on Michigan Avenue, the huge **Medical Center** in west suburban Maywood, and the recently opened **Mallinckrodt Campus** in North suburban Wilmette.

Die Loyola University mit einem Universitätsgelände, das über die ganze Stadt verteilt ist, ist typisch für die größeren Universitäten in und um Chicago. Das Hauptgelände ist der **Lake Shore Campus** an der North Sheridan Road. Ebenfalls in der Stadt an der Michigan Avenue ist der **Water Tower Campus.** Im westlich gelegenen Vorort Maywood ist das große **Medical Center** und im nördlichen Vorort Wilmette wurde kürzlich der **Mallinckrodt Campus** eröffnet.

LIFE AND LEISURE — LEBEN UND FREIZEIT

University of Chicago

Stuart Hall

Illinois Benedictine College

Education in the Chicago Area
by Dr. M. Roth, IBC

The Chicago metropolitan area provides a full spectrum of opportunities in higher education. Institutions of higher learning include public and private universities, four-year liberal arts colleges, two-year community colleges, and a wide variety of technical and career oriented institutions. Programs for all recognized degrees and certificates are offered within a sixty kilometer radius of Chicago's center, the Loop.

The University of Chicago is an outstanding example of excellence in a private university. Known worldwide for the number of Nobel Prize winners on its faculty, the University of Chicago offers advanced degrees in all major academic areas including business, economics, and politics. Northwestern University, also private, has been ranked first among U.S. graduate business schools in a survey conducted by Business Week magazine. Other private universities include Loyola, DePaul, Roosevelt and Illinois Institute of Technology (IIT). IIT's architecture is a product of Bauhaus Style, Mies van der Rohe.

The University of Illinois at Chicago is the premier state (public) university in the area. It offers a full range of degree and non-degree programs in

Erziehung und Schulausbildung in Chicago
by Dr. M. Roth, IBC

Chicago bietet ein breites Spektrum an höherer Schulausbildung. Dazu gehören öffentliche und private Universitäten, Colleges, die eine Allgemeinausbildung anbieten, einschließlich Mathematik, Naturwisschaften und Soziologie, mit einer Studiendauer von vier Jahren. Gemeinde-Colleges mit einer Studienzeit von zwei Jahren und eine Vielzahl technisch- und handelsorientierter Lehranstalten. Studienprogramme mit anerkannten Abschlüssen werden in einem Umkreis von 60 Kilometern von Chicagos Zentrum, dem Loop, angeboten.

Die 'University of Chicago' ist ein hervorragendes Beispiel für eine private Universität. Weltbekannt für ihre zahlreichen Nobelpreisträger bietet die Universität Abschlüsse in allen akademischen Bereichen einschließlich Betriebs- und Volkswirtschaftslehre und Politologie. In einer Umfrage des Magazins 'Business Week,' stand die Northwestern University, ebenfalls eine private Universität, auf Platz eins auf der Liste der besten Universitäten für Betriebswirtschaft. Zu den privaten Universitäten zählen auch Loyola University, DePaul University, Roosevelt University und das Illinois Institute of Technology (IIT). Die Architektur des IIT ist ein Produkt des Bauhausstiles und stammt von Mies van der Rohe.

Die 'University of Illinois in Chicago' ist die größte der staatlichen Universitäten in der Umgebung. Sie bietet ein weitgefächertes Angebot an Programmen, mit oder ohne Abschluß, in

many aspects of business, economics and politics. Three smaller state universities which provide a less extensive range of programs are Chicago State, Northeastern Illinois and Governor's State. These institutions serve a large percentage of students who live in the Chicago area and do not require residence facilities.

Finally, there are many fine four-year liberal arts colleges providing mostly undergraduate degrees in the arts, sciences, business and premedical fields. These schools are private and attract those who are looking for more personal contact between faculty and students.

Two-year community colleges have both liberal arts and professional courses. Many of their graduates go on to finish bachelor's degrees at four-year colleges and universities.

German students who have finished high school in Germany would qualify to enter any of the institutions of higher learning in the Chicago area. In order to determine their entry level, these students would have to take written examinations, and in some cases, write an essay and be interviewed. In addition to their academic achievement, extracurricular activities would be considered in making an admissions decision. Middle school graduates would do well to apply to a community college from which they would be able to transfer to a four-year institution.

Bereichen wie Wirtschaftswissenschaften und Politologie an. Die drei kleineren staatlichen Universitäten mit einem weniger breitem Angebot sind: Chicago State, Northeastern Illinois und Governor's State. Diese Universitäten werden vor allem von Studenten der näheren Umgebung besucht, die nicht auf dem Universitätsgelände, dem Campus, wohnen.

Schließlich gibt es noch eine Reihe von Colleges mit einer Studienzeit von vier Jahren, die einen undergraduate Abschluß anbieten in Fächern wie Kunst, Wissenschaft, Wirtschaft und Einführungskurse in die Medizin. Diese Schulen sind privat und sprechen vor allem die Studenten an, die auf einen persönlicheren Kontakt zwischen Professor und Student Wert legen.

Colleges mit einer Studienzeit von zwei Jahren bieten sowohl Kurse der Philosophie wie auch berufsorientierte Kurse an. Viele der Absolventen gehen danach zu einem Vier-Jahres-College oder einer Universität, um dort ihren Bachelor's Degree (niedrigsten akademischen Grad) zu erwerben.

Deutsche Abiturienten besitzen unter Umständen genügend Qualifikationen, um mit einem Studium an einer der höheren Lehranstalten in Chicago zu beginnen. Sie müssen allerdings eine schriftliche Aufnahmeprüfung ablegen und in manchen Fällen ein Essay schreiben und sie werden zu einem Gespräch geladen. Außer ihren akademischen Leistungen werden für die Aufnahme auch außerplanmäßige Fächer und Aktivitäten in Betracht gezogen. Realschulabgänger würden gut daran tun, zunächst an einem der Gemeinde-Colleges anzufangen und von dort anschließend auf eines der Vier-Jahres-Colleges überzuwechseln.

The potential student should remember that undergraduate education in the U.S. is general and provides little specialization. German students should investigate the possibility of receiving credit for courses already taken by passing a proficiency exam in subjects like calculus or language. U.S. colleges and universities are famous for their sports teams and other extracurricular activities.

Students will find a great many educational options in the Chicago area. Regardless of their academic, social or cultural orientation, they will find a school to fulfill their expectations. As an example, Illinois Benedictine College in the suburb of Lisle, has a one hundred year history of excellence in arts and sciences. It was one of the first to start an undergraduate program in International Business and Economics. This program is interdisciplinary and draws on resources from all over the world. Its co-ordinator comes from Germany and a number of its students have interned in Germany under the auspices of the Carl Duisberg Gesellschaft.

Tuition costs are substantially higher in the United States than in Germany. Students who come to any U.S. institution of higher education, public or private, can apply for and expect to get some financial aid to cover the costs of tuition and living expenses.

Interessierte Schüler oder Studenten sollten daran denken, daß eine Ausbildung in den USA allgemeiner und weniger spezialisiert ist. Außerdem sollten deutsche Studenten in Erfahrung bringen, ob nicht einige Kurse, z.B. in Mathematik und Sprachen im voraus anerkannt werden. Amerikanische Colleges und Universitäten sind für ihre Sportmannschaften und andere Aktivitäten, die außerhalb des Lehrplans stattfinden, bekannt.

Den Studenten in Chicago bieten sich viele Ausbildungsmöglichkeiten. Ungeachtet ihrer akademischen, sozialen oder kulturellen Orientierungen, können sie eine Ausbildungsstätte finden, die ihren Erwartungen entspricht. Als ein Beispiel kann das Illinois Benedictine College dienen, das im Vorort Lisle liegt und auf eine hundertjährige Tradition der Künste und Wissenschaften zurückblickt. Es war eines der ersten Colleges, die ein undergraduate Programm in Internationales Betriebs – und Volkswirtschaft anboten. Dieses Programm ist interdisziplinär und stützt sich auf Beiträge aus aller Welt. Der Koordinator dieses Programmes stammt aus Deutschland und eine Reihe seiner Schüler studierte unter der Schirmherrschaft der Carl Duisburg-Gesellschaft in Deutschland.

Die Studiengebühren sind in den Vereinigten Staaten bedeutend höher als in Deutschland. Studenten, die zum Studieren an eine amerikanische Lehranstalt kommen, privat oder staatlich, können einen Antrag auf einen finanziellen Studienzuschuß stellen, um die Lebens- und Studienkosten teilweise zu decken.

Living in the Midwest — A Woman's Point of View

by Marlis Schmidt

Wearing pink polyester pantsuits with their hair in rollers: this was my first impression of the *typical* American woman on my trips to the grocery store back in the early 70s. Talk about culture shock! My husband had just been transferred to Chicago, and we were tackling the adventure of living more than 4000 miles from home and the challenge of adjusting to a different lifestyle with tons of expectations and excitement. Yes, of course, it was only to be for a short time and, yes, of course, polyester was in (along with battleships that served as cars, matching plaid flannel jackets for him and her, and every appliance, kitchen utensil and gadget under the sun — as long as it came in avocado green or harvest gold).

Luckily, my English wasn't good enough back then to voice my opinion but, judging from those homesick letters to Mom, I wasn't too impressed with life in the Midwest. A year after our arrival it became obvious that, like it or not, Chicago was to become our home for a long time. I was about to find out first hand what this "land of unlimited opportunities" held for a woman.

It has been twenty years now, lots of things have changed since then, most of all I. From being a mother to going back to college and receiving my degree, from being a housewife to starting my own business ventures — I've done things I'd never thought possible back home. I have come to appreciate this melting pot of a nation with all its shortcomings and craziness which firmly has one foot on the moon — and the other one forever in a log cabin!

Raising kids can be hazardous to your sanity, as any mother will confirm. In the U.S. it's a bit easier, but still a job and a half: *Children Come First!* The society that gave us Mickey Mouse (as well as Beavis & Butthead) always has shown a bigger-than-life attitude towards its offspring. From Saturday morning cartoons to Disneyland, very few Americans really ever outgrow the child inside. How else would you explain that our most popular movie ever was about a short and utterly helpless alien from outer space (ET), and our fascination with kindhearted Arnold Schwarzenegger (who ranks up there right next to Superman)?

It all goes back to those birthday parties, I'm sure. Back in the 70s, when young mothers still took time off to raise their kids (boy, that has changed, too), every mom on the block had a station wagon — *Mom's Cab* we called it. I vividly remember taking truckloads of 4- to 10-year olds to McDonald's, the movies, amusement parks, mini-golfing, video arcades — you name it. There's an entire industry just

Das Leben im Mittleren Westen — Aus der Perspektive einer Frau

von Marlis Schmidt

Rosa Hosenanzüge aus Polyester und Lockenwickel in den Haaren: das war mein erster Eindruck von der *typischen* Amerikanerin bei meinen Lebensmitteleinkäufen Anfang der 70er Jahre. Ein "Kulturschock" ohnegleichen!

Mein Mann und ich waren gerade nach Chicago versetzt worden, und wir mußten uns 7000 km von der Heimat entfernt häuslich einrichten und an einen neuen Lebensstil gewöhnen. Wir gingen beide Herausforderungen mit Elan und hohen Erwartungen an. Zugegeben, ursprünglich sollte unser Aufenthalt nur von kurzer Dauer sein und, zugegeben, Polyester war damals Mode (genau wie Riesenschlitten von Autos, Flanneljacken in Karo, passend für SIE und IHN, sowie alle nur erdenklichen Küchengeräte und Utensilien - solange sie Avocadogrün oder Erntegold waren).

Glücklicherweise war mein Englisch damals noch nicht gut genug, um meiner Meinung nachhaltig Ausdruck zu geben, aber den heimwehkranken Briefen an meine Mutter nach zu schließen, war ich vom Leben im Mittleren Westen nicht gerade überwältigt. Ein Jahr nach unserer Ankunft wurde klar, daß Chicago auf lange Zeit unser Zuhause werden sollte. Ich sollte aus erster Hand erfahren, was eine Frau in diesem "Land der unbegrenzten Möglichkeiten" erwartet.

Seither sind zwanzig Jahre vergangen, und vieles hat sich verändert - am meisten jedoch ich. Erst Mutter, dann College-Absolventin, erst Hausfrau, dann Unternehmerin - ich habe Dinge unternommen, die ich in meiner alten Heimat nie für möglich gehalten hätte. Ich habe dieses Land mit all seinen Mängeln und Verrücktheiten schätzen und lieben gelernt, ein Land, das mit einem Bein fest auf dem Mond – und mit dem anderen noch immer in der Blockhütte steht!

Wer Kinder großzieht, läuft oft Gefahr, den Verstand zu verlieren; jede Mutter wird dies gern bestätigen. In den USA ist diese Aufgabe etwas einfacher, aber dennoch monumental: *Kinder kommen an erster Stelle*! Die Gesellschaft, die uns Mickey Mouse (und Beavis & Butthead) brachte, hatte schon immer ein ganz besonderes Verhältnis zu ihrem Nachwuchs. Von den Cartoons im Fernsehen bis zu Disneyland lassen nur wenige Amerikaner ihre Kindheit je ganz hinter sich. Wie sonst ließe sich erklären, daß der populärste Film aller Zeiten in den USA von einem kleinen und absolut hilflosen Wesen aus dem Weltall (ET) handelte, und daß wir so von Arnold Schwarzenegger fasziniert sind (der Schulter an Schulter mit Superman rangiert)?

An all dem sind die Geburtstagsfeiern von damals schuld, davon bin ich fest überzeugt. In den 70er Jahren, als junge Mütter noch zu Hause blieben, um ihre Kinder großzuziehen (auch das hat sich gewaltig geändert), hatte jede Mutter einen Kombi - *Mutters Taxi* wurde er genannt. Ich erinnere mich noch genau, wie ich Ladungen von 4- bis 10-jährigen zu McDonald's, ins Kino, in Vergnügungsparks, zum Minigolf und in Videohallen fuhr. Eine ganze Industrie ist damit beschäftigt, Geburtstagsfeiern zu versorgen: passende Papierteller, Hüte und Ballons, Themendekorationen, Mietclowns, Partyspiele - einige Restaurants stellen sogar Unter-

catering to birthday parties: matching paper plates, hats & balloons, theme decorations, rent-a-clowns, party games — some restaurants even employ special amusement counselors to keep the kids happy and entertained (and from throwing pies at each other).

Seriously, I'm happy to admit that this country's love for children has its advantages, too. I don't recall ever having seen a "Keep off the Grass" sign on any public lawn, and it never has been a hassle taking the kids out to eat (even if you have three). Most restaurants have baby chairs, kids menus are a regular feature, some places even have their own playgrounds and activity sets. The smaller the little ones are, the bigger the smiles they will draw from the tables around you (makes life a whole lot easier).

If you decide to eat at home — no problem. Most grocery stores are open 24 hours a day (no, it's not a universal law that one has to do one's shopping before 6 p.m.); there's always ample free parking, and usually someone with a friendly smile to pack and load your bags. Eating healthy is in: veggies, low-cal and fatfree are hot items (there are plenty of crunchy potato chips left for the junk food addict in us, trust me). Don't feel like cooking? The freezers are stuffed with tasty and affordable one-step dishes, ready to heat and serve (there are still plenty of cardboard imitations available, no doubt). The main meal is served in the evening when the family finally comes together. The children return from school around 3, and Dad is not alone battling the rush hour — most Moms work, too.

Our visitors often comment that they see less litter and graffiti in downtown Chicago than in many European cities. Well, we could show you other areas, no doubt,but the environmental awareness in the U.S. seems to be rapidly improving, indeed. The city and most of the suburbs try to take good care of their streets and parks (we're not talking about the annual pothole disaster we have to face after every winter).

Recycling has become mandatory, and ever so easy: each household is provided with a bright blue container to discard glass, aluminum and plastic items; paper and cardboard will be picked up from your sidewalk; and one giant garbage can that can be filled to the brim. Everything else, however, now costs money. Extra bins will be emptied only if they display a sticker, grass clippings and yard waste must be placed in special paper bags (both can be purchased at your local grocery store). Driven by the almighty dollar, the local obsession with green front lawns trimmed to perfection (paired with generally rather large properties) has created a brand new hobby: composting and mulching.

Talk about hobbies: often thought to be typical American inventions, they're really don't take too much of our time. I often feel that in this country we work harder and longer hours than anywhere else. Not because we have to (the 40-hour week is standard in most compa- haltungsberater zur Verfügung, die dafür sorgen, daß sich die Kleinen gut amüsieren (und nicht gegenseitig mit Torte bewerfen).

Spaß beiseite, ich gebe gerne zu, daß die Liebe, die dieses Land Kindern entgegenbringt, auch ihre guten Seiten hat. Niemals habe ich auf einem öffentlichen Rasen das Schild "Betreten verboten" gesehen, und die Kinder mit ins Restaurant zu nehmen, war einfach kein Problem (auch wenn man 3 hat). Die meisten Restaurants haben Hochstühle, Speisekarten für Kinder sind an der Tagesordnung, und einige Restaurants bieten sogar Spielplätze und Aktivitäten-Sets. Je kleiner die Kleinen, desto freundlicher das Lächeln an den umliegenden Tischen (was das Leben bedeutend leichter macht).

Auch wenn man beschließt, zu hause zu essen, ist das kein Problem. Die meisten Supermärkte sind rund um die Uhr offen (kein Gesetz schreibt vor, daß man überall auf der Welt vor 18 Uhr einkaufen muß.) An Parkplätzen fehlt es nicht, und meistens wartet schon eine hilfsbereite Seele, um die Einkaufstüten vollzupacken und in das Auto zu laden. Gesundes Essen ist "in": Gemüse, kalorienarme und fettfreie Speisen sind sehr gefragt (allerdings sorgen knusprige Kartoffelchips dafür, daß auch die "junk food"-Süchtigen nicht zu kurz kommen). Heute wird mal nicht gekocht? Die Tiefkühltruhen sind bis zum Rand gefüllt mit schmackhaften und erschwinglichen Fertiggerichten (neben den Pappkartonimitationen, die natürlich immer noch zu finden sind). Die Hauptmahlzeit wird am Abend eingenommen, wenn die Familie endlich wieder vereint ist. Die Kinder waren bis 15 Uhr in der Schule, und Vater muß sich nicht allein durch den Berufsverkehr kämpfen, da Mutter meistens ebenfalls arbeitet.

Unsere Besucher stellen häufig fest, daß sie weniger Abfall und Graffiti im Zentrum von Chicago sehen als in vielen europäischen Großstädten. Sicher könnten wir ihnen auch andere Gegenden zeigen, es stimmt jedoch, daß das Umweltbewußtsein in den USA rapide zunimmt. Die Innenstadt und die meisten Vororte bemühen sich, ihre Straßen und Parks gut instandzuhalten (abgesehen von den Schlaglöchern, die uns nach jedem Winter heimsuchen).

Recycling ist inzwischen obligatorisch und kein Problem: jeder Haushalt erhält einen leuchtend blauen Container für Glas, Aluminium und Plastikartikel; Papier und Pappe werden am Straßenrand abgeholt, und eine Riesentonne kann randvoll gefüllt werden. Alles andere kostet jetzt allerdings extra. Zusätzliche Behälter werden nur geleert, wenn sie mit einem Aufkleber versehen sind, Gras und Gartenabfälle müssen in besondere Papiersäcke gefüllt werden (beides wird im Supermarkt verkauft). Vom allmächtigen Dollar motiviert, hat die Leidenschaft für perfekt manikürte Rasen zusammen mit den relativ großen Grundstücken ein brandneues Hobby geschaffen: Komposten und Mulchen.

Apropos Hobbys: sie gelten zwar als typisch amerikanische Erfindung, nehmen unsere Zeit jedoch nicht allzu stark in An-

LIFE AND LEISURE — LEBEN UND FREIZEIT

nies) but because we have chosen to join the ranks of entrepreneurs. Even for a woman (especially for a woman), being self-employed is a great way to work at your own pace (and to fully satisfy the workaholic within). There is still a lot of pioneer spirit around, especially among first-generation newcomers. While raising my children, going to college, and publishing a book, I started a small translation business from my home. Within a few years, with the help of freelance translators, we offered services in twelve languages. What surprised me, however, was the total lack of bureaucratic restriction: no test or licenses, diplomas, permits or paperwork were required to get started. "Your customers will decide if you stay in business," I was told.

Free enterprise, indeed. Today I'm working as an independent broker, producing (and financing) my own radio program, and publishing a quarterly newsletter, once again facing very few restrictions. America is still *the land of unlimited opportunities*!

Actually, for many women going into business on their own has become a valid alternative to the corporate world. Equal rights for women in the work place is the law, of course! Equal pay — that's another story. Many women in this country still go by the name of their husbands (and would not have it any other way): Mrs. Charles Robert Whatshisname III does not need her own identity, she's proud to be *the wife*. The younger generation, however, is showing a new attitude. Hyphenated double-names, keeping one's maiden name for professional reasons (or not marrying at all) are not yet the rule, but no exception, either.

What happened to those rollers and the pink polyester suits of the 70s? They have been replaced by a walkman and the warm-up suit. However, there's another side to the woman of the 90s. Stop by at any corporate office or take a stroll along Chicago's trés chic Michigan Avenue, and you'll see a bright fashion picture: from mini to sophisticated long, from baggy pants to stirrups, from designer silk to cotton and beads. Yes, even jeans are in and always will be, but not necessarily at the opera anymore or for dining out (the ones spotted in jeans today are most likely the tourists). For the rest of *us* American women: Hillary is in the White House and we, indeed, have come a long way, baby.

spruch. Ich habe oft den Eindruck, daß wir in Amerika länger und härter arbeiten als alle anderen. Nicht nur, weil wir müssen (in den meisten Unternehmen gilt die 40-Stunden-Woche), sondern weil wir zur Gattung der Unternehmer gehören. Sogar für eine Frau - und besonders für eine Frau - bietet freies Unternehmertum eine ausgezeichnete Chance, unabhängig und nach eigenem Tempo zu arbeiten. Der Pioniergeist ist hier noch sehr lebendig, vor allem unter den Einwanderern der ersten Generation. Während ich meine Kinder großzog, aufs College ging und ein Buch veröffentlichte, startete ich ein kleines Übersetzungsbüro in meinem Haus. Mit Hilfe freiberuflicher Übersetzer boten wir innerhalb weniger Jahre Dienstleistungen in zwölf Sprachen an. Was mich jedoch erstaunte, war das Fehlen jeglicher bürokratischer Einschränkungen: keine Prüfungen oder Lizenzen, Diplome, Zulassungen oder Unterlagen wurden verlangt, um ins Geschäft zu kommen. "Ihre Kunden werden entscheiden, ob Ihr Geschäft weiterbesteht", wurde mir gesagt. Freies Unternehmertum par excellence! Heute produziere und finanziere ich als unabhängige Maklerin mein eigenes Radioprogramm und veröffentliche ein vierteljährliches Radio-Magazin, alles wieder mit einem Minimum an Beschränkungen. Amerika ist nach wie vor das Land der unbegrenzten Möglichkeiten!

Für viele Frauen ist der Einstieg in das selbständige Unternehmertum durchaus eine Alternative zur Arbeit in einer Firma. Gleichberechtigung für Frauen am Arbeitsplatz ist gesetzlich vorgeschrieben, mit der Bezahlung sieht es anders aus! Viele Amerikanerinnen tragen immer noch den Namen ihres Mannes (und wollen das auch): Mrs. Charles Robert Soundso III braucht keine eigene Identität; sie ist stolz darauf, *Gattin* zu sein. Die jüngere Generation sieht das jedoch etwas anders. Doppelnamen mit Bindestrich, Beibehaltung des Mädchennamens aus professionellen Gründen (oder überhaupt keine Eheschließung) sind zwar noch nicht die Regel, aber auch keine Ausnahmen mehr.

Was ist aus all den Lockenwickeln und rosa Polyester-Hosenanzügen der 70er Jahre geworden? Sie wurden durch den Walkman und Jogginganzug ersetzt. Die Frau der 90er Jahre ist jedoch nicht ausschließlich auf diesen Look beschränkt. Ein Blick in Firmenbüros oder ein Spaziergang auf der Michigan Avenue, der Nobelstraße von Chicago, ergibt ein buntes Modebild: vom Mini bis zum eleganten langen Rock, von weiten Flatterhosen bis zu Steghosen, von Designer-Seide bis zu Baumwolle und Holzperlen. Sogar Jeans sind Mode und werden das wohl immer bleiben, aber nicht mehr unbedingt in der Oper oder beim eleganten Abendessen (der uniforme Jeansanzug verrät heute meistens die Touristen). Für *uns* Amerikanerinnen gilt: Hillary ist im Weißen Haus, und wir haben es in der Tat weit gebracht.

Gifts *Geschenkartikel*	Liqueur *Spirituosen*	Chocolates *Schokoladen*	Magazines *Zeitschriften*
Sausages *Wurstwaren*	Delicacies and Beer	Wines *Weine*	Preservatives *Konfitüre*
Cakes *Kuchen*	Party Trays *Aufschnitt Platten*	Cheeses *Käse*	Condiments *Verschiedenes*
Coffee *Kaffee*	Waukeegan near Lake Cook	Friendly Expert Service • *Freundliche Bedienung*	Cosmetics

Kuhn's International Delicatessen

116 South Waukegan Road
Waukegan near Lake Cook
Deerfield, IL 60015
Telephone 708/272-4198

749 West Golf Road
Golf Road near Elmhurst Road
Des Plaines, IL 60016
Telephone 708/640-0223

Up-to-date resources for shopping and other activities
Informationsquellen zum Einkaufen und anderen Aktivitäten

Shopping in Chicagoland

Going shopping, usually, is a very satisfying experience, and a great pastime of Americans.

Americans have a love-hate relationship with shopping: when they purchase necessities, it's a chore; when they buy optional items, it is a fun thing to do, but when they shop only for something to do, it becomes a form of entertainment.

Let's assume, we are looking for bargains in grocery merchandise. Shoppers will buy most items "on sale" when purchasing for a family with children. Such items are marked down to attract shoppers to come to their stores and, hopefully, purchase other, full priced merchandise. Sale merchandise is available at all times, and often includes very timely items.

The choice of products is overwhelming: high to low priced goods, domestic (made in USA) and imported merchandise, high quality and cheap stuff, outrageously extravagant to ultra conservative.

Einkaufen in Chicagoland

Einkaufen wurde, weil so beliebt, zu einem neuen Sport in Amerika.

Die Amerikaner haben eine Haß-Liebe zum Einkaufen: heißt es, lebensnotwendige Dinge einzukaufen, dann wird es zur Aufgabe. Geht man aber jedoch Luxusgegenstände einkaufen, dann macht es Spaß. Geht man aber nur einkaufen, um sich die Zeit zu vertreiben, dann ist es eine Art Erholungssport.

Besonders für Familien mit Kindern sind Sonderangebote in der Lebensmittelabteilung und Schlußverkäufe eine Voraussetzung, ihre Einkäufe innerhalb ihres Budgets zu halten. Bestimmte Waren werden zu herabgesetzten Preisen angeboten, um den Käufer in den Laden zu locken und ihn dann zum Kauf von anderen Waren zum vollen Preis zu bewegen. Jede Woche gibt es neue Sonderangebote, manchmal sind sogar aktuelle Artikel darunter.

Die Auswahl ist überwältigend: von teuren bis zu billigen Waren, einheimischen Produkten (Made in USA) und importierten Produkten, Qualitätsprodukten und billigem Zeug, vom sehr Extravaganten bis zum Ultrakonservativen.

Deswegen sind die Shopping Malls so beliebt. Man kann dort zwischen den einzelnen Geschäf-

That's why shopping malls are so popular. One has a chance to compare, 3 to 6 shoe stores, for instance, within easy walking distance, one stop, free parking, a very pleasant environment at any time of year.

Despite the abundant choices, we find ourselves still shopping at the same stores as established places of business. It has to do with confidence in the establishment, personal attention and convenience. Whether it is a gasoline purchase, a suit, a car or insurance, we usually go back to those we know and who treat us well.

Experimenting with restaurants, movie theaters, golf and bowling, where we boat and bike, or how and where we spend our vacation is recreationally challenging. Shopping for leisure activity is fun, and usually an eye opening or eyebrow raising experience.

Oak Brook Shopping Mall: As much color and music as stores and sales

Einkaufzentrum in Oak Brook: Mehr Blumen und Musik als Geschäft

ten Vergleiche ziehen und sich zum Beispiel einen Schuhladen nach dem anderen anschauen. Die Geschäfte liegen alle in unmittelbarer Nähe voneinander. Die Atmosphäre und Umgebung zum Einkaufen sind das ganze Jahr über angenehm, da sich alles in einem Gebäudekomplex abspielt. Parken ist frei.

Trotz einer übermäßigen Auswahl, gehen die meisten Käufer immer wieder zu den ihnen vertrauten Geschäften. Das liegt wohl an dem Geschäft, der persönlichen Bedienung und der Bequemlichkeit. Egal ob es sich um das Kaufen von Benzin handelt oder um einen Anzug, ein Auto oder Versicherung, man bleibt in vertrauter Umgebung, wo man die Leute kennt und wo man gut bedient wird.

Es ist eine Art Sport, Erholung und Herausforderung zugleich, die verschiedenen Restaurants, Kinos, Golfplätze und Bowlingplätze auszuprobieren. Beliebt sind Bootsfahrten, Fahrradfahren oder sich Gedanken zu machen, wo man den nächsten Urlaub verbringen soll. Schon allein für Freizeit und Urlaub einkaufen zu gehen ist eine Abwechslung und vor Überraschungen ist man dabei keineswegs sicher.

SHOPPING IN CHICAGOLAND — EINKAUFEN IN CHICAGOLAND

Buying a car is an even more involved process:

Before you enter the showroom of a dealer, you need to be sure you know what you want, how much your car's trade-in is worth, and how much you want to spend for the difference in monthly or cash payments.

American cars are very comfortable, safe, and easy to maintain. A 10-minute lubricating job every 3,000 miles will do wonders for performance and longevity. With low speeds on US highways — 55 to 60 miles per hour — speed and power in a car are less important than performance for passing, rough roads and stop-and-go driving.

When you purchase a major ticket item, you must make sure you get the best warranty; sometimes you may want extended warranty. You want the best service policy, hopefully bumper-to-bumper. And you want assurance that the dealer has a good reputation for helping you out when something goes wrong with the vehicle.

If you buy a used car from a private party, your purchase is final — no warranty nor service. If you know the person who you bought the car from, and the car as well, you can expect a good bargain for a reasonable price.

Ein Autokauf ist ein noch viel komplizierterer Vorgang:

Ehe man den Verkaufsraum eines Autohändlers betritt, muß man sich darüber im klaren sein, was man will, wie hoch der Tauschwert des Autos ist und wieviel mehr man sich monatlich an Autozahlungen leisten kann.

Amerikanische Autos sind sehr bequem, sicher und leicht instand zu halten. Alle 3000 Meilen ein kurzer Check-up und Ölwechsel wirken Wunder und erhalten das Auto lange in gutem Zustand. Da die Geschwindigkeitsbegrenzung auf amerikanischen Straßen bedeutend niedriger ist — 55 bis 60 Meilen, oder 88 bis 96 km pro Stunde — spielen Geschwindigkeit und Leistungsfähigkeit des Motors keine so große Rolle wie die Überholfähigkeit, gute Straßenlage und leichtes Anfahren.

Wenn man ein großes und teures Auto kauft, ist eine gute Garantie ratsam. Manchmal ist es eine gute Idee, eine Zusatzgarantie abzuschließen. Wichtig sind gute Wartungskonditionen, wenn möglich eine Versicherung, die alles deckt. Es ist ebenso wichtig, daß der Autohändler einen guten Ruf hat und er, wenn das Auto Mängel aufweist, dafür gerade steht.

Wenn man einen Gebrauchtwagen von einer Privatperson kauft, gilt der Kauf als endgültige Abgabe ohne Garantie oder Service. Es hilft, wenn man die Person kennt, von der man den Gebrauchtwagen kauft. Vielleicht läßt sich sogar ein

Car dealers handle several brands

Autohändler führen mehrere Marken

In general, we Americans like to haggel and dicker, in antique stores, at garage sales (unwanted household items) and flea (miscellaneous merchandise) markets.

When the stakes are high, such as in real estate, shopping around and negotiating becomes a long term and complex process. But it is challenging, nevertheless, because:

- we have unlimited choices of what and where we want to buy or rent.
- we can rest assured that a decision is not final and that family circumstances and job opportunities may dictate moves to different locations.
- we can invest in real estate for future use or speculation depending on our resources.

While most young couples may start out renting an apartment or buying a condominium, as soon as children arrive, a starter house in an appropriate neighborhood may be in order.

Such a house may be new or pre-owned. It oftentimes has two or three bedrooms, a garage and a fair-sized basement for the children to play in during inclement weather. There is a larger living room, a dining area and a compact kitchen. Two bedroom homes may have one full bathroom, three bedroom homes may have a full and one-half bathroom. A starter house with property, a lot size of approx. 60 x 100 ft., costs around $100,000 to $150,000 depending on location, new or older construction, urban or suburban area, etc. Payments work out to approximately $1,000 a month, with interest and property taxes included. If you rent, a small house may be priced at $1,200 to $1,500 a month. In the city or by the lake it may cost up to twice as much, depending on location, the view, proximity to shopping, restaurants and entertainment, the environment, neighborhood, and such.

günstigerer Preis dabei heraushandeln.

Im allgemeinen lieben es die Amerikaner zu feilschen, in Antiquitätenläden, Flohmärkten oder auf dem „Garage Sale". Ein Garage Sale ist ein von einer oder mehreren Familien organisierter Trödelmarkt, der in der eigenen Garage stattfindet und wo Familien ihr Sammelsurium verkaufen.

Wenn es sich um größere Investitionen handelt, wie z.B. der Erwerb von Grundbesitz, dann wird das „Shopping around" und das damit verbundene Verhandeln ein langzeitiges und kompliziertes Projekt. Es ist gar nicht so leicht, denn

— es gibt eine unendliche Auswahl von dem, was und wo man kaufen oder mieten kann.
— oft ist es keine endgültige Entscheidung; Familienumstände oder eine Versetzung an einen anderen Arbeitsplatz machen oftmals einen Umzug unumgänglich.
— Grundbesitz kann eine langfristige Versicherung für die Zukunft sein oder als Anlage für Spekulationszwecke dienen.

Die meisten jungen Ehepaare fangen mit einer Mietwohnung an oder sie kaufen sich eine Eigentumswohnung. Sobald das erste Kind ankommt, wird vielleicht ein „Starter" Haus in der richtigen Nachbarschaft (sprich: Viertel) gekauft.

A cozy home for young people. *Gemütliches Zuhause.*

Es gibt neue und alte Häuser. Die meisten haben 2 bis 3 Schlafzimmer, eine Garage und einen ziemlich großen Keller, in dem die Kinder bei schlechtem Wetter spielen können. Ein großes Wohnzimmer, eine Eßecke oder Eßzimmer und eine Einbauküche. Häuser mit zwei Schlafzimmern haben ein Badezimmer, Häuser mit drei Schlafzimmern haben meistens ein Badezimmer und eine Gästetoilette. Ein Starterhaus mit einer Grundstücksfläche von ca. 60 x 100 Fuß kostet um die $100.000 bis $150.000. Das hängt von der Lage ab, ob es neu oder alt ist, in der Innenstadt oder der Vorstadt liegt usw. Die monatlichen Zahlungen für die Hypothek betragen rund $1.000 pro Monat, Zinsen und Grundsteuern mit inbegriffen. Die Miete für ein kleines Haus kann um die $1.200 bis $1.500 monatlich liegen. In der Stadt oder am See kann es zweimal soviel kosten, das ist nicht nur von der Lage abhängig, sondern auch von der Aussicht, der Nähe von Einkaufsmöglichkeiten, Restaurants und Unterhaltung, Umwelt, Nachbarschaft und dergleichen mehr.

As children get older and entertain high school friends, they need more space. So, a 3 to 5 bedroom place is more appropriate: it will have more recreation space — in addition to the basement, a family room, an outdoor patio, and perhaps a pool. One bedroom is often converted to an office. Entertaining guests is popular and a most enjoyable experience. The larger house with a 2-car garage, and plenty of storage area, is located on a third of an acre lot with landscaping. Costs, all inclusive, can be $200,000 to $300,000. We can expect to pay about $2,500 a month and up, also because of varying property taxes.

A custom home, built to specifications, has individual character and is very spacious and comfortable, efficient, often built on a private lot in the vicinity of good shopping, schools and recreational facilities. It would have special provisions for a home office, feature guest and servant quarters, an indoor pool, a tennis court, a (winter) garden, 3-car garage and storage for a boat, or stables for horses. Beautiful landscaping would enhance the appearance and value of the mansion. Price is estimated at $500,000. and up.

Very popular are homes away-from-home. Whether a cottage by the lake, or a modest trailer in the country, it is still a place to relax, to entertain family and friends over a weekend and on holidays. A house boat on our many lakes and rivers may be an option for those enjoying the pleasures of water recreation. Many people maintain a second residence, a condo, home or park model trailer in moderate or warm climates.

Wenn die Kinder älter werden und Freunde mit nach Hause bringen, braucht man meistens mehr Platz. Deshalb ist ein Haus mit 3 bis 5 Schlafzimmern, einem Keller, einem Aufenthaltsraum, einer Terrasse und einem Swimming-Pool schon vorteilhafter und man hat mehr Platz für Freizeitaktivitäten. Oftmals wird eines der Schlafzimmer als Büro genutzt. Wenn man gerne Gäste unterhält, braucht man mehr Platz. Ein größeres Haus mit einer Garage, die Platz für 2 oder mehr Autos bietet, steht meistens auf einem halben Hektar Land und kostet um die $200.000 bis $300.000, wobei die Hypothek ca. $2.500 pro Monat oder mehr beträgt. Die monatlichen Zahlungen hängen natürlich von den Grundsteuern ab, die in Amerika bedeutend höher sind.

Ein nach Kundenwünschen gebautes Haus hat mehr individuellen Charakter, mehr Platz und ist bequem und praktisch ausgelegt, meistens auf einem Grundstück in der Nähe von guten Einkaufsgelegenheiten, Schulen und Fitnesszentren. Vielleicht mit eigenem Büro, Gästezimmer und Wohnung für die Hausangestellten, einem Pool im Haus, einem Tennisplatz, einem Wintergarten, einer großen Garage und einem Bootsschuppen oder Pferdestall. Schöne Gartenanlagen erhöhen Ansehen und Wert der Villa. Die Preise fangen um die $500.000 an.

Sehr populär sind Wochenendhäuser. Ob es sich um eine Hütte am See handelt oder um einen kleinen Wohnwagen auf dem Land, es ist ein Ort wo man sich mit seiner Familie und Freunden übers Wochenende entspannen kann. Eine weitere Möglichkeit wäre ein Hausboot auf einem der vielen Seen und Flüsse für die Wassersportliebhaber. Viele Leute unterhalten auch ein zweites Heim oder eine Zweitwohnung in einer Gegend mit wärmerem Klima.

Grundbesitz war schon immer eine gute Anlage, aber nur wenn er genutzt wird und in einer guten Gegend liegt.

Die Amerikaner ziehen oft um und leben sich schnell ein. Für sie ist Komfort, ein guter Lebensstil und Annehmlichkeiten sehr wichtig. Aber genauso

This custom home in Oak Brook's Hunters Trails is $750,000 including land
Dieses nach Kundenwünschen gebaute Haus in Oak Brook's Hunter Trail kostet zusammen mit Grundstück über $750.000.

Real Estate has always been a good investment. It should be fully utilized, serving a genuine purpose, be of manageable size, comfortable, a home with neighbors close by, a place to call your own.

Americans are mobile people and change locations according to circumstances, adapt and prosper. The important things are our well-being and life-styles. Our relationship to relatives, our children, friends — and convenient amenities.

The choices we have in investing, shopping and recreation are made so easy, one can easily over-extend finances. Credit is readily available everywhere at reasonable interest rates.

America, which provides freedom in every respect, invites people to enjoy its great prosperity, its many forms of recreation, its abundance of products, its unlimited cultural events, its countless festivities, the splendor of its parks and diverse regions.

wichtig sind die Beziehungen zu Verwandten, zu den Kindern, Bekannten und Freunden.

Die Auswahl an Investitions- und Einkaufsmöglichkeiten und Freizeitaktivitäten ist wirklich sehr groß und kann schnell zu hohen Schulden führen, denn Kredit ist überall leicht zu bekommen.

Amerika genießt in jeder Hinsicht eine gewisse Freiheit und lädt uns ein, an seinem Wohlstand teilzuhaben, seine vielseitigen Freizeitsangebote zu nutzen, sein Überangebot an Produkten, seine unzähligen kulturellen Veranstaltungen und Feste und die Pracht seiner Parks zu genießen und seine verschiedenen Religionen auszuüben.

Zum Einkaufen gehört mehr als nur guter Service:

Es fängt mit der Bequemlichkeit an, der Weg zum Laden, die zugängigen Parkgelegenheiten, ein freundlicher Gruß, genügend Information, um das Einkaufen zu erleichtern.

Mit der freundlichen Hilfe eines erfahrenen Verkäufers wird die Wahl leicht und angenehm gemacht. Aber auch Selbstbedienung kann, wenn alles gut ausgeschildert ist, viel Spaß machen.

A home away from home, a peaceful place.

Zur Ruhe, ein Plätzchen im Wald.

Part of shopping is service. And service includes much more than just maintaining the goods we buy:

It starts with convenience, the way a store is laid out, location, available parking and accessibility, a friendly greeting, information as to facilitate purchases.

The selection process, with the help of an experienced sales clerk, can be enriching. Self service is satisfactory, as long as merchandise is marked in detail, and it usually is.

Fashions and jewelry, as well as personal items may require the individual touch and advice of good sales people.

Quick and easy follow-up with alterations and enhancements, accessories and possible gift wrapping are all part of the purchase, the service — and perhaps an extra sale.

Delivery, installation, pick-up of old appliances are important service aspects — made easy and convenient, they keep customers coming back for more, building a lasting relationship with the establishment.

In the grocery store, items are always expertly packed for the customer in paper or plastic bags of the customer's choice, and often carried out to the car.

With so many brands of products being similar in quality, service by the individual store often makes the difference to discriminating shoppers.

Examples of unlimited choices:

Americans buy and use cars with great interest; it is one of the most talked about subjects besides sports, work and computers.

Cars are often the only means of transportation to work, to shop and to leisure pursuits. Travel distances are substantial and public transportation is not always conveniently available in the suburbs.

Bei Modeartikeln und Schmuck braucht man vielleicht eher die Hilfe eines guten Verkäufers.

Änderungen, Accessoires und eventuell Geschenkverpackungen sind ein integraler Teil des Kundendienstes.

Um dem Kunden noch mehr Annehmlichkeiten zu bieten, und um eine langfristige Beziehung zwischen dem Käufer und dem Kaufhaus aufzubauen, werden Anlieferungen, Installation und das Abholen alter Geräte ebenfalls angeboten.

In den Lebensmittelgeschäften wird die Ware sachgemäß in Papier-oder Plastiktüten verpackt und nach Wunsch bis ans Auto getragen. Mit den vielen Markenprodukten auf dem Markt, ist gute Beratung in den einzelnen Geschäften für den anspruchsvollen Käufer unerläßlich.

Ein Beispiel um dies zu verdeutlichen:

Die Amerikaner haben eine große Liebe für Autos. Neben Sport, Arbeit und Computern ist das Auto ein beliebtes Gesprächsthema.

Für viele ist das Auto oft das einzige Verkehrsmittel, das zur Verfügung steht, um zur Arbeit zu kommen, einkaufen zu gehen oder zum Fitnesszenter zu fahren. Die Entfernungen sind groß und in den Vororten gibt es kaum öffentliche Verkehrsmittel.

In der Stadt Chicago haben wir die CTA (die Chicagoer Verkehrsgesellschaft) und die RTA (die Regionale Verkehrsgesellschaft) mit ihren silbrig-glänzenden Vorortszügen: Die North-Shore-Linie, die North-Western-Linie, die Burlington-Linie und die South-Shore-Linie. Die Hochbahn verbindet die Randbezirke mit dem Loop. Die Untergrundbahn verbindet die Stadt mit dem Flughafen und anderen Stadtvierteln. Ein enges Netz an Bussen zieht sich

Lachner "CHICAGOLAND"

The city of Chicago, however, is served by the CTA and RTA, the Chicago and Regional Transit Authorities link any urban community with slick commuter trains to and from different locations: The North Shore, the North-Western, the Burlington, and the South-Shore System. The Elevated Train serves the outskirts and connects to the Loop. Underground subways connect the airports and other local neighborhoods to the City and vice versa. There is also a very close-knit network of buses all over the city and in the near suburbs. Cabs fill in the gaps, with limousines and buggy rides providing exclusive and entertaining transportation.

Renting a car is a viable and popular alternative, a practical way to get around when travelling away from the home or office.

A word about Credit Cards should be enlightening:

Almost everyone owns and uses credit cards for travel, shopping and other services. A valuable asset, which makes life easy and convenient. Credit card companies do not charge interest if the bill is paid within 30 days. They also offer a number of auxiliary services, which can be very helpful: special discounts, damage and theft protection, travel insurance and cash. It all depends on the carrier, card and financial status.

Renting a car with a U.S. Driver's License and a credit card is most convenient at any location. There are many choices of rental agencies, cars and pricing. Advance reservations for a car is a must, easy with today's 800 toll-free phone numbers.

Corporations often lease their vehicles for delivery personnel, salesforce and executives. It does not require a great investment of capital, maintenance is included, and cars are upgraded to new models on a regular basis. There are a number of accounting details to be considered which are best discussed with an accountant or tax advisor.

Typische Kreditkarten

Our world is full of consultancies, experienced people who offer advice for a fee. It is difficult to estimate the value of such services. Therefore, always know what is needed, wanted or required, before asking for advice. Consultants can better and more efficiently assist if they know exactly what is expected of them.

A guide to shopping and restaurants with German speaking personnel follows this section.

über die Stadt und die anliegenden Vororte. Dort, wo es an Verkehrsmitteln mangelt, findet man immer ein Taxi. Limousinen und Pferdekutschen sind extravagante Alternativen.

Autovermietung ist ebenfalls sehr beliebt und bequem.

Vielleicht sollte auch kurz ein Wort zu Kreditkarten gesagt werden:

Es gibt wohl kaum einen Amerikaner, der keine Kreditkarte sein eigen nennt und sie zum Reisen, Einkaufen, und für andere Zwecke benutzt. Sie ist ein notwendiges Übel, das das Leben erleichtert. Man braucht auf die Belastung keinen Zins zahlen, wenn man die Rechnung innerhalb von 30 Tagen nach Belastung bezahlt. Die Kreditkartengesellschaften bieten darüber hinaus zusätzlichen Service an, der oftmals sehr von Nutzen ist: Sonderrabatte, Schaden- und Diebstahlschutz, Reiseversicherung und Bargeld. Es hängt von dem Unternehmen, der Karte und der Kreditwürdigkeit des Kunden ab.

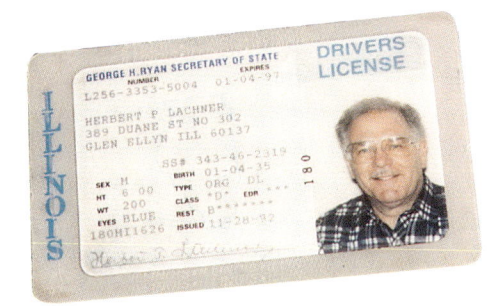

Amerikanischer Führerschein

Mit einer Kreditkarte und einem Führerschein kann man überall ein Auto mieten. Und die Auswahl an Autovermietungen ist groß. Das Auto sollte aber vorbestellt werden, was mit den neuen gebührenfreien 800-Telefonnummern eine Leichtigkeit ist.

Größere Firmen leasen oftmals ihre Wagen für Lieferungen, für das Verkaufspersonal und für die leitenden Angestellten. Man braucht dazu wenig Kapital und die Wartung ist umsonst. Die Modelle werden regelmäßig erneuert. Das dazu erforderliche Rechnungswesen sollte am Besten mit einem Wirtschaftprüfer besprochen werden.

Auto Nummernschild

Unternehmensberater bieten ihre Dienste für ein Honorar an. Es ist schwierig, den Wert dieser Dienste abzuschätzen und es ist empfehlenswert, sich schon vorher im Klaren zu sein, was man eigentlich braucht, bevor man einen Unternehmensberater hinzuzieht. Er kann sie besser beraten, wenn er genau weiß, was von ihm erwartet wird.

Im Anschluß an dieses Kapitel folgt ein Führer zu Geschäften und Restaurants mit deutschsprachiger Bedienung.

SHOPPING IN CHICAGOLAND — EINKAUFEN IN CHICAGOLAND

JF
International Fashions by *Ingrid*

Trachten
Knitwear (Men & Ladies)
Skirts • Blouses
Suits • Dresses
Sizes 8 to 20

**4710 N. Lincoln Avenue
Chicago, Illinois 60625**

Phone 312/878-8382
Fax 312/878-8148

Deutsche Markenschuhe, hervorragend in Qualität und Paßform.

German Quality Shoes for over 30 years

SALAMANDER *of Chicago*

**4762 N. Lincoln Avenue
Chicago, IL 60625**
312/784-SHOE • 312/784-7463

Welcome to Lincoln Square Mall...

Deutsche Wohnkultur im Chicagoland

Northern Home Furnishings

**4662 North Lincoln Ave.
Chicago, IL 60625
312/561-6910**

Chicagoland's largest and most complete selection of fine European furniture

---

"Lincoln Square" Mall

A German speaking oasis in Chicagoland.

It has become the center of the German retail community.

Here you can have a great time at the Chicago Brauhaus: good German food, a live band to German songs and melodies, fellowship with those you know and views you appreciate.

Stores with goods you have known from your childhood year, from the apothecary to the German deli, the fashion and giftstore to magazines and furniture.

Come to *Lincoln Square* Mall when you visit Chicagoland. It is like a trip to the old country.

All stores are inviting you into their world of tradition, yet up-to-date as they are in Europe.

Lincoln Square Einkaufszentrum

Eine deutschsprachige Oase im Chicagoland.

Es ist das Zentrum des deutschen Einzelhandels.

Hier kann man sich im Chicago Brauhaus amuesieren. Gute deutsche Kueche, eine Kapelle, die mit Gesang und Musik Stimmung macht. Geselligkeit mit Menschen, die man versteht und deren Meinung man teilt.

Geschaefte mit Waren, die man oft seit seiner Kindheit nicht mehr gesehen und genossen hat. Von der Apotheke zum Schlachter, von Trachten und Geschenken zu den Zeitschriften, Romanen und Moebeln.

Besuchen auch Sie einmal den *Lincoln Square* Platz wenn Sie in der Gegend sind. Es ist wie ein Ausflug in die alte Heimat.

Alle Geschaefte laden Sie zu einem Bummel durch Klein-Deutschland ein, eine Welt voller Tradition und dem besten aus Europa.

Large Selection
IMPORTED/DOMESTIC
Sausages • Meat
Cheeses • Fish
Salads • Breads
Cookies • Candies
Juices • Jams • Jellies
Honey • Coffee • Tea
Wine • Liquor • Beer
Champagne
Cosmetics
Households Utensils
Gift Baskets
Party Trays

Delicatessen MEYER

4750 N. Lincoln Avenue
Chicago, Illinois 60625
Tel: 312/561-3377

Home of Stiegl Columbus Beer

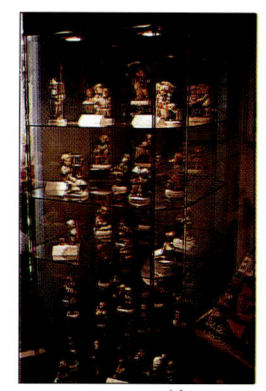

Phone: 312/561-8281

European IMPORT CENTER

European Crystal • China • Linens and other Imported Gift Items
German Language Magazines • Newspapers and Greeting Cards

4752 N. Lincoln Avenue • Chicago, Illinois 60625

Lincoln Square Mall bietet sich an

Excellent German & American Cuisine

Live Entertainment Nightly and Saturday & Sunday Afternoon

Open for Lunch & Dinner

Closed Tuesdays

Chicago Brauhaus RESTAURANT & LOUNGE

4732-34 N. Lincoln Avenue • Chicago, Illinois 60625
Tel. 312-784-4444 • Fax 312-784-2092

Latest Top European and Vintage Frames:
– Cazal
– Giorgio Armani
– Hugo Boss
– Neostyle
– Porsche
– Rodenstock
– Silhouette
– Zeiss
– and More...

Board Certified Opticians

QUALITY OPTICAL

4718 N. Lincoln Avenue
Chicago, IL 60625
Tel: 312/561-0870 Fax: 312/561-4185

Eyes Examined — Children's Vision — Glasses Fitted — Contact Lenses

German Speaking Restaurant Guide

Chicago

Berghoff Restaurant Co.
17 W. Adams Street
Chicago, IL 60603
312/427-3170

Chicago Brauhaus Inc.
4732 N. Lincoln Avenue
Chicago, IL 60625
312/784-4444

Fondue Stube
2717 W. Peterson
Chicago, IL 60659
312/784-2200

Heidelberger Fass
4300 N. Lincoln Avenue
Chicago, IL 60618
312/478-2486

Hüttenbar
4721 N. Lincoln Avenue
Chicago, IL 60625
312/561-2507

Laschet's Inn
2119 W. Irving Park Road
Chicago, IL
312/478-7915

Schulien Restaurant & Salon
2100 W. Irving Park Road
Chicago, IL 60618
312/478-2100

Zum Deutschen Eck
2924 N. Southport
Chicago, IL 60657
312/525-8121

Near North Suburbs

Black Forest Chalet
8840 Waukegan Road
Morton Grove, IL 60053
708/965-6830

Far North Suburbs

Chef Karl's Edelweiss Inn
411 E. Park Avenue
Libertyville, IL 60048
708/367-9696

Jensen House Restaurant
1185 Main Street
Antioch, IL 60002
708/395-6474

Wunder-Bar Restaurant
40805 N. Route 83
Antioch, IL 60002
708/395-8282

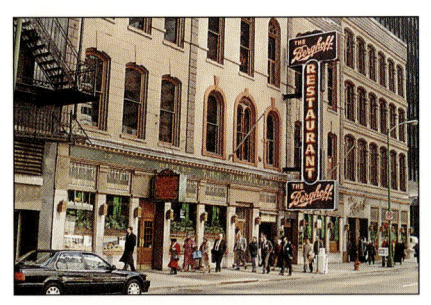

The Berghoff Restaurant

The Schulien Restaurant

The Bistro 1800

Arlington Place Restaurant

Gasthaus "Zum Loewen"
1958 W. Roscoe
Chicago, IL 60657
312/477-5510

Golden Ox Restaurant
1578 N. Clyborn
Chicago, IL 60622
312/664-0780   944-0284

German American Restaurant
642 N. Clark Street
Chicago, IL 60610
312/642-3244

Metro Club
3032 N. Lincoln Avenue
Chicago, IL 60657
312/929-0622

Mirabell Restaurant
3454 W. Addison
Chicago, IL 60618
312/463-1962

Resi's Bierstube
2034 W. Irving Park
Chicago, IL 60618
312/472-1749

Bistro 1800
1800 Sherman
Evanston, IL 60201
708/492-3450

Old Munich Inn
582 N. Milwaukee Avenue
Wheeling, IL 60090
708/537-1222

Schwabencenter (Banquethall)
301 N. Weiland
Buffalo Grove, IL 60089
708/541-1090

Northwest Suburbs

Arlington Place
902 E. Northwest Highway
Arlington Heights, IL 60004
708/253-2190

Christl's German Inn
45 W. Slade Street
Palatine, IL 60067
708/991-1040

Dieterle's Restaurant
550 S. McLean Place
Elgin, IL 60123
708/697-7311

Deutschsprechendes Restaurants

Fritzl's Country Inn
900 Ravinia Terrace
Lake Zurich, IL 60047
708/540-8844

Gasthaus Zur Linde
15 N. Grove Avenue
Elgin, IL 60120
708/695-8828

Hans Bavarian Lodge
931 N. Milwaukee Avenue.
Wheeling, IL 60090
708/537-4141

Edelweiss Restaurant
7650 W. Irving Park
Norridge, IL 60634
708/452-6040

Klas Restaurant
5734 Cermak Road
Cicero, IL 60650
708/652-0795

Little Bavaria
2521 Central Avenue
Cicero, IL 60650
708/863-9752

Schatzie's Restaurant & Lounge
16 E. North Avenue
Northlake, IL 60164
708/562-0160

Weinkeller Brewery
651 Westmont Drive
Westmont, IL 60559
708/789-2236

William Tell Restaurant
6201 Joliet Road
Countryside, IL 60525
708/352-1101

Rhine Inn
1995 Bloomingdale Road
Glendale Heights, IL 60139
708/351-6606

South Suburbs

Rosemarie's German Kitchen
2445 Ridge Road
Lansing, IL 60438
708/895-9789

Gasthaus zur Linde

Hans Bavarian Lodge

Bar at the Golden Ox

The Black Forest Restaurant

Near West Suburbs

Bohemian Crown Restaurant
7249 Lake Street
River Forest, IL 60305
708/366-8140

Bohemian Crystal
639 Blackhawk Drive
Westmont, IL 60559
708/789-1981

Czech Plaza Restaurant
7016 Cermak Road
Berwyn, IL 60402
708/795-6555

Little Bohemian Restaurant
25 E. Burlington Street
Riverside, IL 60546
708/442-1251

Moldau Restaurant
9310 Ogden Avenue
Brookfield, IL 60513
708/485-8717

Pilsner Restaurant
6725 W. Cermak Road
Berwyn, IL 60402
708/484-2294

Far West Suburbs

Bohemian Garden
980 75th Street
Downers Grove, IL 60515
708/960-0078

Dumpling Villa Restaurant
300 E. St. Charles Road
Villa Park, IL 60181
708/834-9565

Heidelberg International Delicatessen & Restaurant
122 S. York Road
Elmhurst, IL 60126
708/530-5115

Joliet Region

Bohemian Corner
700 Ruby Street
Joliet, IL 60435
815/722-9633   723-7770

Cafe Bohemian
15756 S. Bell Road
Lockport, IL 60441
708/301-3339

Die Bier Stube
42 Kansas Street
Frankfort, IL 60423
815/469-6660

Gift Shops
Andenken- und Geschenkeläden

Austrian Station
3504 N. Elston
Chicago, IL 60618
312/583-8288

European Import Center
4752 N. Lincoln Ave.
Chicago, IL 60625
312/561-8281

European Imports
7900 N. Milwaukee Ave.
Niles, IL 60714
708/967-5253

Salamander Shoes
4762 N. Lincoln Ave.
Chicago, IL 60625
312-784-7463

Schmidt Imports
4606 N. Lincoln Ave.
Chicago, IL 60625
312/561-2871

Sound & Image Inc.
4728 N. Lincoln Ave.
Chicago, IL 60625
312/334-3212

Optical
Brillen und Optik

Quality Optical
4718 N. Lincoln Ave.
Chicago, IL 60625
312/561-0870

European Bakeries

Chicago

Beil's Bakery
4229 W, Montrose Avenue
Chicago, IL 60641
312/725-0021

Cafe Selmarie
2327 W. Giddings
Chicago, IL 60625
312/989-5595

Dinkel's Bakery
3329 N. Lincoln Avenue
Chicago, IL 60625
312/281-7300

Chicago Brauhaus

Enisa's European Pastry
4701 N. Lincoln Avenue
Chicago, IL 60625
312/271-7017

North Star Bakery
4545 N. Lincoln Avenue
Chicago, IL 60625
312/561-9858

Lutz Continental Cafe & Pastry Shop
2458 W. Montrose Avenue
Chicago, IL 60614
312/478-7785

Europäische Konditoreien und Bäckereien

Rolf's Patisserie
2634 N. Laramie Ave.
Chicago, IL 60639
312/804-0400

Schmeissing Bakery
2679 N. Lincoln Avenue
Chicago, IL 60614
312/525-3753

Vienna Pastry Shop
5411 W. Addison
Chicago, IL 60641
312/685-4166

Zum Deutschen Eck

Wagner's Bakery
2148 W. Cermak
Chicago, IL 60608
312/847-8180

Weber's Bakery
7055 W. Archer
Chicago, IL 60638
312/586-1234

Near West Suburbs

Cukraren Fine European Pastries
677 N. Cass Avenue
Westmont, IL 60559
708/325-1727

Fingerhut's Chas Bakery
9110 Bway Ave.
Brookfield, IL 60513
708/485-8480

Reuter's
7177 W. Grand Avenue
Chicago, IL
312/889-1414

Schwaegerman's Bakery
104 W. Calendar Avenue
La Grange, IL 60525
708/354-2253

Schmeissing Bakery

Veseckey's Bakery
6634 W. Cermak Road
Berwyn, IL 60402
708/788-4144

Far West Suburbs

Amann's Bakery
488 Spring Road
Elmhurst, IL 60126
708/832-2289

Buettner's Bakery
601 E. Irving Park Road
Roselle, IL 60172
708/529-6607

Lilac Pastry Shop & Bakery
348 S. Main Street
Lombard, IL 60148
708/627-1310

Noack's European Pastries
6 N. Island Street
Batavia, IL 60510
708/879-3323

Northwest Suburbs

Central Continental Bakery
101 S. Main Street
Mt. Prospect, IL 60056
708/870-9500

Fritzl's Country Inn

Daneggar's Pastry Shop
18 N. Dryden Avenue
Arlington Heights, IL 60004
708/255-3160

Oergel's Bakery & Cafe Inc.
1735 W. Golf Road
Mt. Propsect, IL 60035
708/439-6969

Old World Bakery Inc.
64 N. Old Rand Road
Lake Zurich, IL 60047
708/438-7233

Sauer's Bakery Shop
532 W. Dundee Road
Wheeling, IL 60090
708/537-4050

Near North Suburbs

Amy Joy Donuts
7248 N. Milwaukee Avenue
Niles, IL 60714
708/647-9819

Doerner's Bakery
1405 Waukegan Road
Glenview, IL 60025
708/724-8975

Vienna Pastry Shop

Niles Pastry Shop
7633 Milwaukee Avenue
Niles, IL 60714
708/967-9393

Somenek's European Pastry
1221 W. Dundee Street
Buffalo Grove, IL 60089
708/870-0960

Somenek's European Pastry
7900 N. Milwaukee Avenue
Niles, IL 60714
708/965-5680

Far North Suburbs

Bernhardt's Bakery
536 N. Milwaukee Avenue
Libertyville, IL 60048
708/362-2355

Bernhardt's Bakery
1550 Grand Avenue
Waukegan, IL 60085
708/662-4065

Bernhardt's Bakery
775 Main Street
Antioch, IL 60002
708/395-9355

Lutz Continental Cafe and Pastry Shop

South Suburbs

Baden-Baden Bakery Inc.
13010 Western Avenue
Blue Island, IL 60406
708/388-7222

Baumann's Bakery
12250 Harlem Avenue
Palos Heights, IL 60463
708/448-1440

Fleckenstein's Bakery
19225 La Grange Road
Mokena, IL 60448
708/479-5256

Butchers
Fleischereien

Chicago

Black Forest Meat Market
2002 W. Roscoe
Chicago, IL 60618
312/472-7720

Paulina Market
3501 N. Lincoln Ave.
Chicago, IL 60657
312/248-6272

The Alpine Market

Near North Suburbs

Schmeisser's Home Made Sausage Incorporated
7649 Milwaukee Avenue
Niles, IL 60714
708/967-8995

Zier Premium Meats
813 Ridge Road
Wilmette, IL 60091
708/251-4000

Butchers

South Suburbs

Eckert Brothers Meat Market
5267 W. 95th Street
Oak Lawn, IL 60543
708/422-4630

Far West Suburbs

Otto's Old Time Meat Market
125 Addison Ave.
Elmhurst, IL 60126
708/832-2079

Black Forest Meat Market

Northwest Suburbs

Schaltz Enterprise
73 Fountain Square Plaza
Elgin, IL
708/697-6606

Thueringer Meats
624 S. Arthur Ave.
Arlington Heights, IL 60005
708/253-4111

Koenemann's Sausage Co., Inc.
27090 W. Rt. 120
Volo, IL 60073
815/385-6260   1-800-662-5584

Delicatessen

Chicago

Alpine Meat Market
4030 N. Cicero Avenue
Chicago, IL 60641
312/725-2121

Black Forest Market
2002 W. Roscoe
Chicago, IL 60618
312/348-3660

Inge's Delicatessen
4724 N. Lincoln Avenue
Chicago, IL 60625
312/561-8386

Edelweiss Delicatessen

Kuhn's Delicatessen
3053 N. Lincoln Avenue
Chicago, IL 60657
312/525-9019   525-4595

Meyer Delicatessen
4750 N. Lincoln Avenue
Chicago, IL 60625
312/561-3377

Meyer Import Delicatessen
3306 N. Lincoln Avenue
Chicago, IL 60659
312/281-8979

Olga's Delicatessen
3209 W. Irving Park Road
Chicago, IL 60618
312/539-8038

Near North Suburbs

Black Forest Delicatessen
8840 Waukegan Road
Morton Grove, IL 60053
708/965-3113

Delikatessen Linger, Inc.
Oak Mill Mall
7900 N. Milwaukee Avenue
Niles, IL 60714
708/967-0180

A. F. Meyer

Kuhn's Imports
3118 McArthur Boulevard
Northbrook, IL 60062
708/480-9698

Kuhn's International Delicatessen
116 S. Waukegan Road
Deerfield, IL 60015
708/272-4197

Far North Suburbs

Ann's Bavariahaus
114 W. Peterson Road
Libertyville, IL 60048
708/367-5933

Far West Suburbs

Heidelberg International
122 S. York Road
Elmhurst, IL 60126
708/530-5115

Near West Suburbs

Kuhn's Imports Inc.
9503 Winona Street
Schiller Park, IL 60176
708/678-0850

Prague Sausage
6312 Cermak Road
Berwyn, IL 60402
708/795-0250

Northwest Suburbs

Black Forest Deli
1129 N. Roselle Road
Hoffman Estates, IL 60195
708/882-5822

Continental-Delikatessen & Imports
10 S. Evergreen
Arlington Heights, IL 60004
708/259-9544

Edelweiss Delicatessen
136 W. Northwest Highway
Palatine, IL 60007
708/359-7030

Kuhn's Delicatessen
749 W. Golf Road
Des Plaines, IL 60016
708/640-0222

Taste of Europe Delicatessen
674 S. Barrington Road
Streamwood, IL 60107
708/372-0063

Distributors of German Food & Beverages

Deutsche Lebensmittelgroßhändel

Barton Beer Ltd.
55 E. Monroe St.
Chicago, IL 60603
312/346-9200
(1)

Baum Wine Imports, Inc.
485 Thomas Drive
Bensenville, IL 60106
708/616-1690
(2)

Berg & Sons Co.
4949 Elston Avenue
Chicago, IL 60630
312/283-1370
(16)

Charlotte Charles, Inc.
5990 W. Touhy Ave.
Niles, IL 60714
708/647-0787
(6, 7, 15, 20)

Chicago Importing Co.
1144 Randolph St.
Chicago, IL 60607
312/421-5177
(4, 7, 10, 12, 13, 14, 17, 19, 21)

Consolidated Distilled Products
3247 S. Kedzie Ave.
Chicago, IL 60623
312/254-9000
(2, 3)

Dae-Julie, Inc.
1665 E. Birchwood Ave.
Des Plaines, IL 60018
708/296-1800
(6, 8, 13, 20)

European Imports Ltd.
1334 W. Fulton St.
Chicago, IL 60607
312/226-8060
(8, 16)

Food Brokers, Inc.
3330 Dundee Road
Northbrook, IL 60062
708/291-1450
(16)

Gies Import
3345 N. Southport Ave.
Chicago, IL 60657
312/472-4577
(1, 2)

Gorski Distributors, Inc.
46 State Street
Lemont, IL 60439
708/257-5441
(1)

Judge & Dolph Ltd.
680 N. Lake Shore Drive
Chicago, IL 60611
312/280-8700
(2, 3)

Kehe Food Distribution, Inc.
333 S. Swift Road
Addison, IL 60101
708/953-2829
(4, 7, 10, 12, 13, 14, 17, 18)

Kreiner Imports
3155 South Shields
Chicago, IL 60616
312/225-5100
(4, 6, 11, 13, 14, 18, 20)

Kuhn's Import, Inc.
3118 McArthur Blvd.
Northbrook, IL 60062
708/480-9698
(5,6,7,8,9,10,11,12,13,14,15,16,18,20)

Labatt's U.S.A. Inc.
1110 Lake Cook Road
Buffalo Grove, IL 60089
708/459-0101
(6)

Lohmiller Wine Distributors
3817 N. Francisco Ave.
Chicago, IL 60618
312/267-7326
(2)

Paterno Imports Ltd.
2701 S. Western Ave.
Chicago, IL 60608
312/247-7070
(1)

R.J. Imports, Ltd.
6250 N. River Road, Suite 8000
Rosemont, IL 60018
708/692-2280
(1)

Ragold, Inc.
500 N. Michigan Ave., #1700
Chicago, IL 60611
312/222-1888
(13)

Reimann Company
1304 Cooper Drive
Papatine, IL 60067
708/991-1366
(5,6,7,8,9,10,11,12,13,14,15,16,18,20)

Skandia Foods, Inc.
615 E. Brook Drive
Arlington Heights, IL 60005
708/364-9704
(7, 14, 15, 16)

Strock USA L.P.
500 N. Michigan Ave., #844
Chicago, IL 60611
312/467-5700
(13)

WeinBauer, Inc.
8340 Center Street
River Grove, IL 60171
708/452-0585
(1)

Westdale Foods Co.
7825 S. Roberts Rd.
Bridgeview, IL 60455
708/458-7774
(13, 14)

Winesellers Ltd.
9933 N. Lawler Ave.
Skokie, IL 60077
708/679-0121
(1)

Zuercher & Co.
1032-34 W. Fulton St.
Chicago, IL 60607
312/666-6992
(16)

Key

(1)	Beer	(12)	Vinegar, mustard, condiments
(2)	Wine	(13)	Confections, candies, chocolates
(3)	Spirits	(14)	Cakes, cookies, crackers
(4)	Coffee	(15)	Bread
(5)	Fruit juices	(16)	Cheese
(6)	Other non-alcoholic beverages	(17)	Potato products
(7)	Fish products	(18)	Pudding and desserts, baking aids
(8)	Meat products	(19)	Health and dietetic foods
(9)	Ready-to-serve dishes	(20)	Pasta products
(10)	Canned fruits, vegetables, jams	(21)	Miscellaneous
(11)	Pickled preserves, sauerkraut		

Karneval

From New Year's Eve till Ash Wednesday is the "Merryment Season" in Germany; from the North Sea to the Boden Sea and the Alps, and especially in the Rhineland the spirit of "Karneval" (Mardi Gras) is high. This custom was not invented yesterday, but many centuries ago when people started celebrating Karneval along the banks of the mighty Rhine River. It is in the character of the people of that area to make the most of the festivities and to take advantage of the time just before the Lenten Season of fasting before Easter for one last fling, to intensely eat, drink, and be merry. It is at that time that the Merrymakers (Narren und Närrinnen) rule and everything seems like a fairy tale of carefree happiness. Everyone kindles on the sparkling moods of the other and gets carried along in a certain longing, for non-stop fun and unburdened merryment. Karneval is in itself a spiritual medium, tied in together with long and seriously taken traditions. Among all joys of life, Karneval is a very special kind of play. Only people who are free from within can truly devote themselves and be submissive to this happy and merry strength and let that power take them over. Therefore, the Rheinischer Verein von Chicago does not want to keep its members and friends from such joy and so it has been for the last 104 years, and so may it be today that we will follow our motto:

"Everyone well and pain to no one"

and that we keep up the tradition of one of the most beautiful and oldest German "Volksfests" here in the "New World."

In the name of the "Rheinische" spirit we wish all our guests to this year's Karneval Sessions pleasure and good humor.

The Board Members of the Rheinischer Verein of Chicago 1890

S.T. Prinz Albert I. and I.L. Prinzessin Monica I. with family and friends, Karneval 1994.

Zum Deutschen Eck

Once just a bar on the corner of Southport and Oakdale, *Zum Deutschen Eck* was always a piece of home and haven for German immigrants. In the shadow of the neighborhood churches St. Alphonsus and St. Luke, many guests found here a hearty meal, sound advice and made valuable connections.

In 1956, Al Wirth Sr. founded *Zum Deutschen Eck* which has been owned and operated by the Wirth Family ever since. Through the years it has been transformed into a beautiful Bavarian Chalet, with two dining rooms, a unique bar and three banquet rooms for 24 to 400 patrons, a true Chicago landmark.

Many people met their spouses here and celebrated their weddings and other family events.

Today, after serving three generations of customers, *Zum Deutschen Eck* still nurtures the tradition with continental cuisine, live, weekly entertainment...a place to celebrate.

Your host, Al Wirth Jr. continues this feeling of "Gemütlichkeit" and would like to welcome you to enjoy great food, great times and great atmosphere.

Your Host Al Wirth

Die Bar an der Ecke Southport und Oakdale, das spätere *Zum Deutschen Eck*, war schon immer ein Stück Heimat und Zuflucht für deutsche Immigranten. Hier, im Schatten der Nachbarschaftskirchen St. Alphonsus und St. Luke fanden viele Gäste ein köstliches Mahl, einen guten Ratschlag und knüpften wertvolle Verbindungen.

Im Jahre 1956 gründete Al Wirth Sr. das *Zum deutschen Eck*, welches seither von der Familie Wirth besessen und bewirtschaftet wurde. Über die Jahre hat man es in ein bezauberndes bayrisches Chalet mit zwei großen Esszimmern, einer aussergewöhnlichen Bar und drei Festsälen fuer 24 bis 400 Personen verwandelt, geradezu ein Wahrzeichen der Stadt Chicago.

So manche Menschen haben hier ihren Lebenspartner gefunden und haben hier Hochzeit und andere Familienfeste gefeiert.

Heute, nach drei Generationen von treuen Kunden, pflegt das *Zum deutschen Eck* immer noch die alte Tradition mit europäischer Küche und einer Kapelle, die wöchtlich spielt...eben ein Lokal zum feiern.

Ihr Wirt, Al Wirth Jr., ladet ein zur Gemütlichkeit, und er würde auch Sie gerne begrüßen zu einem festlichen Essen bei guter Unterhaltung in großartiger Atmosphäre.

Wein Stube

Continental Banquet Room

2924 North Southport Avenue • Chicago, Illinois 60657 • (312) 525-8121

Club Life in Chicagoland

American Friends of Austria
Henry Glass, Präsident
Tel.: 708-446-1358
Loretta Fleischmann, Sekretärin
Tel.: 708-696-2878, 312-583-8288

Deutsche Tag-Vereinigung
Erich Himmel, Präsident
Tel.: 312-561-8670
Marianne Wehrle, Sekretärin
Tel.: 312-267-7326

Karnevals-Gesellschaft Rheinischer Verein von Chicago
Al Kaczmarek, Präsident
Ulrike Graf, Sekretärin
Tel.: 312-478-2948

Hamburg Chicago Club
Renate Bonde, Präsidentin
Uwe Bonde, Sekretär
Tel.: 708-462-6943

Berliner Bären
Guenther Jacoby, Präsident
Tel.: 708-593-8349
Liesel Jacoby, Sekretärin
Tel.: 708-593-8349

D.A.N.K.-Hauptgeschäftsstelle
Ernst Ott, Nationalpräsident
Tel.: 312-275-1100

D.A.N.K.-Gruppe-Nord
Siegfried Reinke, Präsident
Tel.: 312-561-9181

D.A.N.K.-Gruppe-West
Siegfried Endlichofer, Präsident
Tel.: 708-246-6824

General Von Steuben Float
1993 General Von Steuben Parade

German American Heritage Institute
Gary Neubieser
Tel.: 708-366-0071

Damengruppe des Rheinischen Vereins
Elisabeth Kraus, Präsidentin
Tel.: 708-679-5887
Mirdza Raane, Sekretärin
Tel.: 312-774-8340

Niedersachsen-Club Chicago
Wilfried Guntermann, Präsident
Werner Raasch, Sekretär
Tel.: 708-366-3996

Steuben Society of America Unit No. 30
Harold Kekstadt, Chairman
Tel.: 312-761-4488

Schwaben-Verein von Chicago
Walter Sanders, Präsident
Tel.: 708-383-7928
Rudolf Kaiser, Sekretär
Tel.: 708-397-3806

Vereinsleben

American Aid Society of German Descendants
Hans Gebavi, Präsident
Tel.: 312-763-1323
Joseph Stein, Sekretär
Tel.: 708-381-7915
Elizabeth Gebavi, Sekretärin & Museum Curator
Tel.: 312-763-1323

American Aid Society Jugendruppe:
Joseph Stein
Tel.: 708-381-7915

American Aid Society Kindergruppe:
Elsa Walter
Tel.: 708-381-1385

Banat-Brestowatzer Vergnügungs-Verein
John Kraus, Präsident
Tel.: 708-679-5887
Margaret Rally, Sekretärin
708-963-4635

Vereinigung der Donauschwaben
Niklaus Kreiling, Präsident
Tel.: 708-818-9785
Helga Blaumueller, Sekretärin
Tel.: 708-729-7675
Franz Winteer, Festpräsident
Tel.: 312-685-1683

German-American Club of Antioch
Karl Pokorny, Präsident
Tel.: 708-587-5707
Susanne Tanachovsky, Sekretärin
Tel.: 708-395-5008

Parade of Flags - Glenview Naval Air Base 1993 General Von Steuben Parade

Schuhplatter-Verein "Edelweiss"
Richard Anetsberger, Präsident
Walter Huber, Sekretär
Tel.: 312-472-8575

Schuhplatter-Verein "D'Lustigen Holzhacker-Buam"
Lloyd E. Wevang, Präsident
Tel.: 312-286-5661
Irma Wevang, Sekretärin
Tel.: 312-286-5661

Vereinigte Deutsch-Amerikanische Chöre von Chicago und Umgebung
Rudi Dick, Präsident
Tel.: 312-763-1833
Wolfgang Reich
Tel.: 708-635-8418

Elmhurst Männerchor
Klaus Schmidt, Präsident
Tel.: 708-833-3466
Gerhard Henke, Sekretär
Tel.: 708-544-1506

Rheinischer Gesangverein
Hans Strauch, Präsident
Tel.: 708-541-9639
Dieter Jacobshagen, Sekretär
Tel.: 708-893-3609

Schiller Liedertafel
Fritz Baumgart, Präsident
Tel.: 708-803-9471
Klaus Scheiweke, Sekretär
Tel.: 708-747-4574

CLUB LIFE IN CHICAGOLAND

Club Life continued...

Schleswig-Holsteiner Sängerbund
Tel.: 312-763-9554
Otto Drews, Präsident
Tel: 708-272-8598
Hans Berndt, Sekretär
Tel.: 708-965-3196

Schwäbischer Sängerbund
Heinz Krauth, Präsident
Tel.: 708-991-3267
Walter Sanders, Sekretär
Tel.: 708-383-7928

Elmhurst Damenchor
Brigitte Lenke, Präsidentin
Tel.: 708-665-3137
Uschi Kundmann, Sekretärin
Tel.: 708-766-0320

Damenchor Lorelei
Berta Ulich, Präsidentin
Tel.: 312-248-5275
Rita Wehrle, Sekretärin
Tel.: 312-267-7326

Steirer Damenchor
Hella Meyer, Präsidentin
Tel.: 312-973-2425
Grace Peterson, Sekretärin
Tel.: 708-290-8801

Deutsch-Amerikanischer Kinderchor, Inc., Chicago, IL
Ruth Schuebel, Präsidentin
Roxane Ellwanger, Sekretärin
Tel.: 312-736-5015
Helen Reichard, Koordinator
Tel.: 312-282-3482

D.A. Sänger von Chicago
Bob Lichtenvoort, Präsident
Tel.: 708-823-0810
Charlotte Tantius, Sekretärin
Tel.: 708-272-0076

1993 Germanfest Weekend - Guest Chorus
Shanty Chor Nordstrand; Kreis Nord Friesland, Deutschland

Österreichischer Gemischter Chor (Austrian Mixed Chorus)
Walter Fleischmann, Präsident
Tel.: 708-696-2878
Walter Pomper, Sekretär
Tel.: 312-892-3590

Schubert-Lyra Chor
Hans Bauer, Präsident
Tel.: 708-674-7437
Thomas Bauer, Sekretär
Tel.: 708-675-6120

Harlem Männer und -Damenchor
Marvin Schlichting, Präsident,
Tel.: 708-366-7991
Monika Foster, Sekretärin
Tel.: 708-682-3969

Alpine Ski Club
Hans Kendl, Präsident
Tel.: 708-991-5345
Irene Spanroff, Sekretärin
Tel.: 706-426-3764

German American Police Assoc.
Roger Haas, President
Laura Tischhauser, Secretary
Tel.: 312-539-2023

Schwaben A.C.
Mike Lemonidis
Tel.: 708-382-3986
Fran Pope, Sekretärin
Tel.: 708-394-4736

St. Hubertus Jagd Club
Jakob Zimmermann, Präsident
Tel.: 312-775-7912
Heinrich Hummelbeck, Vizepräsident
Tel.: 312-282-5034

Brandenburger Schützenverein Chicago, Inc.
Werner Huepper, Präsident
Tel.: 708-808-8286
Peter Wrehde, Vizepräsident
Tel.: 708-255-7938

Introduction of Officers and 1993 Cornflower Queen
1993 Germanfest Weekend

Vorstand und 1993 Kornblumenkönigin German Fest Wochenende

Plymouth High School Marching Band; Plymouth, Wisconsin
1993 General Von Steuben Parade

Horse & Wagon (Sponsored by Louis Glunz Distributors)
1993 General Von Steuben Parade

CLUB LIFE IN CHICAGOLAND

Lachner "CHICAGOLAND"

Hamburg – Sister City 1994   4318 Miles – 6960 km east of Chicago   Hamburg – Partner-Stadt 1994

Hamburg – Chicago's German Sister City
Hamburg – Chicagos Deutsche Partnerstadt

The opinion is unanimous: Hamburg is beautiful. More and more visitors are coming each year to Germany's second city (1.7 million residents) and are taking home fond memories. For Chicagoans who are planning to visit their sister city, there's a lot to see and a lot to do; allow us to show you:

Numerous parks and tree-lined avenues make Hamburg one of Europe's greenest cities. You've probably heard of

Die Meinung ist einstimmig: Hamburg ist wunderschön. Jedes Jahr kommen mehr und mehr Besucher nach Hamburg, einer der schönsten Städte Deutschlands (1,7 Millionen Einwohner) und Partnerstadt Chicagos, und nehmen schöne Erinnerungen mit nach Hause. Für die Chicagoer, die einen Besuch in der deutschen Partnerstadt planen, gibt es viel zu sehen und zu unternehmen. Hier ein paar Tips:

Die vielen Parkanlagen und Alleen haben Hamburg in eine der grünsten Städte Europas verwandelt.

Port of Hamburg — 15,000 ocean-going vessels dock in Germany's largest seaport yearly, carrying over 50 million tons of cargo. It is still 65 miles up the Elbe River to the North Sea from here.

Der Hamburger Hafen - 15 000 Ozeanriesen, die über 50 Millionen Tonnen Fracht transportieren, legen jährlich in Deutschlands größter Hafenstadt an. Von hier sind es noch 104 km weit die Elbe hoch bis zur Nordsee.

Suell Hill near Blankenese is famous for its view onto the Elbe River, and is home to many retired captains.

Vom Süllberg in Hamburgs berühmtem Vorort Blankenese hat man einen wundervollen Blick auf die Elbe. Dort ist auch die Heimat vieler Kapitäne, die sich zur Ruhe gesetzt haben.

Sailboats on the Alster, an idyllic mini-lake in the middle of the City

Segelboote auf der Alster, ein idyllischer kleiner See inmitten der Stadt.

View from Lombards Bridge across the Inner Alster to the City Hall and Nicolai Church

Sicht von der Lombardsbrücke, die über die Innen-Alster führt, zum Rathaus und zur Nicolaikirche.

When the sun shines it seems like Sunday

Wenn die Sonne scheint, wird jeder Tag zu einem Sonntag

Hamburg is surrounded by heath, hills and lakes. Along the Elbe river are very fertile vegetable and fruit regions with picturesque farm buildings such as this thatched house during cherry blossom time.

Hamburg ist von Heide, Hügeln und Seen umgeben. An den Ufern der Elbe liegen fruchtbare Gemüse- und Obstgärten mit idyllischen Bauerngehöften, wie dieses strohgedeckte Haus hier während der Kirschblütenzeit.

"Planten un Blomen", a 115-acre green oasis within a stone's throw from the Damtor Station. Trees, bushes and lawns are a sight for sore eyes. Every spring, the air is filled with the scent of 85,000 crocuses, narcissi and tulips in bloom. At the Stephansplatz entrance, you'll find the Japanese Gardens, complete with magical streams, lakes and waterfalls. The tropical greenhouses are also well worth visiting, and there are numerous fine restaurants right in the park that invite you to take it easy.

Trees and flowers, parks and woods are as much a feature of Hamburg's cityscape as the canals and waterways that criss-cross the city on the Elbe river.

„Planten un Blomen" ist eine 46 ha große, grüne Oase nur einen Steinwurf vom Damtor Stadion entfernt. Bäume, Büsche und Rasenanlagen sind eine Augenweide. Im Frühjahr ist die Luft erfüllt mit dem Duft von 85 000 Krokussen, Narzissen und Tulpen in ihrer vollen Blütenpracht. Am Eingang zum Stephansplatz liegen die Japanischen Gärten mit ihren zauberhaften Bächen, Teichen und Wasserfällen. Das tropische Gewächshaus ist ebenfalls eine Attraktion, die man sehen sollte und über den ganzen Park verteilt stehen einladende Restaurants.

Bäume und Blumen, Parks und Wälder gehören genauso zum Stadtbild Hamburgs wie die Kanäle und Wasserwege, die sich durch die Stadt an der Elbe ziehen.

Wußten Sie schon, daß Hamburg eigentlich mehr Brücken hat als Venedig und Amsterdam zusammen? Und nicht zu vergessen die unvergleichliche Alster, ein wahres Wunderland der Erholung inmitten der Stadt. Die Alster entspringt in Schleswig-Holstein und plätschert zunächst als Bach gen Süden auf die große Stadt zu. Während sie an Größe, Geschwindigkeit und Kraft zunimmt, wird sie mitten im Hamburger Stadtgebiet durch einen Staudamm gedämmt. Sogar stocksteife Hamburger werden sentimental, wenn sie das Loblied der Alster singen. Sie alle, Wassersportler und Landratten zugleich, sind sehr stolz auf ihr Paradies des Erholungssports. Der angrenzende Alsterpark mit seinen majestätischen alten Bäumen, der Blumenpracht, einem Ententeich und den sorgfältig gepflegten Rasenflächen lädt zum Picknick und Ballspielen ein. Jogging und Fahrradfahren entlang der Alster gehört zum alltäglichen Leben. An ihrem Ufer stehen noble Clubs, deren

Actually, Hamburg has more bridges than Venice, Amsterdam and London together. Did you know that? Not to forget the unequalled Alster, that recreational wonderland, right in Hamburg's center. Starting as a spring in Schleswig-Holstein, the Alster heads south as a babbling brook, toward the big city. Growing in size, speed and strength, it is finally restrained by a dam in mid-metropolis. Even the most stiff upper-lipped Hamburger people have been known to show signs of faithful emotion where epithets for the Alster are concerned. There is no mistaking their pride in this leisure paradise for water sports enthusiasts and landlubbers alike. The surrounding Alsterpark with its fine old trees, flowers, a duck pond and neatly-mown lawns invites for picnics and ball games. Jogging and cycling along the Alster has become a recreational must. The shoreline

Called the "Venice of the North", Hamburg has more bridges than Venice and Amsterdam combined.

Hamburg, das Venedig des Nordens, hat mehr Brücken als Venedig und Amsterdam zusammen.

The Hamburg "Rathaus": Seat of the Senate and City Council

Das Hamburger Rathaus: Sitz des Senats und der Stadtverwaltung

Namen eng mit Tradition verbunden sind. Dazu gehören 23 Sportclubs und 3 Segelschulen. Und wenn man keine Yacht besitzt -nun dann mietet man eben eine! Oder ein Ruderboot, Tretboot oder Kajak. Eine Flotte von weißen Alster-Schiffen liegt am Jungfernstieg und bietet Fahrten für jeden Geschmack an: die Alstertour mit Führer, zwei Kanaltouren, einen Ausflug in der Abenddämmerung, die Vierlandetour, die Brückentour und natürlich die Fähre. Sie können von der einen Seite zur anderen überwechseln oder eine Rundfahrt machen, die 2 Stunden dauert - Sie können an neun Anlageplätzen ein- und aussteigen. Und wenn

HAMBURG – SISTER CITY — HAMBURG – PARTNER-STADT

Riverside Cafe on the Alster Creek, where people relax and reminisce

Ein Strandcafé an den Ufern der Alster zum Entspannen und zum Träumen.

is dotted with respectable clubs whose names are redolent with tradition, including 23 sports clubs and 3 yachting schools. If you don't own a yacht — rent one! Or a row boat, pedal boat or canoe. A fleet of white Alster cruise ships starts at the "Jungfernsteig" landings, offering something for everyone: the Alster guided tour, two canal tours, the twilight tour, the Vierlande tour, the bridges tour and the ferry service. You can cross from one side to the other or take 2-hour round trips — with nine jetties to get on and off. If you like to fish — the Alster is definitely an angler's delight, with carp, pike, eel, bitterling and tench. If that's too much work, stop by at any of the many cafes, bars or restaurants to enjoy some R&R right in the heart of the bustling city. The Port is undeniably one of Hamburg's major attractions.

It is not only the largest in Germany, with roughly 500 berths for seagoing ships, a surface area of 63 square

Sie gerne angeln gehen - die Alster ist ein wahres Anglerparadies mit Karpfen, Hechten, Aalen, Bitterlingen und Schleien. Meinen Sie, das ist zu anstrengend, nun dann können Sie jederzeit in einem der vielen Cafés, Bars oder Restaurants haltmachen, um sich inmitten der geschäftigen Stadt zu erholen und zu entspannen.

Der Hafen ist zweifellos Hamburgs größte Attraktion. Er ist nicht nur Deutschlands größter Hafen mit rund 500 Anlegeplätzen für seetüchtige

Schiffe, einer 63 km² großen Fläche und 60 Docks, sondern er kann sich mit den größten Häfen der Welt messen. Stundenlang kann man dem Treiben zuschauen, vom Verladen von Teppichballen, die mit Ladekränen in die Lagerhäuser der Stadt transportiert

kilometers and a choice of 60 docks - it can hold its own with the largest ports in the world. There's so much to see, from bales of carpets being moved by crane in the Warehouse City to the breathtaking speed at which containers are loaded and unloaded. Shipping on the Elbe can be closely watched from vantage points ashore such as the riverside "balcony" behind the Rathaus in Altona.

Boating on the Alster is so popular, there is little space to maneuver.

Da Bootfahren auf der Alster so beliebt ist, bleibt einem wenig Platz zum Manövrieren.

For an even closer look at the big ships you can tour the Port by launch from the Landungsbruecken', St. Pauli, or take the ferry across the river to Finkenwerder. You can also tour the Port, or at least part of it, by car,

werden, bis zu der atemberaubenden Geschwindigkeit, mit der Containerschiffe be- und entladen werden. Man kann dem Treiben auf der Elbe aber auch von bestimmten günstigen Aussichtspunkten am Ufer zuschauen, zum Beispiel von der Uferballustrade hinter dem Rathaus in Altona. Bei einer Hafentour in einem Küstenboot, das von der Landungsbrücke St. Pauli abfährt, kann man die Schiffe aus nächster Nähe betrachten. Oder man nimmt die Fähre über den Fluß nach Finkenwerder. Man kann teilweise das Hafengelände mit dem Auto, dem Fahrrad oder zu Fuß erkunden. Denken Sie dabei daran, daß Sie die Zollgrenzen passieren und wenn sie den Freien Hafen mit einem Perserteppich über die Schulter geschlungen verlassen wollen, kann es leicht passieren, daß der Zollbeamte Ihnen Schwierigkeiten macht. Spaß macht es auch, durch den alten Elb-Tunnel zu laufen oder durch die historische Lagerhausstadt zum Monument des mittelalterlichen Seeräubers und Volkshelden Claus Stoertebeker am Brooktor.

Auslassen darf man auf keinen Fall Hamburgs Seedenkmal an der St. Pauli Landungsbrücke, die Windjammer „Rickmer Rickmers," die 1896 gebaut wurde. Heute ist es ein Museum und Restaurant. Und da Sie nun schon einmal im Hafenviertel sind, sollten Sie sich Nord-Deutschlands bedeutendste Barockkirche anschauen, die St. Michaelis-Kirche, besser bekannt als „Michel." Die Kirche wurde zwischen 1751 und 1762 erbaut mit einer Kirchturmspitze die 132 m hoch ist. Vom Turm aus hat man eine herrliche Sicht über die Stadt und den Hafen.

Machen Sie jetzt einen Spaziergang entlang der historischen Deichstraße mit Lagerhäusern und Bürogebäuden

by bike or on foot. Keep in mind, though, that you might be crossing customs borders — if you leave the Free Port with a Persian carpet slung over your shoulder, you might have difficulties convincing the customs officers you were just passing through. On foot it's great fun walking through the old Elbe Tunnel or wandering around historic Warehouse City to the monument of the mediaeval buccaneer and folk hero Claus Stoertebeker at Brooktor.

Don't miss Hamburg's maritime landmark at the St. Pauli Landungsbruecken, the "Rickmer Rickmers", a windjammer built in 1896. It is now a museum and restaurant and open for tours and dining. Since you are in the port's vicinity, take a look at Northern Germany's most significant baroque church structure, St. Michaelis. Better known as "Michel", this church was built 1751-62, its spire is 132 m high (almost 400 feet). A viewing platform gives you a splendid panorama of the city and port.

Take a stroll along historic Deichstrasse with warehouse and office buildings dating back to the 17th/18th century, and don't miss the "Rathaus", the magnificent sandstone edifice in the neo-renaissance style, built 1886-97, seat of the Senate and City Council. With its 647 rooms (6 more than Buckingham Palace) and splendid interior, it makes for an enjoyable tour.

Tired of sightseeing?

aus dem 17. und 18. Jahrhundert. Und nicht zu vergessen, das Rathaus, der herrliche Sandsteinbau im Stil der Neurenaissance, der 1886-97 erbaut wurde und der Sitz der Stadtverwaltung und des Senats ist. Mit seinen 647 Räumen (6 mehr als der Buckingham Palast) und der prächtigen Innenausstattung, ist das Rathaus ein sehenswürdiger Teil der Tour.

Wenn Sie jetzt der Stadtbesichtigung überdrüßig sind, nun, Hamburg ist ja auch die Stadt mit den größten überdachten Einkaufsarkaden angefüllt mit den teuersten und geschmackvollsten, exklusivsten und auserwähltesten, ältesten und modernsten Kostbarkeiten. 10 Arkaden liegen allein zwischen der Mönckebergstraße und dem Gänsemarkt. Sehr interessant ist ein Abstecher ins „trendy" Pöseldorf, einer Mischung aus eleganter Wohngegend, Einkaufszentrum und Künstlerkolonie.

Für die Nachtschwärmer und für die Frühaufsteher hat sonntags um 7 Uhr morgens die Stunde geschlagen, wenn der Fischmarkt in St. Pauli seine Tore öffnet. Händler, Einkäufer und Touristen schieben sich durch die Auktionshalle. Bananenbündel werden in die Menge geworfen. Kaninchen wechseln den Besitzer. Topfpflanzen werden gekauft und wie Jagdtrophäen davongetragen. Obwohl heutzutage Fisch nur eine der vielen Waren ist, so wurde der Markt ursprünglich zum erstenmal 1703 gehalten, damit die Fischer ihre schnellverderblichen Waren am Tag des Herren verkaufen konnten. Es stimmt, wenn man sagt: Hamburg ohne Fisch ist wie München ohne Bier.

Wenn Sie glauben, Sie bleiben etwas länger in unserer Partnerstadt Hamburg, dann empfehlen wir die „Hamburg Karte" mit der Sie in allen Bussen und mit der Untergrundbahn fahren

Hamburg is also the city with the most covered shopping arcades in Europe, filled with the costly and tasteful, the exclusive and select, the antique and fashionable — ten arcades between Moenckebergstrasse and Gaensemarkt alone! And there's always trendy Poeseldorf — a cross between high-class residential area, shopping center and artist colony.

For late night outers and early risers, seven o'clock on Sunday morning is the time when the Fishmarket opens in St. Pauli. Traders, shoppers and tourists mill around the auction hall. Bunches of bananas are thrown into the crowd. Rabbits change hands. Potted plants are bought and carried away like hunting trophies. Although fish is just a sideline these days, the market was first held in 1703 so fishermen could sell their perishable ware on the Lord's Day. It's true what they say: Hamburg without fish is like Munich without beer.

Should you plan to spend some time in our sister-city, we recommend the "Hamburg Card", allowing for travel on busses and the underground, free admission to eleven museums and up to 40% deductions on city tours, Alster cruises and harbour tours. Ask for it at your Hamburg hotel. Enjoy your stay!

Information and pictures courtesy of the Hamburg Tourist Office edited by Marlis Schmidt

können. Dazu erhalten Sie freien Eintritt zu 11 Museen und eine 40%ige Ermässigung für Stadttouren. Fragen Sie in ihrem Hamburger Hotel danach. Und jetzt viel Spaß!

Information und Bilder mit Genehmigung des Hamburger Touristenbüros.

A scenic harbor tour will enchant you with modern container ships and highsea tankers as well as tour and tug boats and an occasional windjammer clipper. Ahoy!

Auf einer malerischen Hafentour begegnen einem moderne Containerschiffe, Hochseetanker, Ausflugsdampfer oder Schleppkähne. Vielleicht gelegentlich auch ein Windjammer-Segelschiff. Ahoy!

Chicago's Beginnings

Chicago's History and the German Community
by Richard Lindberg

Of all the early explorers whose names are connected with the Chicago area, the best known are Pere Jacques Marquette (1636-75) and Louis Jolliet, both French. The civil servant and the explorer-priest complemented each other in exploration of the territory.

Rene Robert Cavelier, Sieur de La Salle, famed explorer of the French territories in the United States, used the Chicago area as a short cut from Lake Michigan to the Mississippi River in 1681 after hearing of Marquette's experience. The short cut was by way of the portage, a swampy piece of land over which travelers could carry their canoes, and make the connection from the Chicago River to the Des Plaines River, leading to the Illinois River and the Mississippi.

During the early 1700's this Portage was a passageway for the French who traded with the Miami and Potawatomi Indians in the area. The French continued to claim the territory until it was ceded to England in 1763.

Although settlers in the Illinois territory were sparse at the time of the Declaration of Independence, in 1776, the strategic importance of the Chicago area was widely recognized. The possession and

Die Anfänge Chicagos

Die Geschichte Chicagos und Seinen Deutschen Bevölkerung
von Richard Lindberg

Von allen Entdeckern, die man mit dem Gebiet um Chicago in Verbindung bringt, ragen zwei ganz besonders heraus. Die beiden Franzosen Pater Jacques Marquette (1636-75) und Louis Jolliet, taten sich zusammen, um das Gebiet zu erforschen. Der eine ein Entdecker und Priester, ein Händler der andere.

Rene Robert Cavelier, Sieur de LaSalle, berühmter Entdecker des französischen Territoriums in den Vereinigten Staaten, versuchte, 1681 seinen Weg vom Michigansee zum Mississippi über Chicago abzukürzen, nachdem er von Marquettes Erlebnissen hier hörte. Dieser Weg, der durch die Portage führte, d.h. die seichten Stellen in Sumpflandschaften, durch die die Bootsfahrer ihre Boote oder Kajaks tragen mußten, verband den Chicago River mit dem Des Plaines River, der wiederum in den Illinois River und schließlich in den Mississippi floß.

Diese Portage war in den ersten Jahren des 18. Jahrhunderts eine Verbindungsstraße für die Franzosen, die mit den in diesem Gebiet lebenden Miami und Potawatomi Indianern handelten. Das Gebiet war bis zur Übergabe an England im Jahre 1763 unter französischer Herrschaft.

Obwohl die Anzahl der Kolonisten im Illinois-Territorium zur Zeit der Unabhängigkeitserklärung im Jahre 1776 sehr spärlich war, gewann das Gebiet um Chicago an strategischer

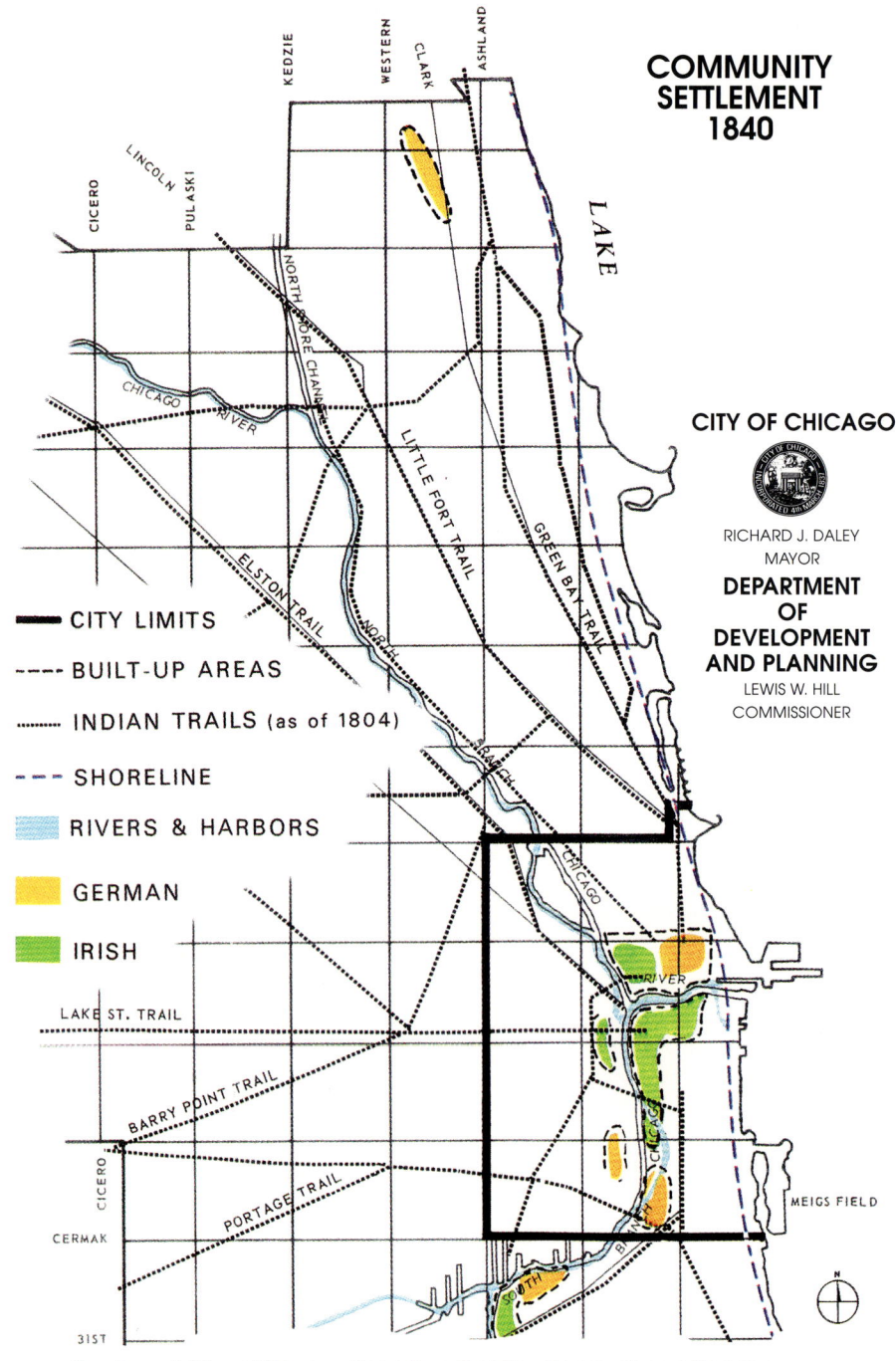

COMMUNITY SETTLEMENT 1840

CITY OF CHICAGO

RICHARD J. DALEY
MAYOR

DEPARTMENT OF DEVELOPMENT AND PLANNING
LEWIS W. HILL
COMMISSIONER

- CITY LIMITS
- BUILT-UP AREAS
- INDIAN TRAILS (as of 1804)
- SHORELINE
- RIVERS & HARBORS
- GERMAN
- IRISH

Courtesy of City of Chicago Department of Development and Planning.

COMMUNITY SETTLEMENT 1860

Legend:
- CITY LIMITS
- BUILT-UP AREAS
- HORSE CAR LINES
- SHORELINE

- RIVERS & HARBORS
- GERMAN
- IRISH
- SWEDISH
- NORWEGIAN
- DUTCH
- CZECH/SLOVAK
- BLACK
- SCOTTISH
- POLISH
- ITALIAN

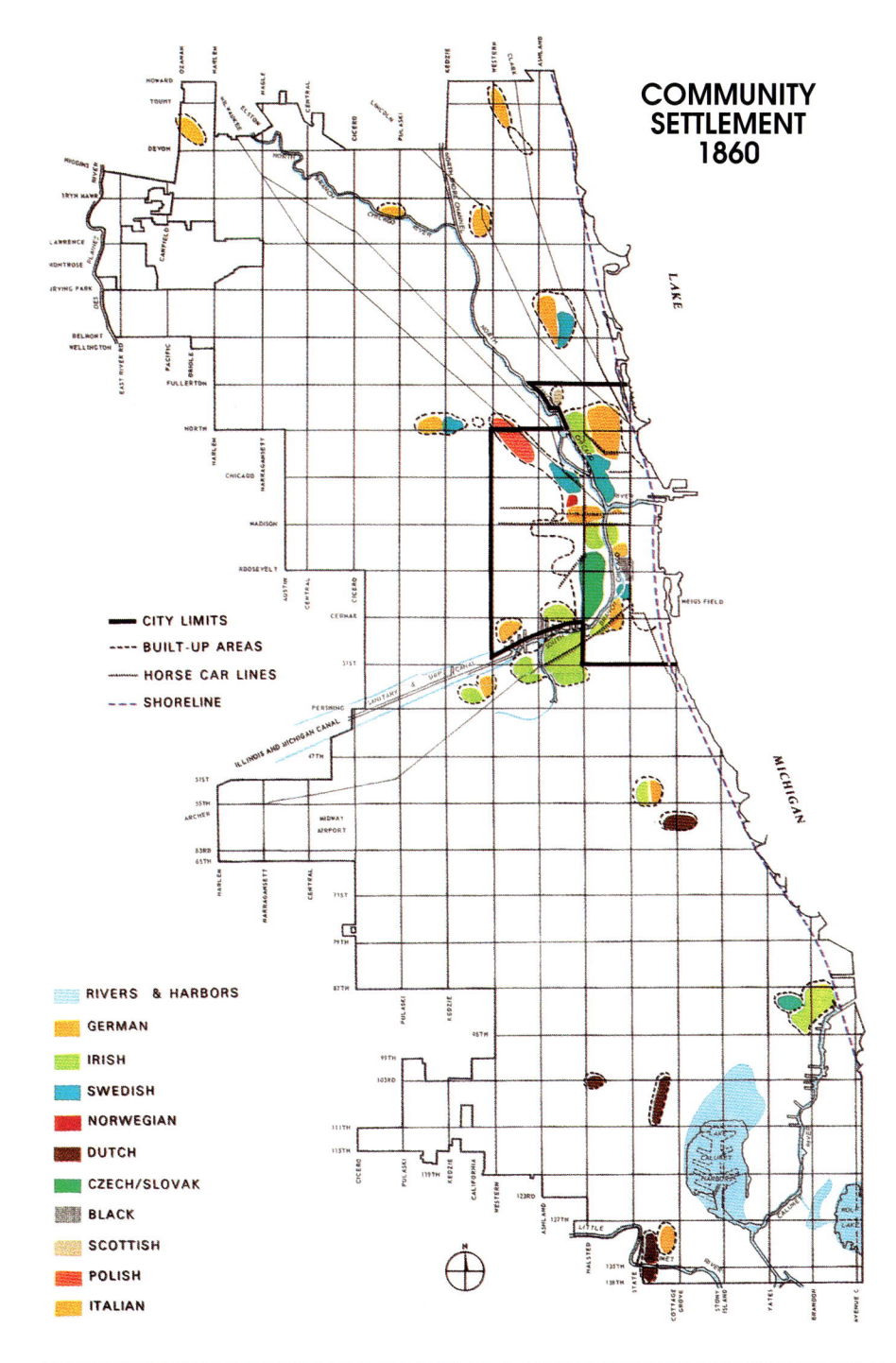

fortification of the Midwest would hopefully serve to defuse any British-inspired Indian uprisings on the western boundaries of the country.

In 1803, Fort Dearborn was built at the mouth of the Chicago River as a trading post and to encourage settlement. In 1812, however, the fort was burnt by the Indians, and 52 people were massacred. The fort was soon rebuilt, and with military protection, settlers returned to the Chicago area. The number of pioneers to Illinois increased, and when the population reached 40,000, a formal petition to Congress for statehood was made. On December 3, 1818, Illinois entered the Union as the 21st state.

On March 4, 1833, the town of Chicago was incorporated, population, about 350. Chicago became a city in 1837 with 4,000 residents; five years later, the population was 8,000.

Work began in 1836 on the Illinois - Michigan Canal to replace the portage, connecting Lake Michigan and the Mississippi. The Bridgeport community developed on Archer Road and the Canal as construction workers settled along the south fork of the Chicago River.

A glue factory, slaughter house, and masonry factory were established in Bridgeport. Among the earliest manufacturing plants were a tannery and a saw mill on the north branch of the Chicago River.

Chicago's first brewery, the Chicago Brewery, was established

Bedeutung. Eine Festigung des Mittelwestens sollte gegen eventuelle Aufstände der von den Briten dazu ermutigten Indianern an der westlichen Grenze des Landes schützen.

1803 wurde eine Festung, das Fort Dearborn, an der Mündung des Chicago Rivers errichtet. Sie sollte als Handelsplatz dienen und vorbeiziehende Ansiedler dazu ermutigen, sich hier niederzulassen. Die Festung wurde jedoch bereits 1812 von den Indianern niedergebrannt und 52 Menschen fielen diesem Massaker zum Opfer. In kürzester Zeit wurde die Festung wieder aufgebaut und die Siedler kehrten unter Militärschutz wieder in die Chicagoer Region zurück. Die Anzahl der Ansiedler in Illinois stieg rapide an und als die Bevölkerungszahl 40.000 erreichte, wurde beim Kongreß ein offizieller Antrag gestellt, Illinois zum Staat zu erklären. Am 3. Dezember 1818 trat Illinois als 21. Staat der Union der Vereinigten Staaten bei.

Am 4. März 1833 wird Chicago als Stadtgemeinde eingetragen. Seine Bevölkerung zählt jetzt 350 Einwohner. 1837 wird Chicago Stadt und zählt 4000 Einwohner. Fünf Jahre später ist die Einwohnerzahl auf 8000 angestiegen.

1836 begannen die Arbeiten am Illinois-Michigan-Kanal, um die Furt, die sog. Portage, zu ersetzen, die den Michigansee mit dem Mississippi verband. Die Bauarbeiter des Kanals ließen sich am südlichen Arm des Chicago Rivers nieder und entwickelten so die Bridgeport-Gemeinde an der Archer Road am Kanal.

Eine Leimfabrik, ein Schlachthaus und eine fettverarbeitende Fabrik ließen sich in Bridgeport nieder. Zu den ersten

---

CHICAGO'S BEGINNINGS — DIE ANFÄNGE CHICAGOS

Cannstatter-Volksfest-Weinschenke
Schwaben-Verein
Chicago

in September, 1839, by German Americans William Haas and William Lill. By 1857, it was the largest brewery in operation west of Cincinnati.

In 1848, the Illinois — Michigan Canal was completed. In places, it cut through solid bedrock and swamps. The hopes and dreams of the Canal supporters were realized as shipping and trading dramatically increased. Sugar, agricultural and other products from the South, machine goods from the East, lumber and farm produce from the Midwest, all passed through the Canal.

Also in 1848, a locomotive named "The Pioneer", of the Galena and Chicago Union Railroad, began a 10 mile run from Chicago to the Des Plaines River and back.

The Canal and the railroads converging on Chicago insured the City's importance as the main gateway to the West. The Chicago and Northwestern Railroad, the former Galena and Chicago Union, advertised for immigrants to settle the lands and become railroad customers.

The rapid settlement of the Old Northwest Territory made Chicago a major transportation and commercial center. Developing agriculture in the state of Illinois, meant that farmers turned to Chicago as the place to dispose of their harvest and to buy farm equipment and manufactured goods. Chicago provided faster

Fertigunsanlagen gehörten eine Ledergerberei und ein Sägewerk am nördlichen Arm des Chicago Rivers.

Chicagos erstes Brauhaus war die Chicagoer Brauerei, die 1839 von den beiden Deutsch-Amerikanern William Haas und William Lill gegründet wurde. Bis 1857 hatte sich die Brauerei schon zur größten Brauerei westlich von Cincinnati hochgearbeitet.

1848 wurde der Illinois-Michigan-Kanal fertiggestellt. An verschiedenen Stellen wurde das Flußbett durch Grundgestein gebrochen und durch Sumpflandschaften geführt. Als die Schiffahrt und der Handel durch den Kanal dramatisch zunahmen, sahen seine Förderer ihre Hoffnungen und Träume erfüllt. Zucker, landwirtschaftliche Erzeugnisse und andere Produkte vom Süden, Maschinen vom Osten, Bau- und Nutzholz sowie Milch- und Vieherzeugnisse vom Mittelwesten wurden alle durch den Kanal verfrachtet.

Ebenfalls im Jahre 1848 nahm eine Lokomotive, „The Pioneer" genannt, der Galena und Chicago Union Railroad, den Betrieb der 16 km langen Strecke zwischen Chicago und dem Des Plaines River auf.

Der Kanal und die Eisenbahnlinie, die beide nach Chicago führten, verhalfen der Stadt, als Tor zum Westen, eine wichtige Stellung einzunehmen. Die Chicago und Northwestern Railroad, ehemals die Galena und Chicago Union-Linie, warben die Immigranten an, sich auf dem umliegenden Land niederzulassen und dann Kunden der Eisebahnlinie zu werden.

Die schnelle Besiedlung des alten Nordwest-Territoriums verwandelte Chicago in ein großes Transport- und

Chicago and North Western Station at Wells and Kinzie Sts., 1885

The Chicago River at North Ave. around the turn of the century.

Der Chicago River an der North Ave. um die Jahrhundertwende

Photos courtesy of the Chicago Historical Society

CHICAGO'S BEGINNINGS — DIE ANFÄNGE CHICAGOS

and better access to eastern markets than the circuitous Mississippi to Gulf of Mexico route. Soon it became the chief grain market of the United States, handling over 20 million bushels annually.

In 1847, Cyrus Hall McCormick moved his reaper factory from Cincinnati to the north banks of the Chicago River near the Lake. The McCormick reaper revolutionized farm production of grain, and by 1849 his company was producing 1,500 reapers a year.

Chicago was the logical place for settlers arriving by steamship, lake schooner or railroad to stop for supplies before venturing West. Wagon shops, plow and hoe factories, lumber yards and dry goods stores grew prosperous outfitting farmers and homesteaders.

By 1841, with the export of farm products, two-way lake traffic began to develop. Over 10,000 vessels arrived in the port of Chicago in 1865.

Railroads were expanding too, and by 1855, almost 100 trains were entering the city every day. By 1860, Chicago was the center of the largest railroad center in the country, consisting of nearly 3,000 miles of track. In 1865, the Union Pacific Railroad began operations, linking Chicago to the West.

The German Community

German and Irish immigrants had come to Chicago since the 1830s. The German Evangelical Association encouraged large numbers of Germans and German Americans from Pennsylvania to settle in the Chicago area.

In 1843, over 800 Chicago residents had immigrated from Norway or Germany. By 1860 more than 22,000 Chicagoans were from Germany. Industry, labor, politics, culture and religion were all shaped to a degree by these vigorous people.

The Germans who settled in Chicago during the 1840's and 1850's were civic minded and adept at organizing. The German Immigrant Society was one of many organizations founded by nationality groups to aid families newly arrived in the United States and Chicago. Other early German societies were the Coachmakers' Association, Carpenters' Association, Tailors' Association, Men's Singing Club and Association for Arts and Sciences. Much of the trade union movement was organized on the basis of nationality.

Letters, such as one written in 1856 to friends in Germany by Jacob Gross, an immigrant to Chicago, provide a picture of life at that time: "As to our present circumstances, we can truthfully say, they are good. In the summer we must pay $6.00, in the winter $4.00 for rent, but we have 1° acres of land around the house. And besides raising vegetables for our own use, we sold $ 18.00 worth ... As to our employment: Theodor and I make

---

Handelszentrum. Die Bauern der sich schnell entwickelnden Landwirtschaft im Staat von Illinois, erkoren Chicago als ihren Marktplatz aus, um dort ihre Ernten zu verkaufen und Landwirtschaftsgeräte und andere Güter einzukaufen. Chicago gewährleistete zu den östlichen Märkten einen bedeutend schnelleren Zugang als die Mississippi - Golf von Mexiko-Route. Bald wurde es der Hauptgetreideumschlagplatz der Vereinigten Staaten, auf dem über 7 Millionen Tonnen an Getreide jährlich umgeschlagen wurden.

1847 verlagerte Cyrus Hall McCormick seine Mähmaschinenfabrik von Cincinnati zum Nordufer des Chicago Rivers in der Nähe des Sees. Die Mähmaschinen von McCormick gestalteten die Getreidelandwirtschaft von Grund auf neu. Schon um 1849 stellte die Firma 1 500 Mähmaschinen pro Jahr her.

Für die Kolonisten, die per Dampfschiff, Schoner oder der Eisenbahn kamen, war Chicago der natürlichste Halteplatz, um Vorrat einzukaufen, eh sie ihre Reise in den Westen antraten. Stellmacher, Pflug- und Hackenhersteller, Sägereien sowie Textil- und Schnittwarengeschäfte, die die Bauern und Ansiedler versorgten, wurden dabei wohlhabend.

Mit dem Export von landwirtschaftlichen Erzeugnissen entwickelte sich um 1841 ein reger Seeverkehr. Über 10 000 Schiffe legten im Jahr 1865 im Hafen von Chicago an.

Auch die Eisenbahnlinien dehnten sich aus und um 1855 fuhren täglich fast 100 Züge in die Stadt. Um 1860 war Chicago das Zentrum des Eisenbahnverkehrs und hatte ein Schienennetz, das sich über fast 4 500 km erstreckte. 1865 wurde die Union Pacific Railroad eröffnet, die mit ihren Zügen Chicago mit dem Westen des Landes verband.

Die Deutsche Gemeinde

Deutsche und irische Einwanderer kamen schon um 1830 nach Chicago. Der Deutsche-Evangelische Verband förderte es, daß eine große Anzahl an Deutschen und Deutsch-Amerikanern aus Pennsylvania sich im Großraum Chicago ansiedelten.

Um 1843 lebten über 800 Einwanderer aus Norwegen und Deutschland in Chicago, aber um 1860 waren es schon über 22 000 Deutsche, die in Chicago lebten. Diese tatkräftigen Menschen sollten zu einem gewissen Grad Industrie, Arbeit, Politik, Kultur und Religion prägen.

Die Deutschen, die sich in den 40er und 50er Jahren des letzten Jahrhunderts in Chicago ansiedelten, waren bürgerlicher Gesinnung und geschickt im Organisieren. Die Deutsche Einwanderergesellschaft war eine von vielen Organisationen, die von den verschiedenen Nationalgruppen gegründet wurde, um den neuangekommenen Familien in den Vereinigten Staaten und in Chicago zu helfen. Andere deutsche Vereinigungen waren der Kutschen- oder Stellmacher-Verband, die Zimmermacher-Gilde, die Schneidergilde, der Männergesangsverein und die Gesellschaft für Kunst und Wissenschaften. Die Bewegung des

"Pionere der Chicago Turngemeinde..." by Kurz & Allison. (Courtesy of the Chicago Historical Society)

Portions of this chapter are based on the book "Historic City — The Settlement of Chicago". It was published in 1976 by the City of Chicago, Richard J. Daley, Mayor, and the Department of Development and Planning, Lewis W. Hill, Commissioner and are gratefully acknowledged by this publisher.

wood in the City. The cord brings 10 to 12 shillings, but the measure is two feet shorter than yours.

"Theodor wanted to learn a trade, but I could not spare him. Leopold is learning plastering and whitewashing and gets 10 shilling or 3 gulden a day, but without board. Otto is learning the butcher trade and gets 12 dollars a month and board — he is strong and has grown tall.

"It will take us a while to be able to have again the many things we gave away in Germany. Every beginning is hard. But we never have had to battle with Want and Hunger, and if the Good Lord lets us keep our health, we have good prospects."

German Churches

Chicago's first German religious communities appeared just north and south of the Chicago River and in Bridgeport.

French-born and newly ordained Fr. John St. Cyr was assigned to Chicago from St. Louis in 1833. German and Irish immigrants became his most numerous communicants at St. Mary's, the first Catholic Church of Chicago. By 1840, the number of immigrants from Germany had substantially increased. Many spoke and understood only German, so Fr. St. Cyr was given an assistant, Fr. Leander Schaffer, to tend to their needs in their own language.

In 1843, about 40 families organized St. Paul Evangelical

Madison St. at Clinton St. in 1860. (Daily News photograph, courtesy of the Chicago Historical Society)

Handwerkerverbandes hatte hauptsächlich nationalen Ursprung.

Briefe wie der, der 1856 von Jacob Gross, Immigrant in Chicago, an Freunde in Deutschland geschrieben wurde, gibt Einsicht in das Leben seiner Zeit: „Ich kann ehrlich sagen, daß es uns unter den gegenwärtigen Umständen entsprechend gut geht. Im Sommer müssen wir $6,00 für Miete bezahlen, im Winter sind es $4,00. Aber dafür steht das Haus auf 60 Ar Land, genug, daß wir nicht nur Gemüse für unseren eigenen Bedarf anbauen konnten, sondern sogar für $18,00 Gemüse verkaufen konnten ... In bezug auf Arbeit: Theodor und ich machen Holz in der Stadt, das Klafter für 10 bis 12 Schillinge, aber das Maß ist hier 2 Fuß kürzer als bei Euch.

„Theodor will ein Handwerk erlernen, aber ich brauche ihn. Leopold lernt das Verputzen und Wändeziehen und erhält 10 Schillinge oder 3 Gulden pro Tag, aber ohne Unterkunft. Otto ist in der Metzgerlehre und bekommt 12 Dollar im Monat und Unterkunft - er ist groß geworden und kräftig.

„Es wird schon noch eine Weile dauern, bis wir wieder alles haben, was wir in Deutschland hatten. Aber jeder Anfang ist schwer. Jedenfalls haben wir nie Hunger gelitten und, wenn Gott will, bleiben wir bei guter Gesundheit und werden es schaffen."

Deutsche Kirchen

Die ersten deutschen Kirchengemeinden in Chicago bildeten sich nördlich und südlich vom Chicago River und in Bridgeport.

Der gerade zum Priester geweihte Frère John St. Cyr aus Frankreich wurde 1833 von St. Louis nach Chicago

Lutheran Church and St. Paul United Church of Christ. Both congregations shared a pastor for two years, Rev. August Selle, and built a wooden church and school in 1846 at LaSalle and Ohio Streets.

In 1846, Bishop Quarter, Chicago's first bishop, authorized the foundation of St. Peter's parish for German Catholics. Fr. John Jung was the first pastor. The original church was on Washington Street between Wells and Franklin, but later moved to Polk and Clark Streets. Today, the new St. Peter's is located on Madison Street between Clark and LaSalle, where the Franciscan Friars offer Mass every morning and noon for people working in the Loop.

St. Joseph's parish was also founded in 1846, for German Catholics living around Chicago and Wabash Avenues near the present Holy Name Cathedral. The first church was a temporary frame structure, and the parish boasted a one room school.

St. Michael's parish was organized in 1852 on the near northside by a group of German Catholics and the Very Rev. Anthony Kopp, vicar general and pastor at St. Joseph's parish. Michael Diversey donated a parcel of land on which a small frame church was built. It was named St. Michael's in honor of Diversey's patron saint. The Redemptionist Fathers took charge in 1860. The church was rebuilt after the Great Chicago Fire

versetzt. Deutsche und irische Immigranten stellten den größten Teil seiner Kirchengemeindemitglieder der St. Mary Kirche, der ersten katholischen Kirche in Chicago. Um 1840 hatte sich die Anzahl der Immigranten aus Deutschland um ein Vielfaches vergrößert. Viele von ihnen sprachen und verstanden nur Deutsch, und Frère St. Cyr bekam einen Assistenten, Frère Leander Schaffer, der sich um ihre Bedürfnisse in ihrer eigenen Sprache kümmern sollte.

Rund 40 Familien gründeten 1843 die St. Paul Evangelisch-Lutheranische Kirche und die St. Paul United Church of Christ. Beide Gemeinden teilten sich 2 Jahre lang denselben Pastor, den Reverend August Selle. 1846 bauten sie eine Holzkirche und Schule an der Kreuzung der LaSalle und Ohio Streets.

1846 erteilte Bischof Quarter, Chicagos erster Bischof, die Genehmigung, die St. Peter-Gemeinde für deutsche Katholiken zu gründen. Frère John Jung war ihr erster Pastor. Die erste Kirche stand auf der Washington Street zwischen Wells und Franklin. Später zog sie zur Polk Ecke Clark Street um. Heute steht die neue St. Peters Kirche auf der Madison Street zwischen Clark und LaSalle, wo die Franziskaner-Priester jeden Morgen und Mittag für die Leute, die im Loop arbeiten, die Messe lesen.

Die St. Josephs-Gemeinde wurde ebenfalls 1846 für deutsche Katholiken gegründet, die in der Nähe der Chicago und Wabash Avenues lebten, nahe der Holy Name Cathedral. Die erste Kirche war ein vorübergehendes Holzgebäude, und die Gemeinde verfügte nur über eine aus einem Klassenzimmer bestehende Schule.

Teile dieses Kapitels basieren auf dem Buch „Geschichtliche Stadt — Die Besiedlung von Chicago". Es wurde 1976 von der Stadt Chicago, Bürgermeister Richard J. Daley, und der Abteilung für Entwicklung und Planung, Kommissar Lewis W. Hill herausgegeben. Dieses wird durch den Herausgeber dieses Buches dankend bestätigt.

Chicago's most sumptuous mansion: Potter Palmer's castle on Lake Shore Drive between Schiller and Banks Sts., 1900. (Courtesy of the Chicago Historical Society)

Chicagos prächtigste Villa: das Potter Palmer Schloß am Lake Shore Drive, zwischen Schiller und Banks Street, 1900 (mit Genehmigung der Chicago Historical Society)

of 1871. The present gothic church located in the Old Town area, features a 200 foot tower with five bells.

The oldest German parish on the westside was St. Francis of Assisi, built in 1853 at 11th and Clinton Streets. It is no longer in existence.

In 1864, St. Boniface parish was founded on the near northside. Mass was first celebrated in a little frame building on Noble near Chestnut Street. In 1867, the Franciscan Sisters of Joliet arrived to staff the school. Fr. Clement Venn became pastor in 1869. In time, St. Boniface became the largest German Catholic parish in Chicago. St. Boniface Cemetery, at Clark and Lawrence Avenue, is the oldest cemetery in Chicago.

Many Protestant churches with predominantly German congregations also flourished. In 1852, the Van Buren German Methodist Episcopal Church was founded on Van Buren Street between Clark and Wells.

Others established between 1860-70 were the Zion United Evangelical Lutheran Church, Salem United Evangelical Lutheran Church, Clybourn German Methodist Church, First Zion Evangelical Lutheran Church and St. James Evangelical Lutheran Church.

Die St. Michaels-Gemeinde wurde 1852 auf der Nordseite Chicagos von einer Gruppe deutscher Katholiken und dem Reverend Anthony Kopp gegründet. Rev. Kopp war Hauptvikar und Pastor der St. Josephs Kirche. Michael Diversey schenkte der Kirche ein Stück Land, auf das eine kleine Holzkirche gebaut wurde. Zu Ehren von Diverseys Schutzheiligem wurde sie St. Michaels genannt. Die „Redemptionist Fathers" übernahmen die Kirche im Jahre 1860. Nach dem Großbrand von 1871 wurde die Kirche wieder aufgebaut. Heute steht die im gotischen Stil gebaute Kirche in der Altstadt, der sogenannten Old Town. Ihr fast 70 Meter hoher Kirchturm beherbergt fünf Glocken.

Die älteste deutsche Gemeinde auf der Westseite war St. Francis von Assisi, die 1853 an der 11. und Clinton Street errichtet wurde. Sie existiert heute nicht mehr.

1864 wurde die St. Bonifazius Gemeinde auf der Nordseite gegründet. Die erste Messe wurde in einem kleinen Holzhaus auf der Noble Street nähe Chestnut Street gelesen. Die Franziskaner Schwestern kamen dann 1867 aus Joliet, um die Schule zu leiten. Frère Clement Venn wurde 1869 ihr Pastor. St. Boniface entwickelte sich später zur größten deutschen katholischen Kirchengemeinde in Chicago. Der St. Boniface-Friedhof an der Clark und Lawrence Avenue ist der älteste Friedhof in Chicago überhaupt.

Viele protestantische Kirchen mit vorwiegend deutschen Gemeindemitgliedern blühten auf. 1852 wurde die deutsche Van Buren Methodist-Episcopal Kirche auf der Van Buren Street zwischen Clark und Wells gegründet.

German Integration

The year 1855 was the year of the "German Beer Riots". These started when Mayor Levi Boone ordered the closing of all saloons and beer gardens on Sundays. To German workers, whose Sundays traditionally were days on which to relax and enjoy a stein of beer, this was outrageous. Saloon keepers ignored the edict, and 200 were arrested. Angry Germans marched downtown to protest. Before peace was restored, one person died, several were hurt, and scores arrested.

It was the generation known as the "49ers" that left the greatest imprint on Chicago's history. Because of the political, social and economic upheaval in Hessen, Baden and Wuttemberg, and the subsequent dissolution of the Frankfurt Parliament in 1849, Germans came to the United States and to Chicago in record numbers. Within a few years the Germans were second only to the Irish as the most dominant ethnic group in the City.

These German immigrants found work in the packing houses adjacent to the Union Stockyards on the South Side; some helped build the Illinois-Michigan Canal; still others found employment in the building trades, manufacturing and public service.

Andere, neu-gegründete Kirchen um 1860-70 waren die Zion United Evangelical Lutheran Church, Salem United Evangelical Lutheran Church, Clybourn German Methodist Church, First Zion Evangelical Lutheran Church und St. James Evangelical Lutheran Church.

Die Deutschen in Chicago

1855 war das Jahr der „German Beer Riots," der deutschen Bieraufstände. Sie hatten ihren Anfang nachdem Bürgermeister Levi Boone sonntags die Schließung aller Saloons und Biergärten anordnete. Für die deutschen Arbeiter, für die der Sonntag schon immer ein Tag der Erholung war, an dem man sich den Genuß eines Kruges Bier gönnte, war das absolut nicht tragbar. Als sich dann die Saloon Keepers, also die Bierhallenbesitzer, nicht nach der Anordnung richteten, wurden 200 von ihnen verhaftet. Wütend marschierten die Deutschen nach Downtown, um dagegen zu protestieren. Ehe aber wieder Friede und Ordnung hergestellt werden konnten, wurde eine Person getötet, viele verletzt und unzählige verhaftet.

Es war die Generation, die als die „49iger" bekannt wurde, die den größten Eindruck auf Chicagos Vergangenheit machte. Viele Deutsche kamen wegen der politischen, sozialen und wirtschaftlichen Unruhen in Hessen und Baden-Württemberg und der darauffolgenden Auflösung des Frankfurter Parlamentes im Jahre 1849 in großen Zahlen nach USA und nach Chicago. Innerhalb nur weniger Jahre nahm die deutsche Bevölkerung nach den Iren den 2. Platz unter den ethni-

CHICAGO'S BEGINNINGS — DIE ANFÄNGE CHICAGOS

Overleaf:
Photo, Panaromic view of the Century of Progress, 1933. Photo by Chicago Aerial Survey.

Hundert Jahre Fortschritt Weltausstellung 1933. Foto: Chicago Aerial Survey

Three monuments of Chicago architecture on Michigan Ave.: (left to right) the Auditorium, the Fine Arts Building, and the old Art Institute, 1889. (Courtesy of the Chicago Historical Society)

Drei markante Gebäude an der Michigan Avenue: Das Auditorium, das Kunstgewerbe Gebäude und das alte Kunstmuseum, 1889.

Two days after President Lincoln issued his call to arms in 1861, 105 members of the Chicago Turnverein organized the Turner Cadets and volunteered for service in the Union Army.

As a result of steady immigration, the German population in Chicago tripled between 1870 and 1900. At the turn of the century, there were over 400,000 men, women and children of German descent, representing a quarter of the City's population. The largest German community continued to be east of the Chicago River's north branch between Diversey and Devon Avenues. Many smaller communities were in Hyde Park, South Shore, Humboldt Park and Albany Park.

German contributions to the development of Chicago were many, especially in music. In 1860, Hans Balatka, a well-known Austrian director, came to Chicago and organized the Philharmonic Society. The Schiller Theater was built by the German Opera House Company and opened in 1892. It was renamed the Garrick and continued to operate until 1989.

The Orchestra Association was founded in 1891. The 90 member, largely German, symphony orchestra opened its first season with Theodor Thomas conducting. Thomas was born in Hanover, immigrated to America and later made his home in Chicago, where he became musical director of the

schen Gruppen der Stadt ein.

Diese deutschen Einwanderer fanden Arbeit in den Packhäusern neben den Unions-Schlachthöfen auf der Südseite. Einige arbeiteten am Bau des Illinois-Michigan-Kanals mit. Wieder andere fanden Arbeit auf dem Bau, in der Fertigung und im öffentlichen Dienst.

Zwei Tage nach dem Aufruf Präsident Lincolns, 1861, zu den Waffen zu greifen, organisierten sich 105 Mitglieder des *Chicago Turnverein*, die Turner Kadetten und stellten sich freiwillig in den Dienst der Unions Armee.

Aufgrund des ständigen Einwandererstromes hatte sich die deutsche Bevölkerung in Chicago zwischen 1870 und 1900 verdreifacht. Um die Jahrhundertwende machten 400 000 Männer, Frauen und Kinder deutscher Herkunft ein Viertel der Chicagoer Bevölkerung aus. Die größte deutsche Gemeinde existierte weiterhin östlich des nördlichen Armes des Chicago Rivers zwischen Diversey und Devon Avenues. Andere, kleine deutsche Gemeinden befanden sich in Hyde Park, am South Shore, im Humboldt Park und Albany Park.

Die Deutschen leisteten ihre Beiträge hauptsächlich in der Musik. 1860 kam Hans Balatka, ein bekannter österreichischer Intendant, nach Chicago, um die Philharmonische Gesellschaft zu gründen. Das Schiller Theater wurde von der German Opera House Company gebaut und öffnete 1892 seine Türen. Es wurde später in Garrick umbenannt und schloß 1989 seine Türen.

Die Orchestra Association wurde 1891 gegründet. Das Symphonie Orchester mit seinen 90, vorwiegend deutschen Musikern, eröffnete seine

Glaubensbekenntnis an Amerika

Die Tatsache, dass wichtige Aufgaben noch ungelöst vor uns stehen, sollte jeden Amerikaner deutscher Abstammung anspornen, sich öffentlich für die Ziele des D.A.N.K. einzusetzen. Sie sind ein Glaubensbekenntnis an das wahrhafte Amerika und stehen im Einklang mit der offiziellen Auffassung der Regierung in Washington. Mit Gottes Segen, Idealismus und Fleiss, werden wir sie gemeinsam früher oder später meistern. Hier die Präambel der D.A.N.K.-Satzungen.

Im Geiste der amerikanischen Verfassung, ihrer grundlegenden Prinzipien der Freiheit, Demokratie und Menschenrechte;

In Würdigung des hervorragenden Anteils deutscher Einwanderer im Kampfe für die Unabhängigkeit, am Aufbau, an der Entwicklung der Vereinigten Staaten zu einer führenden Nation;

Im Bewusstsein der Pflicht der Deutsch-Amerikaner, ihren Anteil an der Verantwortung für die Zukunft der Vereinigten Staaten auf sich zu nehmen, im Einklang mit der Tatsache, dass unsere Heimat Amerika in ihren Wurzeln eine Schöpfung auch deutschen Geistes ist;

In Anbetracht des Umstandes, dass andere Nationalitäten des gemeinsamen amerikanischen Vaterlandes sich zu Gemeinschaften vereinigen, um ihre Bestrebungen wirksam zu vertreten, hat der Deutsch-Amerikanische National-Kongress (Inc.) es sich zur Aufgabe gemacht, die schöpferischen und gestaltenden Fähigkeiten der Amerikaner deutscher Abstammung mehr als bisher im öffentlichen Leben der Nation zur Geltung zu bringen.

Distributed by D.A.N.K., 27012 Hilliard Blvd., Cleveland, Ohio 44145, U.S.A.

Germans as Fellow Americans for 300 Years

Hail to Posterity!
Hail, future men of German-America!
Let the young generation yet to be
look kindly upon this.
Think how your fathers left their native land,
In Patience planned
New forest homes beyond the mighty sea,
There undisturbed and free
To live as brothers in one family.
What pains and cares befell,
What trials and what fears,
Remember! And wherein we have done well
Follow our footsteps, men of coming years!
Where we have failed to do
Aright, or wisely live,
Be warned by us, the better way pursue,
And knowing we were human, even as you,
Pity us and forgive!
Farewell, Posterity! Farewell, Germany!
Forevermore farewell!

Franz Daniel Pastorius
Father of German-America

CONCORD

The AMERICAN HERITAGE POSTER
Copyright © 1985 by F. Dornstaedter

THE ARRIVAL OF THE FIRST GERMAN SETTLERS IN PHILADELPHIA — 1683

1893 World's Columbian Exposition. Orchestra Hall was built in 1905 to house his orchestra. In 1991, the Chicago Symphony Orchestra celebrated its 100th birthday with a concert at Orchestra Hall.

Germans maintained several organizations to assist newly arrived countrymen. In addition to the German Immigrant Society, there were groups which helped people who came from a particular state or city, such as Bavaria, Baden and Berlin.

The United Evangelical Orphan Asylum in Bensenville was supported solely by contributions from the German Evangelical Association. The first Alexian Brothers Hospital, founded in 1866, was operated by members of the German Order. The hospital is still in existence in the suburb of Elk Grove Village.

October, 1871 is remembered as the time of the Great Chicago Fire. The fire is believed to have started when a cow kicked over the lantern in Mrs. O'Leary's barn, on De Koven Street near Jefferson, just south of the Greyhound Bus Terminal and near today's Chicago Fire Academy.

Fanned by strong southwest winds, the fire jumped the River at Polk Street and soon all of Chicago was ablaze. The wooden buildings burned rapidly; ships on the River caught fire. The fire jumped the River again at Wacker and burned north all the way to Lincoln Park. On the second day of the fire, a heavy rain finally put out the flames.

The devastation was terrible. An area of 3° square miles had burned to the ground, 300 people died, 100,000 were left homeless and 18,000 buildings destroyed. Property damage totaled 200 million dollars.

During the conflagration, German immigrant, Frank Trautmann, saved the city waterworks from destruction. For 30 years he was chief engineer for the Chicago water department. When flames threatened the pumping station at Michigan and Chicago Avenues, Trautmann and his assistants covered it with woolen blankets and canvas sails soaked in lake water. Two days later, Trautmann was able to restore water to the City. The pumping station and St. Peter's Church were the only buildings that survived the Great Fire.

Saison mit Theodor Thomas als Dirigent. Thomas, der in Hannover geboren war, wanderte nach Amerika aus und ließ sich später in Chicago nieder, wo er der musikalische Intendant der Columbus Welt-Ausstellung 1893 wurde. 1991 feierte das Chicago Symphony Orchestra seinen 100. Geburtstag mit einem Konzert in der Orchestra Hall.

Die Deutschen in Chicago unterhielten mehrere Organisationen, um den Neuankömmlingen aus Deutschland unter die Arme zu greifen. Neben der Deutschen Einwanderergesellschaft gab es Gruppen der verschiedenen Regionen, wie zum Beispiel Bayern, Baden und Berlin.

So wurde die United Evangelical Waisenkinderanstalt in Bensenville nur durch Spenden der Deutschen Evangelischen Gesellschaft unterstützt. Das erste Alexian Brothers Hospital wurde 1866 gegründet und es wurde ausschließlich von Mitgliedern des Deutschen Ordens unterhalten. Das Krankenhaus steht noch heute im Vorort Elk Grove Village.

Der Oktober 1871 ging in die Geschichte als die Zeit des Großen Brandes von Chicago ein. Man vermutet, daß das Feuer durch eine Kuh verursacht wurde, die eine Laterne in Mrs. O'Learys Stall umstieß. Dieser Stall stand auf der De Koven Street nahe der Jefferson Street, südlich hinter dem Greyhound Bus Terminal, wo heute Chicagos Feuerakademie steht.

Von einem starken Südwestwind angefacht, sprang das Feuer über den Fluß bis zur Polk Street und bald stand ganz Chicago in Flammen. Die Holzhäuser brannten schnell ab. Sogar die Schiffe auf dem Fluß fingen Feuer. Das Feuer sprang nochmals am Wacker Drive über den Fluß und breitete sich nördlich bis zum Lincoln Park aus. Endlich, am zweiten Tag dann, löschte ein starker Regen das Feuer.

Die Verheerung war groß. Eine 3° Quadratmeilen große Fläche brannte bis auf den Grund ab. 300 Menschen kamen dabei um, 100 000 wurden obdachlos und 18 000 Häuser wurden zerstört. Der Schaden betrug 200 Millionen Dollar.

Ein deutscher Einwanderer, Frank Trautmann, rettete das Wasserwerk der Stadt während der Feuerbrunst vor Zerstörung. 30 Jahre lang war er der Leiter der Chicagoer Wasserwerke. Als die Flammen sich der Pumpstation auf der Michigan und Chicago Avenue näherten, deckten Trautmann und seine Helfer die Pumpstation mit in Wasser getränkten Wolldecken und Segeltüchern ab. Nach zwei Tagen schon konnte Trautmann die Wasserversorgung der Stadt wieder herstellen. Die Wasserpumpstation und die St. Peters Kirche waren die einzigen Gebäude, die den Großbrand überlebten.

Rebuilding the Central Business District, View N.E. from LaSalle & Madison Streets, 1872. (Courtesy of the Chicago Historical Society)

Blick nach Nord-Osten von der LaSalle und Madison Street, 1872

CHICAGO'S BEGINNINGS — DIE ANFÄNGE CHICAGOS

German Neighborhoods

By the end of the 19th century, families of German descent had been in Chicago for more than 70 years. They prospered and settled in various parts of the City. The largest German community was on the northwest side along Lincoln Avenue, an area which still retains the flavor of early days.

By 1910, the children of German immigrants outnumbered their parents two to one. Already there were third and fourth generations of German families in Chicago who were well integrated in the life of the City.

German churches, both Catholic and Protestant, maintained schools for the preservation of the German language and literature. Since 1865 German was taught in the public schools. In the heat of feelings, generated by World War I, however, the State Legislature voted to outlaw educational instruction in German.

When war erupted in Europe in 1914, Chicago's German and Austro-Hungarian communities were drawn closely together and raised funds for the relief of refugees and the homeless in Germany.

Americans of German heritage were quick to respond to President Wilson's appeal for neutrality. Once the United States entered the war in 1917, German Americans supported the war effort. The Illinois Staats-Zeitung summed up the German community's position by stating: "We shall be proud if no German

Deutsche Nachbarschaften (Viertel)

Ende des 19. Jahrhunderts lebten die Nachkommen deutscher Einwanderer schon seit über 70 Jahren in Chicago. Sie ließen sich in verschiedenen Teilen der Stadt nieder und wurden dort Grundbesitzer. Die größte deutsche Gemeinde befindet sich heute auf der Nordwestseite auf der Lincoln Avenue. Diese Gegend hat auch heute noch den Charakter ihrer Anfangszeit.

1910 hatte sich die Zahl der Kinder deutscher Einwanderer gegenüber ihren Eltern verdoppelt, und in der Zwischenzeit lebte schon die 3. oder 4. Generation in Chicago. Die Familien deutscher Herkunft hatten sich in das Leben der Stadt integriert.

Die deutschen Kirchen, katholische und evangelische, unterhielten deutsche Schulen, um die deutsche Sprache und Literatur aufrechtzuerhalten. Deutsch wurde seit 1865 in den öffentlichen Schulen unterrichtet. Aufgrund der Ereignisse des 1. Weltkrieges entschloß sich das Parlament von Illinois, den Deutschunterricht zu verbieten.

Als 1914 der Krieg in Europa ausbrach, haben sich die deutschen und österreichisch-ungarischen Gemeinden zusammengeschlossen, um für Flüchtlinge und die Heimatlosen Gelder zu sammeln.

Die Amerikaner deutschen Ursprungs haben schnell auf Präsident Wilsons Aufruf zur Neutralität reagiert. Als die Vereinigten Staaten 1917 in den Krieg zogen, wurden sie dabei von den Deutsch-Amerikanern unterstützt. Die Illinois Staats-Zeitung illustrierte die Stellung der deutschen Gemeinde, als sie schrieb: „Wir wären stolz, wenn kein Deutsch-Amerikaner versuchen wird, sich dem Militär-

Reservists at German Counsul's, Sept. 5, 1914. (Courtesy of the Chicago Historical Society)

Reservisten beim deutschen Konsul, 5. September 1914

American looks for an excuse to escape military duty". It was a painful time, however, for those who had come to the United States recently and who had relatives fighting on the other side. German Americans serving in the American army fought bravely and with distinction. Of the six World War I Congressional Medal of Honor winners, three bore German surnames.

Chicago's neighborhoods tell the history of the urban and industrial side of America. Spanish, Korean or English may be the language today in neighborhoods where it was once German, Swedish or Italian; but the older neighborhoods remain and are still vigorous, each preserving its own history and culture.

The richness of cultural variety is one of the things that makes American cities unique, invigorating and stimulating. People, who in other parts of the world have fought each other in wars, go into business with each other in America. In the United States, people of different nationalities marry each other and think of themselves as Americans. The dynamics of American society move people in the direction of accommodation and integration.

From Chicago's earliest days, Germans have left their imprint upon the City's diverse ethnic culture: a legacy of hard work and resourcefulness and pride in its institutions.

dienst zu entziehen." Allerdings war es für die frisch eingewanderten Deutschen sehr schmerzhaft, denn ihre Familien und Verwandten kämpften auf der anderen Seite. Die Deutsch-Amerikaner, die der amerikanischen Armee dienten, kämpften mutig und ehrenvoll. Drei der sechs "Congressional Medals of Honor" (höchste Tapferkeit auszeichnung) des 1. Weltkrieges trugen deutsche Namen.

Die Nachbarschaften Chicagos reflektieren die städtische und industrielle Entwicklung Amerikas. Spanisch, Koreanisch oder Englisch mag heute in den Nachbarschaften gesprochen werden, wo früher Deutsch, Schwedisch oder Italienisch gesprochen wurde. Aber die alten Nachbarschaften sind erhalten geblieben und sind genauso energiegeladen wie eh und je, wobei jede ihre eigene Vergangenheit und Kultur aufrecht erhalten hat.

Der Reichtum an verschiedenartigen Kulturen ist es, was die amerikanischen Städte von anderen unterscheidet. Dieses Erbe ist belebend und anregend.

Menschen, die auf anderen Teilen der Erde gegeneinander in den Krieg zogen, machen in Amerika miteinander Geschäfte. In den Vereinigten Staaten heiraten Menschen von verschiedenen Nationalitäten und betrachten sich als Amerikaner. Die Dynamik der amerikanischen Gesellschaft wirkt ausgleichend und integrierend.

Die Deutschen aus den Anfangstagen der Stadt haben das ihrige getan, einen Eindruck auf die ethnisch vielseitige Kultur zu hinterlassen: ein Erbe harter Arbeit und Einfallsreichtums und Stolz auf ihre Institutionen..

Germania Club photo by Barnes-Crosby, 1904 (Courtesy of the Chicago Historical Society)

Das Germania Club Haus war jahrzehntelang Zentrium deutscher Geselligkeit.

CHICAGO'S BEGINNINGS — DIE ANFÄNGE CHICAGOS

GOETHE-INSTITUT CHICAGO

The Goethe Institute was founded in 1951 to promote a wider knowledge of the German language abroad and to foster cultural cooperation with other countries. It is a worldwide non-profit organization with 157 institutes in 73 countries. The Chicago office offers a series of language courses, as well as complete library services.

Through close collaboration with local cultural and educational institutions it regularly presents programs in the arts and humanities in Chicago and throughout the Midwest. Unless otherwise noted, all events at the Goethe Institute are open to the public and free of charge.

Das Goethe-Institut wurde 1951 zur Pflege der deutschen Sprache im Ausland sowie zur Förderung der internationalen kulturellen Zusammenarbeit gegründet. Der gemeinnützige Verein ist mit 157 Instituten in 73 Ländern vertreten. Das Goethe-Institut in Chicago bietet Sprachkurse auf verschiedenen Ebenen an und verfügt über eine komplette Bibliothek.

In enger Zusammenarbeit mit Kultur-, Erziehungs- und Bildungsinstitutionen vor Ort organisiert das Goethe-Institut regelmäßig Programme in den verschiedenen Bereichen der Kunst und Geisteswissenschaften in Chicago wie auch im gesamten Mittleren Westen. Falls nicht anderweitig angegeben, sind alle Veranstaltungen des Goethe-Instituts der Öffentlichkeit zugänglich und kostenlos.

401 North Michigan Avenue, Chicago, Illinois 60611
Tel. 312/329-0915 / Fax 312/329-2487 / TLX 494-6142 UW / 342-5013 MCI

Schwäbischer Sängerbund, 40. Jubilaum, Lincoln Turner Halle, Chicago, April 8, 1934, photo by Kaufmann & Fabry (Courtesy of the Chicago Historical Society)

AT YOUR SIDE THERE WERE GERMANS TOO

by

KONRAD KREZ

Not as burdens to these shores we throng,
    From our cherished German Fatherland.
Indeed, we have brought so much along,
    Unknown to you, yet by our hand.
And when from the dense forestal shields,
    and the open wilderness you
wreath'd your vast and verdant fields,
    At your side there were Germans too.

    So much of that which in earlier days
        you brought here from across the sea,
    We taught you how to prepare, and ways
        to produce more goods, yes, 'twas we.
    Dare not forget this, deny it n'er —
        Say not that we did not so do,
    For a thousand forges witness bear:
        At your side there were Germans too.

And though your art and your sciences now
    bring their strength and power to this land,
Their fame rests still on the German brow,
    'Twas mostly done by German hand,
And when from your songs melodies ring
    memories of hearts once so true,
'Tis known to me, in the songs you sing
    is much put there by Germans too!

    Thus, with great pride on this soil we stand,
        Which from the wilds our strength brought claim,
    Ever wonder then, what kind of land,
        'twould be if n'er a German came!
    And so we declared in Lincoln's day,
        And that day freedom's horn first blew —
    Yes, we dare undeniably say:
        At your side there were Germans too!

Translated from the German original by Dr. Robert E. Ward.

Distributed by D.A.N.K., 27012 Hilliard Blvd., Cleveland, Ohio 44145, U.S.A.

Spirits of 1776
—And 1976

Da waren Deutsche auch dabei

Als Bettler sind wir nicht gekommen
Aus unserem deutschen Vaterland.
Wir hatten manches mitgenommen,
Was hier noch fremd und unbekannt.
Und als man schuf aus dichten Wäldern,
Aus öder, düstrer Wüstenei
Den Kranz von reichen Feldern,
Da waren Deutsche auch dabei.

Gar vieles, was in früheren Zeiten
Ihr kaufen müsstet überm Meer,
Das lehrten wir euch selbst bereiten,
Wir stellten manche Werkstatt her.
Oh, wagt es nicht, dies zu vergessen,
Sagt nicht, als ob das nicht so sei,
Es künden's tausend Feueressen,
Da waren Deutsche auch dabei.

Und was die Kunst und Wissenschaften
Euch hier verlieh'n an Kraft und Stärk',
Es bleibt der Ruhm am Deutschen haften,
Das meiste war der Deutschen Werk.
Und wenn aus vollen Tönen klinget
Ans Herz des Liedes Melodei,
Ich glaub' von dem, was ihr da singet,
Ist vieles Deutsche auch dabei.

Drum steh'n wir stolz auf festem Grunde,
Den unsere Kraft der Wildnis nahm,
Wie wär's mit eurem Staatenbunde,
Wenn nie zu euch ein Deutscher kam?
Und wie in Bürgerkriegestagen,
Ja schon beim ersten Freiheitsschrei:
Wir dürfen's unbestritten sagen,
Da waren Deutsche auch dabei.

Konrad Krez (b. 1828 in Landau
d. 1897 in Milwaukee)

Copyright © 1974 by the German-American National-Congress, Cleveland, Ohio U.S.A.

The American BICENTENNIAL German Scroll

AMERICAN REVOLUTION BICENTENNIAL 1776-1976

CHICAGO'S BEGINNINGS — DIE ANFÄNGE CHICAGOS

Carnival...

The Chicago Karneval draws visitors from nearby States as well as from abroad. Here the "Husaren" from Hamilton, Ontario, Canada...

Der Chicagoer Karneval zieht Besucher aus den umliegenden Staaten und sogar aus dem Ausland an. Hier die Husaren aus Hamilton, Ontario, Canada...

...and a delegation greeting from Milwaukee, Wisconsin

...und eine Delegation aus Milwaukee, Wisconsin

1993 Carnival Royalty Prince Joseph I and Princess Irene (Mr. & Mrs. Rotter).

1993 Seine Hoheit Prinz Joseph I und Prinzessin Irene (Rotter).

Alaaf - Helau !

"Karneval am Rhein ?" No — it's Carnival at the shores of Lake Michigan.

It's one of the biggest annual events of the German American community: Chicago's Rheinischer Verein with its "Fanfarenzug", the drum and bugle marching corps, the "Amazonen" girls dance group, and, of course, Carnival's Prince and Princess, including their large entourage. The Rheinischer Verein is the main organizer of the many social affairs during the Carnival period. Even the youngsters don't want to miss the masquerade Mardi Gras at the D.A.N.K. house.

Of course, a policeman is always present to ensure law and order.

Ein Polizist ist natürlich auch dabei, um nach Recht und Ordnung zu schauen.

Lachner "CHICAGOLAND"

The "Amazonen" Dance Group of the Rheinischer Verein.

Die Tanzgruppe, die Amazonen des Rheinischen Vereins.

MC. Erich Himmel, Mrs. Pat Michalski, Assistant to Governor Edgar and Consul General Guenter Wasserberg.

Zeremonienmeister Erich Himmel, Frau Pat Michalski, Assistentin des Gouverneurs von Illinois Jim Edgar, und Generalkonsul Günter Wasserberg.

Karneval ...

Alaaf - Helau !

„Karneval am Rhein ?" Nein, es ist Karnevalszeit an den Ufern des Michigansees.

Bei weitem die größte Veranstaltung der Deutsch-Amerikanischen Gemeinde: Chicagos Rheinischer Verein mit Fanfarenzug, Amazonen-Tanzgruppe und, nicht zu vergessen, Karnevalsprinz und -prinzessin mit Gefolge. Der Rheinische Verein ist Zentralorganisator vieler Veranstaltungen wähend der Karnevalszeit. Auch die Kleinen sind bei der Mardi Gras-Maskerade im D.A.N.K.-Haus dabei.

Kinder Karneval is a highlight of the German language weekend school at D.A.N.K. Chicago North. Here the Children's Prince and Princess are being crowned.

Kinder-Karneval ist einer der Höhepunkte der deutschen Wochenendschule der D.A.N.K.-Gruppe Chicago-Nord. Hier werden Kinderprinz und -prinzessin gekrönt.

GERMAN AMERICAN HERITAGE — DAS DEUTSCH-AMERIKANISCHE ERBE

The *"Schwaben Verein"*, one of Chicago's oldest German American societies, celebrated their 116th Cannstatter Volksfest in 1993. The Schwaben Center at Buffalo Grove includes an attractive Club House, a soccer field and ample room for many outdoor activities.

Der Schwaben Verein ist einer der ältesten Deutsch-Amerikanischen Vereine und feierte 1993 das 116. Cannstatter Volksfest. Das Schwabenzenter in Buffalo Grove bietet ein attraktives Klubhaus, einen Fußballplatz und ausreichend Platz für die vielen Feste und Veranstaltungen.

The welcome sign is out...
Der Schwabenclub öffnet die Türen ...

...the store is open ...
...nur hereinspaziert ...

and Alderman Eugene Schulter (right) is bringing greetings from the Chicago City Council, and presenting Schwaben President Walter Sanders Mayor Daley's Proclamation, honoring the German American Society.

und Stadtrat Eugene Schulter (rechts) übermittelt Grüße des Stadtrats von Chicago und überreicht dem Präsidenten des Schwabenvereins, Walter Sanders, eine Proklamation von Bürgermeister Daley, zur Ehrung des Deutsch-Amerikanischen Vereins.

German American Heritage

by Ernst Ott, National President, D.A.N.K. – The German American National Congress

Chicago, the "Capital of America's Heartland" is a very ethnic city. Immigrants of many nationalities and races give the city and greater metropolitan area a distinct character. German-Americans or Americans of German heritage — as some preferred to be called — represent the largest segment of the ethnic diversity as it does throughout the state, and for that matter the entire United States. According to the latest national census (1990) fifty-seven (57) million Americans profess to be of German ancestry and, if you include Austrian and Swiss-Germans, the total figure approaches 60 million. The next closest group are the Irish with 38 million.

Great immigration waves took place during the turn of the century, after World War I and again after World War II. But early German settlers go back to the 17th century. They contributed greatly to the development, struggle for independence, and were champions for the abolition of slavery, for freedom of the press and religion.

Many of the German immigrants left their homelands because of persecution — religious or political — or economic hardships. Others were brought here by their pioneering spirit or simply seeking greater opportunity.

The shadow of two world wars, and the suppression of German

Das Deutsch-Amerikanische Erbe

von Ernst Ott, Präsident des Nationalen D.A.N.K.-Verbandes – Der Deutsch-Amerikanische Nationalkongreß

Chicago, die „Hauptstadt Mitten im Herzen von Amerika," ist eine Stadt vieler Völkergruppen. Immigranten aller Nationalitäten und Rassen geben der Stadt und dem angrenzenden Großraum einen sehr unterschiedlichen Charakter. Deutsch-Amerikaner oder Amerikaner deutscher Herkunft - wie manche es bevorzugen, genannt zu werden - repräsentieren den größten Anteil der Nationenvielfalt im gesamten Staat und überhaupt in ganz Amerika.

Gemäß der letzten Volkszählung (1990), bekennen sich 57 Millionen Amerikaner zu ihrer deutschen Herkunft und, wenn man die Österreicher und Schweizerdeutschen mit hinzuzählt, sind es beinahe 60 Millionen. Die Iren mit 38 Millionen sind die zweitgrößte Bevölkerungsgruppe nach den Deutschen.

Große Immigrationswellen fanden um die Jahrhundertwende, nach dem ersten Weltkrieg und erneut nach dem zweiten Weltkrieg statt. Aber die ersten deutschen Einwanderströme reichen zurück ins neunzehnte Jahrhundert. Sie haben viel zur Entwicklung beigetragen, wie auch im Kampf um die Freiheit und waren Verfechter im Kampf um die Abschaffung der Sklaverei. Sie setzten sich ebenfalls für Presse- und Religionsfreiheit ein.

Viele der deutschen Immigranten mußten ihr Heimatland wegen Verfolgung verlassen - religiöser oder politischer Natur - oder wegen wirtschaftlich harter Zeiten. Andere hat ihr Pioniergeist hierher gebracht oder einfach die Suche nach besseren Möglichkeiten.

Der Schatten zweier Weltkriege und die

German Customs and Traditions run deep in Chicagoland.

activities during, and, to some extent, even after the two wars left a definite mark on German Americans. But, while they were politically largely reticent, they continued to nourish and cultivate their German heritage.

Today's German-American organizations are rather diverse. Several go back 100 and more years and managed to endure through several generations. However, most that are active today were founded after the last large-scale immigration wave during the 1950s. They include many former "Volksdeutsche", German ethnic groups from eastern and southeastern European nations. These displaced people came to America with little more than a suitcase and a few dollars in their pockets, but eager to build a new life in the Land of Unlimited Opportunities.

Indeed, most prospered and became good American citizens. Many young men and women served in the Korean and Vietnam wars. Others went back to Europe as part of the NATO forces.

In Chicagoland, the economic growth was fueled largely by the industrious German-American element. The German heritage is also evident by various towns, which carry German names, such as Schaumburg, Lake Zurich and Mundelein. A good number of German streets exist in Chicago, the most prominent Mannheim Road, Schiller and Goethe Streets. German

Unterdrückung deutscher Aktivitäten hat bis zu einem gewissen Grad bei den Deutsch-Amerikanern einen bestimmten Charakterzug hinterlassen. Aber, während sie sich politisch größtenteils zurückhaltend verhielten, haben sie nicht aufgegeben, ihr deutsches Erbe zu pflegen und zu kultivieren.

Heute gibt es deutsch-amerikanische Organisationen sehr unterschiedlicher Natur. Mehrere sind schon hundert Jahre alt oder älter und haben mehrere Generationen überdauert.

Wie auch immer, die meisten Vereine, die heute noch aktiv bestehen, wurden nach der letzten größeren Immigrationswelle, während der 50iger Jahre gegründet. Sie schließen viele ehemalige „Volksdeutsche" mit ein, sowie deutsche Völkergruppen aus ost- und südösteuropäischen europäischen Nationen.

Die so Vertriebenen kamen mit selten mehr als einem Koffer und ein paar Dollar in der Tasche nach Amerika, jedoch immer bestrebt, ein neues Leben im Land der unbegrenzten Möglichkeiten aufzubauen.

Tatsächlich, die meisten hatten Erfolg und wurden gute amerikanische Bürger. Viele junge Männer und Frauen dienten im Korea- und Vietnamkrieg. Andere kehrten als Teil der Nato-streitkräfte nach Europa zurück.

Das wirtschaftliche Wachstum wurde im Großraum Chicago größtenteils durch industrielle deutsch-amerikanische Elemente angetrieben. Die deutsche Herkunft läßt sich auch in den Namen

One of Chicago's outstanding German Americans, Mr. Karl Laschet (right) is being honored here for his services to the German American Community by German Day Association President Erich Himmel. Mr. Laschet owned the authentic and cozy Laschet Inn in Chicago; a street has been named after him.

Einer der bekanntesten Deutsch-Amerikaner von Chicago, Herr Karl Laschet (rechts) wird anläßlich seiner für die Deutsch-Amerikanische Gemeinde geleisteten Dienste durch den Präsidenten der Vereinigung des Deutschen Tages, Herrn Erich Himmel, geehrt. Herr Laschet war der Besitzer des originalgetreuen und gemütlichen Laschet Inn. Eine Straße in Chicago wurde ebenfalls nach ihm benannt.

Chicago's "D'lustigen Holzhacker Buam" are maintaining their Bavarian dances with the ever popular "Schuhplattler".

„D'lustigen Holzhacker Buam" von Chicago bleiben ihren Bayrischen Tänzen mit dem altbekannten „Schuhplattler" treu.

Austrian and German men of all ages still enjoy wearing their richly decorated "Lederhosen" and costumes.

Österreichische und deutsche Männer aller Altersgruppen tragen noch heute ihre reich verzierten Lederhosen und Trachten.

Deutsche Sitten und Gebräuche haben sich tief in Chicagos Geschichte verankert

Milwaukee's D.A.N.K. folksingers and dancers perform at "German Fest, Milwaukee", America's largest German American Summer Festival.

Die Volkssänger und Tänzer der Milwaukee D.A.N.K.-Gruppe treten auf dem „Deutschen Fest in Milwaukee" auf, dem größten deutsch-amerikanischen Sommerfest.

GERMAN AMERICAN HERITAGE — DAS DEUTSCH-AMERIKANISCHE ERBE

Rain or shine, the Steuben Parade goes on. From left Mrs. Pat Michalski, Assistant to Governor Edgar, TV personality Harry Volkman, Erich Himmel, German Day Association President, Eugene Schulter, Alderman and Chicago's Mayor Richard M. Daley.

Ob bei Regen oder Sonnenschein, die Steubenparade findet statt. Von links nach rechts sind folgende Persönlichkeiten zu sehen: Frau Pat Michalski, Assistentin des Gouverneurs Jim Edgar; Harry Volkman, bekannter Fernsehansager; Erich Himmel, Präsident der Vereinigung des Deutschen Tages sowie Alderman Eugene Schulter und Chicagos Bürgermeister Richard M. Daley.

Chicago's Annual Steuben Parade is probably the largest and longest in the country. Almost every German American Society is represented. Visiting groups from out of state and Germany participate in their colorful costumes

The Donauschwaben of Greater Chicago.

Die Donauschwaben aus Großchicago

heritage organizations, particularly in larger towns, serve as a meeting place where one can congregate, enjoy good fellowship and hold social and cultural functions.

In the metropolitan Chicago area there are some 50 German-American societies, numerous restaurants and several German language publications and radio programs. The German section at Lincoln and Lawrence Avenues, at the near north side of the City, is a busy hub of German activities, even though many German Americans have migrated to other suburbs.

Located near the corner of Lawrence and Lincoln, at 4730 North Western Avenue, are the headquarters of the German American National Congress (D.A.N.K.). The German House, owned by the D.A.N.K. Chapter North, is a six story building which serves as a cultural center, not only for D.A.N.K. but also for about two dozen German-American societies.

The German American National Congress is today the largest German-American umbrella organization with some 50 chapters and almost 80 associated member organizations from coast to coast. While it is not a political organization and concentrates on cultural, social and educational programs, it does endeavour to represent German Americans on a national level.

D.A.N.K. was founded in 1958 when a group of German-Americans from various organizations decided to take a more active part in American public life and give Germans a stronger voice in matters of local, state and national affairs. Soon the organization spread from Chicago over the entire country. It also publishes a monthly newspaper, "The

Contiuned on page 228

vieler umliegender Orte nicht verleugnen, wie z.B. Schaumburg, Lake Zurich und Mundelein. Es gibt eine Reihe von deutschen Straßennahmen in Chicago, die bekanntesten darunter sind wohl die Mannheim und Kirchoff Roads, Goethe und Schiller Streets, Ernst und Ferne Courts, Mies van der Rohe Way. Und zwei Oberschulen heißen: Baron von Steuben und Karl Steinmetz Oberschule. Organisationen deutschen Ursprungs, hauptsächlich in größeren Städten, dienen als Treffpunkte, um sich zu versammeln, Freundschaften und Beziehungen zu pflegen und gesellschaftliche und kulturelle Funktionen wahrzunehmen.

Im Großraum Chicago gibt es mehr als 50 deutsch-amerikanische Vereine, eine große Anzahl an Restaurants und mehrere deutschsprachige Publikationen, sowie Radioprogramme. Das deutsche Viertel auf der Lincoln- und Lawrence Street, auf der nördlichen Seite der Stadt, ist ein geschäftiger Knotenpunkt in dem sich die deutschen Aktivitäten noch immer konzentrieren, obwohl viele Deutsch-Amerikaner in die Vororte gezogen sind.

Ecke Lawrence- und Lincoln, auf 4730 Nord Western Avenue, befindet sich die Hauptgeschäftsstelle des Deutsch-Amerikanischen Nationalkongreßes (D.A.N.K.). Das deutsche Haus, dessen Besitzer die Gruppe Nord des D.A.N.K.s ist, ist ein sechsstöckiges Gebäude, das als kulturelles Zentrum dient und nicht nur dem D.A.N.K., sondern auch ungefähr zwei Dutzend anderen deutsch-amerikanischen Vereinen zur Verfügung steht.

Continued on page 228

The "Shanty Choir Nordstrand" from Germany delighted their audience with traditional sailors' songs

Der „Shanty Chor Nordstrand" aus Deutschland hat die Zuhörer mit traditionellen Seemannsliedern begeistert.

Chicagos jährliche Steuben Parade ist wahrscheinlich die größte und längste in ganz Amerika. Beinahe jede deutsch-amerikanische Gesellschaft ist vertreten. Besuchergruppen von außerhalb des Staates und aus Deutschland nehmen in ihren farbenprächtigen Kostümen daran teil.

The D.A.N.K. Sparrows have become famous for their German folk songs. Under the direction of founder Pradella-Ott, they have performed widely in America and Germany.

Die D.A.N.K.-Spatzen sind durch ihre deutschen Volkslieder berühmt geworden. Unter der Leitung ihrer Gründerin, Frau Pradella-Ott, sind sie bereits in ganz Amerika und Deutschland aufgetreten.

GERMAN AMERICAN HERITAGE — DAS DEUTSCH-AMERIKANISCHE ERBE

In Washington, on October 6th, 1993 German Americans celebrated their 7th annual German American Day.

As in previous years, the Congressional Study Group on Germany and the German American Parlamentary Group of the Bundestag hosted their reception at the Senate Caucus Room.

Foreign Minister Dr. Kinkel and Ambassaror Dr. Immo Stabreit were the hosts of the evening reception at the German Embassy. Guests of Honor included the Honorable Thomas S. Foley, Speaker of the House, Deputy Secretary of State Peter Tarnoff, Chairman of the Congressional Study Group on Germany, Representative Doug Bereuter. Speaker for the German Americans was German American Joint Actions Committee Co-Chairman and D.A.N.K. National President Ernst Ott.

Making introductions at the Embassy reception (from left) D.A.N.K. National President Ernst Ott, Speaker of the House Thomas Foley, Foreign Minister Dr. Klaus Kinkel and Chairman of the Congressional Study Group on Germany, Representative Doug Bereuter
(Photo: G. Kainz, Washington Journal)

Vorstellung der Gäste beim Botschaftsempfang (von links) Ernst Ott, Nationaler Präsident vom D.A.N.K., Präsident des Repräsentantenhauses Thomas Foley, Außenminister Dr. Klaus Kinkel und Repräsentant Doug Bereuter, Vorsitzender der Kongreß-Studiengruppe Deutschland
(Foto: G. Kainz, Washington Journal).

Am 6. Oktober 1993 haben die Deutsch-Amerikaner in Washington ihren siebten jährlichen Deutsch-Amerikanischen Tag gefeiert.

Wie auch schon in vorherigen Jahren, hat die Congressional Studiengruppe Deutschland und die Deutsch-Amerikanische Parlamentsgruppe des Bundestages einen Empfang im Caucus-Zimmer des Senats gegeben.

Außenminister Dr. Kinkel und Botschafter Dr. Immo Stabreit waren die Gastgeber des Abendempfangs in der deutschen Botschaft. Ehrengäste waren der Honorable Thomas S. Foley, Präsident des Repräsentantenhauses, der stellvertretende Bundesaußenminister Peter Tarnoff und der Vorsitzende der Kongreß-Studiengruppe Deutschland und Abgeordnete des Repräsentantenhauses Doug Bereuter. Sprecher für die Deutsch-Amerikaner war Ernst Ott, Mitvorsitzender des Deutsch-Amerikanischen Joint Actions Committees und Präsident des D.A.N.K.

Proudly exhibiting the Presidential Proclamation (from left) D.A.N.K. National President Ernst Ott; Ambassador Dr. Immo Stabreit; Director, United German American Committee Marlene Stock and National Chairman Steuben Society of America, Heinz Obry
(Photo: Robert Stock)

Hier wird stolz die Proklamation des Präsidenten gezeigt (von links): Ernst Ott, Nationaler Präsident des D.A.N.K., Botschafter Dr. Immo Stabreit; Direktorin des United German American Committees Marlene Stock und Nationaler Vorsitzender der Steuben-Gesellschaft von Amerika Heinz Obry (Foto: Robert Stock)

Lachner "CHICAGOLAND"

One of the celebrity visitors to Chicago in 1993 was the President of the Federal Republic of Germany, Richard von Weiszäcker. He met with leaders of the German American community at the city's Mayfair Hotel.

The meeting, arranged by the German Embassy in Washington and Chicago's Consulate General office, was the first opportunity for many German American leaders of the Midwest to meet face-to-face with the German President.

Einer der berühmten Besucher 1993 in Chicago war Bundespräsident Richard von Weizsäcker. Er traf sich mit leitenden Persönlichkeiten der deutsch-amerikanischen Gemeinschaft der Stadt Chicago im Mayfair Hotel.

Diese Versammlung, die von der Deutschen Botschaft in Washington und dem Deutschen Konsulat in Chicago organisiert worden war, gab vielen Deutsch-Amerikanern des Mittelwestens die Chance, den deutschen Bundespräsident persönlich kennenzulernen.

D.A.N.K. President Ernst Ott presented Bundespraesident von Weizsäcker a memento of his visit to Chicago. (Photo: Eintracht)

D.A.N.K.-Präsident Ernst Ott überreicht dem Bundespräsidenten von Weizsäcker ein Erinnerung an seinen Besuch in Chicago. (Foto: Eintracht).

In Chicago, German-Americans congregated October 10th 1993 again, to celebrate German American Day at St.Benedict Church which was filled to capacity. German Day Association President Erich Himmel and Vice President Irene Rotter welcomed the numerous representatives of the German American community. Many societies brought their organization's flags and banners. The men's and ladies' choirs under the direction of David Crane and George Bell presented a festive musical program for this event.

In Chicago versammelten sich die Deutsch-Amerikaner am 10. Oktober 1993 wieder, um den Deutsch-Amerikanischen Tag in der St. Benedict Kirche zu begehen. Die Kirche war bis auf den letzten Platz gefüllt. Der Präsident des Deutschen-Tag-Verbandes, Erich Himmel, und Vize-Präsidentin Irene Rotter hießen die verschiedenen Vertreter der deutsch-amerikanischen Gemeinschaft willkommen. Viele Vereinigungen waren mit Vereinsfahnen und -banner vertreten. Zu diesem Anlaß boten der Männer- und Frauenchor unter der Leitung von David Crane und George Bell ein festliches Musikprogramm.

The "Siebenbuerger Sachsen" maintain their traditions in their new home country.

Die Siebenbuerger Sachsen bewahren ihre Tradition in ihrer neuen Heimat.

GERMAN AMERICAN HERITAGE — DAS DEUTSCH-AMERIKANISCHE ERBE

German Unification Day in Chicago

Tag der Deutschen Vereinigung in Chicago

Under the sponsorship of the Consul General's office, a small combined ensemble of Chicago's Symphony Orchestra and the Berlin Philharmonic performed a special program on the occasion of the 3rd anniversary of German Unification with special guest Daniel Barenboim (fourth from right). After the performance Consul General Gabriele von Malsen-Tilborch (pictured) invited several hundred guests to a cocktail reception in the ballroom of Orchestra Hall. It was a memorable evening, indeed, to celebrate German Unification.

Unter der Sponsorschaft des Deutschen Konsulats boten, aus Anlaß des 3. Jahrestages der Vereinigung Deutschlands, ein kleines Ensemble des Chicago Symphonie Orchesters und der Berliner Philharmoniker, unter der Gastleitung von Daniel Barenboim (vierter von rechts), ein Sonderprogramm. Nach der Vorstellung lud Generalkonsulin Gabriele von Malsen-Tilborch (abgebildet) mehrere hundert Gäste zu einem Cocktail-Empfang in den Ballsaal der Orchestra Hall. Die Feieraus Anlaß der Vereinigung Deutschlands war wirklich ein denkwürdiger Abend.

Illinois Senator Moseley-Braun (D) with Mrs. Pradella-Ott (right) discuss German American activities.

Illinois Senatorin Moseley-Braun (D) und Frau Pradella-Ott (rechts) sprechen über deutsch-amerikanische Aktivitäten.

German American Journal", mostly in English, since many of its members are of 2nd, 3rd and older generation German-Americans. An Education Fund and the German-language weekend schools were founded. Ten D.A.N.K. schools in various states and a children's choir in Chicago, "Die D.A.N.K. Spatzen", the D.A.N.K. Sparrows, keep promoting German language and music. A youth exchange program between Germany and America has brought over 1,000 German youngsters to the U.S. in recent years. Various American groups had a good time in Germany as well.

A long cherished dream became reality when Congress declared October 6th, 1987 the first German-American Day, and then President Reagan signed the proclamation in a Rose Garden ceremony. It was mainly due to D.A.N.K.s efforts, and those of former D.A.N.K. National President Elsbeth Seewald, that the necessary votes in both the Senate and House of Representatives were obtained to ensure passage of the resolution. German American Day has been celebrated annually since that day with representatives from Germany and the U.S. government participating.

Another German-American event of national prominence is the Annual General von Steuben Parade. It was this Prussian officer who trained General Washington's unexperienced troops that eventually defeated the British forces and achieved independence for the United States. In Chicago it is celebrated on the 3rd weekend in September, in conjunction with the German Fest. Various bands and other groups from Germany have come and joined the parade.

D.A.N.K.s German House accom

Der Deutsch-Amerikanische Nationalkongreß ist heute der größte deutsch-amerikanische Dachverband mit ungefähr 50 lokalen Gruppen und beinahe 80 eingeschriebenen Mitgliedsorganisationen von Küste zu Küste. Obwohl er keine politische Organisation ist und sich hauptsächlich mehr auf kulturelle, gesellschaftliche und erzieherische Programme konzentriert, bemüht er sich doch, den Deutsch-Amerikaner auf nationaler Ebene zu vertreten.

Der D.A.N.K. wurde 1958 gegründet, als sich eine Gruppe von Deutsch-Amerikanern verschiedener Organisationen dazu entschloß, einen aktiveren Anteil am öffentlichen amerikanischen Leben zu nehmen und den Deutschen ein stärkeres Gewicht in Bezug auf lokale, staatsweite und nationale Belange zu verleihen. Sehr bald schon dehnte sich die Organisation von Chicago über das ganze Land aus. Der D.A.N.K. veröffentlicht eine monatliche Zeitung - den Deutsch-Amerikaner - hauptsächlich in englischer Sprache, da viele der Mitglieder bereits in der zweiten, dritten oder einer noch älteren Generation Amerikaner sind. Ein Unterrichts-Fonds und die deutschsprachige Wochenendschule wurden gegründet. Zehn D.A.N.K. Schulen in verschiedenen Staaten und ein Kinderchor in Chicago, die D.A.N.K. Spatzen, fördern die deutsche Sprache und Musik. Ein Jugend-Austauschprogramm zwischen Deutschland und Amerika hat in den letzten Jahren über 1000 Jugendliche in die USA gebracht. Verschiedene amerikanische Gruppen wiederum haben Deutschland besucht.

Ein lang gehegter Wunschtraum wurde Wirklichkeit, als der Kongreß am 6. Oktober 1987 den ersten Deutsch-Amerikanischen Tag ins Leben rief und Präsident Reagan in der Rose-Garden-Zeremonie die Proklamation unterschrieb. Das ist hauptsächlich den Bemühungen des D.A.N.K.s und seiner ehemaligen, nationalen Präsidentin Elsbeth Seewald zu verdanken, die dafür sorgten, daß die nötigen Stimmen sowohl im Senat als auch im Repräsentantenhaus eingeholt werden konnten. Seither wird der Deutsch-Amerikanische Tag jährlich unter Teilnahme von Vertretern der deutschen und amerikanischen Regierungen gefeiert.

German Ambassador Dr. Immo Stabreit addresses members of the German American community during his visit to the "Windy City".

Der deutsche Botschafter Dr. Immo Stabreit spricht zu Mitgliedern der deutsch-amerikanischen Gemeinschaft bei einem Besuch in der „windigen Stadt."

Attending the Ambassador's reception were (l.t.r.) Veronika Steingraber, Patricia Kemper, Carola Kupfer (Members of the Columbia Club), Elsbeth M. Seewald (D.A.N.K. Honorary National President), Marlis Schmidt (Producer of the German radio program "Continental Journal" and publisher of "Tune-In" magazine), Renate Friedemann (Consul) and Gunella Griletz (Producer of the radio program "Sound of Europe").

Anwesend beim Empfang des Botschafters waren von links nach rechts Veronika Steingraber, Patricia Kemper, Carola Kupfer (Mitglieder des Columbia-Clubs); Elsbeth M. Seewald (D.A.N.K. Honorary National President); Marlis Schmidt (Rundfunkproduzentin des Radioprogramms in deutscher Sprache „Continental Journal und Herausgeber der Zeitschrift „Tune-In"); Renate Friedemann (Konsulin) und Gunella Griletz (Rundfunkproduzentin des Radioprogramms in deutscher Sprache „Sound of Europe").

GERMAN AMERICAN HERITAGE — DAS DEUTSCH-AMERIKANISCHE ERBE

Pictured are members of the D.A.N.K. organization, the Consul General, representatives of the U.S. Army and a German Navy detachment during the solemn ceremony.

Abgebildet sind Mitglieder der D.A.N.K.-Organisation, die deutsche Generalkonsulin, Vertreter der US-Armee und ein Sonderkommando der deutschen Marine bei der Feierlichkeit

Volkstrauertag, German Memorial Day ceremony at Fort Sheridan is being observed annually and honors the German World War II Prisoners of War who died there during captivity. D.A.N.K. has looked after these graves and maintained this tradition over the years.

Der Vokstrauertag wird jährlich am Fort Sheridan eingehalten und ehrt die Gefangenen und Gefallenen des 2. Weltkrieges. D.A.N.K. pflegt die Gräber seit Jahren und erhält die Tradition aufrecht.

Christmas Celebrations are a time of joy and hope for young and old.

Das Weihnachtsfest ist eine Zeit der Freude und Hoffnung für alt und jung.

Residents at the Altenheim Nursing Home at Forest Park are visited by Santa Claus. Here Mrs. Elsa Gay with Mr. and Mrs. "Santa Claus".

Santa Claus besucht die Bewohner des Altenheims in Forest Park. Hier sehen wir Elsa Gay mit Herrn und Frau Santa Claus.

Anxiously awaiting the arrival of Santa Claus, children show off their musical talents at D.A.N.K.'s Christmas Party.

Kinder auf einer D.A.N.K. Weihnachtsfeier demonstrieren ihre musikalischen Talente und warten auf den Weihnachtsmann.

modates in addition to the National Executive Office, a 500 seat capacity ball room with kitchen and bar facilities, a European type cafe, the German language weekend school meeting rooms for some 20 German associations, the Willy Scharpenberg Museum, a library and movie theater. While the house is frequented throughout the week, it is mainly on the weekends that most educational and social events take place.

Dances, theater performances, German and U.S. holiday festivities, Christmas parties, New Year's celebrations and carnival costume balls are, of course, major events that bring German Americans and their friends together at the D.A.N.K. Haus.

Ein anderes deutsch-amerikanisches Ereignis mit nationaler Prominenz ist die jährliche General-von-Steuben-Parade. Es war dieser Preußische General, der Washingtons unerfahrene Truppen exerzierte, die dann erfolgreich gegen die britischen Truppen eingesetzt wurden und für die Unabhängigkeit der Vereinigten Staaten kämpften.

Dieses Ereignis wird in Chicago am dritten Wochenende im September gefeiert, zusammen mit dem deutschen Fest. Verschiedene Musikbands und andere Gruppen kommen aus Deutschland, um an der Parade teilzunehmen.

D.A.N.K.s Deutsches Haus beherbergt nicht nur die D.A.N.K.-Verwaltung, sondern auch einen großen Ballsaal, der Platz für 500 Gäste bietet, mit Küche und Bar, einem europäischen Café, die Klassenzimmer der deutschen Wochenendschule sowie Platz für weitere 20 deutsche Vereine, das Willy Scharpenberg-Museum, eine Bücherei und ein Filmtheater. Obwohl das Gebäude während der Woche gut besucht ist, finden Schulunterricht und gesellschaftliche Veranstaltungen hauptsächlich an den Wochenenden statt.

Tanzveranstaltungen, Theateraufführungen, deutsche und amerikanische Feiertagsaktivitäten, Weihnachsfeiern, Neujahrsparties und Karnevals-Kostümbälle, sind natürlich die Hauptveranstaltungen, die Deutsch-Amerikaner und ihre Freunde im D.A.N.K. Haus zusammenbringen.

At the D.A.N.K Haus, many Sunday afternoons during the winter were enlightened by a program of operetta music, dance and chanties. The audience enjoyed these get togethers with good German coffee and a piece of traditional Black Forest Torte. Georg Lieder also produces the weekend programs "Musical trip around the world" on WVVX 103.1 FM.

Im D.A.N.K.-Haus werden viele Sonntagnachmittage im Winter mit den Operetten-, Tanz und Lieder-Programmen erhellt. Das Publikum genießt diese Zusammenkünfte bei deutschem Kaffee und einem Stück traditioneller Schwarzwälderkirschtorte. Georg Lieder ist auch der Produzent des Wochenend-Radioprogramms „Musikalische Reise um die Welt" auf WVVX 103.1 FM.

Lieder's operetta group performing for an enchanted audience.

Lieders Operettengruppe vor einem vezauberten Publikum.

A formal duet performing at the D.A.N.K. ballroom.

Ein Duett im D.A.N.K. Festsaal.

"Sing and the world will sing with you, cry and you cry alone!"

„Singe und die Welt singt mit Dir, weine und Du weinst allein!"

Lachner "CHICAGOLAND"

Alderman Eugene Schulter, the City of Chicago representative in German American affairs, here with children at Lincoln Avenue Mall.

Stadtrat Eugene Schulter, Vertreter für deutsch-amerikanische Angelegenheiten in der Stadt Chicago, hier mit Kindern auf der Lincoln Avenue Mall.

The City of Chicago is well informed about German American activities and is a strong supporter of the many functions in the City.

Die Stadt Chicago ist gut über die deutsch-amerikanischen Veranstaltungen, die sie fördert, informiert.

German-American Media

During the last week of January 1994, German-American History was made in Chicago's business community. Through the intermediary of Bert Lachner, the first German Media Exhibit was opened in the James R. Thompson Center, the former State of Illinois Building. It was a memorable premiere. Looking back on a history of 256 years, the German press was recognized and the Governor honored the newspaper business for bridging the gap between the old and the new world, as well as acting as intermediary in the integration of German immigrants on this continent.

The first bridge was built by Johann Christopher Saur of the Palatinate Ladenburg. He was the first and probably most important printer in America in the 18th Century who acquired a piece of property in Germantown, Pennsylvania in 1783, on which he built a house and a print shop. From the letter foundry in Frankfurt, Saur secured the Gothic lettering system, which gave him an edge over other printers such as the famous Benjamin Franklin. On August 20, 1739, the „Hoch-Deutsch Pennsylvanische Geschichtsschreiber" (High-German Pennsylvania Reporter of History) appeared for the first time, and in 1743 the first Luther Bible printed in German appeared in America.

During an impressive ceremony in the James R. Thompson Center - a revolutionary architectural creation by German-American Helmut Jahn - and in the presence of numerous guests of honor and representatives from German-language newspapers and radio stations, the German media was honored and its merits recognized. The 'Illinois Staatszeitung,' founded in 1848, together with twelve other German-language papers were reported to have given the deciding support in the election of Abraham Lincoln as President of the United States of America. 100 years ago there were roughly 850 German-language papers in print in the United States.

Today almost seventy German-language newspapers and monthly journals are published by a few idealists. This is why this First German Media Exhibit in the James R. Thompson Center is of such great importance.

And this is precisely the reason why Bert Lachner, author of this book, receives his justly deserved dues by being honored by a wide circle of people.

Werner Baroni

Deutschamerikanische Medien

In der letzen Januarwoche 1994 wurde im Hauptgeschäftsviertel von Chicago deutschamerikanische Geschichte geschrieben. Durch Vermittlung von Bert Lachner eröffnete Gouverneur Jim Edgar im State of Illinois Building die 1. Deutsche Medienausstellung. Es war eine denkwürdige Premiere. In der 256 jährigen Geschichte der deutschsprachigen Presse würdigte der Gouverneur die Brückenfunktion der Zeitungen zwischen der alten und der neuen Heimat, sowie ihre Vermittlerdienste bei der Integration deutscher Einwanderer in die neuen Verhältnisse auf einem 10 Millionen qkm grossen Kontinent.

Der erste Brückenschlag wurde von Johann Christopher Saur aus dem pfälzischen Ladenburg gemacht. Er war in Amerika, Anfang des 18. Jahrhunderts, der erste und wohl bedeutendste Drucker, der 1738 in Germantown/Pennsylvanien ein Grundstück erwarb auf dem er ein Wohnhaus errichtete und eine Druckerei betrieb. Saur beschaffte sich in Deutschland aus der Schriftgießerei Luther in Frankfurt die Frakturschrift, wodurch er gegenüber anderen Druckern, zum Beispiel dem berühmten Benjamin Franklin, einen Vorsprung erhielt. Am 20. August 1739 erschien zum ersten Mal der „Hoch-Deutsch Pennsylvanische Geschichtsschreiber" und 1743 die erste Lutherbibel, die in Amerika in deutscher Sprache gedruckt wurde.

Während der eindrucksvollen Feierstunde im State of Illinois Building, ein epochales Werk des Deutschamerikaners Helmut Jahn, wurde im Beisein zahlreicher Ehrengäste, sowie deutschsprachiger Zeitungs- und Radiovertreter, die Verdienste der Medien gewürdigt. Der 1848 gegründeten Illinois Staatszeitung darf bescheinigt werden, 1860 mit zwölf anderen deutschsprachigen Zeitungen Abraham Lincoln bei der Wahl zum Präsidenten der Vereinigten Staaten entscheidend unterstützt zu haben. Vor 100 Jahren gab es in den Vereinigten Staaten ca. 850 deutschsprachige Zeitungen.

Heutzutage werden ca. siebzig deutschsprachige Zeitungen, einschließlich der Monatshefte, von einigen wenigen Idealisten hergestellt. Schon deshalb kommt der 1. Deutschen Medienausstellung im James R. Thompson Zentrum eine besondere Bedeutung zu.

Dafür gebührt Bert Lachner, der Herausgeber dieses Buches ist, der Dank weiter Kreise.

Werner Baroni

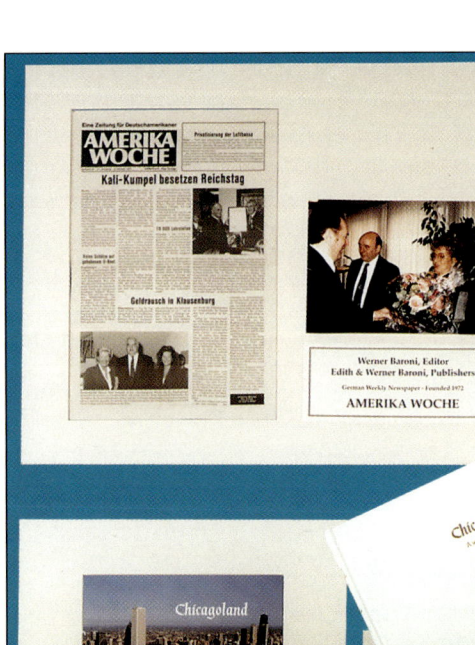

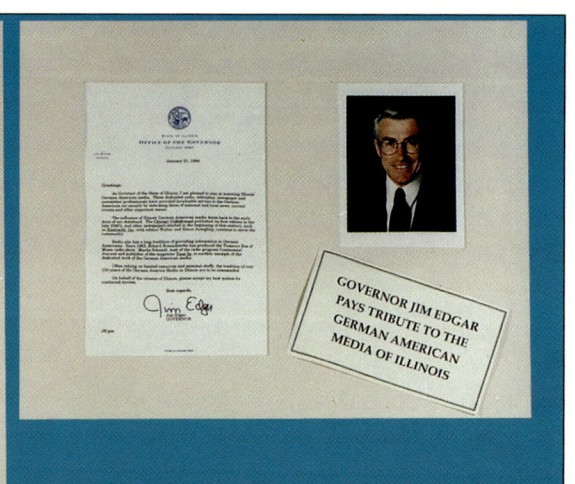

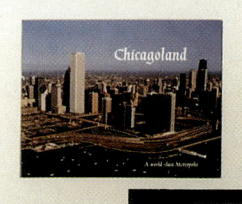

AMERIKA WOCHE
Werner Baroni, Editor
Edith & Werner Baroni, Publishers
German Weekly Newspaper · Founded 1972

EINTRACHT, INC.
Klaus & Walter Juengling,
Editors & Publishers
Weekly German Newspaper · Founded 1923

GOVERNOR JIM EDGAR PAYS TRIBUTE TO THE GERMAN AMERICAN MEDIA OF ILLINOIS

CHICAGOLAND, A WORLD-CLASS METROPOLIS
Bert Lachner, Editor
German Media Group, Publisher
English & German
Publishing Date: May, 1994

GERMAN AMERICAN BUSINESS JOURNAL MIDWEST
Niels G. Friedrichs, Editor & Publisher
Bimonthly English Magazine · Founded 1982 · Official Publication of German-American Trade & Commerce Promotion

D.A.N.K. AURORA NEWSLETTER
William Fuchs, President
Darlene Fuchs, Editor
English & German Newsletter · 3 times a year · Founded 1988

THE GERMAN-AMERICAN JOURNAL
Ernst Ott, Editor & President
Monthly English & German Newspaper · Founded 1960
Official Publication of German-American National Congress

EINTRACHT, INC. AMERIKA WOCHE WASHINGTON JOURNAL
Isabella Erbe Przysiezny, Journalist

TUNE IN
Marlis Schmidt, Editor & Publisher
Quarterly English & German Radio Newsletter
Founded 1987

EXECUTIVE CHRONICLES
Dr. Karl Hnilicka, Editor
English and German Quarterly Magazine · Founded 1989

THE GERMAN AMERICAN POLICE ASSOC. NEWSLETTER
Roger Haas, President
Mike Haas, Editor
Bimonthly English Newsletter · Founded 1975

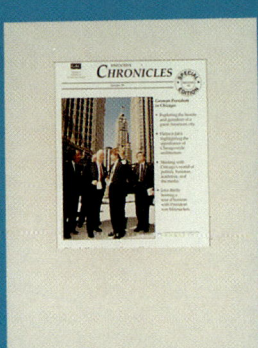

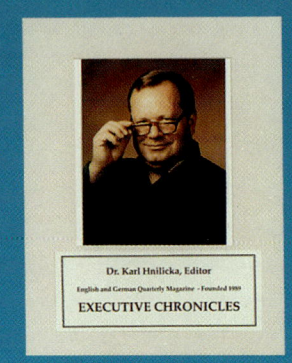

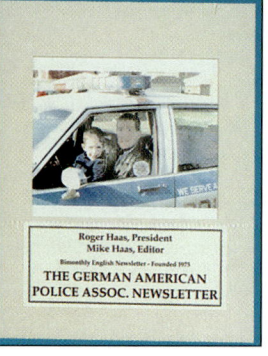

234   Lachner "*CHICAGOLAND*"

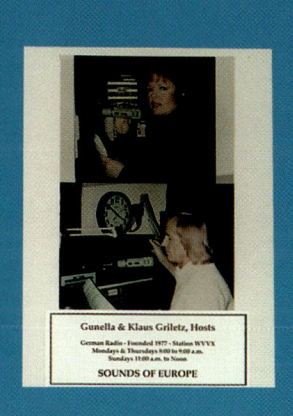

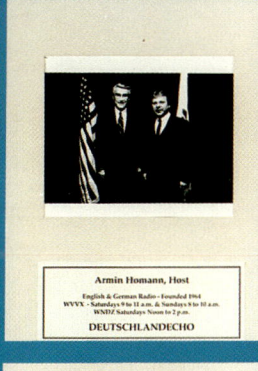

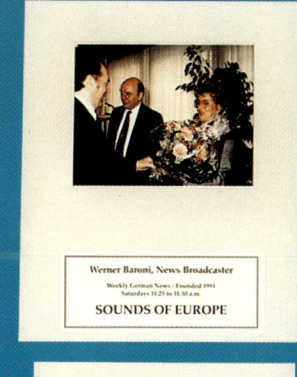

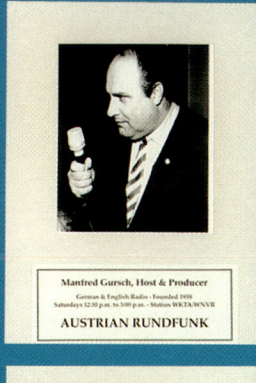

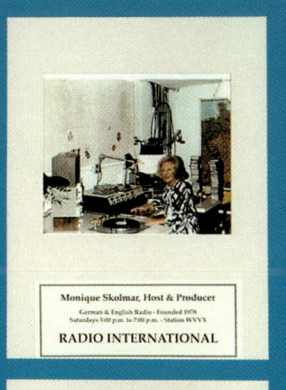

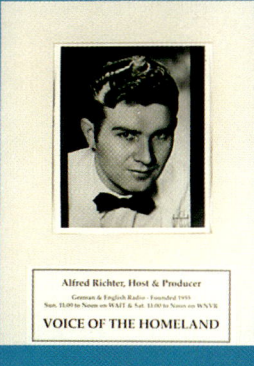

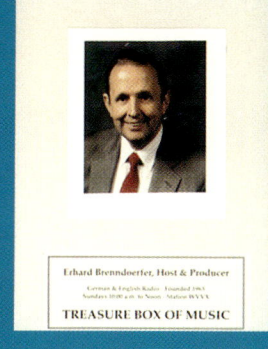

The German community in Chicagoland enjoys a lively press corp and many hours of German music and other radio programs, including news, interviews and documentaries.

This display of profiles was taken from German American Media Week, January 21 to 28, 1994 at the James R. Thompson Center at Randolph and Clark Streets. Governor Jim Edgar made the proclamation and 200 media people and community leaders attended the ribbon cutting ceremony.

Deutsch-Amerikaner in Chicagoland erfreuen sich einer aktiven Presse und vieler Stunden deutscher Radio Musik.

Diese Tafeln wurden zum Anlaß der Deutsch-Amerikanischenen Media Woche vom 21. bis 28. Januar 1994 im James R. Thompson Zentrum an der Ecke Randolph und Clark ausgestellt. Gouverneur Jim Edgar machte die Proklamation und etwa 200 Gäste der Media, Wirtschaft, Industrie und Kultur waren zur Eröffnung erschienen.

GERMAN AMERICAN HERITAGE — DAS DEUTSCH-AMERIKANISCHE ERBE

Chicagoland's future looks exciting

Chicagoland sieht einer vielversprechenden Zukunft entgegen

The City and its suburbs continually improve their infrastructure and services to benefit its growing population.

In recent years, a Lake water distribution network was completed. O'Hare Airport went through a multiyear improvement process, which ended in 1993 with the opening of the gleaming new International Terminal. The road and highway systems in and around Chicago are constantly being renewed and expanded.

In the City, the Chicago Mercantile Exchange opened a second floor with more trading facilities. The new Harold Washington Public Library, at Dearborn Street and Congress Parkway in the South Loop, was opened in 1992.

Soon, the Deep Tunnel

Die Infrastruktur der Stadt und ihrer Vororte ist laufend einer Weiterentwicklung unterworfen, um den Bedürfnissen der ständig wachsenden Bevölkerung gerecht zu werden.

Vor ein paar Jahren wurde ein Wasserverteilernetz fertiggestellt, das Wasser vom Michigansee in alle Richtungen Chicagolands verteilt. Der O'Hare Airport wurde einem viele Jahre während Sanierungsprogramm unterworfen, das 1993 mit der Eröffnung seines neuen Internationalen Terminals abgeschlossen wurde. Das Schnellstraßennetz in und um Chicago wird ununterbrochen saniert und erweitert.

In der City hat die Chicago Mercantile Exchange ein zweites Stockwerk zur Erweiterung der Börsensaalfläche hinzugefügt. Die neue Harold Washington Stadtbibliothek an der Dearborn Street Ecke Congress Parkway im Süd-Loop öffnete 1992 ihre Tore.

Project will be completed, controlling flooding problems in the City. Also, Chicago will soon have a new, state-of-the-art Main Post Office.

The McCormick/Navy Pier Authority predicts completion of the Navy Pier project with its Crystal Garden, Ferris Wheel and Festival Hall, by 1995.

A third McCormick Place exhibition and convention complex, currently the largest construction project in the region, will be completed in 1997.

With plenty of space for expansion and growth, Chicago and its metropolitan area offer the investor excellent opportunities to do business. Whether it's manufacturing, distribution or services, Chicagoland is an ideal place for national and worldwide enterprise.

Other projects on the agenda include:

- Extension of the Elgin - O'Hare Expressway with a West Entrance to the airport
- Heartland International, an airport designed to serve the whole Midwest, on Chicagoland's south side.
- A network of Highspeed Trains connecting the regional centers of Milwaukee, Minneapolis, Indianapolis, St. Louis and Detroit with the City and the airports of Chicagoland.

Auch das Tief-Tunnel-Projekt befindet sich in seiner Abschlußphase. Seine Aufgabe wird es sein, Überflutungsprobleme in der Stadt in die Hand zu bekommen. Ein neues und ultra-modernes Hauptpostamt steht ebenfalls vor seiner Vollendung.

Die zuständige Planungsbehörde für McCormick Place und Navy Pier sieht für 1995 das Ende des Navy Pier-Projekts vor, mit einem Kristall Garten, Riesenrad und Festhalle.

Eine dritte McCormick Place-Ausstellungshalle steht gegenwärtig als größtes Bauprojekt der Gegend an, dessen Abschluß für 1997 geplant ist.

Da Chicago über ausreichenden Platz verfügt, sich auszubreiten und weiter zu wachsen, bietet es Anlegern hervorragende Gelegenheiten für Investitionen. Ob Herstellung, Vertrieb oder Dienstleistungen, Chicagoland ist ein idealer Ort für landes- und weltweite Unternehmen.

Andere Projekte, die auf der Tagesordnung stehen, sind:

- Verlängerung der Elgin - O'Hare Schnellstraße mit einer West-Ausfahrt zum Flughafen
- Heartland International, ein Flughafen auf der Südseite von Chicago, der dem gesamten Mittelwesten dienen soll.
- Ein Netz von Inter-City-Zügen, das Milwaukee, Minneapolis, Indianapolis, St. Louis und Detroit mit Chicago und seinen

- A double-deck Midtown Expressway may be constructed, connecting O'Hare airport with Heartland, to provide fast, limited access to and through the City for commercial and passenger traffic.
- In the City, the process of expanding and rejuvenating the elevated and subway systems will continue. More stations may integrate directly into malls and stores, keeping pedestrians out of weather and off the busy streets.
- Buildings may be connected with more sky bridges and lower level malls providing easy and comfortable access for business and shopping in the downtown area.

In 1908, Daniel H. Burnham said, "Make no little plans, they have no magic to stir men's blood".

The Chicago "I Will" spirit has resulted in many civic accomplishments in the 19th and 20th Centuries. Looking ahead to the 21st Century, more than seven million Chicagolanders hope for more and greater progress, prosperity and opportunities for all men and women, when the Windy City, the City of the Big Shoulders, the proud, world-class metropolis on the shore of Lake Michigan, celebrates its 200th birthday in the year 2033.

Flughäfen verbindet.

- Eine „Doppeldecker" Midtown Schnellstraße ist in der Planung, um den O'Hare Flughafen mit dem Heartland zu verbinden und schnellen, aber begrenzten Zugang zur und durch die Stadt für Kommerziellen- und Passagierverkehr möglich zu machen.
- In der Stadt wird das Erweiterungs- und Verjüngungsprojekt der Hoch- und Untergrundbahnsysteme weiter angetrieben. Mehrere Bahnhöfe planen, direkten Zugang zu Malls und Kaufhäusern zu gewährleisten, so daß der Fußgänger sich nicht mehr dem Wetter oder überfüllten Straßen auszusetzen braucht.
- Brücken und Subterrian-Malls zwischen den Gebäuden sind im Planungsstadium, um Einkaufen in der Innenstadt für den Kunden leichter zugänglich und bequemer zu gestalten.

Daniel H. Burnham sagte im Jahre 1908: „Denkt großzügig, denn mickrige Pläne lassen die Leute kalt."

Der Chicagoer Charakterzug „ich werde es schaffen" hat im 19. und 20. Jahrhundert Berge versetzt. Mehr als 7 Millionen Chicagoer sehen dem 21. Jahrhundert mit der Hoffnung und dem Gedanken eines größeren Fortschrittes, Wohlstandes und besseren Möglichkeiten für alle entgegen, wenn die windige Stadt, die Stadt der breiten Schultern, die stolze Weltmetropole an den Ufern des Michigansees ihren 200. Geburtstag im Jahre 2033 feiern wird.

Bibliography — Referenzen

Bach, Ira and Wolfson, Susan. *Chicago On Foot*. Chicago: Review Press, 1987

Berger, Miles. *They Built Chicago*. Chicago: Bonus Books, 1992

Flinn, John. *The Standard Guide to Chicago*. New York: The Standard Guide Co., 1992.

Gilbert, Paul and Byron, Charles. *Chicago & Its Makers*. Chicago: Felix Mendelshon Publishers, 1953.

Grossman, Ron. *Guide To Chicago Neighborhoods*. Chicago: New Century Publishers, 1981.

Hayner, Don and McNamee, Tom. *Streetwise Chicago, A History of Chicago Street Names*. Chicago: Loyola University Press, 1988.

Hayner, Don and McNamee, Tom. *Metro Chicago Almanac*. Chicago: Chicago Sun Times and Bonus Books, 1993.

Hinz, Greg. *Recovery Zone*. Chicago, Chicago Magazine, July 1993.

Holli, Mellvin and Jones, Peter. *Ethnic Chicago*. Chicago: Wm. Easrdman's, 1984.

Lindberg, Richard. *Passport's Guide To Ethnic Chicago*. Chicago: Passport Books, 1953.

Lowe, David. *Chicago Interiors*. Boston: Houghton Mifflen, 1975.

Mayer, Harold and Wade, Richard. *Chicago, Growth of A Metropolis*. Chicago: Universtiy of Chicago Press, 1970.

Schnedler, Jack. *Chicago*. Oakland, CA: Compass American Guides, 1993.

Paciga, Dominic and Sherrett, Ellin. *Chicago, City of Neighborhoods*. Chicago: Loyola University Press, 1986.

Franz Schulze and Kevin Herrington. *Chicago's Famous Buildings*. The University of Chicago Press, Chicago & London.

Encyclopaedia Britannica, Jr. Vol. IV. Publ. by Encyclopaedia Britannica, Inc., New York, 1934.

Historic City, The Settlement of Chicago. Publ. by the Department of Development and Planning, Chicago, 1976.

Chicago History Magazine of the Chicago Historical Society, Fall-Winter 1973, Vol. II, No. 4, Isabel S. Grossner, Editor.

AAA Map Chicago and Vicinity, 1992 edition. Publ. by American Automobile Association, Heathrow, FL.

Meet the Family, The Gekler Family History 1833-1966. Publ. privately by Mary F. Gekler.

Participants — Beteiligte Firmen

BMW of North America, Inc.	59
Lufthansa	61
Harting Connectors	63
Mercedes-Benz of North America, Inc.	65
Schenker International	67
Audi/of America, Inc.	69
Automatic Liquid Packaging, Inc.	72/73
Irving Press, Inc.	81
Air France	91
Siemens	93
United Airlines	95
Flitz Metal Polish	97
Chicago Resorts	99
Erfurt, Inc.	101
Merz Apothecary	105
Kuhn's Delicatessen	173
Lincoln Square Mall	182/183
International Fashions by Ingrid	
Salamander Shoes of Chicago	
Northern Home Furnishings	
Delicatessen Meyer	
European Import Center	
Chicago Brauhaus	
Quality Optical	
Zum Deutschen Eck	190/191

The support of our participants is greatly appreciated.

Wir danken für die Unterstützung der beteiligten Firmen.

Photo Acknowledgements

We wish to acknowledge the following organizations and individuals, whose courtesy and cooperation in supplying us with photographs, maps and graphics of their facilities or records is greatly appreciated.

In order of their first appearance:

Chicago Historical Society 3, 204, 207, 211, 215, 216, 217, 218

Edelmann PR, Chicago
(Illinois State Tourist Office) 5, 8, 9, 17, 19, 39, 40, 41, 43, 45, 47, 48, 49, 50, 52, 53, 54, 64, 66, 85, 98, 100, 102, 104, 109, 110, 114, 122, 124, 125, 126, 127, 128, 129, 136, 139, 140, 145, 148

City of Chicago
(Department of Tourism) 11

Airpix, Chicago 12, 21, 47, 79, 113, 115

Bert Lachner, Author 12, 26, 27, 28, 29, 31, 32, 33, 34, 35, 36, 37, 38, 40, 41, 42, 43, 44, 49, 51, 60, 64, 71, 80, 86, 87, 92, 94, 96, 102, 09, 110, 111, 112, 116, 118, 120, 129, 139, 143, 144, 147, 149, 152, 153, 154, 155, 156, 157, 160, 161, 174, 175, 176, 177, 178, 179, 180, 181

Marc Segal 14/15

City of Chicago
(Department of Aviation) 16, 88, 134, 137

Rand McNally 18

Alfred Blumenthal, Photographer 23

Illinois & Michigan Canal
(National Heritage Commission) 24

CTA, Chicago Transit Authority 25

Mary Gekler, Editor
(Private Collection) 30, 74, 133, 148

Chicago Convention and Tourism Bureau, Inc. 30/31, 46, 108, 124, 125, 131, 132, 133, 165

Ed Michals, Editor 44, 62, 80, 146, 150, 151, 236

German American Chamber of Commerce of the Midwest
Niels G. Friedrichs, Co-Author 55, 57

Chicago Tribune 58
BMW 59
Lufthansa 61
Harting Connectors 63
Mercedes-Benz 65
Chicago Board of Trade 68
Chicago Mercantile Exchange 68
Audi / Volkswagen 69
Chicago Stock Exchange 70
Automatic Liquid Packaging 72/73
Orchestra Hall 74
Irving Press 81
World Trade Center 85
City of Chicago
(McPier Authority) 89, 106, 107
Air France 91
Siemens 93
Trans Tech America 95
Flitz Polish 97
Chicago Resorts 99, 116, 117
Erfurt 101
Jens Friedrich, Photographer 103
Merz Apothecary 105

Marriott Lincolnshire 117
Brookfield Zoo 119, 149
Frank Lloyd Wright Homes 119

Fotoquellen

Wir möchten hiermit den folgenden Organizationen und Personen für die Bereitstellung der Fotos, Karten und Grafiken ihrer Einrichtungen und Informationen sehr danken.

In der Reihe ihrer ersten Erscheinung:

Fermi Lab 120
Arlington International 121
Medieval Times 121
Six Flags, Great America 123

United Airlines 135
Midway Airport, City of Chicago
(Department of Aviation) 138

State of Illinois
(Chicago Tollroad Authority) 140

Bob Horsch, Photographer 141, 142, 164, 240, Cover photos

Lyric Opera 145

James A. Rasmussen, Photographer 162
Chicago Bears   (Football)   164
Chicago Cubs   (Baseball)   164
Chicago Power   (Soccer)   165
Chicago White Sox (Baseball)   165

Northwestern Memorial Hospital 166
University of Illinois at Chicago 166
Loyola University 167
University of Chicago 168
Illinois Benedictine College 168

Kuhn's Delicatessen 173
International Fashions by Ingrid 182
Salamander Shoes of Chicago 182
Northern Home Furnishings 182
Delicatessen Meyer 183
European Imports Center 183
Chicago Brauhaus 183
Quality Optical 183
Berghoff Restaurant 184
Schulien Restaurant 184
Bistro 1800 184

Arlington Place 184
Gasthaus zur Linde 185
Hans Bavarian Lodge 185
Golden Ox 185
Black Forest Restaurant 185
Chicago Brauhaus 186
Zum Deutschen Eck 186
Schmeissing Bakery 186
Fritzl's Country Inn 187
Vienna Pastry Shop 187
Lutz Continental 187
Alpine Market 187
Black Forest Meat Market 188
Edelweiss Delicatessen 188
A.F. Meyer 188

Zum Deutschen Eck 190/191

German Day Association
Erich Himmel, President 192, 193, 194, 195

Hamburg– Sister City
Hamburg Tourist Office, New York 196, 197, 198, 199, 200, 201

City of Chicago
(Department of Development and Planning) 202, 203

Ed Michals, Editor
(Private Collection) 205, 208, 209, 212

D.A.N.K.,
German American National Congress
Ernst Ott, National President 213, 219, 220, 221, 222, 223, 224, 225, 226, 227, 228, 229, 230, 231, 232, 233

Beach & Barnes, Photo Studio 234, 235

Index

A
Adler Planetarium 45, 48, 130, 131
Air France 91
Airlines 61, 91
Airports 88
Amoco Building 14, 104
Amtrac 100
Andersen, Arthur Co. 92
Aquarium, Shedd 45, 48, 102
Architecture 84, 131
Argonne National Laboratory 119
Arlington International Race Course 114, 121
Art Institute 44, 45, 132, 133
Auditorium Building 212
Auditorium Theater 146
Automatic Liquid Packaging 72

B
Baderbrau Brewing 121
Bahai Temple 122
Ballooning 140
Berghoff's Restaurant 81
B M W 59
Board of Trade Building 41, 68
Bridgeport 203
Bristol Renaissance Faire 123
Brookfield Zoo 119, 149
Buckingham Fountain 28, 104
Burlington Northern Railroad 110
Burnham Park Harbor 22, 8
Burnham Plan 84
Butchers 187

C
Cantigny Memorial Park 120
Chicago Bears 47, 164
Chicago Blackhawks 164
Chicago Bulls 164
Chicago Civic Center 40, 43, 129

Chicago Convention & Tourism Bureau 53
Chicago Cubs 164
Chicago Cultural Center 32, 147
Chicago Fire 60, 125
Chicago's Future 236
Chicago Historical Society 147
Chicago Loop 38
Chicago Lyric Opera 74, 145
Chicago Mercantile Exchange 68
Chicago Northwestern Railroad 206
Chicago Police 37, 39, 51
Chicago Power 165
Chicago River 32, 36
Chicago Stadium 164
Chicago Stock Exchange 70
Chicago Symphony Orchestra 31
Chicago Sun-Times 71, 143
Chicago Theater 44, 146
Chicago Transit Authority 25, 110
Chicago Tribune 71, 143
Chicago White Sox 165
Chicago Yacht Club 14
Churches 144, 209
Civic Opera House 35, 74
Columbia Yacht Club 14
Commerzbank 69, 96
Congress Parkway 30
Continental National Bank 41, 68
Credit Cards 181
Cuneo Museum 122, 147

D
Daley, Richrad M (Mayor 10, 26
Dan Ryan Expressway 109
Delicatessens 188
DePaul University 168
Department of Planning & Development 76, 77
Deutsche Bank 90

Diamond Star Motors 62
Dresdner Bank 60, 96
DuPage County Airport 139

E
Edens Expressway 109
Edgar, Jim (Governor) 9
Education 161, 163
Eisenhower Expressway 109
Ethnicity 202, 217
European Bakeries 186
Exports 62
Expressways 108, 109

F
Federal Center 124
Federal Reserve Bank 96
Fermilab 120
Field, Marshall 80
Field Museum of Natural History 45, 132, 147
Fishing 53, 114
Flatzek, Peter 57
Football, Bears 47, 164
Ford Motor Co. 82
Fort Dearborn 38, 203
Friedrichs, Neil 57
Futures & Options Exchange 236

G
German American Chamber of Commerce 56
German American Day 226]
German American Heritage 222
German Churches 208
German Clubs 192-195
German Community History 202, 206
German Consul 10
German Gift Shops 186
German Integration 210

Alphabetisches Verzeichnis

German Media Group 112, 234
German National Associations of Commerce 58
German National Congress (DANK) 229
German Sister City 198
German Speaking Restaurants 184, 185
Germania Club 217
Glen Ellyn 118
Golf 150
Grant Park 14, 28 128
Grant Park Garage 26
Great America Amusement Park 123
Greyhound Bus Terminal 110

H
Hanburg 198
Hancock Center 14, 104
Harting Connectors 65
Highways of Chicago Region 108, 109
Halloween 128
Hilton Airport Hotel 135, 136
Hockey, Blackhawks 197
Horse Racing 114
Hospitals 161
Hotels 60

I
Illinois Benedictine College 168
Illinois Institute of Technology 64, 168
Illinois & Michigan Canal 24, 203, 205
Illinois, University of, at Chicago 166
Indian Lakes Resort 99, 117
Intercontinental Hotel 92

J
Jahn, Helmut 8, 35, 41, 82
Jazz 27
Jazzfest 27
John Hancock Center 40

K
Karneval 190, 220
Kennedy Expressway 109
Kingery Expressway 108

L
LaSalle Street 41, 62
Labor Day 128
Lachner, Bert (Publisher) 13
Lake Cruises 151
Lake Calumet Harbor 24
Lake Michigan 22, 24, 29, 30, 51, 53, 126
Lake Shore Drive 14, 30, 52
Licoln Park 80
Lincoln Park Conservatory 132, 148
Lincoln Park Lagoon 125
Lincoln Park Zoo 80
Lincoln Square Mall 182
Locks in Chicago River 36
Loop 17
Loyola University 166
Lufthansa 611
Lyric Opera 79, 145

M
Mackinac Island Regatta 14
Magnificent Mile 52
Maps 18, 31, 56, 58, 102
Marriott Lincolnshire Resort 117
Marshall Field & Co. 80
McCormick Place 46, 89, 90, 107
Medieval Times 121
Meigs Field 47, 139, 141
Mercedes-Benz 63, 86
METRA (Metropolitan Rails) 110
Michigan Avenue 57
Michigan Avenue Bridge 33
Midway Airport, 25, 89, 138, 139
Mies van der Rohe, Ludwig 46
Monroe Building 57
Morton Arboretum 120, 148, 151
Motorola 64, 83

Museum of Braodcast Communications 147
Museum of Contemporary Art 147
Museum of Science and Industry 130, 147

N
Navistar 88, 92
Navy Pier 49, 106
Neighborhoods 56
Newspapers 71, 143
Nordic Hills Resort 99, 117
North Lake Shore Drive 52
Northwestern University 122

O
O'Hare Airport 16, 25, 88, 90, 135
O'Leary's Barn 60, 214
Oak Park 119
Oak Brook 113
Oak Brook Country Club 115
Oak Brook Hills Resort 99, 116
Oak Brook Shopping Center 113, 116
Oakbrook Terrace Tower 112
Oktoberfest 129
Opera, Lyric (Civic) 74, 145
Orchestra Hall 31, 74, 145
Outer (Lake Shore) Drive 14, 30, 52

P
PACE 110
Pal-Waukee Airport 140
Petrillo Band Shell 14
Picasso, Pablo Ststue 2, 40, 43
Picnics 150
Police, Harbor 51
Polo 51
Planetarium, Adler 48
Population Statistics 17, 58
Prudential Plaza 14
Potter Palmer Mansion 209

Q
Queen Elizabeth 28
Quaker Oats Co. 78

R
Railroads 10
Restaurants 154
    American 154
    Chinese 156
    Continental 156
    French 158
    German 158
    Greek 158
    Italian 158
    Japanese 160
    Mexican 160
    Seafood 161
    Steak & Beef 161
Richard J. Daley Plaza 40, 43
Roosevelt University 168

S
St. Michael's Church 144, 209
Sailing 114, 127
Sanitary Ship Canal 24
Sears Tower 29, 42
Shedd Aquarium 47, 48
Shipping 24, 89
Shopping 174
Sister City, Hamburg 143
Six Flags Great America Amusement Park 123
Soldier Field 46, 47
Spiegel 48, 87
Sports 164
State Street 39, 80
State of Illinois Center 8
Stevenson Expressway 109
Steuben Parade 224, 225

T
Taste of Chicago 26, 27
Telephone Area Codes 76, 77
Telephone Timing 83
Temperatures, Average 131
Terminals at O'Hare Airport 136
Thanksgiving 129
Thomas, Theodore 31
Thompson, James Center 8
Trans Tech America 95
Three Thirty Three West Wacker Building 104, 133
Three Eleven South Wacker Duilding 14

U
Union Station 110
United Airline 135
University Club 57
University of Chicago 166
University of Illinois at Chicago 166

W
Washington, Harold Library 80
Water Tower Place 76, 104
Water Tower Pumping Station 104
Weights & Measures 82
Weisberg, Lois 74
White Sox 165
Woman's Point of View 170
World Cup '94 47
World Trade Center 35, 85
World's Fair, Century of Progress 211
World's Tallest Building 29
Wright, Frank Lloyd 119
Wrigley Field 164
Wrigley Building 71

Z
Zoos 149
    Brookfield Zoo 149
    Lincoln Park Zoo 149

ALPHABETICAL INDEX — ALPHABETISCHES VERZEICHNIS

Lachner "*CHICAGOLAND*"

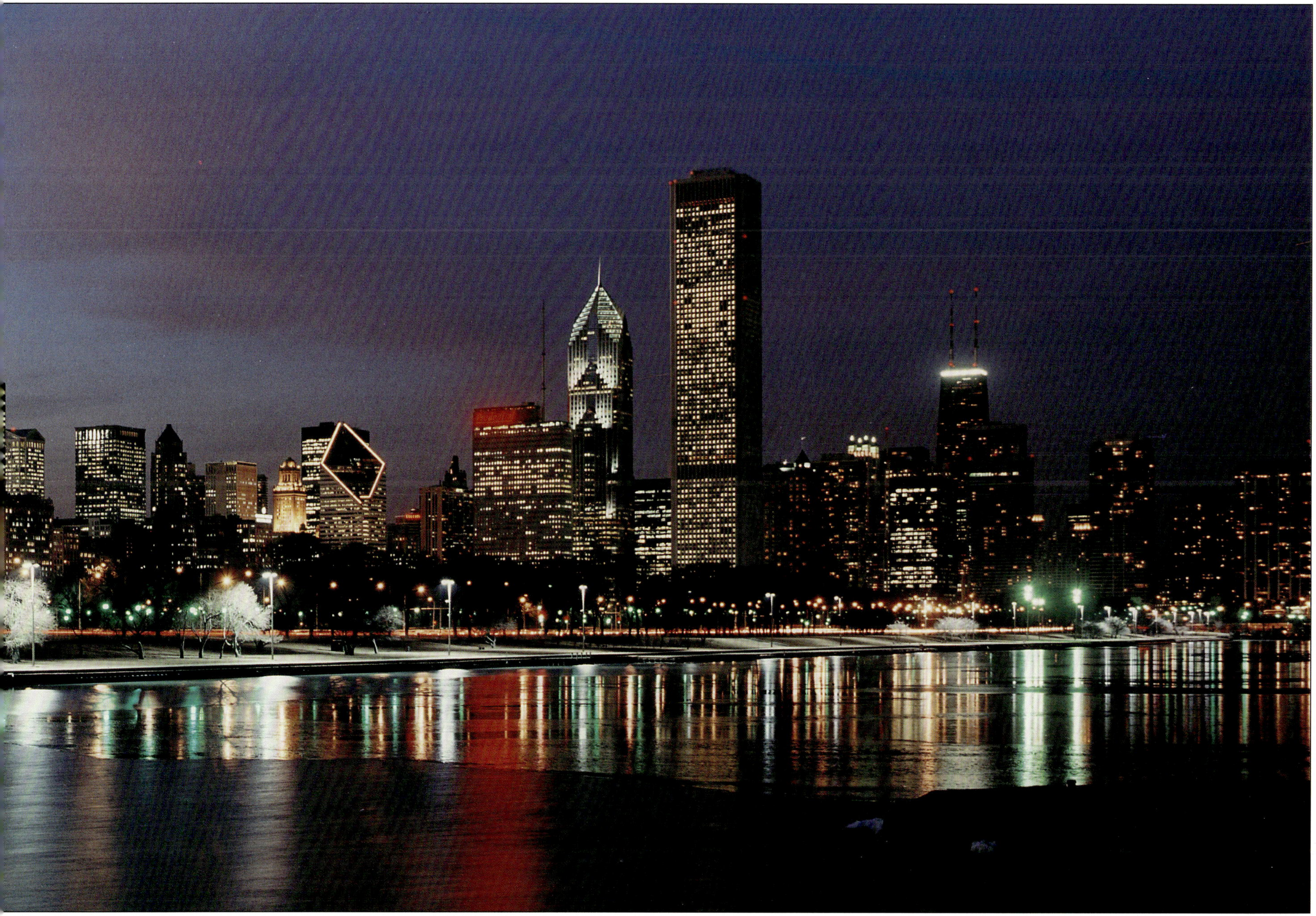

NOTES

NOTES

$49.50

ISBN: 0-964-06590-8

Printed on Recycled Paper

Printed in USA

Aoki
Morning sky
Oct. 18